C0-CCP-663

JOURNAL FOR THE STUDY OF THE NEW TESTAMENT SUPPLEMENT SERIES

99

Sheffield Academic Press

Paul's Language about God

Neil Richardson

Journal for the Study of the New Testament
Supplement Series 99

Published by Sheffield Academic Press Ltd
Mansion House
19 Kingfield Road
Sheffield, S11 9AS
England

Typeset by Sheffield Academic Press
and
Printed on acid-free paper in Great Britain
by Bookcraft
Midsomer Norton, Somerset

British Library Cataloguing in Publication Data

A catalogue record for this book is available
from the British Library

ISBN 1-85075-485-3

CONTENTS

ACKNOWLEDGMENTS

Paul's Language about God is an abridged and lightly revised version of a dissertation presented to Bristol University in 1992. I should like to express my warm thanks to Dr John Ziesler, who, as my supervisor, gave me invaluable help and encouragement.

I am very grateful, too, to the Revs. A.R. George, S. Jackson and A. Maguire, who generously helped me with the task of proof-reading. And, lastly, I wish to acknowledge my debt to my wife, Rhiannon, and to my sons, Mark, James and Simon, for their continual support and understanding.

ABBREVIATIONS

AnBib	Analecta biblica
BAGD	W. Bauer, W.F. Arndt, F.W. Gingrich and F.W. Danker, *Greek–English Lexicon of the New Testament*
Bib	*Biblica*
BJRL	*Bulletin of the John Rylands University Library of Manchester*
BZNW	Beihefte zur *ZNW*
EpwRev	*Epworth Review*
EvT	*Evangelische Theologie*
ExpTim	*Expository Times*
JBL	*Journal of Biblical Literature*
JSNT	*Journal for the Study of the New Testament*
JSNTSup	*Journal for the Study of the New Testament* Supplement Series
JTS	*Journal of Theological Studies*
NovT	*Novum Testamentum*
NRSV	New Revised Standard Version
NTS	*New Testament Studies*
REB	Revised English Bible
SBLDS	SBL Dissertation Series
SJT	*Scottish Journal of Theology*
ST	*Studia Theologica*
TGl	*Theologie und Glaube*
WBC	Word Biblical Commentary
ZNW	*Zeitschrift für die neutestamentliche Wissenschaft*

The abbreviations used for the works of Philo are those listed in Schürer 1987, (Vol. III.2), pp. 812-3.

INTRODUCTION

The mystery of God is the central mystery of Christian faith. Other mysteries, the Incarnation and the Resurrection, derive from this one central mystery. So it is not surprising, and not before time, that the question of God has been increasingly recognised in the late twentieth century as the central question for Christian theology.[1] It is not the central purpose of this study to investigate the reasons why this is so, still less to offer 'answers', however tentative, from a philosophical or theological standpoint. But contemporary questions about God, whether by Christians or by others, are the background against which this inquiry is conducted, and therefore it may be useful to outline the kind of questions which are almost certainly an inevitable part of any culture or society where the word 'god' is used.

'It seems that the word "God" means different things, even different kinds of things, to different people.'[2] This is due not least to the fact that the word has no clear or obvious referent. The same statement could hardly be made about a table or a chair, for example. Many, indeed, would question whether the word 'God' means anything at all to people in the Western world. Some would go further, and argue that the word 'God' is not only incomprehensible but also uninteresting.[3]

There are at least three interrelated tasks here. First, there is the task of wrestling with the ultimate question of the *reality* of God. As Gerald Kaufman puts it: 'the problem now is not, *pace* Bultmann, demythologising ultimate reality, but whether there is a "beyond" at all...So either "metaphysical dualism" must be surrendered or we must restate it in a way which shows it is still possible and significant to speak of

1. Thus, for example, R.M. Grant, *The Early Christian Doctrine of God* (Charlottesville, 1966), p. 1.

2. R. Morgan and J. Barton, *Biblical Interpretation* (Oxford: Oxford University Press, 1988), p. 19.

3. A. Lindemann 'Die Rede von Gott in der paulinische Theologie', *TGl* 69.4 (1979), p. 373.

"God".'[1] As we shall see, however, the question of *whether* God exists was not an issue for the writers of the New Testament, including Paul.

Secondly, there is the task of exploring and expounding the nature of *God-language*. Here the inquirer is concerned with questions such as: What does theological language express ? How does it represent? How does it communicate?[2] Thirdly, there is the task of making God *credible*. This is more a practical than a theoretical question,[3] and it is noteworthy that W. Hordern, in his discussion of language about God, cites approvingly the view of Bonhoeffer that a renewal of theological language can only come about through prayer and service.[4]

These three tasks constitute a massive challenge to the Christian Church, and the first two a challenge to any would-be apologist for the Christian faith. How can anyone begin to speak *tout court* about God, unless he/she and his/her listeners have some shared understanding, or at least the possibility of a shared understanding, of what the word 'God' means? The question 'What is meant by "God"?' seems not to have received the attention it deserves in an environment where God can no longer, so to speak, be taken for granted.

Two basic points are worth making at this stage. First, as Paul Tillich frequently emphasized, 'God' refers, not to a being, but to 'the ground of our being'. This last phrase may not be a particularly attractive definition of the word 'God', but Tillich is fundamentally correct in his reminder that God is the *ens realissimum*. This fundamental distinction between God as Being and God as a being is made in Richard Niebuhr's celebrated essay 'Faith in Gods and in God'.[5] The emphasis on God as

1. G. Kaufman, *God the Problem* (Cambridge, MA: Harvard University Press, 1972), pp. 43-44.

2. J. MacQuarrie, *God-Talk* (London: SCM Press, 1967), p. 79. Cf. P. van Buren, *The Edges of Language* (London: SCM Press, 1972), especially ch. 8.

3. N. Lash, *A Matter of Hope* (London: Darton, Longman & Todd, 1981), p. 286.

4. W. Hordern, *Speaking of God* (London: Epworth,1964), p. 160.

5. Reprinted in R.A. Eckardt (ed.), *The Theologian at Work* (London: SCM Press, 1968) pp. 44-58. Another notable 'definition' of God is to be found in G. Theissen's *Psychological Aspects of Pauline Theology* (ET; Edinburgh: T. & T. Clark, 1987) p. 55:

> Behind the pressure of reality in selection, historical catastrophes, and crises of identity, we experience a given central reality that places clear limits on human self-will, that imposes a harsh education toward reality, and that often proceeds gruesomely and inexorably—but that simultaneously makes possible and permits an infinite multiplicity

Being is given powerful expression in the following paragraph:

> What is it that is responsible for this passing, that dooms our human faith to frustration? We may call it the nature of things, we may call it fate, we may call it reality. But by whatever name we call it, this law of things, this reality, this way things are, is something with which we must all reckon. We may not be able to give a name to it, calling it only the void out of which everything comes and to which everything returns, though that is also a name. But it is there—the last shadowy and vague reality, the secret of existence by virtue of which things come into being, are what they are, and pass away. Against it there is no defense. This reality, this nature of things, abides when all else passes. It is the source of all things and the end of all. It surrounds our life as the great abyss into which all things plunge and as the great source whence they all come. What it is we do not know save that it is and that it is the supreme reality with which we must reckon.[1]

It follows from this, secondly, that 'God' is not a name, since only creatures and things can be named.[2] Not surprisingly, there has been a long tradition (by no means confined to Christianity) of apophatic theology—that is, one may more easily say what God is not than what he is. Nevertheless, an apologist for 'God' (Christian or not) can hardly rest content with that, and it is interesting to note that in one of the very few passages in the New Testament which can be called apologetic we have a statement which at least approximates to a definition of God: 'in him we live and move and are' (Acts 17.28). With this may be compared a modern writer's reference to God as our 'environment', and the title of

> of organisms, cultural patterns, and self-interpretations, so that we are as astonished at its apparently boundless liberality as we are appalled at its severity. This central reality is ultimately the 'creator' of our life-world. Everything found within us is an experiment attempting to correspond to it. All organic, psychic, and intellectual structures are attempts to adapt to it. Is it so inexplicable that some human beings intuitively sense this, become conscious of it, and wish to lead their life as an echo of this hidden transcendent reality? Is it unjustified to call this reality God?

The merit of Theissen's language here is that it takes seriously the process of evolution. But this is to be expected from the author of *Biblical Faith* (ET; London: SCM Press, 1984).

1. Eckardt, *Theologian*, pp. 53-54.

2. Cf. Thomas Aquinas on the question 'Is the name "God" peculiar to God alone?', in I.T. Ramsey (ed.), *Words about God* (London: SCM Press, 1971) pp. 47-49.

one of the most notable theological works of recent years, *God as the Mystery of the World.*[1]

The sermon at Athens, however, is the exception, not the norm in the New Testament, and that for at least two reasons. First, all the New Testament documents, probably without exception[2] were written to believers. Secondly, the society into which Jesus was born can fairly be said to have taken God 'quite for granted'.[3] (Whether this was as true of the more cosmopolitan and sophisticated circles in which Paul sometimes moved as a missionary is a matter which will concern us later on.) At the very least, one may wonder whether there was any general agreement about the referent of words such as 'God', 'gods' and 'the divine'. But as far as Judaism was concerned, in spite of the growing recognition of Judaism's diversity,[4] it was uniformly monotheistic.

Perhaps it is this 'unquestioning assurance' which is partly responsible for the apparent neglect of the New Testament concept of God. Certainly, it is remarkable how little the language of the New Testament about God has been investigated by scholars. Compared with the vast outpourings on Christology, eschatology, and many other subjects, the paucity of books, or even sections of books devoted to what New Testament writers have to say about God is astonishing. Lindemann is probably correct when he alleges that one reason for this neglect has been the widely held view that the Old Testament Jewish understanding of God is regarded as the framework within which New Testament talk of God is associated only as it were secondarily. This *tendenz* in New Testament scholarship he defines as follows:

1. E. Jüngel *God as the Mystery of the World* (ET; Edinburgh: T. & T. Clark, 1983).

2. The literary form and style of Lk. 1.1-4 might suggest a wider public than a Christian church or churches (see, for example, the similarity of Luke's preface with that of Josephus), but the contents of Luke–Acts as a whole strongly suggest a Christian readership. (Thus also R. Maddox *The Purpose of Luke–Acts* [Edinburgh: T. & T. Clark, 1982], pp. 12-15.)

3. H. Cadbury, *The Peril of Modernizing Jesus* (London: SPCK, 1962), p. 188. Compare also K. Rahner, *Theological Investigations I* (ET; London: Darton, Longman & Todd, 1965), pp. 77-148, '*Theos* in the New Testament'. Rahner refers to the unquestioning assurance that God is simply there (p. 95). Compare also, in his more recent investigation, B. Haymes *The Concept of the Knowledge of God* (London: Macmillan, 1988), p. 120.

4. See now J. Neusner, W.S. Green and E. Frerichs (eds.), *Judaisms and their Messiahs* (Cambridge: Cambridge University Press, 1987).

> The idea that one cannot in the end provide a distinctively Christian understanding of God, but that Christian language about God must, basically, be concentrated on inscribing specifically Christian features on to a preconceived general understanding of God.[1]

Such a view helps to explain the very small amount of space devoted to the 'idea of God' in several well-known New Testament theologies. Bultmann, for example, devotes less than four pages to Jesus' idea of God.[2] When we turn to the Pauline section of these theologies, the list of contents is even more striking. Bultmann has two sections on 'The Righteousness of God' and 'Grace'.[3] Conzelmann devotes some 13 pages to 'God's Saving Action in Christ',[4] and some six pages and two and a half pages to δικαιοσύνη θεοῦ and 'The Wrath of God' respectively.[5] Kümmel's *Theology of the New Testament* is similar. Under the title 'The Christ Event'[6] he deals with the language Paul uses about Christ (mainly titles), inquires briefly into the meaning of the righteousness of God,[7] and devotes a paragraph[8] to arguing that Jesus and Paul are essentially at one in their idea of God.

These sections do not exhaust all that these scholars have to say about

1. Lindemann, 'Die Rede von Gott', p. 358.

2. R. Bultmann, *Theology of the New Testament* (London: SCM Press, 1952), pp. 22-26. Jesus' idea of God is not the focus of our study, but this, too, has not received the attention it should have had. Cadbury's study, noted earlier, especially pp. 76-79, is a notable exception. Bultmann, it should be said, wrote at greater length about Jesus' idea of God in his earlier study *Jesus* (Berlin: Deutsche Bibliothek, 1929; translated into English in 1934 as *Jesus and the Word*), but his work in both studies is flawed in two ways: first, as is often recognized now, less than justice is done to Judaism (e.g. 'God had retreated far off into the distance as the transcendent heavenly King', *NT Theology I*, p. 23), and, secondly, Jesus' message is consistently interpreted through the lens of modern existentialism. An anti-Jewish *tendenz*, however, may come to expression in other ways, as perhaps in K. Holl's assertion 'I have never understood how anyone could doubt that Jesus taught a new idea of God as compared with the Old Testament' (K. Holl, *The Distinctive Elements in Christianity* [ET; Edinburgh: T. & T. Clark, 1937], p. 17).

3. Bultmann, *NT Theology*, pp. 270-87 and 288-314.

4. H. Conzelmann, *An Outline of the Theology of the New Testament* (ET; London: SCM Press, 1969), pp. 199-212.

5. Conzelmann, *Outline*, pp. 239-41.

6. W.G. Kümmel, *Theology of the New Testament* (ET; London: SCM Press, 1974), pp. 151-72.

7. Kümmel, *Theology*, pp. 196-98.

8. Kümmel, *Theology*, p. 248.

the New Testament concept of God, but the headings of the various sections of these works are indicative of the relatively marginal place given to this subject. When we examine other treatments of Paul's theology, the situation is no different. One of the most widely used books in Britain over the last 25 years has been Whiteley's *The Theology of St Paul*. He devotes a special section to 'The Wrath of God',[1] and the whole of the second chapter to 'The Created Order',[2] but, again, the arrangement of the material suggests that no particular questions about God arise. (The General Index is revealing, in that there is a long list of entries under 'Christ, Person of', and seven entries under 'Spirit of God', but the word 'God' is not entered separately.) Another very influential study of Paul has been W.D. Davies' *Paul and Rabbinic Judaism*. Here Davies devotes two paragraphs to 'the idea of God in 1st century Judaism',[3] arguing that Jewish apocalyptic was the predominant influence on Paul, and that 'the idea of God in apocalyptic leans mostly to the side of transcendentalism' (p. 12). Even if it is true, as Beker and others have argued, that Jewish apocalyptic was a major influence on Paul, the view that the God of apocalyptic was remote has been recently challenged.[4] In any case, the traditional dichotomy between the transcendent and the immanent is, at best, unhelpful, and possibly misleading, in an exploration of the biblical language about God.[5]

It may be questioned whether a more recent study does justice to Paul's *theo*logy. J.A. Fitzmyer in his book *Paul and his Theology*[6] asserts that Paul's experience near Damascus 'did not alter his

1. D.E.H. Whiteley, *The Theology of St Paul* (Oxford: Basil Blackwell, 1964) pp. 61-72.

2. Whiteley, *Theology*, pp. 17-44.

3. W.D. Davies, *Paul and Rabbinic Judaism* (London: SPCK, 1948, 1955, 1970), pp. 11-13.

4. L. Hurtado, *One God, One Lord* (Philadelphia: Fortress Press, 1988).

5. At the very least, 'transcendence' needs careful definition, as MacQuarrie indicates in his discussion of Pseudo-Dionysius's thought, suggesting that God's true transcendence lies in his 'going beyond himself in generous love and self-giving' (J. MacQuarrie, *In Search of Deity* [London: SCM Press, 1984) p. 79; cf. D.M. MacKinnon, *Themes in Theology: The Threefold Cord* (Edinburgh: T. & T. Clark, 1987), p. 180, and especially ch. 3 of C.A. Holbrook, *The Iconoclastic Deity: Biblical Images of God* [Lewisburg: Bucknell University Press, 1984], in which the author notes the ambiguities in the word 'transcendent', and the need for clarification when it is used of the God of the Bible).

6. J.A. Fitzmyer, *Paul and his Theology* (Princeton, NJ: Prentice-Hall, 1987).

fundamental commitment to the "one God", but that whilst his 'basic *theo*logy did not change, his Christology did'.[1] But can one differentiate so readily between Paul's *theo*logy and his Christology? This is a question I hope to explore in this study, particularly in Chapter 5. Indeed, Paul's use of language about God must be explored in the light of the ways and contexts in which Paul uses it. John Barton, in his recent Bampton lectures,[2] discusses 'The Question of the Canon', referring to 'the new work God has accomplished' through Jesus. He goes on:

> This is not primarily a point about the meaning of texts: it is a matter of a new community, a new ethos, a new understanding of God—a new creation, Christians said. But it does have an effect on texts. It draws them into fresh conjunctions, destroys existing threads of connection, and establishes new ones.[3]

Although Barton is thinking primarily of the relation of the Old Testament to the New, his last sentence in this quotation, if applied to Paul's language about God, provides part of the agenda for this study. What is the significance of the linguistic patterns in Paul's God-language, and of the contexts in which they are used? And *is* there a new understanding of God here?

To return to Fitzmyer, in a subsequent chapter he goes on to argue that what Paul asserts about God 'is usually asserted in contexts dealing with his salvific activity... Even when Paul speaks of the qualities or attributes of God, they almost always depict God as such and such *for us, on our behalf*'.[4] This is a very sweeping generalization about a wide range of God-language, and does not significantly affect my contention that New Testament scholarship has largely overlooked this area.

Lindemann[5] suggests three reasons why the question of Paul's understanding of God plays so small a role in scholarly discussion. First, Paul's thought from his conversion onwards, is perceived to have become more christocentric; according to this school of thought, 'God disappears—not entirely, of course, but in Pauline thought he moves into the far distance'. Here Lindemann cites the work of W. Bousset and P. Ferne as typical of many.[6] Secondly, it has been widely held that

1. Fitzmyer, *Paul*, p. 30.
2. J. Barton, *People of the Book?* (London: SPCK, 1988).
3. Barton, *People*, p. 33.
4. Fitzmyer, *Paul*, p. 42.
5. Lindemann, 'Die Rede von Gott', p. 359.
6. The well-known work of L. Cerfaux, *Christ in the Theology of St Paul* (ET;

Paul's teaching about God was not distinctive; rather the apostle 'moves entirely within the lines already laid down by the tradition in which he stood'. Here Lindemann cites Deissmann: 'A new attitude to God, not new teaching about God'. A more recent example of this school of thought can be found in E.P. Sanders, *Paul and Palestinian Judaism* where Sanders echoes the Bultmannian view that 'anthropology' is Paul's 'principal contribution to theological thought'. Sanders goes on:

> From him we learn nothing new or remarkable about God. God is a God of wrath and mercy, who seeks to save rather than to condemn, but rejection of whom leads to death. One could, to be sure, list further statements made by Paul about God, but it is clear that Paul did not spend his time reflecting on the nature of the deity.[1]

Whether there is a sound basis for such a view will be one of the major concerns of the ensuing study. Before I turn to a survey of more recent contributions by scholars in this field, we must note the third reason which Lindemann gives for the scholarly neglect of the Pauline understanding of God. There was no need, so this argument goes, for Paul 'to develop his thinking about God more fully', because all Paul's letters were written to people who already had a theistic world view. This last point was no doubt true, but whether it follows that such people did not need teaching about God is much more questionable.

In recent years the situation in New Testament scholarship has begun to change. N.A. Dahl, in particular, has drawn attention to the neglect of the New Testament understanding of God.[2] In fact, two very recent

New York: Herder & Herder, 1959) should almost certainly be added to this group.

1. E.P. Sanders, *Paul and Palestinian Judaism* (London: SCM Press, 1977), p. 509. Cf. G. Schneider, 'Urchristliche Gottesverkündigung in hellenistischer Umwelt', *ZNW* 13 (1969), pp. 59-75, who argues from the sermons of Acts 14 and 17 and from Pauline texts such as 1 Thess. 1.9-10 and 1 Cor. 8.6, that early Christian preaching began with the proclamation of the one God, and that the christological kerygma was inserted into this (e.g. pp. 64-65). This almost certainly oversimplifies, and neglects the possibility of interaction between what was predicated about God and what was predicated about Jesus.

2. Noted by L.E. Keck, 'Towards the Renewal of New Testament Christology', *NTS* 32 (1986), pp. 362-67. The same neglect is noted also by J. Giblet in J. Coppens (ed.), *La Notion biblique de Dieu. Le Dieu de la Bible et le Dieu des Philosophes* (Leuven: Leuven University Press), pp. 231-32 and p. 331. But is Giblet correct in going on to say 'Le NT ne nous offre guère de discours sur Dieu'? One may agree with his assertion that it offers a new sense of God and of the conditions for communion with him.

works go some way towards remedying this neglect in a more general way. R.M. Grant's *God and the Gods* gives valuable background material,[1] whilst L. Hurtado's *One God, One Lord* offers a corrective to widely-held but mistaken views of Judaism.[2] As for the Pauline concept of God, two important studies have emerged in recent years, both focusing on the letter to the Romans. The more wide-ranging of the two, H. Moxnes's *Theology in Conflict*[3] argues that Paul's statements about God in their context 'would bring to light an implicit theology which we may describe as Paul's understanding of God'.[4] Moxnes contends that Paul employed God-language to create a new identity for a community consisting of Jewish and non-Jewish Christians.[5] Paul achieved this by using traditional statements about God in contexts which gave them new, controversial meanings. So, for example, Paul uses a traditional formula in Rom. 4.17 (θεοῦ τοῦ ζῳοποιοῦντος τοὺς νεκροὺς καὶ καλοῦντος τὰ μὴ ὄντα ὡς ὄντα) to accomplish a drastic reinterpretation of the tradition.[6] In effect, Paul *redefines* the people of God with the help of traditional God-language. 'That God gives life to the dead, and calls the non-existent into being, are themes connected with the founding of Christian communities.'[7] Thus, in a reversal of Bultmann's well-known dictum, Moxnes argues that 'for Paul, to speak about God is to speak about his people'.[8] Moxnes' own work relates closely to certain aspects of this study, and I shall have cause to refer to his work again, but for the moment I simply note this renewed interest in the significance of Paul's so-called traditional statements about God.

J.M. Bassler's study *Divine Impartiality*[9] has a narrower focus than that of Moxnes, but she notes the neglect of traditional theological statements in Paul, linking this with the general neglect of the *theo*logical

1. R.M. Grant, *Gods and the One God: Christian Theology in the Graeco-Roman World* (London: SPCK, 1986), ranges considerably beyond the New Testament period, but much of his material is relevant to the New Testament understanding of God.
2. Hurtado, *One God*, pp. 22-39.
3. H. Moxnes, *Theology in Conflict* (Leiden: Brill, 1980).
4. Moxnes, *Conflict*, p. 9.
5. Moxnes, *Conflict*, p. 14.
6. Moxnes, *Conflict*, ch. 8 *passim*, but especially pp. 233 and 274.
7. Moxnes, *Conflict*, p. 281.
8. Moxnes, *Conflict*, p. 99.
9. J.M. Bassler, *Divine Impartiality* (SBLDS, 59; Chico, CA: Scholars Press, 1982).

statements of the New Testament.[1] Bassler's particular contribution is to show the 'pivotal' place in Paul's argument of Rom. 2.11: οὐ γάρ ἐστιν προσωποληµψία παρὰ τῷ θεῷ. Whereas in Old Testament and inter-testamental literature the theme of divine impartiality is used to explain the ailing fortunes of Israel,[2] Paul in Romans correlates impartiality in judgment with impartiality in grace.[3] Thus, in Bassler's view, the theological statement in 2.11 is 'pivotal', summing up the preceding section, and introducing the theme of the following one.[4]

It is clear from these two studies alone that the significance of Paul's language about God has been greatly underestimated,[5] and yet we still have no overview of Paul's teaching about God. Such a study, however, is urgently required. In a period when we have been taught to reassess our perceptions of and opinions about ancient Judaism, and to explore more carefully the continuities and discontinuities between Judaism and the new Christian faith, very little exploration seems to have been undertaken on Christian language about God. How new or distinctive was it? Did the coming of Jesus affect the language about God which the very first believers inherited from their mother faith? If so, in what ways? Did they use traditional God-language in new ways and in new contexts, as Moxnes and Bassler claim?

One particular question, therefore, with reference to Paul, presents itself: how far were Paul's concept of and language about God changed by his conversion to the Christian faith? Clearly Paul must count as the most important individual case-study of the general questions posed in the previous paragraph. Closely related to this question is the question of the extent to which ideas and language about God shaped Paul's understanding of Christ and the language which Paul used about Christ.

There is an important point about method to be made here. Although

1. Bassler, *Impartiality*, p. 1.

2. Bassler, *Impartiality*, e.g. pp. 21 and 44.

3. Compare 2.1-11, and especially v. 11, with 3.21-31 and 10.12-13.

4. Bassler, *Impartiality*, p. 152. Bassler concludes that the fundamental importance of the theme of divine impartiality in Romans supports the view that the Collection was an important factor in the purpose of the letter.

5. This is not to ignore the useful material in the study by D. Ford and F. Young, *Meaning and Truth in 2 Corinthians* (London: SPCK, 1987), notably chs. 6 and 9, nor the chapter in R.F. Collins, *Studies in the First Letter to the Thessalonians* (Leuven: Leuven University Press, 1984), devoted to an examination of God-language in 1 Thessalonians. Collins himself (pp. 230-31) notes the frequency with which commentators on Paul avoid a specific presentation of Paul's doctrine of God.

Paul's language about Christ has been explored again and again, such explorations have usually proceeded without sufficient attention to the way in which Paul's language about God and his language about Christ are so thoroughly intertwined. It may be questioned whether that which the apostle so thoroughly 'joined together' should be 'put asunder' by methodologies which all too often have the effect of marginalizing Paul's language about God. One of the merits of L.J. Kreitzer's study *Jesus and God in Paul's Eschatology*[1] is the attention it pays to the relationship in Paul's thinking between what Kreitzer calls theocentricity and christocentricity.[2] Kreitzer's own work focuses on Paul's eschatology, and I shall need to discuss his findings more fully in Chapter 5.

How then, is the task of examining Paul's language about God to be done? Some of the points urged by L.E. Keck in a study of method in the exploration of New Testament Christology[3] may be made *mutatis mutandis* of New Testament *theo*logy. All too often, Keck claims, New Testament scholars have reduced christology to a history of ideas in the early church, and, even more, to a cataloguing of the history of christological titles, which, in the case of St Paul, takes us 'past his Christology'.[4] Keck calls for a new approach which 'respects the grammar of christological discourse', a task which involves attending to 'the correlates of Christology', because the New Testament does not have a separate christological section, but always expresses the identity and significance of Jesus in relation to something else—doxology, paraenesis, cult narrative, and so on. Secondly, such a task involves taking seriously the form and function of the texts.

There are some important pointers here for my own study. Of course, Paul's understanding of God could hardly be studied by an analysis of the different words or titles he uses for God, since he is remarkably consistent in his use of the word *theos*.[5] Nevertheless, it will be important not to reduce this investigation to a search for abstract ideas, such

1. L. Kreitzer, *Jesus and God in Paul's Eschatology* (Sheffield: JSOT Press, 1987).

2. Kreitzer, *Jesus and God*, especially pp. 15, 21-22, 28-29, 163-64, and 165-70. Cf. Ford and Young, *Meaning and Truth*, p. 241.

3. Keck, 'Towards the Renewal' (see p. 18 n. 2 above).

4. Keck, 'Towards the Renewal', p. 369.

5. There are a few exceptions, notably in the participial phrases such as Gal. 5.8, in some LXX quotations (e.g. 2 Cor. 6.18), and in the use of the *hapax legomenon* θειότης at Rom. 1.20.

as the 'omnipotence' of God. These are simply not Paul's categories of thought.[1]

In rejecting the titular approach to New Testament Christology, Keck refers to James Barr's dictum: 'It is in sentences that real theological thinking is done'.[2] This is an important corrective to older methodologies—whether in Christology or theology. However, there are insights to be gained by an analysis of smaller grammatical units, since such units can reflect, however unintentionally, the theological presuppositions of the writer. In the chapters which follow, therefore, I shall be paying particular attention to the *context* of Paul's language about God without neglecting the smaller units of which that language is made up. This approach does mean, however, that I shall not be concerned primarily with the history and development of such language, except insofar as it illuminates Paul's own use of it. Nor is the development of Paul's own thought my primary concern, although the possibility cannot be ruled out that Paul's understanding of God developed during the period covered by his letters.[3]

I turn, then, to the methods adopted in the following study. Clearly the extent of the area to be explored is a major problem, and it will hardly be possible to discuss thoroughly all the relevant material. Indeed, one of the difficulties is defining what *is* the relevant material.[4] This particular inquiry, however, is primarily a linguistic one. I shall be focusing

1. H. Boers, *What is New Testament Theology?* (Philadelphia: Fortress Press, 1979), p. 18, argues that one of the most serious dilemmas in Christian thought was the Bible's inability to provide 'the formal categories of thought on which a theological system could be built'. Hence, when such a system was built, its categories were alien to the Bible.

2. Quoted in Keck, 'Towards the Renewal', p. 368. The quotation comes from J. Barr, *The Semantics of Biblical Language* (Oxford: Oxford University Press, 1961), p. 234.

3. For the purposes of this study, the following letters are treated as Pauline: Romans, 1 and 2 Corinthians, Galatians, Philippians, 1 Thessalonians and Philemon. Aspects of the language of Ephesians, Colossians, 2 Thessalonians and the Pastorals will be discussed in Appendices 2 and 4, and although it is not the purpose of the Appendices to argue that these letters are deutero-Pauline, it will be suggested there that the evidence examined points in that direction.

Pauline chronology is too vast a subject to enter into here, and, as my discussion of methodology below will indicate, not of major importance for this study. It is assumed, however, that 1 Thessalonians was written c. CE 50–51, and that the remaining Pauline letters were written within a decade or so of this letter.

4. Ford and Young, *Meaning and Truth*, pp. 235-36.

on the *language* which Paul uses about God, rather than his understanding of God, although I shall be concerned with exploring what experience and understanding of God lies behind the language.

This still leaves a vast amount of material, of course. I shall begin, therefore, by selecting *samples* of Paul's theological language. But before proceeding to a preliminary discussion of which passages have been chosen, and why, a few more remarks are necessary on the parameters of Paul's theological language. Can it, in fact, be defined? First, there is Paul's explicit theological language. Here we must obviously include Paul's use of θεός. The fact that this word was not a specifically Christian word[1] makes all the more necessary an exploration of *how* and *in what contexts* Paul uses it. But despite the overwhelming preponderance of θεός in Paul's God-language,[2] I shall need to note other features of his God-language, including participial clauses, which clearly refer to God, and 'divine passives' (i.e. implying the action of God) even though the very concept of a 'divine passive' has recently been questioned.[3] But whilst the danger of finding divine passives where there are none must be acknowledged, it is difficult to avoid the conclusion that the action of God is implicit in at least some of the passive verbal forms in Paul's writings, notably Paul's use of ἐγήγερται in 1 Corinthians 15.

A more important and difficult question is whether the words 'lord'(κύριος) and 'spirit' (πνεῦμα) fall within the terms of the inquiry. The view taken here is that these two words should be investigated, and that for two reasons. First, the phrase 'the Spirit of God' occurs in the Old Testament and in later Jewish writings, and therefore, although that particular expression is not very common in Paul's writings[4] there is, to say the least, a *prima facie* case for regarding πνεῦμα as a God-word. The place of κύριος is more complicated since in LXX quotations it usually, but not always, denotes God, whilst elsewhere it usually, but not always, denotes Christ, and there are a number of verses where it could

1. Cf. MacQuarrie, *Deity*, p. 230.

2. 548 occurrences (R. Morgenthaler *Staistik Des Neutestamentlichen Wortschatzes* (Zürich: Gotthelf-Verlag, 1958), p. 105).

3. C. Macholz, 'Das "Passivum Divinum"—seine Anfänge im Alten Testament un der "Hofstil"', *ZNW* 81 (1990), however, finds the origin of the 'divine passive' in the way in which superiors, and especially the king, were addressed.

4. Rom. 8.9, 14; 1 Cor. 2.11, 14; 6.11; 7.40; 12.3; 2 Cor. 3.3; Phil. 3.3 (and 'his Spirit' at, e.g., 1 Thess. 4.8).

denote either God or Christ.[1] So there are two reasons for investigating the place of κύριος in Paul's language about God: first, it *was* part of Paul's God-language, as one might expect in the case of a Jew, and secondly, κύριος is a very important part of the linguistic evidence in my investigation in Chapter 5 of the relationship between Paul's language about God and his language about Christ. As will become clear in Chapter 5, it is not always easy to determine the precise significance of κύριος applied to Christ, but since it is undoubtedly a 'God word' in the Old Testament, it requires investigation.

The second reason why πνεῦμα and κύριος must be included within the scope of this inquiry lies in the fact that, whatever their precise meaning and function, they are too closely intertwined, like Paul's Christ-language, with the language he uses about God to be detached from it without serious risk of misunderstanding the whole.

I turn, then, in the following chapters to selected passages from Paul's writings. Here it will be necessary briefly to outline the reasons for the selection which has been made. I begin with Romans 9–11 for three reasons. First, the letter to the Romans has first claim on our attention as the letter in which Paul mentions God more frequently than in any other letter.[2] Secondly, the question of God is central to Paul's agenda in these chapters, which comprise a sustained argument by Paul about the place of Israel within the providence of God. The theological concern however is paramount: 'Romans 9–11 are driven by a concern for the integrity and consistency of God'.[3] There is also a third reason for studying these particular chapters. Because the language and arguments are very Old Testament-centred and include many references to God, Jewish literature provides an ample basis for comparison and contrast with Paul's language here. This will enable us to get to grips with our first question, namely to what extent, if any, Paul's language about God differs from that of the Old Testament and of later Jewish writings.

Chapter 2 is concerned with the language Paul uses about God in 1 Corinthians 1.18–3.23. There are two reasons for selecting this

1. J. Ziesler's comment (*Paul's Letter to the Romans* [London: SCM Press, 1989], p. 56) is noteworthy at this stage: 'This is a term difficult to define in relation to God'.

2. E.g. Moxnes, *Conflict*, pp. 15-16.

3. E.E. Johnson, *The Function of Apocalyptic and Wisdom Traditions in Romans 9–11* (Atlanta: Scholars Press, 1987), p. 138. The theological issues, as Johnson notes (e.g. p. 123), are adumbrated in Rom. 3.1-8.

passage. First, it is remarkable for its 'clusters' of God-language. For example, the word θεός occurs four times in 1.20-21, and four times in 1.24-25. Similar 'clusters' occur in 3.6-9, and 3.16-17. Although other passages in Paul's writings contain frequent references to God, these 'clusters' are particularly noteworthy. As I hope to show, Paul seems to go out of his way in these verses to use θεός as frequently as he does, and I shall explore the possible reasons for this. But there is a further reason for examining these verses. They contain perhaps the most startling example of the 'intertwining' of God- and Christ-language in Paul's writings, and one of the sharpest paradoxes in Paul:

> τὸ μωρὸν τοῦ θεοῦ σοφώτερον τῶν ἀνθρώπων ἐστὶν καὶ τὸ ἀσθενὲς τοῦ θεοῦ ἰσχυρότερον τῶν ἀνθρώπων (1.25).

Once again, I shall be concerned with the question of continuity and discontinuity of Christian language about God with that of Judaism, with particular reference to the language of power and weakness. In this discussion it will be necessary to include what Paul has to say about his apostleship, since the language of power and weakness used in 1 Corinthians 1.18-25 is closely paralleled in other passages in the Corinthian correspondence.[1]

Chapter 3 focuses on a passage in which the word πνεῦμα occurs, 2 Corinthians 2.14–4.6. Several other such passages could have been chosen, of course (notably Rom. 8.1-30; 1 Cor. 12.1-13; Gal. 5.16-25), but the choice of this passage makes it possible to bring another of Paul's *Hauptbriefe* more fully into the discussion, as well as offering further examples of Paul's use of θεός. The polemical use of God-language will be a particular concern here. But it will be necessary to broaden the scope of the inquiry in this chapter to explore the wider question of the origin and significance of Paul's πνεῦμα-language, since it is especially important for our understanding of Paul's concept and language about God.

In Chapter 4 I examine Pauline paraenesis, beginning with a detailed analysis of the God-language in what is generally regarded as the most extended paraenetical section in the Pauline corpus, namely Rom. 12.1–15.7. This passage has an extra importance for study in its concentrated use of κύριος in 14.1-12, thus offering further instances of the 'mixing' of *theo*-[2] and christological language. The survey in this

1. Notably 1 Cor. 4.8-13; 2 Cor. 4.7-12 and 6.3-10.
2. It will be observed that in this study *theo*logy will mean language or thought

chapter will broaden to include other examples of Pauline paraenesis, and a comparison with Jewish and Graeco-Roman paraenesis.

It is perhaps necessary at this point to address the question of why two samples from Romans should be included in my selection, and none from Galatians, Philippians, 1 Thessalonians and Philemon. First, it is an interesting fact that God-language is less plentiful in Galatians, Philippians and Philemon than in the other letters.[1] There are two explicit references to God in Philemon, while in the other two there are none of the concentrations of God-language (with the possible exceptions of Gal. 4.4-9 and Phil. 4.6-9 and 18-20) which have been identified in the longer letters. This is less true of 1 Thessalonians,[2] but this letter does not actually provide concentrations of *both* θεός-language *and* κύριος-language in the way in which Rom. 12.1–15.7 does. I shall, however, be drawing on the evidence of these other letters as the study proceeds.

Chapter 5 surveys the various ways in which Paul's language about God and his language about Christ interact with each other. I drew attention earlier in this introduction to the extraordinary neglect in New Testament scholarship of what the New Testament has to say about God, and to a related problem of *methodology* in the study of New Testament Christology. Christology, in fact, is a misleading term, in that it might imply that statements or words about Christ can somehow be studied in isolation from their surrounding language. It is my contention that a writer's language about God and his language about Christ are best studied *together*. So this chapter attempts to identify some basic linguistic patterns before concluding with studies of 2 Cor. 5.19 and 1 Cor. 8. 6.

Finally, I summarize my findings and attempt to draw some conclusions.

A final word about method may be necessary here. Clearly it is difficult to set limits to a study of this kind. If one is to do justice to Paul's understanding and concept of God, it is essential to take into account not only the *explicitly theo*logical language, but also the implicitly theological. This study, however, is primarily a linguistic one,

about *God* (as opposed to language or thought about Christ), whilst 'theology' will have its normal, wider meaning.

1. Galatians has 149 verses, but only 31 occurrences of θεός, while Philippians has 104 verses, but only 24 occurrences of θεός.

2. The word θεός occurs 35 times in the 89 verses of 1 Thessalonians.

concentrating primarily on Paul's explicit statements about God, with particular reference to the passages which I have selected. At the same time, I shall be concerned to draw out as far as possible the wider theological implications of Paul's language, and to make connections with other kinds of language in his letters.

Chapter 1

GOD-LANGUAGE IN ROMANS 9–11

As I noted in the Introduction, θεός occurs more frequently in Romans than in any other of Paul's letters, except for the short 1 Thessalonians.[1] This fact alone gives Romans a particular importance in this inquiry, although I have offered reasons for selecting chs. 9–11 for particular close study. But there are preliminary questions to be addressed first, especially in view of a tendency until recently to view Romans 9–11 as a digression or 'untypical' of Paul.[2] Whether these chapters are typical of Paul—and, in particular, whether their language about God is consistent with, if not identical to language about God used by Paul elsewhere in Romans, and in other letters, is a question which can only be answered as this study proceeds.

As for the place of these chapters in Romans, there is a growing consensus amongst scholars that they are integral to the argument of the epistle, and not a digression or appendix after the climax of 8.31-39.[3] The difficult section 3.1-8 appears to anticipate the agenda of chs. 9

1. Thus also L. Morris, 'The Theme of Romans', in *Apostolic History and the Gospel* (ed. W.W. Gasque and R.P. Martin; Exeter: Paternoster, 1970), pp. 249-63, esp. pp. 251 and 263.

2. An extreme expression of this view can be found in Holl, *Distinctive Elements*, p. 36, where the author regards these chapters as reflecting a concept of God formed by Paul in his Pharisaic days.

3. Thus, e.g., C.E.B. Cranfield, *The Epistle to the Romans* (Edinburgh: T. & T. Clark, 1979), II, p. 445; C.K. Barrett, *The Epistle to the Romans* (London: A. & C. Black, 1957), p. 175; O. Michel, *Der Brief an die Römer* (Göttingen: Vandenhoeck & Ruprecht, 1978), p. 289, W.S. Campbell, 'Why Did Paul Write Romans?', *ExpTim* 85.9 (1974), pp. 268-69, and 'The Romans Debate', *JSNT* 10 (1981), pp. 19-28; J. Jervell, *The Unknown Paul: Essays in Luke–Acts and Early Christian History* (Minneapolis: Augsburg, 1984), p. 33; Johnson, *Apocalyptic and Wisdom Traditions*, pp. 116-23.

to 11, a point acknowledged by most recent exegetes.[1] Some of the questions raised there Paul has already dealt with (v. 8 in 6.1-11, for example), but some unfinished business remains, notably the problem of Israel's unbelief.[2]

But if the connection of chs. 9–11 with the preceding chapters is clear, the purpose of the epistle as a whole and the situation to which it is addressed are not. Yet here, too, there is a growing consensus that the purpose of Romans is to be sought in the situation at Rome.[3] Gamble[4] rightly points out that to conclude that Paul did not know what was going on in the church at Rome from the fact that he had not yet visited it is a *non sequitur*. A full discussion of this question is not directly relevant to my study, but there seems to be good grounds for recognizing that (a) Jew–Gentile relations are a central theme;[5] (b) the edict of Claudius, expelling the Jews from Rome (referred to in Acts 18.2), is therefore relevant to the purpose of the letter.[6] (Weifel[7] has examined the evidence for the history of the Jewish community in Rome, perhaps at this time as large as 40,000,[8] and while his contention that Paul's

1. Campbell, 'Romans Debate', p. 39; U. Wilckens, *Der Brief an die Römer* (Zürich: Benziger Verlag; Neukirchen–Vluyn: Neukirchener Verlag, 1980), II, pp. 191-92; J. Munck, *Christ and Israel* (Philadelphia: Fortress Press, 1967), pp. 56-57; S.K. Williams, 'The "Righteousness of God" in Romans', *JBL* 99/2 (1980), p. 280; A.J.M. Wedderburn, *The Reasons for Romans* (Edinburgh: T. & T. Clark, 1988), p. 112.

2. Cranfield, *Romans*, II, p. 180, prefers the translation 'unbelief' to 'unfaithfulness'.

3. Some of the issues are discussed in K.P. Donfried (ed.), *The Romans Debate* (Minneapolis: Augsberg, 1977). Wedderburn, *Reasons*, *passim,* mounts a powerful case for the particular reasons (he stresses the plural) behind the writing of Romans .

4. H. Gamble, Jr, *The Textual History of the Letter to the Romans* (Grand Rapids, MI: Eerdmans, 1977), pp. 135-36.

5. Thus also, for example, Campbell, 'The Romans Debate', p. 37; Michel, *An die Römer*, p. 290.

6. W. Marxen, *Introduction to the New Testament* (Philadelphia: Fortress Press, 1968), pp. 98-100; cf. Gamble, *Textual History*, pp. 136-37.

7. W. Weifel, 'The Jewish Community in Ancient Rome and the Origins of Roman Christianity', in Donfried (ed.), *Debate*, pp. 100-19.

8. The estimate of D. Georgi in *The Opponents of Paul in 2 Corinthians* (Edinburgh: T. & T. Clark, 1986), p. 84 for the beginning of the Christian era, although he acknowledges that estimates differ widely.

views changed is questionable,[1] his reconstruction of the pattern of events is convincing).

This growing recognition by scholars of the particularity of the letter to the Romans accords well with the arguments which Paul develops in Romans, and enables us to place Romans more clearly in the context of Paul's total career, with all the controversies and conflicts which that career generated.[2]

This is not to say that other factors were not at work. Paul's impending visit to Jerusalem (15.25-26, 30-32) may have influenced the writing of Romans as, clearly, did his plans for missionary work in Spain (15.22-24, 28).[3] The first of these visits, of course, was highly significant, practically and symbolically, for Jew–Gentile relations within the Church (v. 27).[4] These considerations, therefore, in addition to the links between chs. 9–11 and the earlier chapters of Romans, strengthen the view that chs. 9–11, which treat of the place of both Jew and Gentile in the purpose of God, are an integral part of the epistle.

But all the specific reasons for writing Romans created their own theological agenda. What is at stake is nothing less than the righteousness of God (δικαιοσύνη θεοῦ, e.g. 1.17), the reliability of God (ἡ ἀληθεία τοῦ θεοῦ, 3.7, 15.8), and the faithfulness of God (τὴν πίστιν τοῦ θεοῦ, 3.3).

Before I turn to a study of the God-language of these chapters, one more preliminary question must be addressed. To whom is Paul directing his remarks? At this point we need to consider the form and style of Romans 9–11. S.K Stowers[5] has presented a powerful argument for the view that the *diatribe*, the literary 'genre' in which most of these chapters is couched, was not Paul's preaching style.[6] More importantly,

1. Thus Weifel links the apparent difference between 1 Thess. 2.15 and Rom. 11 with what he considers to be Paul's revised eschatology, reflected, for example, in the apparent contrast between 1 Thess. 4 and 5 and 2 Cor. 5.1-11 (Donfried, *Debate*, pp. 114-15).

2. Michel's comment (*An die Römer*, p. 288) is appropriate to a good deal of earlier exegesis of Romans: '*wie oft die Abstraktion*... *die Konkretion*... *ersetzt*'.

3. The view of J. Jervell and others that Romans was really a letter to Jerusalem seems unlikely.

4. Well brought out by W. Nickle in *The Collection* (London: SCM Press, 1966).

5. S.K. Stowers, *The Diatribe and Paul's Letter to the Romans* (Chico, CA: Scholars Press, 1981).

6. *Contra* Bultmann, whose earlier conclusions in his *Der Stil der paulinischen*

the *diatribe* was not a polemical, but a paedagogical means of communication. With reference to the important role of objections and false conclusions in Romans 9–11,[1] Stowers concludes:

> Their intent is not polemical but paedagogical... it is as if Paul were instructing a classroom of Jews and various sorts of Christians in the gospel and its implications.[2]

If Stowers is correct, the implications for our understanding of this section of Romans are far-reaching. At one point Paul's addressees are named as 'Gentiles' (11.13), but have they been the addressees throughout this section? If Weifel's and Marxen's reconstructions are on the right lines, it is probably correct to say that the dialogue in Romans 9–11 is primarily between Paul and the Roman Gentile Christians about Israel's role in salvation history and the attitude of Gentile Christians to Israel.[3] It is difficult to exclude altogether the view that Paul, in at least some sections of Romans, is countering Jewish objections to his preaching of the gospel (especially 3.7 and 6.1-2). But it is probably true to say that the role of the supposed Jewish opposition in the composition of the whole has been exaggerated.[4]

But accepting Stowers's main conclusions does not preclude the strong possibility that Paul was drawing on, and reworking, Jewish exegetical traditions in these chapters. Building on the work of E.E. Ellis, W.R. Stegner[5] argues that Romans 9–11 show midrashic features. However, it is 'not a case of either *diatribe* or midrash' since there were similarities in style between them. As we shall see, the points of contact

Predigt und die kynisch-stoische Diatribe (Göttingen: Vandenhoeck & Ruprecht 1910) had been widely accepted, as, for example by R. Scroggs, 'Paul as Rhetorician: Two Homilies in Romans 1-11', in R. Hamerton-Kelly and R. Scroggs (eds.), *Jews, Greeks, and Christians* (Leiden: Brill, 1976), pp. 271-98.

1. Stowers concludes that this role in Rom. 9–11 is 'unparalleled' both in the diatribe and even in Philo (*Diatribe*, pp. 150-51). Stowers's survey includes the writings of Teles(bion), Lucius (Musonius Rufus), Arrian (Epictetus), Dio Chrysostom, Plutarch, Maximus of Tyre, Seneca and Philo.

2. Stowers, *Diatribe*, p.153 (cf. p. 117).

3. Thus also Campbell, 'Freedom and Faithfulness', pp. 37-39.

4. As, for example, in Wilckens, *An die Römer*, II, pp. 181 and 190, and Munck, *Christ and Israel*, p. 44.

5. W.R. Stegner, 'Romans 9.6-29: A Midrash', *JSNT* 22 (1984), pp. 37-52 (cf. Campbell, 'Freedom', p. 42 n. 20).

with the Old Testament and other Jewish traditions in Romans 9–11 both in form and content are many.[1]

I turn, then, to an examination of what Paul says and implies aboout God in these chapters. The principal method adopted here will be to compare and contrast what Paul has to say with passages in Jewish writers dealing with the same subjects or expressing the same or similar ideas. Some conclusions will be briefly drawn at the end of the survey. The view that each chapter in this section of Romans is self-contained whilst at the same time laying the foundation for the next one seems to be substantially correct. The chapters, therefore, will be examined in sequence. Sanders, however, is surely right in linking 9.30-33 with ch. 10.[2]

1. *Paul's Language about God in Romans 9.1-29*

a. *Verses 1-13*

Before I begin this survey of Paul's main argument, it is necessary to examine Paul's use of the word θεός in Rom. 9.5. It comes at the end of a short section (vv. 1-5) in which Paul has expressed his grief about the rejection of the gospel by his fellow-Israelites (vv. 1-3), before going on to enumerate their privileges (vv. 4-5a). The list of privileges ends with a reference to the messiah, and a brief concluding doxology:

> ἐξ ὧν ὁ χριστὸς τὸ κατὰ σάρκα, ὁ ὢν ἐπὶ πάντων θεὸς εὐλογητὸς εἰς τοὺς αἰῶνας, ἀμήν.

This is a familiar *crux interpretum*. Does θεός here refer to the preceding χριστός, or is the doxology in asyndeton? One of the most commonly adduced arguments in favour of the first view is a stylistic one: εὐλογητός in such doxologies is almost always the first word of the sentence.[3] On the other hand, it is rightly pointed out that nowhere else does Paul directly call Jesus God. It is not easy to decide between

1. Johnson, *Function*, *passim*, argues for the presence of *both* apocalyptic *and* wisdom traditions in Rom. 9–11.

2. E.P. Sanders, *Paul, the Law and the Jewish People* (Philadelphia: Fortress Press, 1983), p. 37. So also Munck, *Christ and Israel*, pp. 75-79, and C.K. Barrett, 'The Fall and Responsibility of Israel', in *Essays on Paul* (London: SPCK, 1982), pp. 132-53.

3. Cranfield, *Romans*, II, p.467, notes 'the one known exception': the LXX version of Ps. 68 (LXX 67).19, where κύριος ὁ θεὸς εὐλογητός has been inserted before εὐλογητὸς κύριος.

these two alternatives, as a survey of scholarly opinion shows.[1] Munck regards the doxology as christological not only on the stylistic grounds already mentioned, but because a doxology addressed to God 'would seem out of place in a context that deals with God's gifts and their rejection by unbelievers'.[2] Munck himself, however, goes on to note[3] that to describe Christ as God in this way would be offensive to Jews. In fact, the context, including Paul's language and style in Romans 9–11, tells heavily against the christological interpretation. On balance, Käsemann's view is to be preferred: 'There is a parallel in the doxology in 11.33-36, and such a doxology impressively manifests the solidarity of the apostle to the Gentiles with his people'.[4] If this interpretation is correct, Paul's first reference to God in this section of Romans is a very traditional Jewish one.

With the list of religious privileges, listed in vv. 4 and 5a, enjoyed by the people of Israel, Paul has already established a link with two rhetorical questions which he asked earlier in the epistle:

> τί οὖν τὸ περισσὸν τοῦ 'Ιουδαίου ἢ τίς ἡ ὠφέλεια τῆς περιτομῆς; (3.1).

In ch. 3 of the epistle these questions were answered in the affirmative:

> πολὺ κατὰ πάντα τρόπον. πρῶτον μὲν (γὰρ) ὅτι ἐπιστεύθησαν τὰ λόγια τοῦ θεοῦ (v.2).

This last expression τὰ λόγια τοῦ θεοῦ anticipates the statement in 9.6 with which Paul begins his discussion of the place of Israel within the purpose of God:

> οὐχ οἷον δὲ ὅτι ἐκπέπτωχεν ὁ λόγος τοῦ θεοῦ (v.6a).

1. Among those favouring the christological interpretation are W. Sanday and A.C. Headlam, *The Epistle to the Romans* (Edinburgh: T. & T. Clark, 1902), pp. 237-38, who argue that Paul's language is fluid, and that he had 'no dogmatic reason' for not using such an expression of Christ. More recently, G. Delling, 'Partizipiale Gottespradikationen in den Briefen des Neuen Testaments', *ST* 17 (1963), pp. 1-59, accepts this interpretation, but he tends to assume it rather than argue for it (pp. 38-39, cf. p. 10 n. 2), and the main findings of his paper seem generally to favour the alternative view.
2. Munck, *Christ and Israel*, p. 3.
3. Munck, *Christ and Israel*, p. 33.
4. E. Käsemann, *Commentary on Romans* (London: SCM Press, 1980), p. 260.

The phrase ὁ λόγος τοῦ θεοῦ is used elsewhere by Paul, but always with reference to the gospel or to Christian preaching,[1] whereas it is used here to denote 'the declared purpose of God',[2] with particular reference, in the first place, to the history of Israel. Its occurrence here, therefore, is more in keeping with Old Testament and Jewish usage, although the most important factor is the meaning it acquires in the course of Paul's argument. And to that I now turn.

Paul attempts to make a distinction within Israel,[3] using the Old Testament figures of Abraham, Isaac, Jacob and Esau as types. Although Isaac and Ishmael were physically both Abraham's sons, it was to Isaac that the promise was given. Two Old Testament quotations, one drawn from Gen. 21.12 and the other from Gen. 18.10a and 14b illustrate the point:

> ἐν Ισαὰκ κληθήσεταί σοι σπέρμα (v.7b).
> κατὰ τὸν καιρὸν τοῦτον ἐλεύσομαι καὶ ἔσται τῇ Σάρρᾳ υἱός (v.9b).

Secondly, Isaac also had two sons, of whom Jacob was preferred to Esau

> τὸν Ἰακὼβ ἠγάπησα, τὸν δὲ Ἠσαῦ ἐμίσησα (v.13)[4]

and this not because either had deserved or forfeited divine favour, but in order that 'God's elective purpose might stand firm':[5]

> μήπω γὰρ γεννηθέντων μηδὲ πραξάντων τι ἀγαθὸν ἢ φαῦλον, ἵνα ἡ κατ' ἐκλογὴν πρόθεσις τοῦ θεοῦ μένῃ, οὐκ ἐξ ἔργων ἀλλ' ἐκ τοῦ καλοῦντος (vv. 11-12).

I shall shortly examine Jewish versions of the Genesis passages which Paul cites, or to which he refers, but first the significance of the phrase ἡ κατ' ἐκλογὴν πρόθεσις must be noted.[6] Sanday and Headlam go so

1. 1 Thess. 2.13 (cf. 1.8 and 4.15); 1 Cor. 14.36; 2 Cor. 2.17; 4.2; and Phil. 1.14 (where, however, not all MSS read τοῦ θεοῦ).

2. Sanday and Headlam's translation, adopted by Cranfield, *Romans*, II, p. 473. Cranfield suggests that it would be a mistake to make a 'hard distinction' between this phrase as it is used here and as it is used elsewhere in the New Testament.

3. Stegner, 'Midrash', p. 38, argues that vv. 6-7 give this 'midrash' its theme and 'initial text'.

4. This is an exact quotation of Mal. 1.3b.

5. Barrett's translation (*Romans*, p. 180).

6. The use of πρόθεσις, as here, to denote God's purpose, is confined to

far as to call these words the key to Romans 9–11, and 'suggest the solution of the problem before St Paul'.[1] Cranfield comments: 'It is one of Paul's definitive expressions for the divine election'.[2]

The juxtaposition of the two nouns ἐκλογή and πρόθεσις is unique not only in Paul, but in the New Testament. Again, the full meaning of these words, particularly πρόθεσις, will only be disclosed by the totality of Paul's argument in chs. 9 to 11, but it is noteworthy that Paul's 'God-language' is here reaching beyond the bounds of Septuagintal language.

One more word in this first section of the midrash (vv. 6-13) concerns us here. It would be difficult to overestimate the significance of the verb καλέω in Paul's God-language. It is used by him many times.[3] Here it functions as a keyword in the midrash,[4] occurring not only in the crucial comment in v.11b and 12a,

> ἵνα ἡ κατ' ἐκλογὴν πρόθεσις τοῦ θεοῦ μένῃ, οὐκ ἐξ ἔργων ἀλλ' ἐκ τοῦ καλοῦντος

but also in the first of Paul's Old Testament quotations in this section,

> ἐν Ἰσαὰκ κληθήσεταί σοι σπέρμα (v.7b).

Here, as Wilckens rightly observes,[5] κληθήσεται is a divine passive, and must be linked with the καλοῦντος of v.12. A further comment by Wilckens on this verb is noteworthy. After surveying its occurrences in the epistles of the New Testament, Wilckens observes,

> Therefore God in early Christian tradition has simply the name ὁ καλέσας, as the one who binds himself by his call to the ones he has called, and makes them worthy of fellowship with him (2 Thessalonians 1.11).[6]

Pauline and deutero-Pauline writings in the New Testament (Rom. 8.28; 9.11; Eph. 1.11; 3.11; 2 Tim. 1.9). πρόθεσις is also used of human purpose and devotion (e.g. Acts 11.23), and in the cultic sense of 'setting forth' (e.g. Mk 2.26). This is its usual meaning in the LXX until the Maccabean writings, where there is a possible parallel to its use here (*3 Macc*. 5.29; cf. 2 Macc. 3.8; *3 Macc*. 1.22; 2.26; 5.12). The source of this later meaning is probably secular Greek, since πρόθεσις is commonly used from Aristotle onwards to express purpose (Sanday and Headlam, *Romans*, p. 244).

1. Sanday and Headlam, *Romans*, p. 244.
2. Cranfield, *Romans*, II, p. 478.
3. 1 Thess. 2.12; 4.7; 5.24; Gal. 1.6, 15; 5.8, 13; 1 Cor. 1.9; 7.15, 17-18. 20-22, 24; Rom. 4.17; 8.30; 9.7, 12, 24-26.
4. Stegner, 'Midrash', p. 38.
5. Wilckens, *An die Römer*, II, p. 192.
6. Wilckens, *An die Römer*, II, p. 206.

Delling[1] goes so far as to suggest that καλῶν is the divine characteristic in the New Testament which parallels ἁγιάζων in the Old Testament. This, however, is doubtful, since καλέω is used often enough in the LXX of God, particularly in Deutero-Isaiah.[2] Nevertheless, the relative (compared with the Old Testament) infrequency of ἁγιάζω in the New Testament with God as the explicit or implicit subject may be significant,[3] and there can be no doubt from Paul's writings of the new role of καλέω in indicating what might be considered the primary divine activity (Rom. 4.17).

In evaluating Paul's language about God in Rom. 9.6-13, however, we have to take account not only of his choice and use of individual words or phrases, but also how these function in the argument as a whole. In order to appreciate the distinctiveness of Paul, or, alternatively, his lack of it, I turn to those Jewish sources which have a bearing on this study. I examine first the book of *Jubilees*, which a recent study has dated around the middle of the second century before Christ.[4] The version of Gen. 18.1-15 which we find here is told in the first person plural. Thus, whereas Genesis 18 begins with a reference to 'God' appearing to Abraham by the oak of Mamre, *Jubilees* (16.1) has 'we appeared to Abraham'. This section of *Jubilees* is, in fact, a considerably abbreviated version of Genesis, reducing Gen. 18.1-15 to a mere four verses (16.1-4). Thus the two verses (Gen. 18.10 and 14) from which Paul draws his quotation in Rom. 9.9 become in the *Jubilees* version 'and (that) when we returned to her at a specific time she should have conceived a son' (*Jub*. 16.4).

The Genesis quotation used earlier by Paul (Rom. 9.7), occurs later in Genesis (21.12). Here the equivalent passage in *Jubilees* is as follows:

1. Delling, 'Partizipiale', p. 31.
2. Isa. 41.2, 4, 9; 42.6; 43.1 etc.
3. *Only* God is the subject (NB the passives) of ἁγιάζω in Paul (Rom. 15.16; 1 Cor. 1.2; 6.11; 7.14; 1 Thess. 5.23).
4. O.S. Wintermute in J.H. Charlesworth, *Old Testament Pseudepigrapha* (London: Darton, Longman & Todd, 1985), II, p. 44; G.L. Davenport, *The Eschatology of the Book of Jubilees* (Leiden: Brill, 1971), posits three possible dates, but all these are regarded by him as within a period spanning the latter part of the third century and c.104 BCE, (pp. 14-16); cf. G.W.E. Nickelsburg, *Jewish Literature between the Bible and the Mishnah* (London: SCM Press, 1981), pp. 78-79, who regards c.175 and 100 BCE as 'the outer limits', with particular pointers towards a date around 168.

> (As for) everything which Sarah said to you, obey her words and do (it) because it is through Isaac that a name and seed will be named for you (*Jub*. 17.6).

Two points are worth making here. First, with reference to the first passage, most Jewish writers faced with the apparent ambiguity in the Genesis story arising from the alternating references to 'the Lord' (Gen. 18.1 and 13), 'three men' (vv. 2-8, 9 and 16) and 'he' (v. 10), describe Abraham's visitors consistently as angels. Paul's reference to the passage is much briefer, and for his particular purpose a reference to divine action is needed.[1] Secondly, with reference to the two writers' use of Genesis 21, Paul retains the, to him, all-important word 'call', whereas *Jubilees* does not. Thus, while the writer of *Jubilees* does not depart significantly from the text, Paul fastens on the word 'call', and, to a considerable extent, builds his midrash upon it.

When we turn to *Jubilees*' version of the Jacob and Esau stories, we find some significant differences from the Genesis narratives. First, the writer implies that *from the beginning* Jacob was more deserving of divine favour than Esau:

> And in the sixth week in the second year Rebecca bore two children for Isaac, Jacob and Esau. And Jacob was smooth and upright, but Esau was a fierce man and rustic and hairy. And Jacob used to dwell in the tents and the youths grew up and Jacob learned writing, but Esau did not learn because he was a rustic man and a hunter, and he learned war, and all of his deeds were fierce (*Jub*. 19.13-14).

The position of this description in the narrative is important. It is the equivalent in *Jubilees* of Gen. 25.24-27, a passage which immediately follows the text quoted by Paul but omitted by *Jubilees*,

> ὁ μείζων δουλεύσει τῷ ἐλάσσονι (Rom. 9.12b, Gen. 25.23).

Thus the reference to Jacob's uprightness precedes the blessings pronounced by Abraham upon Jacob (*Jub*. 22.10-24). It is not explicitly stated that the blessing is the reward for Jacob's uprightness, but the order of events in the narrative carries that implication. A similar theological implication may lie behind the sequence in 22.14-15, part of Abraham's blessing on Jacob, in which a reference to the 'cleansing' of

1. Paul's references to angels are unusually unfavourable, by comparison with many (other) Jewish writers. Thus, the angels of Rom. 8.38, 1 Cor. 4.9 and 11.10 are hostile or potentially hostile. (The references in Gal.1.8, 4.14 and 1 Cor. 13.1 are rhetorical, while Gal. 3.19 refers to angels as mediators of the Law.)

Jacob from sin precedes a reference to God's renewal of the covenant with him:

> May he cleanse you from all sin and defilement,
> so that he might forgive all your transgressions, and your erring through ignorance.
> May he strengthen and bless you,
> and may you inherit all of the earth.
> And may he renew his covenant with you,
> so that you might be a people for him.

Thus, while Sanders[1] is correct in his emphasis that in *Jubilees* 'election is the basis of salvation', that is not the whole picture. He rightly stresses the importance of Jacob,[2] but overlooks the evidence noted above.[3] In particular, the descriptions of Jacob and Esau in *Jub.* 19.13-14 seem to be examples of later beliefs about the two brothers colouring the portrayal of their earliest years, although this opens the way for a misunderstanding of the basis of God's choice of Jacob. Here, it must be said, Paul is more faithful to the substance of the Genesis narrative. But Sanders is probably correct in his conclusion about *Jubilees*[4] that 'the author's view is not the kind of legalism which is summed up in the phrase "works righteousness", for salvation depends on the grace of God'. But it is more questionable whether Sanders is correct in saying that 'God of his own will chose Israel is the predominant theme in *Jubilees*'.[5] It is clearly *a* prominent theme, as one would expect in a document clearly based on the Genesis narrative. But another theme has been introduced, namely the worthiness of the patriarchs. While Sanders acknowledges that 'the author can also say that Abraham chose God and his dominion (12.19)', adding, 'as always, in Judaism, the divine choice does not eliminate freedom of action',[6] one may wonder whether

1. Sanders, *Paul and Palestinian Judaism*, p. 368.
2. Sanders, *Paul and Palestinian Judaism*, p. 363.
3. In a subsequent discussion (pp. 380-83) Sanders notes the frequency of the word 'upright' and related words in *Jubilees* (words applied to Jacob at 27.17 and 35.12), but does not consider the *sequence* of the statements in *Jubilees* and its theological implications.
4. Sanders, *Paul and Palestinian Judaism*, p. 383.
5. Sanders, *Paul and Palestinian Judaism*, p. 363. The same point might be made with reference to the author's description of the birth of Abraham (*Jub.* 11.14-16).
6. Sanders, *Paul and Palestinian Judaism*, p. 363.

Sanders has done justice to the overall picture presented by *Jubilees*.

Other Jewish pseudepigraphical work concerns us here, namely *4 Ezra* 3.13-16.[1] This passage comes from the first vision of the apocalypse, and forms part of the seer's review of history, beginning with Adam (3.4), and ending with the deliverance of Jerusalem into the hands of God's enemies (3.27).[2] In vv. 13-16 he refers to the patriarchs:

> And when they were committing iniquity before you, you chose for yourself one of them, whose name was Abraham; and you loved him and to him only you revealed the end of times, secretly by night. You made with him an everlasting covenant, and promised him that you would never forsake his descendants; and you gave to him Isaac, and to Isaac you gave Jacob and Esau. And you set apart Jacob for yourself, but Esau you rejected; and Jacob became a great multitude' (3.13-16).

Although it is probably correct to see in the figures of Jacob and Esau references to Judaism and Rome, it is important not to exaggerate the differences between Paul and *4 Ezra* here.[3] Even though the writer of *4 Ezra* later goes on to protest 'what nation has kept your commandments so well?' (3.35b; cf. vv. 32-33), the earlier passage is remarkable in what it does *not* say about God's call of the patriarchs (i.e. no character references here), and to that extent it bears a closer resemblance to Paul's version than the accounts in *Jubilees*.

I turn next to the Targums. Identifying the provenance of these, and establishing the age of the material to be found within them is a widely recognized problem. For that reason it cannot be assumed without question that we are dealing with material which is pre-Pauline or even contemporary with Paul. Nevertheless, the view should be noted of a recent editor of the Palestinian Targums that both *Targum Pseudo-Jonathan* and the traditions behind *Codex Neofiti I* contain ancient material of relevant interest 'for a comparison with the NT'.[4] They do, however, contain later additions (e.g. a reference to the daughter of

1. Cited by Wilckens, *An die Römer*, II, p. 195.

2. This sentence is a clear indication that the author has in mind not just the fall of Jerusalem in 587 BCE at the hands of Babylon, but also the fall of Jerusalem to Rome in 70 CE (cf. 3.28) .

3. As Käsemann, *Romans*, p. 264, seems to do.

4. N. McNamara, *The New Testament and the Palestinian Targum* (Shannon: Irish University Press, 1968), pp. 15-16, argues that a pre-Christian date is probable for the Palestinian Targum or targums (cf. p. 167).

Mahomet in *Targ. Ps.-J.* Jo Gen. 21.21[1]), and therefore have to be used with some care.

Attention will focus chiefly on *Targum Pseudo-Jonathan* and *Targum Neofiti I*, rather than *Targum Onqelos*. Whether Onqelos was originally Palestinian is debated,[2] but we should note its 'offical' status,[3] and hence its quality as 'certainly the most accurate Aramaic translation of the Hebrew Scriptures'.[4] This needs to be borne in mind when the total evidence is evaluated, for while the other Targum versions sometimes give quite striking departures from, and additions to the Masoretic text (MT), they were clearly not the only scriptural interpretations in currency, and still less, it seems, 'official' interpretations.

The particular concern of this study is to note the Targumic versions of the passages cited by Paul in Romans from the Pentateuch. But first, it is important to note the purpose of the Targums, and the consequences for the language they use (and refrain from using) about God. 'If, as seems certain, [*Targ. Onq.*] was designed for the instruction and edification of the masses...it was essential to alter or eliminate expressions and phrases which were unacceptable to rabbinic theology and *Halakha*'.[5] One of the most prominent features of this kind is the elimination of anthropomorphisms in language about God.[6] As we shall see later, however, anthropomorphisms do not seem to have been an issue for Paul.[7]

In examining the Targumic evidence, it will be necessary to concentrate on those renderings which provide a significant comparison with Old Testament texts cited or referred to by Paul. And first I turn to the

1. M. Aberbach and B. Grossfeld, *Targum Onkelos to Genesis* (New York: Ktav, 1982), pp. 36 and 211 n.12.

2. This is the majority view (Aberbach and Grossfeld, *Targum*, p. 9; cf. R. le Déaut, *Targum du Pentateuque Tome i Genèse* [Paris: Les Editions du Cerf: 1978], p. 21), although it is generally agreed that its final redaction occurred in Babylonia.

3. Le Déaut, *Targum*, p. 20.

4. Aberbach and Grossfeld, *Targum*, p. 9.

5. Aberbach and Grossfeld, *Targum*, p. 10.

6. Among countless examples which could be given, we note the rendering by *Targum Onqelos* of a phrase in Gen.12.7: where the MT has 'was seen': Onqelos renders 'and the Lord *revealed himself* to Abraham'. Cf. McNamara, *New Testament*, pp. 93-94.

7. Paul's LXX quotations contain anthropomorphisms not found elsewhere in his writings. (See the comment on Rom. 10.21 on p. 75 below, and compare also 2 Cor. 6.2).

rendering of Gen. 21.12, quoted by Paul in Rom. 9.7b: ἐν Ἰσαὰκ κληθήσεταί σοι σπέρμα. The rendering of *Targum Pseudo-Jonathan* (henceforward, JO[1]) is translated by Le Déaut as follows:

> It is through Isaac, in fact, that your sons will be called, since this son [sc. Ishmael] of your slavegirl will not be reckoned as your descendant (in your genealogy).[2]

In the preceding verse, however, JO has introduced a quite new thought into the narrative. The Genesis text suggests that Abraham did not wish to expel Hagar and Ishmael from his household: 'And the thing was very displeasing to Abraham on account of his son'(Gen. 21.11). JO, however, explicitly says that the cause of Abraham's displeasure was Ishmael's idolatry: 'The thing greatly displeased Abraham [lit. caused displeasure in the eyes of Abraham] because of his son Ishmael who had devoted himself to the cult of idols'.[3] In fact, both JO and *Neofiti I (N)*, in an elaboration of an earlier verse, accuse Ishmael of trying to lure Isaac into idolatry,[4] and JO goes on to say (v. 12) that Ishmael had departed from the teaching he had received from Abraham.

All of this may seem a far cry from the God-language of Paul, but in fact it is not. For although we are not dealing with explicit God-language or explicit theology (any more than in *Jubilees*), the overall effect is to compromise the freedom of God to elect whomsoever he chooses irrespective of what they have or have not done. But this is clearly the thrust of Paul's argument, even though he does not make explicit in the case of Isaac what he later says (vv. 11 and 12a) of Jacob and Esau.

In the case of other verses from Genesis quoted by Paul in Romans 9, both JO and N retain the first person singular in their renderings of Gen. 18.10 and 14 (Rom. 9.9) with very few alterations, and so they need not concern us here. However, at Gen. 25.23 (Rom. 9.12b), JO again provides the most significant departure from the MT. The RSV renders the verse as follows:

> Two nations are in your womb,
> and two peoples, born of you, shall be divided:

1. The abbreviation of Le Déaut's edition.
2. Le Déaut, *Targum*, p. 209.
3. Le Déaut, *Targum*.
4. The reference in Gen. 21.9 to Ishmael 'playing' (מצחק) (the Hebrew does not have 'with Isaac') is ambiguous (G. Von Rad, *Genesis* [London: SCM Press, 1961], p. 227).

> the one shall be stronger than the other,
> the elder shall serve the younger.

There are two significant features in JO's rendering of this verse (only the last part of which is quoted by Paul). First, it introduces the word 'kingdom' (מלכות) (as also does N), where the MT has 'peoples'(לאמים). But secondly, and more importantly, JO adds a condition at the end of the saying: the elder shall serve the younger 'if the sons of the younger keep the commandments of the Law'.[1] It is important to recognize, of course, that there are many examples in the Old Testament of promises with conditions attached, but here in one Targumic rendering of verses quoted by Paul, we have elaborations which, in effect, compromise the unconditionality of the divine promise.

In the writings of Philo it is more difficult to track down the texts, or the contexts, from which Paul draws in Romans 9. This is largely because Philo often engages in commentary-like writing, but does not work through the Genesis narratives in the way in which the writer of *Jubilees* (or Josephus)[2] does. First, in *De Sobrietate* Philo uses Genesis 21, and the story of Isaac and Ishmael to illustrate his contention that the term 'elder' is often used by Moses to describe those who, perhaps younger in years, are nevertheless spiritually mature. So, for example, at the age of twenty, says Philo, Ishmael is still a mere child, whereas Isaac is 'full-grown in virtues'.[3] Here Philo's moralizing treatment bypasses

1. Le Déaut, *Targum*, pp. 245-47.

2. There is little relevant to our purpose in Josephus' version of these Genesis passages. In his study of Josephus' treatment of Genesis T.W. Franxman notes how Josephus, with reference to Gen. 1–12, radically reduces the number of direct quotations which Genesis attributes to the Deity. The quotations are either omitted, (as in most of Gen. 1), or reported (as in Gen. 12.1-3). In subsequent chapters, some divine communications are simply omitted (e.g. Gen. 13.14-17). All other direct quotations are reduced to being reported, except a small portion of God's words to Abraham in Gen. 15, and two colloquies with Jacob (28.13-15 and 46.2-4) (T.W. Franxman, *Genesis and the Jewish Antiquities of Flavius Josephus* [Rome: Biblical Institute Press, 1979], p. 20).

Turning to the Genesis passages from which Paul draws in Rom. 9, we find that the promise of Isaac to Abraham is referred to in *Ant.* 1.183, 191 and 197. It is the last of these three which corresponds with the account in Gen. 18.1-15, from which Paul draws his quotation in Rom. 9.9. Here, Josephus writes consistently of three angels who are 'messengers of God' (*Ant.* 1.198). True to form, Josephus here turns the direct speech of Genesis 18.10 ('I will surely return to you in the spring, and Sarah your wife shall have a son') into indirect speech: 'they declared that they

the theological point drawn out of the Genesis story by Paul.

Secondly, in *De Abrahamo* 22.107-13, Philo discusses the story of Abraham narrated in Gen. 18.1-15. Abraham's three visitors are not identified as God, although their 'diviner' nature is alluded to (θειοτέρας ὄντες φύσεως). Here, however, Philo is concerned to emphasize Abraham's hospitality, which is the product of his 'piety' (θεοσέβεια, 23.114), in contrast to the inhospitality of the Egyptian described earlier. In fact, the promise of a son is described as a reward (ἆθλον) for his hospitality.[1]

Philo alludes to the births of Esau and Jacob in several places.[2] The most significant is the discussion in *De Legum Allegoria* III 29.89, in which Philo emphasizes that while Jacob and Esau were still in the womb God pronounced the one a ruler and the other a slave. However, the reason for this appears to be God's foreknowledge:

> For God the Maker of living things knoweth well the different pieces of his own handiwork, even before He has thoroughly chiselled and consummated them, and their faculties which they are to display at a later time, in a word their deeds and experiences.

Philo goes on to quote Gen. 25.23 ('Two nations are in thy womb') and comments:

would return one day and find that she had become a mother'.

It must be concluded that there are none of the themes here which we found in *Jubilees* and some of the Targums. The alterations are more stylistic, Josephus conscious, perhaps, of a Graeco-Roman readership.

Of the remaining verses quoted by Paul in this section of Romans, the promise incorporated into the story of the expulsion of Hagar (Gen. 21.12; Rom. 9.7b) is passed over by Josephus in his re-writing of the story. Finally, the births of Jacob and Esau are briefly recounted (*Ant.* 1.257-58), Josephus again replacing the divine direct speech of Gen. 25.23 by indirect speech: 'And He told him that Rebecca would give birth to twins, that nations would bear their names, and that he that to appearance was the lesser would excel the greater'.

3. *Sobr.*2.8.

1. Cf. *Cher.* 13.45. Here, however, the point is the gift of the God who is all-sufficient. Clement of Rome provides an interesting parallel to the above reference: 'It was also because of his faith and hospitality that a son was given to him in his old age' (*1 Clement* c.10, translation from M. Staniforth, *Early Christian Writings* [Harmondsworth: Penguin, 1968], p. 28).

2. Philo alludes to the two brothers many times (Colson, Loeb I, p. xxv). Of the passages listed by Colson, the following allude directly or indirectly to their births: *Sacrif.* 17, *Sobr.* 26, *Congr.* 61.

> For in God's judgment that which is base and irrational is by nature a slave, but that which is of fine character and endowed with reason and better is princely and free. And this not only when either is full-grown in soul, but even if their development is uncertain.

Philo's treatment of the Genesis narratives is very different from that of Paul. In the passage just quoted, Philo's emphasis on the foresight of God, rather than what Paul calls ἡ κατ' ἐκλογὴν πρόθεσις τοῦ θεοῦ, together with his moralizing approach, draws a very different lesson from the Genesis narratives.

Finally, with reference to Rom. 9.6-13, I examine relevant passages in the midrash.[1] First, there are few comments on Gen. 21.12 (Rom. 9.7b), and on Gen. 18.10, 14 (Rom. 9.9) relevant to the purpose of the study. There is, however, an interesting comment at *Gen. R.* 53.12 on Gen. 21.12: R. Judah b. Shilum, noting the '*in* Isaac' says 'The "*beth*" (In) denotes two...thus whoever believes in the two worlds shall be called "thy seed"'.[2] This same passage is noted by Stegner,[3] who posits a common exegetical tradition.

Rabbinic comments on the Jacob and Esau stories show some significant differences from Paul. God-language cannot often be directly compared, but the theological implications of statements about the two brothers are important, and form an interesting comparison with what Paul is saying here about God. First, in the midrash, it is clear that Jacob and Esau are 'types' of the later Israelite and Edomite nations, and this has significantly influenced interpretation of the Genesis stories.[4] This means that heinous crimes are attributed to Esau which have no basis in the Genesis narratives at all. For example, when Esau comes in from the field (Gen. 25.29), it was because he had 'violated a betrothed maiden' and 'committed murder' (Deut. 22.25 and Jer. 4.31 being cited in support).[5] Conversely, Jacob's faults and shortcomings are frequently

1. The translation quoted from below is that of H. Freedman and M. Simon (eds.), *Midrash Rabbah* (10 vols.; London: Soncino Press, 1939).

2. *Gen. R.* 53.12 (Freedman and Simon, *Midrash*, p. 471).

3. Stegner, 'Midrash', p. 46. Whether the statement of R. Judah can be called 'precisely Paul's stance in Romans' (ibid.) even though the content of belief differed is more questionable.

4. Munck notes *Jub.* 37–38, and *T. Jud.* 9 in this connection (*Christ and Israel*, pp. 39-43).

5. *Gen. R.* 63.12 (Freedman and Simon, *Midrash*, p. 567).

overlooked or minimized.[1] What is particularly significant for our comparison with Paul is that these interpretations are extended to the prenatal period. Thus whenever Rebecca passed idolatrous temples, Esau 'eagerly struggled to come out'.[2] But whenever Rebecca stood near synagogues or schools 'Jacob struggled to come out.'[3]

Finally, with reference to the verse which Paul quotes from Malachi ('Jacob I loved, Esau I hated', Mal. 1.3, Rom. 9.13), it is interesting to see that this same verse from Malachi is quoted with the comment 'The hated of thy creator is in thy womb'.[4] A second comment, noteworthy in the light of Paul's subsequent discussion of the place of Pharaoh in the purpose of God (Rom. 9.17-18), consists of a pun on the name Esau: 'It is for nought ("*shaw*") that I created him in my universe'.[5] It seems clear, therefore that the identification in later tradition of Esau with (a) the Edomite nation and (b) Rome[6] has been one influence in giving to these interpretations at least an implicit (occasionally explicit) theology quite different from that of Paul. As we saw in the book of *Jubilees*, in the Targums, and in Philo, the introduction of references to the characters of Jacob and Esau shifts the emphasis from God's calling and promise to the virtues and defects of the one called and the one rejected.

Summary. Some of Paul's God-language in vv. 1-13 appears, at first sight, traditional LXX or later Jewish God-language: the doxology of v. 5, 'the word of God' (v. 6), and the inclusion of no less than four examples of divine speech from the LXX (vv. 7, 9, 12, 13). Yet the form

1. For example, the only comment we find on Esau's accusation that Jacob took away the blessing by guile (Gen. 27.35) is: 'R. Johanan said: He (sc. Jacob) came with the wisdom of his *torah*' (67.4).

2. Here Ps. 68.4 is cited ('The wicked are estranged from the womb'). Strack–Billerbeck are therefore basically correct in saying that in the Haggadic literature the pre-natal sin of Esau is a theme (H.L. Strack and P. Billerbeck, *Kommentar zum Neuen Testament aus Talmud und Midrasch* (München: C.H. Beck'sche, 1928), III, p. 266). We note, however, the important and serious criticisms of Strack–Billerbeck by Sanders, concurring with the guidelines and conditions for its use which he argues for (*Paul and Palestinian Judaism*, pp. 234-35; cf. pp. 42-43).

3. Here Jer. 1.5 is cited ('Before I formed thee in the belly I knew thee').

4. *Gen. R.* 63.7 (Freedman and Simon, *Midrash*, p. 561).

5. Esau in Hebrew is עשו, 'emptiness' or 'vanity' is שוא.

6. From what period the identification of Esau with Rome began to be made is difficult to say. Throughout the Talmudic era this equation was made (Aberbach and Grossfeld, *Targum*, p. 151 n.14).

and function are quite distinctive. Paul, in effect, is writing a kind of midrash in which a key word (if not *the* key word) is καλέω (vv. 7 and 12), which he thereby characterizes as a primary and fundamental divine activity. Thus he meets Israel, so to speak, on her own territory, but develops the argument, and the God-language, in a quite distinctive way. The crucial 'piece' of God-language comes in v. 11, in words which are either absent from the LXX (ἐκλογή) or have a different meaning (πρόθεσις). Thus a radical statement about the freedom of God is made.

A marked contrast with all the Jewish writings (except *4 Ezra*) we have examined can be seen. The most important difference lies in the total exclusion from Paul of all references to the character of the patriarchs. In *Jubilees* the *order* of the material implicitly introduces a note of merit; in the Targums the addition of themes extraneous to the Old Testament texts, and in the midrash the identification of Jacob and Esau with contemporary Israel and Edom or Rome have a similar effect. Finally Philo by (a) moralizing and (b) an emphasis on the divine πρόνοια (a word never used by Paul of God) has also blunted the theme of *undeserved* choice which is the nub of Paul's argument.

It would be going too far to say that any of the authors is developing a theology of 'righteousness by works' (they tend to be moralistic rather than legalistic), and no doubt all would consciously reject such a theology. Nevertheless, the effect of many of their additions to, or interpretations of the text is to produce a less 'radical' understanding of the freedom of God than that which we find in Romans, particularly as expressed in 9.11-12:

> μήπω γὰρ γεννηθέντων μηδὲ πραξάντων τι ἀγαθὸν ἢ φαῦλον, ἵνα ἡ κατ' ἐκλογὴν πρόθεσις τοῦ θεοῦ μένῃ, οὐκ ἐξ ἔργων ἀλλ' ἐκ τοῦ καλοῦντος, ἐρρέθη αὐτῇ ὅτι ὁ μείζων δουλεύσει τῷ ἐλάσσονι, καθὼς γέγραπται τὸν Ἰακὼβ ἠγάπησα, τὸν δὲ Ἠσαῦ ἐμίσησα.[1]

b. *Verses 14-29*

Verses 14-29 comprise another section of Paul's argument in which there are significant comparisons to be made with Jewish sources and

1. As a postscript to this section we note the similar findings of G.W. Hansen *Abraham in Galatians: Epistolary and Rhetorical Contexts* (Sheffield: JSOT Press, 1989), Appendix I, pp. 167-74, who draws attention to the *motif* in Jewish tradition of Abraham's supposed obedience to the Mosaic Law, suggesting that Paul's opponents at Galatia used this to argue that by such obedience came Christian perfection. (Cf. Georgi, *Opponents*, pp. 51-52, who notes the stress on Abraham's piety *before*, as well as after, God's call to him, cf. pp. 57-58).

traditions, and with later Christian thought. Paul begins this section by anticipating a question from his students (as Stowers has shown in his study of the '*diatribe*' form)[1], and not opponents, imaginary or otherwise.[2] The question is very like an earlier one posed by Paul in this epistle: τί οὖν ἐροῦμεν; μὴ ἀδικία παρὰ τῷ θεῷ; μὴ γένοιτο (cf. Rom. 3.5). Now, however Paul's exposition of ἡ κατ᾽ ἐκλογὴν πρόθεσις τοῦ θεοῦ gives added urgency to the question. Having established a distinction within Israel which has no basis in human merit at all, but only in the πρόθεσις of God, he now proceeds to offer a positive and a negative example of this. Some commentators have concluded at this point that Paul does not take the question of his imaginary interlocutor seriously,[3] although there is no doubt that a satisfactory answer has been given by the end of ch. 11. Paul, however, is concerned for the moment with a thorough-going exposition of 'the elective purpose of God' in both its positive and negative manifestations.

The first language about God which concerns us here is a quotation from the LXX: τῷ Μωϋσεῖ γὰρ λέγει ἐλεήσω ὃν ἂν ἐλεῶ καὶ οἰκτιρήσω ὃν ἂν οἰκτίρω (Rom. 9.15, Exod. 33.19). Here Paul keeps to the text of the LXX (at least, to a form of the LXX known to us).[4] The Targums, both JO and N, give a rendering significantly different: 'He says…"I will show mercy on the one who is worthy of mercy, and I will have pity on the one who is worthy of pity"'.[5] The same emphasis occurs in the midrash where the following comment occurs:

> Then it was that God showed him all the treasures in which the rewards of the righteous are stored away. Moses asked: 'To whom does all this treasure belong?' 'To those who bring up orphans'... And I will be gracious... namely, unto him to whom I wish to be gracious.[6]

1. See the earlier discussion, pp. 30-31 above.
2. *Contra*, for example, Wilckens, *An die Römer*, II, p. 199. Wilckens more correctly notes the Jewish expression παρὰ τῷ θεῷ, equivalent to עם יהוה.
3. C.H. Dodd, *The Epistle to the Romans* (London: Hodder & Stoughton, 1932), p. 171; J.A.T. Robinson, *Wrestling with Romans* (London: SCM Press, 1979), pp. 115-16.
4. The great variety of textual forms makes it unwise to be dogmatic about which version or versions were known to Paul. Nevertheless, he seems to have followed the normal practice of incorporating interpretation into the text he is quoting.
5. Le Déaut, *Targum*, p. 267.
6. *Exod. R.* 45.6 (Freedman and Simon, *Midrash*, pp. 524-25). It is important to note, however, that the translators add in a footnote, 'Even if he has not earned it'.

This rendering is referred to by Munck[1] as 'the Jewish interpretation', a sweeping generalization. Nevertheless, I note that once again these interpretations produce a tension within the theological convictions of Israel. Although the mystery of Israel's call is also widely recognized within the Jewish literature of the period, it is difficult to avoid the conclusion that the Targumic versions, at least, of Exod. 33.19, introduce the concept of merit.

Paul next provides a summarizing comment on the quotation he has just given: ἄρα οὖν οὐ τοῦ θέλοντος οὐδὲ τοῦ τρέχοντος ἀλλὰ τοῦ ελεῶντος θεοῦ (v.16). There are two features about this verse relevant to this study: both suggest that in these chapters we are encountering Paul at his most Jewish. First, he uses the word ἐλεῶντος, a word very common in the LXX, but which, significantly, rarely occurs in Paul's writings outside Romans 9–11. It is used no less than six times by Paul in these chapters,[2] only four times elsewhere in his writings.[3] Similarly the noun ἔλεος occurs twice in Romans 9–11,[4] and only twice elsewhere.[5] Secondly, Paul's use of the word τρέχοντος, whilst admittedly not a God-word here, may indicate that he is reworking well-known Jewish exegetical traditions. Some Rabbinic comments on Gen. 25.22, 'And the children struggled together within her' (i.e. Jacob and Esau within Rebecca) derive the verb ויתרצצו from the verb רוץ meaning 'to run', as in the comment that 'each ran to slay the other'.[6] Although Paul is no longer speaking directly of Jacob and Esau here, it is possible that the occurrence of τρέχοντος in v. 16 is a reminiscence of the traditions on which Paul was drawing in vv. 6-13. Thus there is further evidence here that Paul is writing from Jewish traditions and

1. Munck, *Christ and Israel*, p. 44 n. 48. It is noted also by Strack–Billerbeck, *Kommentar*, III, p. 268.

2. 9.15, 16, 18; 11.30, 31, 32.

3. Rom. 12.8; 1 Cor. 7.25; 2 Cor. 4.1; Phil. 2.27.

4. 9.23; 11.31. R. Badenas, *Christ the End of the Law: Romans 10.4 in Pauline Perspective* (Sheffield: JSOT Press, 1985), pp. 236-37 n. 108 also notes the importance of this word-group in Rom. 9–11.

5. Rom. 15.9; Gal. 6, 16.

6. *Gen. R.* 63.6 (Freedman and Simon, *Midrash*, p. 559). J. Piper, *The Justification of God. An Exegetical and Theological Study of Romans 9.1-23* (Grand Rapids, MI: Baker, 1983), pp. 132-33, following Noack and Maier, may be correct in regarding τρέχοντος, not as a Greek athletic metaphor, but as a 'Jewish metaphor of moral attainment'. But he is wrong in assuming that Paul is arguing against Jewish legalists here.

using distinctively Jewish language about God.

Paul's next quotation from the Old Testament shows some significant differences from the Septuagint text as we know it.[1] Quoting Exod. 33.19, Paul has εἰς αὐτὸ τοῦτο ἐξήγειρά σε ὅπως ἐνδείξωμαι ἐν σοι τὴν δύναμίν μου καὶ ὅπως διαγγελῇ τὸ ὄνομά μου ἐν πάσῃ τῇ γῇ.[2] There are two noteworthy differences from the LXX text here: first, Paul has εἰς αὐτὸ τοῦτο where the LXX has ἕνεκεν τούτου, and secondly, Paul has the active ἐξήγειρα, stressing the divine initiative and sovereignty, where the LXX has the passive διετηρήθης, admittedly a '*divine* passive', reflecting God's activity, but a less strong expression than ἐξήγειρα. A third difference lies in the fact that Paul has δύναμιν where the LXX has ἰσχύν, δύναμιν being Paul's preferred word for power.[3]

In their rendering of this verse, the Targums are closer to the LXX than to Paul, in that they tend to speak of Pharaoh being *allowed to exist*. Le Déaut translates *Targum Neofiti*:

> But I have not let you exist until now in order that you may live well. No, it is for this reason that I have let you exist until now: to make you see the strength of my power, and so that you may make known my holy name throughout the whole earth.[4]

In short, what Paul has done here is to 'bring out more sharply the sovereignty of the divine purpose'.[5]

Paul now proceeds to offer a theological summary of the illustrations he has so far given: ἄρα οὖν ὃν θέλει ἐλεεῖ, ὃν δὲ θέλει

1. This is a necessary *caveat* to enter about all Paul's LXX quotations.

2. The preamble to this quotation, in view of the quotation's first person singular verbs, is noteworthy: λέγει γὰρ ἡ γραφὴ τῷ φαραώ. It constitutes important evidence that Scripture, for Paul, was the Word of God (cf. J.D.G. Dunn, *Romans* [WBC, 38; Waco, TX: Word Books, 1988], II, p. 553).

3. The word δύναμις is used of the power of God, or of Christ or of the Holy Spirit some twenty times in the Pauline letters, ἰσχύς not at all, although ἰσχύς is used of the power of God or Christ in the deutero-Paulines (Eph. 1.19; 6.10; 2 Thess. 1.9).

4. Le Déaut, *Targum*, pp. 66-68. JO, though somewhat shorter, is essentially the same. Cf. Strack–Billerbeck, *Kommentar*, III, pp. 268-69.

5. Cranfield, *Romans*, II, p. 486; cf. Dunn, *Romans*, p. 554. Piper, *Justification*, pp. 147-48, in a note on ἐξήγειρα, notes the view of Luz that Paul is not so much reverting to the Hebrew as using ἐξεγείρω in its general biblical use. But Piper claims that the Hebrew equivalent here (עמד) is not used in the *hiphil* to mean 'preserve alive', but 'to appoint'.

σκληρύνει (v. 18). The first part of this summary paraphrases that part of Exod. 33.19 which Paul has just quoted. The second half introduces the concept of divine 'hardening' which is vital to Paul's thought and argument at this point. The verb he uses here, σκληρύνει, is the one normally used[1] in Exodus of the Lord hardening Pharaoh's heart.[2]

In the several verses where these expressions occur, the Targums show little elaboration of the MT.[3] (The Exodus narratives themselves show some variations, speaking sometimes of the Lord hardening Pharaoh's heart [e.g. 4.21] and sometimes of Pharaoh hardening his heart [e.g. 8.15].[4]) The midrash, however, reveal some interesting comments on the Exodus narratives. But here there is much greater emphasis on the character of Pharaoh. At *Exod. R.* 8.1, for example, in a comment on Exod. 7.1 ('And the Lord said to Moses, See, I make you as God to Pharaoh') Pharaoh is charged with being one of four men who claimed divinity and thereby brought evil upon themselves'.[5] Several other passages in the midrash emphasize Pharaoh's wickedness. He is variously described as 'wicked' (e.g. 9.1), 'like a serpent' (9.4) ' a fool' (9.7 with reference to Prov. 29.11)[6] and an 'idolater' (9.9).

Midrashic comments on the hardening of Pharaoh's heart are interesting. Some attribute it directly to God: commenting on Exod. 9.12, the midrash states that even if Pharaoh now wished to repent, God would harden his heart 'in order to exact the whole punishment from him'.[7]

1. σκληρύνω occurs in the Exodus narratives with reference to hardening Pharaoh's heart at 4.21; 7.3, 22; 8.15 (LXX 11); 9.12, 35; 10.1.20, 27; 11.10; 13.15; 14.4, 8, 17 (references in Dunn, *Romans*, II, p. 554).

2. σκληρύνω translates three Hebrew verbs in these passages: קשה, meaning, in the *Hiphil*, 'to make difficult' (Exod. 10.1), חזק, meaning in the *Piel* form, 'to make rigid or hard' (Exod. 4.21; 7.22; 8.19; 9.12, 35; 10.20, 27; 14.4, 8, 17, and, thirdly, כבד, in the *Hiphil*, 'to make unresponsive (Exod. 10.1).

3. JO always speaks of the hardening of 'the dispositions of his heart'. The Exodus narratives themselves seem to show some variations, speaking sometimes of 'the Lord hardening' Pharaoh's heart, and occasionally, as at 8.15, of Pharaoh hardening his heart.

4. Noted also by Dunn, *Romans*, II, p. 554.

5. In support of this judgment Ezek. 29.31 and Jer. 44.36 are cited as evidence of Pharaoh's punishment.

6. Prov. 29.11: 'A fool gives full vent to his anger, but a wise man quietly holds it back'.

7. A second, more theological interpretation of Pharaoh's hardening follows at this point.

On the other hand, a more psychologizing explanation is given at 9.8: 'He (sc. Pharaoh) is angry; just as the liver (*kabed*) waxed angry, so has the heart of this man become stubborn. He does not understand, being a fool, for: 'Anger resteth in the bosom of fools' (Prov. 26.3).[1]

On the whole, then, the emphasis in midrashic interpretations falls heavily on the character of Pharaoh; the freedom and sovereignty of God are not usually the focus of attention, as they clearly are in Paul.

A similar pattern can be found in other Jewish writers. Josephus adds some critical character references to his version of the Exodus story. After the Nile has turned to blood, he writes: 'God, seeing that the graceless king, after deliverance from this calamity was no longer willing to be wise'.[2] Similarly Pharaoh 'less fool than knave, though alive to the cause of it all, was matching himself against God as a deliberate traitor to the cause of virtue'.[3] A similar point may be made about the writings of Philo. Several times in his *De Vita Mosis* Philo stresses the character of Pharaoh:

> The king, whose soul from his earliest years was weighed down with the pride of many generations, did not accept a God discernible only by the mind.[4]

referring a little later on to 'the harshness and ferocity and obstinacy of his temper'.[5] So obstinate is Pharaoh, in fact, that Philo describes the Egyptians as protesting to him ὡς πάντων αἰτίου τῶν συμβεβηκότων δεινῶν, although there is no evidence in Exodus of such a complaint.

The references, therefore, in Jewish literature to the Exodus narrative from which Paul quotes reflect the same tendency which was discernible in the Jewish interpretations of the Genesis passages used earlier by Paul. That tendency is to fill out the biblical narratives with character references which they do not contain. Some of these elaborations, particularly those referring to Pharaoh, are a natural deduction from the biblical text, but the effect of all the elaborations, whether they are a natural deduction from the text or not, is to make the interpretations less theocentric than the original scriptural texts. It would be wrong to read into

1. *Exod. R.* 9.8 (Freedman and Simon, *Midrash*, p. 125).
2. *Ant.* 2.296.
3. *Ant.* 2.307, cited by Munck, *Christ and Israel*, p. 48, who dubs it a psychologizing version.
4. *Vit. Mos.* 1.88.
5. *Vit. Mos.* 1.89.

the interpretations a doctrine of 'justification by works', but the overall result is to blur the argument that God's call and promise do not rest on what has been done or not done.[1] The stark theocentricity of Paul's argument is well brought out in the summary of v. 18.

Before I move on to the next stage of Paul's argument, it will be useful to underline the distinctiveness of Paul's language here by a brief look at how other Christian writers have handled the concept of the divine 'hardening'.

Although Paul uses πωρόω synonymously with σκληρύνω (Rom. 11.7-10), σκληρύνω itself is a rare word in the New Testament, occurring, apart from here in Romans, only at Acts 19.9, and Heb. 3.8, 13, 15 and 4.7. The Hebrews references can be ignored here, since the last three are echoes or paraphrases of the original quotation, from Psalm 95 (LXX 94) v. 8: μὴ σκληρύνητε τὰς καρδίας ὑμῶν. This corresponds to that Exodus theme which Paul does *not* take up, namely, that of a human being hardening his heart, and so it offers no parallel to Paul's thought here. The verse from Acts (19.9) is more ambiguous. The setting is the synagogue at Ephesus, and the verse describes the response of some of the Jews there: ὡς δέ τινες ἐσκληρύνοντο καὶ ἠπείθουν κακολογοῦντες τὴν ὁδὸν ἐνώπιον τοῦ πλήθους. Here it is unlikely that a reference to *divine* hardening is intended. Haenchen[2] translates 'some hardened themselves', although the other verses which he cites have no parallel to this particular expression. Bruce, probably more correctly, translates ἐσκληρύνοντο by 'were obstinate' (lit. 'made themselves difficult').[3]

Lampe notes the metaphorical use of σκληρύνω in patristic writings.[4] Once again, however, the themes we have noticed in other writers can be traced. Clement of Rome, for example, writes of a man 'hardening his heart' (σκληρῦναι τὴν καρδίαν αὐτοῦ), and continues:

> as the hearts of those who rebelled against Moses the servant of God were hardened (ἐσκληρύνθη)... Pharaoh, too, and his army... were swallowed up in the Red Sea and perished, for no other reason than that

1. Munck, *Christ and Israel*, p. 43. Cf. Ziesler, *Romans*, p. 243.
2. E. Haenchen, *The Acts of the Apostles* (Oxford: Basil Blackwell, 1971), p. 559.
3. F.F. Bruce, *The Acts of the Apostles* (London: Tyndale, 1951), p. 355.
4. G.W.H. Lampe (ed.), *A Patristic Greek Lexicon* (Oxford: Oxford University Press, 1961), p. 1240, where several references to Pharaoh are listed.

> their foolish hearts were hardened (σκληρυνθῆναι), after God's servant Moses had performed his signs and wonders in the land of Egypt.[1]

Here, although the passive 'were hardened' is used, Clement's earlier expression 'hardening his heart' suggests that ἐσκληρύνθη is not to be taken as a divine passive. Secondly, the moralizing nature of this paraenetic section shifts the centre of attention to Pharaoh's character (NB 'foolish'), rather than divine agency.

Origen, too, in his Homilies on Exodus, notes the expressions 'the heart of Pharaoh was hardened', and 'the Lord hardened Pharaoh's heart', taking the former to mean *quasi sponte induratum.*[2] Origen interprets the language of Exodus here by reference to Rom. 2.4-5. Here however the emphasis falls on human responsibility, rather than divine agency:

> ἢ τοῦ πλούτου τῆς χρηστότητος αὐτοῦ καὶ τῆς ἀνοχῆς καὶ τῆς μακροθυμίας καταφρονεῖς... κατὰ δε τὴν σκληρότητά σου καὶ ἀμετανόητον καρδίαν θησαυρίζεις σεαυτῷ ὀργὴν ἐν ἡμέρᾳ ὀργῆς καὶ ἀποκαλύψεως δικαιοκρισίας τοῦ θεοῦ...

In fact, the fate of Pharaoh is referred to quite frequently in patristic writings,[3] but it is explained *as his own fault*.[4] It thus appears that Paul in his stress on the divine freedom and agency, differs not only from Jewish writers (except the book of Exodus itself), but also from Christian writers as well.[5]

This uncompromising tone does not change in the verses which follow. Here Paul is drawing on motifs and imagery which are very common in Jewish writings. There are several close parallels to the questions posed by Paul in v. 19: Ἐρεῖς μοι οὖν τί (οὖν) ἔτι μέμφεται; τῷ γὰρ βουλήματι αὐτοῦ τίς ἀνθέστηκεν;

This is particularly true of the second question (which is incorrectly translated by both the NRSV and the REB, both of which introduce the word 'can'; as Dunn points out, the issue is not who *can* resist God's

1. Clement of Rome 51.3 (trans. Staniforth, *Writings*, p. 50).
2. M. Borret (trans.), *Origène—Homélies sur L'Exode* (Paris: Editions du Cerf, 1985), IV.2 (p. 120).
3. See Lampe, *Lexicon*, for a full list of references.
4. I owe this observation to Munck, *Christ and Israel*, p. 43 n.45.
5. It must be stressed that I am discussing here Jewish and Christian treatments of a particular Old Testament motif, rather than their general theology.

will, but who *has* resisted[1]).The nearest parallels seem to be Job 9.4 and 19, and Wis. 12.12:

> Who has resisted him and succeeded?... If it is a matter of justice, who can summon him? (Job 9.4b, 19b).
>
> For who will say 'What have you done?' Or will resist your judgment? Who will accuse you for the destruction of nations that you have made? Or who will come before you to plead as an advocate for the unrighteous? (Wis. 12.12).[2]

However, despite the similarity in language, the difference in context is crucial. The verses from Job are part of a bitter, despairing speech in which Job laments his impotence before what he perceives as divine injustice:

> though I am blameless, he would prove me perverse... he destroys both the blameless and the wicked (vv. 20b and 22b).

The verse from Wisdom comes at the end of the writer's description of the fate of the 'ancient inhabitants of your holy land' (v. 3), and forms part of a passage in which the tension between ethnocentricity and a broader universalism is particularly acute.[3]

At first, Paul's terse, swift-moving *diatribe* style gives the impression of harshness, even ruthlessness on the part of God. But while the theme of divine severity undoubtedly runs throughout these chapters,[4] no stage

1. Dunn, *Romans*, II, p. 556. Wilckens, *An die Römer*, II, p. 201 n. 893, calls ἀνθέστηκεν a gnomic perfect.

2. Job 9.4b: τὶς σκληρὸς γενόμενος ἐνάντιον αὐτοῦ ὑπέμεινεν;
Job 9.19b: τὶς οὖν κρίματι αὐτοῦ ἀντιστήσεται;
Wis. 12.12a: Τὶς γὰρ ἐρει Τὶ ἐποίησας ἢ τὶς ἀντιστήσεται τῷ κρίματί σου;

Other parallels to Paul's language are: Job 41.1b, 2; Nah.1.6; Wis. 11.21; Jdt.16.14.

3. In fact, the book of Wisdom seems to provide a notable contrast with Paul's thought, where the point, in the end, is that God does not liquidate the vessels of wrath. We should note, however, the earlier assertion of the writer of Wisdom that 'It is your mastery over all which causes you to spare all' (11.26). Commenting on this last verse, Winston refers to the teaching of R. Joshua b. Levi that God's omnipotence reaches its culmination in the repression of his wrath and in his longsuffering with the wicked (*b. Yom.* 69b, quoted by D. Winston, *The Wisdom of Solomon* [New York: Doubleday, 1979], p. 242). Winston cites a parallel in Ps-Aristeas. It is doubtful whether Sir. 16.11 offers a parallel, as he seems to imply.

4. See the discussion of Rom. 11 in section 3 below.

of the argument can be detached from the conclusion towards which Paul is working in 11.32: συνέκλεισεν γὰρ ὁ θεὸς τοὺς πάντας εἰς ἀπείθειαν, ἵνα τοὺς πάντας ἐλεήσῃ. Barrett's comment on this verse is crucial for a proper understanding of the God-language of ch. 9:

> Here at length the full meaning of Paul,'s 'double predestination' is revealed. God has predestinated *all men* to wrath and he has predestinated *all men* to mercy. If they were not predestinated to the former they could not be predestinated to the latter.[1]

Thus, in the light of 11.32, Barrett, commenting on the harsh language of ch. 9, remarks: 'it is not unimportant that Pharaoh...is regarded as standing within God's purpose, which is a purpose of mercy'.[2] This is so important a point that it is necessary to ask whether Barrett is justified in regarding 11.32 as an interpretative control on ch. 9. It is true that Paul's first readers or hearers may not have been able to anticipate, as they heard or read ch. 9, the conclusion which he reaches in 11.32. But Romans 9–11 is a carefully structured unity, in which the language, for example, of 9.15 and 25 anticipates the conclusion of 11.32. The careful structure of the whole may be seen particularly in the way in which 10.12-13 come almost exactly halfway:

> οὐ γάρ ἐστιν διαστολὴ Ἰουδαίου τε καὶ Ἕλληνος, ὁ γὰρ αὐτὸς κύριος πάντων, πλουτῶν εἰς πάντας τοὺς ἐπικαλουμένους αὐτόν· πᾶς γὰρ ὃς ἂν ἐπικαλέσηται τὸ ὄνομα κυρίου σωθήσεται.

Before this point, much of Paul's language has been 'turning the tables' (i.e. on Israel) language. Thereafter, Paul works back, as it were, to the inclusive conclusion of 11.32. The unity of the argument, therefore, justifies us in accepting 11.32 as an interpretative control on ch. 9.

There are many parallels in Jewish writings to the image of the potter and the clay which now follows in vv. 20 and 21:

> ὦ ἄνθρωπε, μενοῦνγε σὺ τίς εἶ ὁ ἀνταποκρινόμενος τῷ θεῷ; μὴ ἐρεῖ τὸ πλάσμα τῷ πλάσαντι τί με ἐποίησας οὕτως; ἢ οὐκ ἔχει ἐξουσίαν ὁ κεραμεὺς τοῦ πηλοῦ ἐκ τοῦ αὐτοῦ φυράματος ποιῆσαι ὃ μὲν εἰς τιμὴν σκεῦος ὃ δὲ εἰς ἀτιμίαν;

1. Barrett, *Romans*, p. 227. The unity of these chapters is acknowledged, e.g. by Dodd, *Romans*, pp. 23, 161, and Ziesler, *Romans*, p. 38.
2. Barrett, *Romans*, p. 188.

The number of parallels here[1] may help to explain why the wording of v. 20b does not correspond with any one verse in the LXX. The nearest parallels are Isa. 29.16[2] and 45.9:

> You turn things upside down! Shall the potter be regarded as the clay? Shall the thing made say of its maker, 'He did not make me'; or the thing formed say of the one who formed it, 'He has no understanding'? (Isa. 29.16).

> Woe to you who strive with your Maker, earthen vessel with the potter! Does the clay say to the one who fashions it, 'What are you making'? (Isa. 45.9[3]).

In attempting to explore the contexts and function of the potter–clay analogy in these two passages, we come up against obscurities in both. It is probable, however, that 29.16, like v. 15 before it, is directed against the ruling classes in Jerusalem for fomenting rebellion against Sennacherib.[4] In Isaiah 45 it is possible that there has been some textual dislocation, and it may be significant that vv. 9-10 differ from Deutero-Isaiah's usual style,[5] and that they are the only example in Deutero-Isaiah of a woe uttered against Israel in exile. Whybray thinks Westermann exaggerates the difficulties, but both (Westermann more tentatively) favour the view that these verses upbraid Israel for doubts about, or objections to the prophecy of deliverance by means of the foreigner Cyrus.[6]

Two other examples of the potter–clay analogy from Jeremiah and from the Wisdom of Solomon may be briefly noted. In Jeremiah 19 the prophet is commanded to break a flask in the sight of some of the elders and senior priests of Jerusalem (v. 10), and to say:

> So will I break this people and this city, as one breaks a potter's vessel, so that it can never be mended.

1. Wilckens, *An die Römer*, II, p. 202 n. 900, notes several parallels, including a number from the Dead Sea Scrolls.

2. As Dunn, *Romans*, II, p. 556, notes, the first six words μὴ ἐρεῖ τὸ πλάσμα τῷ πλάσαντι correspond exactly with the Greek of Isa. 29.16.

3. Isa. 45.9b: μὴ ἐρεῖ ὁ πηλὸς τῷ κεραμεῖ, τί ποιεῖς ὅτι οὐκ ἐργάζῃ, οὐδὲ ἔχεις χεῖρας; μὴ ἀποκριθήσεται τὸ πλάσμα πρὸς τὸν πλάσαντα αὐτό;

4. Thus O. Kaiser, *Isaiah 13–39* (London: SCM Press, 1974), pp. 275-77.

5. C. Westermann, *Isaiah 40–66* (London: SCM Press, 1974), p. 165.

6. R.N. Whybray, *Isaiah 40–66* (London: Marshall, Morgan & Scott, 1975), pp. 107-109; Westermann, *Isaiah,* pp. 164-66.

Again, the analogy is employed as a word of judgment against Israel. But here the prophet sounds a note of finality, whereas, as I suggested earlier, Paul's language should be interpreted in the light of his final conclusion in 11.32.

In some ways, the book of Wisdom offers the closest analogy of all:

> A potter kneads the soft earth and laboriously molds each vessel for our service, fashioning out of the same clay both the vessels that serve clean uses and those for contrary uses, making all alike; but which shall be the use of each of them the worker in clay decides (Wis. 15.7).[1]

The similarity of detail between Paul and Wisdom is striking, but the writer of Wisdom is embarking on a tirade against the foolishness of the maker of idols, and so the context could hardly be more different.[2]

The two Isaiah parallels, and other instances of this analogy of potter and clay in the prophetic literature, show that there was a well-established tradition for using this analogy in judgment against Israel. Paul's use of it, however, is distinctive. Isaiah of Jerusalem uses it as a warning against a faithless political stratagem; Deutero-Isaiah employs it (it would seem) to criticize faithlessness of a different kind; and Jeremiah uses it to sound a note of finality. In Paul, however, the severity of the language and the negative character of the biblical *topoi* (Esau, Pharaoh) occupy, as it were, a penultimate place in the total structure, the ultimate note, as far as Israel is concerned, being sounded in 11.26: καὶ οὕτως πᾶς Ἰσραὴλ σωθήσεται (cf. vv. 27 and 32). Paul's God-language

1. The translation of Winston, *Wisdom.*

2. C. Romaniuk, 'Le livre de la sagesse dans le Nouveau Testament', *NTS* 14 (1968), pp. 507-508, comments not only on the common motif of Rom. 9.20 and Wis. 15.7, but also the 'similarity of context'. This latter point seems ill-founded, since the point of the potter illustration in Wisdom is to highlight the folly of idol-makers. The article as a whole seems to overestimate the evidence for the view that Paul used the book of Wisdom, despite the remarkable coincidence in language between Wis. 2.24 and Rom. 5.12.

Generally, Paul is much more conservative in the God-language he uses than the writer of Wisdom, but the theology behind the language is not so. The book of Wisdom, for all its rich God-language, retains the traditional Jewish conviction that the people of Israel and the land of Judaea remain God's *preferred* people and land (e.g. 12.7). This particularist conviction affects profoundly the writer's interpretation of divine action in history, and above all the outworking of the divine righteousness: the people of God benefit *at the expense of others*, thanks to God's action on their behalf.

here, therefore, is 'characteristically Jewish',[1] but the context, and particularly the place of these verses in Paul's overall argument, give the God-language a significantly different meaning.

More important (and difficult) language about God follows in the next verses:

> εἰ δὲ θέλων ὁ θεὸς ἐνδείξασθαι τὴν ὀργὴν καὶ γνωρίσαι τὸ δυνατὸν αὐτοῦ ἤνεγκεν ἐν πολλῇ μακροθυμίᾳ σκεύη ὀργῆς κατηρτισμένα εἰς ἀπώλειαν, καὶ ἵνα γνωρίσῃ τὸν πλοῦτον τῆς δόξης αὐτοῦ ἐπί σκεύη ἐλέους ἃ προητοίμασεν εἰς δόξαν.

It will be noted that there is no question mark at the end of these verses, in contrast with the usual interpretation of Paul's language at this point. That is because Siegert's suggestion that v. 23 is the apodosis to the protasis of v. 22 seems very probable—that is 'If God...*this was in order that* (καὶ ἵνα)...'[2] But it is still necessary to ask whether the sense of εἰ δὲ θέλων is concessive or causal. There are, in fact, two good reasons for regarding this expression as causal. First, the theological understanding of wrath which this would imply would correspond more nearly to Rom. 1.18-32, which make clear that God's wrath *is* being revealed, and not restrained.[3] Secondly, this interpretation is supported by the affinity in language of vv. 22 and 17 (ὅπως ἐνδείξωμαι ἐν σοι τὴν δύναμίν μου...),[4] indicating that God *does* demonstrate his power in judgment, and does not refrain from doing so (as the concessive sense of εἰ δὲ θέλων would imply).[5] This means that God's wrath is revealed, and his power made known, precisely *in* his endurance of 'vessels of wrath' (or, in the thought of 1.24-28, his 'handing over' [παρέδωκεν] those 'suppressing the truth').

With these preliminary interpretative remarks, I now turn to investigate whether there is anything distinctive at this point in Paul's

1. Dunn, *Romans*, II, p. 556. Dunn is speaking of the *idea* of creation, but the phrase is equally applicable to Paul's language at this point. Winston, *Wisdom*, pp. 285-86, notes the appearance of the potter–clay theme in Herodotus and other non-biblical writers.

2. Siegert's view is cited and adopted by Ziesler, *Romans*, p. 247.

3. While 1.18-32 refers to the Gentile world, it would undermine Paul's entire argument if he differentiated between Gentile and Jew at this point by arguing that God revealed his wrath upon the Gentiles, but not upon the Jews.

4. ἐνδείκνυμι (vv. 17 and 22), διαγγέλλω/γνωρίζω (vv.17 and 22), δύναμις (v. 17), δυνατόν (v. 22) (cf. Munck, *Christ and Israel*, p. 62).

5. Thus, e.g., Cranfield, Barrett, Käsemann.

God-language, his use of it, and the theology which emerges from it.

The concept of divine wrath, of course, is common both in the Old Testament and in later Jewish writings.[1] In the Old Testament itself, portrayals of Yahweh's wrath vary considerably. Fichtner contends that 'at a later period there is obviously an attempt to loosen and even dissolve too close an assocation of God with wrath'[2] and he instances the absolute use of the word as evidence of this. This seems questionable, although in Philo, especially, there is evidence of a wish to 'distance' God from wrath and destruction.[3] One important development in Hebrew thought, however, was the recognition that God's anger must be differentiated from human anger, 'which has its root predominantly in the domineering ego of man'.[4] Thus God's anger comes to be linked with his longsuffering: God does not always give free rein to his anger.[5]

The juxtaposition of 'wrath' and 'longsuffering' is precisely what we have here in v. 22: ἤνεγκεν ἐν πολλῇ μακροθυμίᾳ σκεύη ὀργῆς... It would be unwise to generalize from Jewish sources at this point. In some texts wrath and mercy are simply juxtaposed, without any attempt to reconcile them, or to explain the relation between the two. So for example, in Sirach we have 'For mercy and wrath are with the Lord'.[6]

Later Jewish apocalyptic offers interesting examples of this kind of

1. According to Sjöberg-Stählin (*TWNT*, V, p. 413), only the Stoic-influenced Letter of Aristeas reflects the view that God governs the world without any wrath. Other expressions in this writing, however, sound more biblical—e.g. 'God destroys the proud' (p. 263), and 'smitten by God' (p. 313). The latter, if not the former, certainly seems to express the view of the writer.

2. *TWNT*, V, pp. 395-96.

3. There is, for example, the argument in Philo, *Fug.* 66 that 'it is unbecoming to God to punish, seeing that He is the original and perfect Lawgiver: He punishes not by His own hands but by those of others who act as His ministers' (Loeb Translation *ad loc.*) cf. also *Agr.* 129, *Conf. Ling.* 179, and *Dec.* 176. Colson (Loeb, III, p. 491) notes also *Op. Mund.* 75 and *Plant.* 53. On this see also D.T. Runia, *Philo of Alexandria and the Timaeus of Plato* (Leiden: Brill, 1986), p. 442. Finally, we should note this tendency to downplay the wrath of God in *Aristeas*, e.g. 192.

4. *TWNT*, V, p. 397.

5. *TWNT*, V, p. 405.

6. Sir. 16.11b. Cf. *Prayer of Manasseh*, 5-6. According to A.T. Hanson, *The Wrath of the Lamb* (London: SPCK, 1957), pp. 13-21, the only places in the Old Testament where a tension or opposition between mercy and wrath are felt are: Hosea, Isa. 57.16-17, 60.10 and Ps. 85.

God-language. In *2 Baruch*[1] a long list of divine qualities occurs in which the phrase 'the suppression of wrath' is followed immediately by 'the abundance of longsuffering'.[2] The thought here seems to be different from that of Paul: wrath is *suppressed* rather than revealed in divine longsuffering. The second passage from *2 Baruch*, however, offers a closer parallel. In ch. 13, as part of his vindication of God's justice, the seer explains that God punished his sons first 'that they might be forgiven' (v. 10). As for the Gentiles 'with them he patiently holds his hand until they have reached the full extent of their sin...' Thus 'God's patience works *against the nations* rather than *for his people*'.[3] Such an understanding of divine wrath seems to be in keeping with the distinction in the Old Testament and subsequent Jewish writing between the historical exercise of God's wrath and its irrevocable, or eschatological, exercise.

Paul's language is strikingly like, and yet unlike, the language of *2 Baruch*. It is superficially similar; there is the same juxtaposition of wrath and longsuffering. But it is different in that there is a stronger eschatological note. This is particularly clear in the passage noted earlier, Rom. 2.4-5, in which the present manifestation of wrath anticipates the final wrath. Paul, in fact, normally conceives of the divine wrath as something final, not temporary. The thought that God's wrath is short-lived, or temporary, is common in both the Old Testament and later Jewish writings.[4] But of Paul, Michel writes:

1. *2 Baruch*, like most apocalyptic writings, was the product of crisis. This crisis was reflected in its God-language (and in that of *4 Ezra*) in the perhaps strident reassertion of precisely those convictions most challenged by the crisis—e.g. the omnipotence and judgment of God.

2. *2 Bar*. 59.4 (trans. Charlesworth, *Pseudepigrapha*, I, p. 642).

3. G.B. Sayler, *Have the Promises Failed?* (Chico, CA: Scholars Press, 1984), p. 56.

4. A.J. Heschel, *The Prophets* (London: Harper, 1962). See, e.g., Dan. 8.19; 2 Macc. 7.33. The language of the book of Wisdom, however, is worth noting. The writer contrasts the fate of God's people with that of the Egyptians: 'The godly also had a taste of death when a multitude were struck down in the wilderness: but the divine wrath did not long continue' (18.20), whereas 'the godless were pursued by pitiless anger to the bitter end' (19.1). (See p. 57 n. 2 above.) The chief difference between Wisdom and Paul here seems to lie in the fact that for Paul Jew and Gentile alike were now experiencing a foretaste of the wrath of the *eschaton* (Rom. 1.18-32; 4.15; 5.9 etc). Michel, *An die Römer*, p. 314 n. 21, refers to Wis. 12.20, noting the new distinction introduced by Paul in Rom. 9.6.

> His wrath is the manifestation of his power. God's wrath in this context is conceived in a radical way: it is not only a reaction to a human action, but a comprehensive judgment which determines human existence from beginning to end.[1]

In this verse, however, Paul speaks not simply of 'wrath', but of 'vessels of wrath' (σκεύη ὀργῆς). The actual phrase occurs in Jeremiah 50.(LXX 27) 25,[2] although there it denotes the tools or weapons of God's anger. The nearest parallel to the concept is probably to be found in the Damascus document, which speaks of

> wrath... towards those who depart from the way and abhor the Precept... For from the beginning God chose them not; He knew their deeds before ever they were created and He hated their generations, and He hid His face from the Land until they were consumed.[3]

Similar language[4] occurs in the *Apocalypse of Abraham*, written probably towards the end of the first century of the Christian era.[5]

In a comparison of Paul's language and thought with Jewish apocalyptic, there are two closely related differences to be noted. First, Paul's language is yet another example of the apostle 'turning the tables' on Israel. Secondly, however, it may be significant, as Cranfield suggests, that Paul does not use a verb with the prefix προ, when writing of the σκεύη ὀργῆς,[6] and, moreover, uses a verb in a passive form κατηρτισμένα (contrast προητοίμασεν, v. 23, of the σκεύη ἐλέους). Indeed, Paul's use of verbs with the prefix προ, predicating

1. Michel, *An die Römer*, p. 314.
2. Noted for example by Dunn, *Romans*, p. 559 . Cf. Isa. 13.5 (Symm.).
3. 2.7ff. (G. Vermes, *The Dead Sea Scrolls in English* [Harmondsworth: Penguin, 1962], p. 98). Cf. 1QH 15.12ff., 'But the wicked Thou didst create for (the time) of Thy (wrath)... ' (Vermes, *Dead Sea Scrolls*, p. 195). (Both passages cited by Michel, *An die Römer*, p. 314 n. 21).
4. See the comments by R. Rubinkiewicz in Charlesworth, *Pseudepigrapha*, II, p. 683.
5. 22.3-5 (Rubinkiewicz's translation): 'And I said, "O sovereign, mighty and eternal! Why are the people in this picture on this side and on that?" And he said to me, "These who are on the left side are a multitude of tribes who existed previously... and after you some (who have been) prepared for judgment and order, others for revenge and perdition at the end of the age. Those on the right side of the picture are the people set apart for me of the people with Azazel; these are the ones I have prepared to be born of you and to be called my people.'
6. Cranfield, *Romans*, II, p. 495. Contrast *TWNT*, V, p. 442.

divine action, is invariably positive.[1] For this reason, and because, as I emphasized earlier, the declared intention of God according to Paul is to show mercy on all (11.32), it is clear that there is nothing immutable about 'vessels of wrath'; they do not have to remain vessels of wrath.[2]

Does this mean, then, that there is no place in Paul's thought for a final, or eschatological exercise of wrath? Clearly, there is, as we have seen. But in relation to this passage 1 Thess. 2.16 constitutes a particular difficulty. Speaking of the Jews who 'all this time...have been making up the full measure of their guilt', Paul writes: ἔφθασεν δὲ ἐπ' αὐτοὺς ἡ ὀργὴ εἰς τέλος. Even if, with Bruce, we translate εἰς τέλος as 'completely' (as in Jn 13.1), it is difficult to reconcile these words with what is said in Rom. 11.25-6. As Bruce says,

> Paul certainly did not believe in AD 57 that irrevocable retribution had overtaken the Jewish people; what had come on them, he said, was a partial and temporary 'hardening' (πώρωσις) which was but the prelude, in the mysterious purpose of God, to the ultimate salvation of 'all Israel' (Rom. 11.25, 26). Unless he changed his mind radically on this subject in the interval of seven years between the writing of 1 Thessalonians and of Romans, it is difficult to make him responsible for the viewpoint expressed here.[3]

It may be better, in view of these difficulties, to translate the εἰς τέλος of 1 Thess. 2.16 as 'until the end' (which is the translation normally given for this phrase in its occurrence at Mk 13.13).[4] One more word in v. 22 deserves notice here. μακροθυμία is used only once elsewhere in Paul, in a verse noted earlier in this discussion (Rom. 2.4). It occurs only five times in the LXX, and is used only once (Jer. 15.15) of

1. προεπηγγείλατο (Rom.1.2), προέγνω (Rom. 8.29, cf. 11.2); προκεκυρωμένην (Gal. 3.17); προευηγγελίσατο (sc. ἡ γραφή, Gal. 3.8); προώρισεν (Rom. 8.29-30; cf. 1 Cor. 2.7; and Eph. 1.5, 11).

2. There may be an interesting parallel here in the Parable of the Sheep and the Goats (Mt. 25.31-46). Admittedly the participle ἡτοιμασμένος is used in the king's words to both the sheep and the goats (βασιλείαν ἡτοιμασμένην, v. 34; πῦρ . . . ἡτοιμασμένον, v. 41) but of the former the kingdom is said to have been prepared 'for you' (ἀπὸ καταβολῆς κόσμου), whereas to the latter, the fire has been prepared τῷ διαβόλῳ καὶ τοῖς ἀγγέλοις αὐτοῦ. The point to note is that the parallelism is not exact.

3. F.F. Bruce, *1 and 2 Thessalonians* (WBC, 45; Waco, TX: Word Books, 1982), pp. 48-49.

4. K.P. Donfried and I.H. Marshall, *The Theology of the Shorter Pauline Letters* (Cambridge: Cambridge University Press, 1993), pp. 69-70.

God's patience. The verb is even more rare, but used with reference to God at Sir. 18.11.[1] The adjective is more common, occurring, for example, in the list of divine characteristics at Exod. 34.6: κύριος ὁ θεὸς οἰκτίρμων, καὶ ἐλεήμων, μακρόθυμος, καὶ πολυέλεος καὶ ἀληθινός.[2] In secular Greek all three words (μακροθυμία, μακροθυμέω, and μακρόθυμος) are extremely rare,[3] and it would seem that biblical usage accounts for the great majority of instances.[4]

Although there are some details to be noted in the God-language of v. 23, its main thought is the positive counterpart to what has been said in v. 22: the purpose of the proleptic display of God's wrath upon the σκεύη ὀργῆς was to show mercy on another group, identified in v. 24 as οὐ μόνον ἐξ Ἰουδαίων ἀλλὰ καὶ ἐξ ἐθνῶν. All the more significant, therefore, is the language which Paul uses about God in v. 23: καὶ ἵνα γνωρίσῃ τὸν πλοῦτον τῆς δόξης αὐτοῦ ἐπὶ σκεύη ἐλέους ἃ προητοίμασεν εἰς δόξαν. Several individual words require a brief comment here.

1. γνωρίζω, a verb infrequent in the LXX outside the books of Psalms and Daniel, is more common in the deutero-Pauline epistles than in the Paulines,[5] but where it is used by Paul, it is usually with some emphasis, as in the virtually identical statements in 1 Cor. 15.1 and Gal. 1.11 γνωρίζω δὲ (γὰρ in Galatians) ἀδελφοί τὸ εὐαγγέλιον. The two occurrences of γνωρίζω in this context (vv. γνωρίσαι in v. 22), however, are the only instances in Paul where God is the subject.

2. τὸν πλοῦτον τῆς δόξης αὐτοῦ: Hauck/Kesch, in their discussion of πλοῦτος,[6] refer to Paul's distinctive usage of this word in applying it to God: 'Riches is for him a term to denote the being of Christ, the work of God in Christ and the eschatological situation of Christ's community'. This is basically correct, although, again, it must be observed

1. Sir. 18.11: 'That is why the Lord is patient with people; that is why he lavishes his mercy upon them' (REB).

2. Cf. Num. 14.18. It is remarkable how little of the God-language of these verses features in Paul's writings.

3. Secular references in Liddell and Scott are very few.

4. The noun μακροθυμία is predicated of God elsewhere in the New Testament only at 1 Pet. 3.20 and 2 Pet. 3.15. (It is used of Christ at 1 Tim.1.16.) Lampe, *Lexicon*, p. 825, cites several examples of noun, adjective and verb used of God.

5. Eph. 1.9; 3.3, 5, 10; 6.19, 21; Col.1.27; 4.7, 9.

6. *TWNT*, VI, pp. 328-29.

that the majority of occurrences are in the deutero-Paulines,[1] and secondly, 'distinctive' here does not mean 'unique', even within the New Testament, as Hauck and Kesch go on to note, citing, for example, Rev. 5.12 and Heb. 11.25-26. Finally, Käsemann's claim that God's πλοῦτος is in the Pauline and deutero-Pauline corpus 'the fulness of his grace not his being'[2] is perhaps an overstatement in the light of its occurrence in the doxology of Rom. 11.33-36. In view of its occurrence there, and the frequency of the concept of 'riches' applied to God in Philo,[3] 'grace' and 'being' should probably not be contrasted at all.

The word δόξα applied to God is, of course, an extremely important word both in the LXX, throughout the New Testament, and not least in Paul. Here it is probably correct to interpret it in the light of its last occurrence in Romans (9.4) where it presumably refers to the *Shekinah*.[4] Here, therefore, as elsewhere in Paul, notably 2 Corinthians 3 and 4.6, it refers to the self-revelation and presence of God.[5]

3. The ἐλεέω word group, and its frequency in Romans 9–11 has already been commented on[6] and so needs no further comment here. Similarly, προετοιμάζω is significant for its prefix, contrasted with κατηρτισμένα of the previous verse.

Before I turn to an examination of the God-language of vv. 25-29, it will be important to evaluate some of the fundamental theological concepts of vv. 22 and 23 in relation to the preceding argument. In particular, what Paul is saying about the wrath and judgment of God must be noted. Here the sequence of vv. 14-18 is crucial. Paul began with a rhetorical question, in *diatribe* style, followed by an emphatic denial: Τί οὖν ἐροῦμεν; μὴ ἀδικία παρὰ τῷ θεῷ; μὴ γενοῖτο. Most commentators overlook the twofold occurrence of γάρ in vv. 15 and 17 which follows this question: τῷ Μωϋσεῖ γὰρ λέγει . . . (v. 15), λέγει γὰρ γραφὴ τῷ Φαραώ...(v. 17).[7] But is this an 'antithetical

1. Eph. 1, 7, 18; 2.7; 3.8, 16; Col. 1.27; 2.2; in Paul, Rom.2.4; 9.23; 11.33; Phil. 4.9. (Cf. πλουτέω of God or Christ, Rom. 10.12; πλούσιος of God and Christ, 2 Cor. 8.9, Eph. 2.4.)

2. Käsemann, *Romans*, p. 271.

3. Cf. *TWNT*, VI, p. 327 n.79.

4. So, e.g., Ziesler, *Romans*, p. 236.

5. This is preferable to Käsemann's view (*Romans*, p. 271) of δόξα as 'the divine majesty'. See the discussion of δόξα in Chapter 3, section 2.

6. See pp. 44-45 above.

7. E.g. Barrett, *Romans*, pp. 183-87.

parallelism', as Käsemann claims?[1] I think not. Cranfield is correct in his observation that 'Paul does not emphasize the contrast between Moses and Pharaoh (as he could have done by using an adversative conjunction at this point), but rather sets God's word to Pharaoh alongside His word to Moses as parallel to it'.[2] But this means that if the double occurrence of γὰρ in vv. 15 and 17 indicates that *both* verses comprise Paul's rebuttal of the charge that there is injustice παρὰ τῷ θεῷ, then the reference to Pharaoh is just as much a vindication of God's righteousness as the reference to Moses. This can only mean that the 'hardening' is a function of God's righteousness.

This naturally invites a further objection: Ἐρεῖς μοι οὖν τί (οὖν) ἔτι μέμφεται; τῷ γὰρ βουλήματι αὐτοῦ τίς ἀνθέστηκεν; (v. 19). The analogy of the potter which then follows (vv. 20 and 21) does not seem to help Paul's case here, but, as Ziesler writes, Paul 'simply assumes that God's judgment is just, and concentrates on the long-term strategy which is within the sovereign freedom of God'.[3] In fact, what Paul goes on to say, both in the immediate context (vv. 22 and 23) and in the final analysis (11.1 and 32), strongly supports the view taken here that the hardening process, and the historical manifestation of God's wrath, are a function of his righteousness. First, Siegert's understanding of the grammar of vv. 22 and 23 ('But if God wanted to show his wrath...*it was* in order to make known the wealth of his glory...') makes much clearer the connection of these verses with what follows, both immediately and in chs. 10 and 11: Israel's rejection of the gospel *is* the demonstration of God's wrath, *and* the means of calling Gentiles (v. 24; 11.11, 30), and *their* entry will be the means of Israel's final salvation (11.26).

The corollary of all this for our understanding of Paul's language about God is this: God's righteousness and wrath are not antithetical,[4] but rather the historical exercise of God's wrath is a function of both his righteousness and patience.[5] However, God's patience now with unbelieving Israel is the same patience which he has shown in the past to Gentiles, and which lies behind the historical expression of his wrath—seen in the hardening of Israel. This leaves an unmistakable tension between the hope expressed in 'univeralist' sounding verses such as

1. Käsemann, *Romans*, p. 267.
2. Cranfield, *Romans*, II, p. 485.
3. Ziesler, *Romans*, p. 246.
4. Cf. the parallel between Rom. 1.16 and 18.
5. Thus the 'omnipotence' of God may be said to consist in his self-control.

Rom. 11.32 (cf., e.g. 1 Cor. 15.32), and the references to eschatological wrath. Strachan's comment on 2 Cor. 5.21 is helpful here: God's wrath is 'the active manifestation of his essential incapacity to be morally indifferent'.[1] But the positive side of this tension, as developed in the argument of Romans 9–11 is this: Paul has carried through more radically than other Jewish writers two fundamental claims about God, which, though present in the Old Testament, are now applied from the Pauline standpoint that in Christ there is neither Jew nor Greek: (a) Nothing happens outside the providence and purpose of God (b) God's purpose is entirely one of mercy.

In the remaining verses of this section (vv. 25-29), most of the God-language comes from the LXX, although in v. 24 there occurs the verb which has been crucial to Paul's argument from the beginning: οὓς καὶ ἐκάλεσεν ἡμᾶς οὐ μόνον ἐξ Ἰουδαίων ἀλλά καὶ ἐξ ἐθνῶν. This same verb occurs in both the quotations from Hosea which now follow:

> καλέσω τὸν οὐ λαόν μου λαόν μου
> καὶ τὴν οὐκ ἠγαπημένην ἠγαπημένην (v. 25b, Hos. 2.25),
> καὶ ἔσται ἐν τῷ τόπῳ οὗ ἐρρέθη αὐτοῖς
> οὐ λαός μου ὑμεῖς
> ἐκεῖ κληθήσονται υἱοὶ θεοῦ ζῶντος (v. 26, Hos. 2.1).

The most important detail here for this study is Paul's substitution of καλέσω for ἐρῶ (as the LXX text has it), a change which underlines still further the importance of this verb for Paul. It is less easy to determine whether Paul replaced ἐλεήσω τὴν οὐ ἐλεημένην by τὴν οὐκ ἠγαπημένην ἠγαπημένην. In view of the frequency of the ἔλεος group of words in this section of Romans, it would be surprising if he had. Lindars, in fact, notes that LXX MS B has ἀγαπήσω,[2] but it is still significant that Paul omits a second future verb (whether ἐλεήσω or ἀγαπήσω) in order to highlight the, in this context, all-important καλέσω.

Finally, with reference to these verses, there is the word ζῶντος. As an epithet for God, it occurs in Paul also at 2 Cor. 3.3, 6.16 and

1. Hanson, *Wrath*, p. 81, quoting Strachan.

2. B. Lindars, *New Testament Apologetic*: *The doctrinal Significance of the Old Testament Quotations* (London: SCM Press, 1961), p. 243 n.1. Lindars thinks Rom. 9.25 'an independent translation from the Hebrew', even though, as he observes in a footnote, LXX MS B has ἀγαπήσω etc. But in his view the grouping of Old Testament texts in vv. 25-27 may be pre-Pauline, the application of them to the Gentile problem being Paul's distinctive use of them.

1 Thess. 1.9. There is some doubt about whether 2 Cor. 6.16 is Pauline,[1] while the language of 1 Thess. 1.9 is widely believed to be the missionary language of Hellenistic Judaism:[2] πῶς ἐπιστρέψατε πρὸς τὸν θεὸν ἀπὸ τῶν εἰδώλων δουλεύειν θεῷ ζῶντι καὶ ἀληθινῷ. There is thus an interesting contrast between Paul on the one hand, and the Old Testament and other Jewish literature on the other, in the infrequency of the participle ζῶν as an epithet for God in Paul's letters. There are, in fact, several words here which comprise ἅπαξ λεγόμενα in the Pauline corpus, indicating that there are some differences between Paul's language about God and that of the Septuagint.[3]

Summary. Once again, much of the God-language in this section of Romans appears *traditional*: ἐλεέω (vv. 16 and 18), θέλω (v. 18), σκληρύνω (v. 18), the question posed in v. 19, the image of the potter and clay (vv. 20-21), ὀργή (v. 22), μακροθυμία (v. 22), δόξα (v. 24), καλέω (v. 24), together with the LXX quotations (vv. 25-29). But, again, there are marked differences, as Paul continues his midrash on the theme of God's call.

1. He has sharpened the emphasis on God's sovereignty (his rendering of Exod. 9.16), and given a much more *theocentric* argument by the total exclusion of all references to Pharaoh's character. Here there is a striking contrast with midrashic statements about Pharaoh, and with Josephus, Philo and several later Christian writers. (Unlike them, Paul seems to have had no difficulty with the Old Testament concept of divine hardening). Similarly, his quotation of Exod. 33.19 is different from the Targumists in its exclusion of any reference to character or worth.

2. The difference of *context* is vital. Though much of the language and imagery is characteristically Jewish, especially the potter–clay analogy as an expression of judgment on Israel, its *function* is not. The carefully structured unity of Romans 9–11 is important here, and the conclusion of Romans 11, especially vv. 26, 27 and 32 has to be anticipated for the full meaning of Paul's argument to be appreciated.

3. Paul's *eschatology* and *universalism* have affected his use of ὀργή and μακροθυμία, which, again, in appearance are characteristically

1. See V.P. Furnish, *II Corinthians* (New York: Doubleday, 1984), pp. 375-83, for a full discussion of the evidence.

2. Schneider, 'Urchristliche Gottesverkündigung', p. 65.

3. See p. 74 n. 4 and p. 75 n. 1 below.

Jewish, but in the use to which he puts them are not so. The tables are turned on Israel who also, like Gentiles, experiences God's wrath. The effects are different (contrast Rom. 1.18-32 and 11.7-10), but both are explicable by the tragedy of God's withdrawal. The context, however, is always strongly eschatological: ὀργῆ is no longer a temporary, short-lived phenomenon, and its historical manifestation in the present is closely related to eschatological wrath.

4. We are left, therefore, with an unmistakable tension in Paul's writings. While God's wrath in its historical manifestation serves the ultimate aim of his righteousness, the eschatological reality of wrath remains simply because God cannot be indifferent to sin. The tension cannot be resolved without compromising the divine holiness, or depriving human beings ultimately of moral responsibility. This tension, however, is not peculiar to Paul, but is to be found elsewhere in the Old and New Testaments.

As with the God-language of 9.6-13, therefore, there are elements of both continuity and discontinuity, when the God-language used by Paul in 9.14-29 is compared and contrasted with the God-language of other Jewish writings.

2. *Paul's Language about God in Romans 9.30–10.21*

A brief glance at the relationship between Rom. 9.1-29 and 9.30–10.21 is necessary before I survey Paul's language about God in this section. On the face of it, Paul seems to devote 9.1-29 to the theme of election and divine freedom, 9.29–10.21 to the theme of human freedom and responsibility. Yet it would be wrong to assume that Paul is thinking in these categories of thought: what appear to us to be antinomies were not necessarily antinomies to him. Barrett argues[1] that Paul is not simply juxtaposing and contrasting divine choice and human freedom, as the Qumran and Wisdom literatures do, but presenting in 9.29–10.21 'a factual account of what is discussed only in theoretical terms in 9.6-29'.[2] This is certainly part of the picture, as 9.30-32 and 10.3 indicate. But the theological exposition also moves on. It is no accident that the centre of these three chapters is christological. Chapter 10.12-13, in fact, seem to have the same key rôle in Romans 9–11 which 2.11 has in an earlier

1. Barrett, *Essays*, pp. 132-56.
2. Barrett, *Essays*, p. 136.

section of the epistle.[1] (I return to this detail in Chapter 5 below). A further, and related factor in Paul's developing theological exposition is the term δικαιοσύνη,[2] and even more, δικαιοσύνη τοῦ θεοῦ.[3] Before we turn to these, however, there are other details to be considered.

The quotation from the Old Testament in 9.33 need not delay us. Here Paul has used an Old Testament text, or, rather, a combination of two,[4] which was widely used in the early churches.[5] Paul has made the quotation more explicitly christological by the addition of ἐπ' αὐτῷ which occurs neither in the MT nor the LXX:

> ἰδοὺ τίθημι ἐν Σιὼν λίθον προσκόμματος καὶ πέτραν σκανδάλου,
> καὶ ὁ πιστεύων ἐπ' αὐτῷ οὐ καταισχυνθήσεται.[6]

In ch. 10 Paul begins by expressing his longing for the salvation of his fellow-Jews:

> Brothers and sisters, my heart's desire and prayer to God (ἡ δέησις πρὸς τὸν θεόν) for them is that they may be saved (v.1).

Here Paul's reference to his prayer for his people is couched in Old Testament language found more frequently in Luke–Acts than in Paul's own writings.[7]

A phrase which occurs in the next verse, ζῆλον θεοῦ ('they have a zeal for God', v. 2), is noteworthy in that ζῆλος and its cognates are often used in Paul of misplaced zeal.[8] In Jewish tradition 'zeal' had become a classical term characterizing a piety modelled after the example of Phinehas and Elijah.[9] But despite Barrett's claim that 'Paul

1. See the reference to Bassler's work in the Introduction, pp. 19-20.
2. 9.30, 31; 10.3, 5, 6, 10.
3. 10.3.
4. Isa. 8.14 and 28.16.
5. 1 Pet. 2.6 (cf. Mt. 21.42).
6. In other respects Paul's text differs from the two Isaianic texts: Paul has τίθημι instead of ἐμβάλλω (Isa. 28.16), and his λίθον προσκόμματος replaces the λίθον πολυτελῆ of Isa. 28.16, without being the exact equivalent of Isa. 8.14's λίθον προσκόμματι... πέτρας πτώματι.
7. δέομαι is used only at Rom. 1.10 and perhaps 2 Cor. 10.2 (C.K. Barrett, *The Second Epistle to the Corinthians* [London: A. & C. Black, 1973], p. 248) of prayer. δέησις (used of prayer) occurs only here and at 2 Cor. 1.11 and 9.14.
8. Gal. 1.14 and Phil. 3.6. Elsewhere in Paul ζῆλος is linked with ἔρις (Rom. 13.13; 1 Cor. 3.3; 2 Cor. 12.20).
9. Käsemann, *Romans*, p. 280.

as a Christian does not speak of having ζῆλος'[1] the word does not seem to have become 'tainted' beyond recall, since Paul uses it of himself at 2 Cor. 11.2.[2] Here, therefore, we have a very familiar Jewish term, used, as often in Paul, in an unfamiliar way. Here the insufficiency, or misguidedness of Israel's 'zeal for God' is due to its being οὐ κατ' ἐπίγνωσιν a statement which Paul now proceeds to explain (NB the γάρ of v. 3) in the verses which follow.

It is impossible to review, or even to summarize, the massive discussion of the phrase δικαιοσύνη τοῦ θεοῦ.[3] Two preliminary observations may help to show the place and significance of this phrase in Paul's language about God. First, the contexts in which Paul uses it matter more than its history. 'When Paul appropriates a concept, he does not necessarily employ it in its conventional meaning. It is not the history of the concept which is decisive, but the context in which it is used.'[4] Secondly, the occurrences of the word δικαιοσύνη and even more of the phrase δικαιοσύνη τοῦ θεοῦ in the New Testament are instructive. δικαιοσύνη occurs infrequently in the gospels: seven times in Matthew, once in Luke, twice in John, and not at all in Mark.[5] It does not occur at all in 1 Thessalonians, the one letter by Paul we know to have been written before the Judaizing crisis.It is also used only once in 1 Corinthians,[6] another letter which has no explicit echoes or references to the Judaizing crisis. What is more, δικαιοσύνη occurs nowhere else in the New Testament with θεοῦ outside Paul, apart from Jas 1.20 (where it is used in a quite different sense). It is possible, therefore, that δικαιοσύνη and δικαιοσύνη τοῦ θεοῦ became part of Paul's vocabulary in the context of (a) the Gentile mission and (b) the Judaizing crisis. This is the conclusion of A.J.M. Wedderburn[7] who contends that chs. 1–11 of Romans is Paul's defence against the charge that the Gospel is 'shameful' (1.16-17), involving a redefining of the

1. Barrett, *Essays*, p. 145
2. Cf. 2 Cor. 7.7, 11 and 9.2.
3. The studies of J.A. Ziesler, *The Meaning of Righteousness in Paul* (Cambridge: Cambridge University Press,1972), and J. Reumann *Righteousness in the New Testament* (Philadelphia: Fortress Press, 1982), provide good surveys of the discussion until 1980.
4. Williams, '"Righteousness of God"', p. 244.
5. Mt. 3.15; 5.6, 10, 20; 6.1, 33; 21.32; Lk. 1.75; Jn 16.8, 10.
6. 1.30.
7. A.J.M. Wedderburn, 'Paul and Jesus: Similarity and Continuity', *NTS* 34/2 (1988), pp. 161-82.

righteousness of God. Thus the language of justification[1] was 'a relatively late development in a particular polemical context'.[2]

This study is focusing on Paul's language about God, and so δικαιοσύνη is not a direct concern. Obviously it is an important word for Paul. It is introduced into Galatians in the context of a discussion about justification (2.21; cf. 2.15-17), and consequently in Paul's exegesis of Gen. 15.6 ('Αβραὰμ ἐπίστευσεν τῷ θεῷ, καὶ ελογίσθη αὐτῷ εἰς δικαιοσύνην) at Gal. 3.6-29 and Rom. 4.3-25. It is also used in ch. 6, where Paul responds to the question ἐπιμένωμεν τῇ ἁμαρτίᾳ ἵνα ἡ χάρις πλεονάσῃ by using δικαιοσύνη in antithetical parallelism with ἁμαρτία (vv. 13-23). It is clear from these and other passages, notably 2 Cor. 5.21, that in Pauline thought the δικαιοσύνη τοῦ θεοῦ leads to δικαιοσύνη in the believer, Christ himself being the embodiment or focus of this δικαιοσύνη ἀπὸ θεοῦ (1 Cor. 1.30). Not surprisingly, perhaps, it is not always easy to delineate the parameters of Paul's God-language here, particularly as in Rom. 6.13-20, δικαιοσύνη becomes virtually a personified power (6.18).[3] Nevertheless, while recognizing this wider network of Paul's δικαιοσύνη language, I turn now to his use of δικαιοσύνη τοῦ θεοῦ.

For the moment the question of whether the θεοῦ with δικαιοσύνη is an objective genitive, a subjective genitive, or a *genitivus originis* must be left aside.[4] (Reumann, however, sensibly observes that θεοῦ may not always be the same kind of genitive.[5]) What *is* clear is that Paul has already used this phrase at significant points in Romans, first, in backing up his claim that the Gospel is the power of God leading to salvation,

> δικαιοσύνη γὰρ θεοῦ ἐν αὐτῷ ἀποκαλύπτεται ἐκ πίστεως εἰς πίστιν, καθὼς γέγραπται ὁ δὲ δίκαιος ἐκ πίστεως ζήσεται (v.17)

and secondly in the passage which anticipates chs. 9–11, namely 3.1-8. After emphatically rejecting the notion that the faithlessness of the Jews

1. In Greek, of course the words 'justify' and 'righteousness' have the same root.

2. Wedderburn, 'Paul and Jesus', p. 170. More recently, M.A. Seifrid, *Justification by Faith: The Origin and Development of a Central Pauline Theme* (Leiden: Brill, 1992) disputes this, placing greater emphasis on Paul's experience at his conversion.

3. So also Reumann, *Righteousness*, p. 81.

4. Williams, '"Righteousness of God"', p. 241.

5. Reumann, *Righteousness*, p. 66.

'annulled' (καταργήσει) the faithfulness of God, Paul goes on to anticipate another question arising from his claim that our 'unrighteousness' 'serves to show'[1] (συνίστησιν) 'the righteousness of God'.

The phrase occurs again in a passage widely recognized to contain a good deal of pre-Pauline material.[2] It is here that δικαιοσύνη receives its fullest definition by Paul:

> νυνὶ δὲ χωρὶς νόμου δικαιοσύνη θεοῦ πεφανέρωται μαρτυρουμένη ὑπὸ τοῦ νόμου καὶ τῶν προφητῶν, δικαιοσύνη δὲ θεοῦ διὰ πίστεως Ἰησοῦ Χριστοῦ εἰς πάντας τοὺς πιστεύοντας, οὐ γάρ ἐστιν διαστολή (3.21-22).

Paul goes on to make two more explicit references to the δικαιοσύνη τοῦ θεοῦ in this section. The second reference seems otiose (the NRSV translates the two Greek phrases εἰς ἔνδειξιν τῆς δικαιοσύνης αυτοῦ, v. 25 and πρὸς τὴν ἔνδειξιν τῆς δικαιοσύνης αὐτοῦ, v. 26 by the one phrase 'to show God's righteousness' in v. 25, omitting, presumably, a translation of the second phrase in v. 26).[3]

A full discussion of this complex passage is beyond the scope of this study. But it is relevant to ask what light these earlier occurrences of δικαιοσύνη τοῦ θεοῦ in Romans throw on its use by Paul in 10.3. In the article to which I have already referred, S.K. Williams concludes that, since Paul nowhere explains the phrase, the Christians at Rome must have already known it, and that can only have been from the Jewish Scriptures.[4] The Jewish Scriptures themselves show that the righteousness of God points to 'God's steadfast adherence to what is right and fitting, his constancy, his trustworthiness, his readiness to save'.[5] So far I agree with Williams. More questionable is his view that in Romans God's faithfulness consists in his faithfulness to his promise to Abraham that in Abraham all the nations of the earth would be blessed.[6] The main difficulty with this view is that that promise is not referred to until 4.17 ('I have made you the father of many nations'), whereas, as we have seen, most of the occurrences of δικαιοσύνη τοῦ θεοῦ are to be found before this point. Similarly, it is not obvious *pace* Williams that the

1. RSV translation; REB: 'serves to confirm'; cf. Käsemann, *Romans*, pp. 82-83.
2. So, for example, Käsemann, *Romans*, p. 92.
3. The REB has 'to demonstrate his justice' twice, implying that the two phrases are identical in meaning.
4. Williams, '"Righteousness of God"', p. 260.
5. Williams, '"Righteousness of God"', p. 263.
6. Williams, '"Righteousness of God"', pp. 263-65.

promise to Abraham is the subject of the midrash in Rom. 9.6-13.[1]

Williams, however, is on firmer ground in drawing attention to the importance of ὑπετάγησαν in 10.3:

> ἀγνοοῦντες γάρ τὴν τοῦ θεοῦ δικαιοσύνην καὶ τὴν ἰδιάν (δικαιοσύνην) ζητοῦντες στῆσαι, τῇ δικαιοσύνῃ τοῦ θεοῦ οὐχ ὑπετάγησαν.

Williams himself concludes that by this expression Paul means that the Jews failed to comprehend *how* God is righteous (i.e. justifying all by faith χωρὶς νόμου).[2] This is surely on the right lines. It is significant that whenever Paul uses the phrase δικαιοσύνη τοῦ θεοῦ, the words 'faith' and 'everyone' or 'all' occur in the same contexts. So in ch. 1 we have δικαιοσύνη τοῦ θεοῦ in v. 17, παντὶ τῷ πιστεύοντι in v. 16 and ἐκ πίστεως εἰς πίστιν in v.17a; in ch. 3 we have πάντας in v. 22 and πάντες in v. 23, and διὰ πίστεως 'Ιησοῦ Χριστοῦ in v. 22; and, finally, in ch. 10 we have the phrase παντὶ τῷ πιστεύοντι in v. 4 (cf. vv. 11-13).

It is now possible to draw some conclusions about the significance of the phrase 'the righteousness of God' in this context in Romans. First, the evidence suggests that this phrase was introduced into Paul's arguments as a result of the Judaizing crisis. Secondly, and this is its main significance in Pauline usage, it comes to denote *both* the continuity *and* the discontinuity between the Old Covenant and the New. The tension comes out most clearly in the twofold reference to the Law in 3.21: the righteousness of God was revealed χωρὶς νόμου yet μαρτυρούμενη ὑπὸ τοῦ νόμου. The phrase δικαιοσύνη τοῦ θεοῦ is thus a 'bridge' term: on the one hand it is an Old Testament expression, indicating God's saving purpose for Israel, but on the other hand it reaches beyond the Old Testament, as Paul's exegesis of the promise to Abraham shows,[3] and as Paul's use of 'everyone' and 'all' in the same contexts as δικαιοσύνη τοῦ θεοῦ clearly shows.

A third point concerns the place of 'the righteousness of God' in Paul's language about God. How significant and determinative is it? Lindemann, in the article noted in the introductory chapter writes as follows:

1. Williams, '"Righteousness of God"', p. 281.
2. Williams, '"Righteousness of God"', pp. 282-83.
3. Williams is right to draw attention to this, but exaggerates its place in the totality of Paul's thought about God's righteousness.

> Pauline theology does not understand God at all in terms of general ideas about God; rather, the Pauline understanding of God is derived entirely from the idea of justification; that is to say, his language about God is derived from his language about the righteousness of God.[1]

Lindemann's view may fairly be said to be representative of a wide swathe of German New Testament scholarship. Yet one may wonder whether Paul is still being seen here, to some extent at least, through the eyes of Luther.[2] It would be more faithful to the evidence we have reviewed to conclude that the phrase δικαιοσύνη τοῦ θεοῦ plays a crucial role in Paul's God-language, but is not the foundation of it all. As we have seen, its occurrences in Paul's writings are relatively few: it was fundamental to the task of delineating both the continuity and the discontinuity between the old and the new in the controversies generated by Paul's law-free Gentile mission.

To return to Romans 10, Paul's use of the term 'the righteousness of God' in v. 3 prepares the way for the first explicit reference to Christ in this section of the epistle: τέλος γὰρ νόμου Χριστὸς εἰς δικαιοσύνην παντὶ τῷ πιστεύοντι (v. 4).[3] The interaction between theological and christological language here and elsewhere in Paul's writings will concern us in Chapter 5. For the moment, I note that Paul is now approaching a kind of watershed in his argument: vv. 11-13 are the climax towards which Paul has been leading, and form the basis from which the remainder of ch. 10 and the whole of ch. 11 proceed.[4]

In the remaining section of ch. 10 (vv. 14-21) let us look briefly at the quotations from the Old Testament which contain language about God.[5]

1. Lindemann, 'Die Rede von Gott', p. 375.

2. On this theme, K. Stendahl's essay, 'The Apostle Paul and the Introspective Conscience of the West' (reprinted in K. Stendahl, *Paul among Jews and Gentiles* [London: SCM Press, 1977], pp. 78-96), remains an important milestone in modern Pauline studies.

3. Since the references to 'Christ' (vv.1 and 3) and to 'the Christ' (v.5) there has been no explicitly Christian language.

4. In this context the comment of Badenas, *Christ the End of the Law*, p. 90, is significant: 'When one looks at Paul's structuring of the material and takes into consideration Paul's features of style in this section—namely his taste for antithesis and paradoxes, his oscillating pattern of thought, his dialectical manner of argumentation, his use of chiasmus, and the epistolary character of the passage—Paul's argumentation appears to be more cohesive than some authors have allowed it to be.'

5. Other LXX quotations in Paul contain 'God-words' which Paul uses nowhere else (e.g. 'the name of God', Rom.2.24; 9.17; and 15.9, and παντοκράτωρ,

First, Paul quotes, with the preamble 'First Moses says', a verse from Deuteronomy (32.21):

> ἐγὼ παραζηλώσω ὑμᾶς ἐπ' οὐκ ἔθνει
> ἐπ' ἔθνει ἀσυνέτῳ παροργιῶ ὑμᾶς (Rom. 10.19).

It is noteworthy that Paul is happy to retain the vivid, lively verbs of the original, without any hint of apology for such anthropomorphic language.[1] In fact, even more anthropomorphic language occurs in the final Old Testament quotation in this chapter (v. 21):

> ὅλην τὴν ἡμέραν ἐξεπέτασα τὰς χεῖράς μου
> πρὸς λαὸν ἀπειθοῦντα καὶ ἀντιλέγοντα (Isa. 65.2).

Finally, Paul's quotation of Isa. 65.1 has a significant difference from both the MT and the LXX, reversing the order of the parallel phrases which comprise the verse. Also, he follows the LXX which translated two Hebrew verbs in the Niphal with a tolerative sense ('I was ready to be sought', 'I was ready to be found') by straightforward aorists: thus

> εὑρέθην (ἐν) τοῖς ἐμὲ μὴ ζητοῦσιν,
> ἐμφανὴς ἐγενόμην τοῖς ἐμὲ μὴ ἐπερωτῶσιν (v.20).

Summary

The middle section of Romans 9–11 furnishes further examples of the 'reminting' of traditional language about God. This can be seen in the reapplication of Isa. 8.14 and 28.16 at 9.33 to Christ (by the addition of ἐπ' αὐτῷ), by the criticism of the ζῆλον θεοῦ which had been a prominent feature of some Jewish piety since the Maccabean period, but, above all, by the re-defining of τὴν δικαιοσύνην τοῦ θεοῦ. This phrase probably entered Paul's vocabulary as a result of the Judaizing crisis, and serves, in effect, as a 'bridge' term between the old and new covenants. It cannot be said, however, to be as seminal and fundamental as many have claimed. Finally, the section 10.1-13 furnishes the first examples in Romans 9–11 of the interplay of God- and Christ-language, and it is significant that they constitute the heart of the whole argument.

2 Cor. 6.18; other such ἅπαξ λεγόμενα occur at Rom. 9.29 and 11.26).

1. Other notable verbs, with God as subject, occurring in an LXX quotation but not elsewhere in Paul's writings, include: νικάω (Rom. 3.4), μισέω (Rom. 9.13), οἰκτείρω (Rom. 9.15), ἀφαιρέω (Rom. 11.27), δράσσομαι (1 Cor. 3.19), and βοηθέω (2 Cor. 6.2).

3. *Paul's Language about God in Romans 11*

The beginning of ch. 11 marks the third and final stage of Paul's argument in this section of Romans. This chapter in turn has three sections which can be clearly distinguished: vv. 1-10, vv. 11-24, and vv. 25-32.[1] I shall examine the statements about God in each of them.

a. *Verses 1-10*

This section has a great deal of Old Testament language once again. The verb in the opening question λέγω οὖν, μὴ ἀπώσατο ὁ θεὸς τὸν λαὸν αὐτοῦ (v.1a) is used frequently in the LXX of God rejecting his people, and, less frequently, of their rejection of him. It occurs infrequently in the New Testament, and only here in Paul. The significance of this clear echo of Old Testament language is heightened in view of the assertion, more than once in the Old Testament, that God will not reject his people. In both 1 Sam. 12.22 and Ps. 94(LXX 93).14, where this assertion is made, ἀπωθέομαι is used.

Paul goes on to reject emphatically the notion that God might reject his people, repeating in v. 2 the language of v. 1: οὐκ ἀπώσατο ὁ θεὸς τὸν λαὸν αὐτοῦ, but now adding 'whom he foreknew' (ὃν προέγνω). The word προγινώσκω is also rare in the New Testament.[2] It is used only twice by Paul, here and at Rom. 8.29. Its significance here is heightened by two factors. First, it picks up the strong emphasis of 9.6-13 on divine election (ἡ κατ' ἐκλογὴν πρόθεσις τοῦ θεοῦ). Secondly, it must be related to Paul's clear preference for the passive of γινώσκω, when talking about God—i.e. Paul prefers to speak of God's knowledge of us, rather than our knowledge of him.[3]

Probably the most important example of language about God in this section of Romans 11 occurs in vv. 5-6:

1. So, for example, Käsemann, *Romans*, p. 298.
2. Only at Acts 26.5, 1 Pet. 1.20 and 2 Pet. 3.17 outside Paul.
3. See especially Gal. 4.9 and 1 Cor. 8.3. The verb προγινώσκω was, in fact, a late-comer to biblical Greek, occurring only three times in the whole of the LXX, and each of those in the late book of Wisdom (6.13; 8.8; 18.6). Another verb which Paul uses here (v. 2b), ἐντυγχάνω, was also a word featuring only in the later books of the LXX (Wisdom, 1, 2 and 3 Maccabees and Dan. 6.12[13]). So here are indications, slight but real, that Paul was by no means limited to the older books of the Jewish Scriptures in his choice of language about God.

> οὕτως οὖν καὶ ἐν τῷ νῦν καιρῷ λεῖμμα κατ᾽ ἐκλογὴν χάριτος γέγονεν· εἰ δὲ χάριτι, οὐκέτι ἐξ ἔργων, ἐπεὶ ἡ χάρις οὐκέτι γίνεται χάρις.

There are no instances of χάρις τοῦ θεοῦ in the LXX. χάρις normally occurs in phrases such as 'find favour (χάριν) in the eyes of'. The nearest parallels to Paul's language occur in Wis. 3.9 and 4.15 where χάρις and ἔλεος are juxtaposed, and in the prophecy of Zech. 12.10, where the prophet speaks of 'a spirit of grace and compassion'. In his study of the significance of χάρις in the theological language of Paul, D.J. Doughty[1] goes so far as to assert that χάρις is almost totally unknown in Jewish literature. In Hellenistic literature the word often denotes the benevolence of the Emperor. It is all the more remarkable that Paul uses the word so often.[2] Doughty claims that Paul usually replaces ἔλεος with χάρις, although this is not true in any literal sense, since χάρις nowhere occurs in any of Paul's Old Testament quotations. It does, however, occur many times with the accompanying genitive θεοῦ, or with θεοῦ understood (so that χάρις sometimes becomes, like δικαιοσύνη, a quasi-personified power).

In Romans 9–11, χάρις occurs only here, although its connection with ἐκλογή (κατ᾽ ἐκλογὴν χάριτος) makes it clear that χάρις is implied in the midrash of 9.6-13. χάρις, however, occurs frequently in earlier chapters of Romans, particularly chs. 4 to 6.[3] Again, as with δικαιοσύνη, the words which tend to occur in the same contexts as χάρις are important clues to its meaning and function in the Pauline writings. First, there is its conjunction with the word 'peace' (εἰρήνη) at 1.7 (cf. 5.1-2); this is Paul's Christianized version of a Jewish and/or secular greeting.[4] χάρις is also used with the word δωρεάν, meaning 'freely' or 'free of charge' (cf. Mt. 10.8), as in 3.24 where Paul writes of believers: δικαιούμενοι δωρεὰν τῇ αὐτοῦ χάριτι διὰ τῆς ἀπολυτρώσεως τῆς ἐν Χριστῷ Ἰησοῦ, and in 5.15, where Paul writes of the grace of God and 'the free gift in the grace of that one man Jesus Christ' abounding for many: πολλῷ μᾶλλον ἡ χάρις τοῦ θεοῦ καὶ ἡ δωρεὰ ἐν χάριτι τῇ τοῦ ἑνὸς ἀνθρώπου Ἰησοῦ Χριστοῦ εἰς τοὺς

1. D. Doughty 'The Priority of ΧΑΡΙΣ. An Investigation of the Theological Language of Paul', *NTS* 19 (1973), pp. 163-68.

2. The imperial connotations of the word *gratia* were a significant dimension in the Augustine–Pelagius controversy.

3. 4.4, 16; 5.2, 15, 17, 20, 21; 6.1, 14, 15. Cf. 1.7 and 3.24.

4. On this, see the discussion in Chapter 4, section 1.

πολλοὺς ἐπερίσσευσεν. χάρις is also frequently used by Paul in antitheses, as in 4.4 (τῷ δὲ ἐργαζομένῳ ὁ μισθὸς οὐ λογίζεται κατὰ χάριν ἀλλὰ κατὰ ὀφείλημα), at 6.14 (οὐ γάρ ἐστε ὑπὸ νόμον ἀλλὰ ὑπὸ χάριν, cf. v.15), and here in 11.6 (εἰ δὲ χάριτι, οὐκέτι ἐξ ἔργων, ἐπεὶ ἡ χάρις οὐκέτι γίνεται χάρις). These antitheses indicate the polemical function of χάρις in certain contexts in Paul.[1] However, unlike δικαιοσύνη, it appears to have a wider function, even when we have discounted its frequent use denoting (a) the grace which is given to the apostle or to believers (as in Rom. 12.3), and (b) an expression of thanksgiving (as in Rom. 7.25). This is true even when allowance is made also for the appearance of χάρις at the beginning and end of all Paul's epistles. In fact, χάρις seems to be the word which denotes more than any other for Paul what he perceives to be the open-handed nature of God, and his lavish generosity. (Here not only is the appearance of δωρεὰν significant, but also the use of the verb περισσεύω (Rom. 5.15; 2 Cor. 4.15; cf. 2 Cor. 8.7; 9.8). The use of χάρις in the antithetical expressions we have noted underscores its significance for Paul: it has a theological affinity with words such as προγινώσκω, ἐκλογή and καλέω in stating Paul's conviction that God himself took the first step, both to the Jewish people and to the Gentiles.[2]

In the remaining verses of this section, the theme of divine hardening recurs. Israel failed to obtain what it sought. The elect obtained it, οἱ δὲ λοιποὶ ἐπωρώθησαν (v. 7d). πωρόω is a rare word in the LXX.[3] The noun πώρωσις, however, occurs at Isa. 6.9-10, which became for the early churches, it would seem, a *locus classicus* for the expression of Israel's unbelief. Thus in Jn 12.40 we have a reference to this passage from Isaiah: καὶ ἐπώρωσεν αὐτῶν τὴν καρδίαν, ἵνα μὴ ἴδωσιν τοῖς ὀφθαλμοῖς.[4] It is possible that other New Testament passages about 'hardening' should be understood in the light of Jn 12.40.[5] However that may be, the active verb in John (ἐπώρωσεν) is mirrored here in Paul by the 'divine passive' ἐπωρώθησαν. That Paul intended this to be understood as *God's* action is made clear by the earlier use of

1. See especially Rom. 6.1; Gal. 1.6, 15; 2.21 and 5.4
2. See Dunn, *Romans*, p. 639.
3. It occurs only at Job 17.7 (of the weakening of the eyes), and perhaps at Prov. 10.20.
4. Cf. Mk 3.5; 4.12; Mt. 13.14-15, Acts 28.26.
5. *TWNT*, V, p. 1026.

σκληρύνει (9.18), a word which was 'exactly'[1] the same as πωρόω.

Paul supports his claim that Israel has been 'hardened' by two more composite quotations from the LXX. First (v. 8) a verse from Deut. 29.3 (v. 4 in some editions) has been negatived, and received from Isa. 29.10 the expression 'a spirit of stupor': ἔδωκεν αὐτοῖς ὁ θεὸς πνεῦμα κατανύξεως ὀφθαλμοὺς τοῦ μὴ βλέπειν καὶ ὦτα τοῦ μὴ ἀκούειν, ἕως τῆς σήμερον ἡμέρας.[2] The 'hardening' of the heart is clearly one effect of the judgment of God, as seen through the eyes of both Old Testament and New Testament writers. Another effect is that of 'blinding', referred to in the second half of Paul's next quotation, in which Paul applies to unbelieving Israel the psalmist's imprecations on his persecutors (Ps. 69[LXX 68].23-24; Rom. 11.9-10). Here the verb used is σκοτίζομαι: σκοτισθήτωσαν οἱ ὀφθαλμοὶ αὐτῶν τοῦ μὴ βλέπειν (v. 10a). A similar expression is used by Paul at Rom. 1.21 ('their senseless minds were darkened [ἐσκοτίσθη]) and at 2 Cor. 4.4, where, however, the agent of the blindness is 'the god of this age'.[3]

All of this language falls strangely on modern ears, but it is an important part of Paul's language about and understanding of God. His use of it here is closely related to his earlier use of this kind of language in ch. 9, and the earlier discussion of its interpretation (section 1.b) is therefore applicable here also.

b. *Verses 11-24*

There is little explicit God-language in this section, but we should not overlook the many passives. While it would be rash to assume that they all indicate the agency of God, the context strongly suggests that they do. There are two verbs which are each used several times in the passive: ἐκκλάω, meaning to 'break off' (vv. 17, 19, and 20), and ἐγκεντρίζω, meaning to 'graft in' (vv. 17, 19, 23 and 24). In addition, the word ἐκκόπτω, meaning to 'cut off', is used twice (vv. 22 and 24). All these verbs build up still further Paul's picture of the freedom of God, and the two-edged character of that freedom: to 'graft in' and to 'break off', to 'elect' and to 'reject'.

In addition to these numerous passives, there are more explicit

1. *TWNT*, V, p. 1030.

2. There are a number of interesting features here about Paul's use of the Old Testament, not least the fact that in Deuteronomy the original words were positive—i.e. now at last they see and hear!

3. Cf. 1 Jn 2.11.

references to God in vv. 21 and 22. They come in the context of a series of stern warnings to Gentile Christians (vv. 13-22): if the work of God consists both of 'grafting in' and 'breaking' or 'cutting off', it is appropriate to speak of both his kindness and severity:

> εἰ γὰρ ὁ θεὸς τῶν κατὰ φύσιν κλάδων οὐκ ἐφείσατο, οὐδὲ σοῦ φείσεται. ἴδε οὖν χρηστότητα καὶ ἀποτομίαν θεοῦ· ἐπὶ μὲν τοὺς πεσόντας ἀποτομία, ἐπὶ δὲ σὲ χρηστότης θεοῦ, ἐὰν ἐπιμένης τῇ χρηστότητι, ἐπεὶ καὶ σὺ ἐκκοπήσῃ (vv. 21-22).

The word χρηστότης is rare in Paul's writings, being used elsewhere of God only at Rom. 2.4.[1] The noun and adjective are used quite frequently in the LXX of God, but *pace* Michel[2] the noun never translates the Hebrew חסד.[3] The equivalent in Hebrew seems to be טוב and related words, as in Psalm 14, which Paul quotes from at Rom. 3.12.

ἀποτομία is a much rarer word. It occurs only here in the New Testament, and does not occur in the LXX, although the adjective ἀπότομος and the adverb ἀποτόμως occur in the book of Wisdom.[4] The noun, too, is rare in non-biblical Greek.[5] Interestingly, the adverb ἀποτόμως is also used by Paul, at 2 Cor. 13.10, a passage where φείδομαι is also used (2 Cor.13.2), as it is here in v. 21. (The phrase εἰ ἐστὲ ἐν τῇ πίστει, 2 Cor. 13.5, provides yet another parallel with this passage—cf. σὺ δὲ τῇ πίστει ἕστηκας, v. 20b.) Paul's use of the adverb in 2 Corinthians 13, in fact corresponds with the general meaning of this word group—judicial severity.

Michel observes that the divine attributes of kindness and severity are often juxtaposed in Rabbinic thought. He himself describes them as 'the two measures of divine righteousness'.[6] In this context Michel compares

1. ἢ τοῦ πλούτου τῆς χρηστότητος αὐτοῦ καὶ τῆς ἀνοχῆς καὶ τῆς μακροθυμίας καταφρονεῖς, ἀγνοῶν ὅτι τὸ χρηστὸν τοῦ θεοῦ εἰς μετάνοιάν σε ἄγει. Paul uses χρηστότης of human conduct at Rom. 3.12, 2 Cor. 6.6 and Gal. 5.22.

2. Michel, *An die Römer*, p. 351.

3. Hatch and Redpath, *Concordance*, II, p. 1375.

4. Wis. 5.20; 6.5; 11.10; 12.9; 18.15; cited by Cranfield, *Romans*, II, p. 570 n.1.

5. In addition to two citations of inscriptions and papyri, Bauer lists Diodorus Siculus 12.16,3; Dionysius Halicarnassus 8.61; Plutarch, *Moralia* 13D, Pseudo-Demetrius, *Eloc.* 292 and Philo, *Spec. Leg.* 2.94 and *Flacc.* 95. In Philo it is a very strong word, with connotations of ruthlessness and cruelty.

6. Michel, *An die Römer*, p. 351; cf. Strack–Billerbeck, *Kommentar*, III,

the difference in the book of Wisdom between God's treatment of the Egyptians and his treatment of Israel. Here in Romans, therefore, we are faced once again with familiar Old Testament and Jewish language about God being employed in surprisingly, and even shockingly, new contexts. The small units of language are not strange, although Paul's use of ἀποτομία is another example of his use of more 'modern' or secular words, alongside the language about God which is much more central to the LXX. Even the analogies and arguments have a familiar ring to them. Paul's choice of the olive tree, for example, was no doubt influenced by its use in the Old Testament as a symbol of Israel.[1] Paul's own presuppositions, however, and his situation, particularly as a Christian missionary to the Gentiles, have the effect of turning familiar language and arguments upside-down (as Michel's reference to the book of Wisdom indicates). As usual, therefore, it is the context and function of Paul's God-language which are particularly significant. Paul was no doubt aware that the last, and the only, passage in Romans in which he had used χρηστότης of God was in the polemical passage against the Jews (ch. 2), referring to God's goodness *specifically* to the Jews. So now, it seems, Gentile and Jew (with the exception of 'the remnant', 11.1b, 4-5) have changed places. Paul's use of the word ἀποτομία confirms this, since Paul's choice of this word may have been influenced not only by its connotations of judicial severity, but also by its linguistic connection with ἀποτέμνω (cf. ἐκκοπήσῃ, v. 22).

c. *Verses 25-36*

Most of this section is concerned with the ultimate salvation of Israel. Paul backs up his conviction that 'all Israel' (v. 26) will be saved, first by the LXX quotations of vv. 26b[2] and 27, and secondly by a reference back to God's election of Israel through the patriarchs (v. 28). This argument is then backed up by the following statement about God: ἀμεταμέλητα γὰρ τὰ χαρίσματα καὶ ἡ κλῆσις τοῦ θεοῦ (v. 29). There is general agreement among commentators that χαρίσματα

p. 292, and Johnson, *Function*, p. 162.

1. Cranfield, *Romans*, II, p. 567.

2. We note the language which Paul draws from the LXX in v. 26, ἥξει ἐκ Σιών ὁ ῥυόμενος, ὁ ῥυόμενος being one of those *hapaxes* in Paul's writings, occurring in an LXX quotation, but not elsewhere. (See p. 74 n. 4 and p. 75 n. 1 above.) Secondly, we note the recurrence of 'divine passives': in v. 30 the verb ἐλέω is twice used in the passive as Paul brings his argument to its climax.

refers back to the privileges of Israel listed in 9.4-5.[1] ἡ κλῆσις illustrates once again the fundamental importance of this word group for Paul's understanding of God. Here it seems best to take it as 'God's calling of Israel to be His special people'.[2]

The word ἀμεταμέλητα is clearly emphatic.[3] It occurs elsewhere in the New Testament only at 2 Cor. 7.10, where it qualifies μετανοίαν, meaning 'the repentance which brings no regret'. Its particular reference here in Romans to God's relationship with Israel means that we cannot conclude that Paul rejected the Old Testament concept of God 'repenting'.[4] It is unlikely that he did, for as Cranfield notes 'all the statements of Scripture about God's repenting...must be seen as embraced within the fundamental and inclusive truth of God's faithfulness to His gracious purpose and to its declaration in His promises'.[5] Very different are Philo's reflections on the immutability of God. Philo is anxious to stress that Gen. 6.5-7 should not be taken to mean that 'the Unchangeable changes',[6] a conclusion he avoids by stressing God's eternity and knowledge of the future.[7]

Von Rad's comment is perceptive: 'It was apparently easier in Old Testament faith to tolerate the danger of lessening God's greatness and

1. So, for example, Wilckens, *An die Römer*, II, p. 258 and Michel, *An die Römer*, p. 358.

2. Thus Cranfield, *Romans*, II, p. 581, against Käsemann, who takes κλῆσις and χαρίσματα to be interchangeable (*Romans*, p. 316), and Michel, *An die Römer* (p. 358), who interprets God's call as the most important of his gifts.

3. Thus Michel, *An die Römer*, p. 357, who cites Rom. 3.3-4, and comments: 'God's constancy and trustworthiness are part of his righteousness'.

4. E.g. Gen. 6.6, where, however, the LXX however has the less colourful verbs ἐνεθυμήθη and διενοήθη. Contrast the assertion that '(God)... is not a man that he should repent' (1 Sam. 15.11, 29) (quoted by Von Rad, *Genesis*, p. 114).

5. Cranfield, *Romans*, II, p. 582 n.1. The whole of this note on God's 'repentance' is excellent.

6. Philo has the Alexandrian reading ἐθυμώθη ('was angry'), where other MSS have the more neutral ἐνεθυμήθη ('laid it to heart'), noted above.

7. 'For God's life is not a time, but eternity, which is the archetype and pattern of time; and in eternity there is no past nor future, but only present existence' (Philo, *Deus Imm.* 33 [cf. 72]). Philo concludes that 'the Existent does not experience repentance' (τοῦ μὴ χρῆσθαι μετανοίᾳ), and his later comment on anthropomorphisms he would no doubt have regarded as applicable to Old Testament language about God repenting: 'the Lawgiver uses such expressions, just so far as they serve a kind of elementary lesson, to admonish those who could not otherwise be brought to their senses' (*Deus Imm.*, 52).

"absoluteness" by human description than to run the risk of giving up anything of God's lively personalness and his vital participation in everything earthly'.[1] While there is a danger of regarding the lively character of Old Testament Hebrew as approximating more nearly to the language of heaven than a more philosophical Greek, nevertheless a modern theologian writes: 'the model of transcendence that eschews anthropomorphisms of all sorts and regards God simply as Being turns out to be the one in which God is less hidden and less mysterious'.[2]

It would be mistaken, of course, to reduce this discussion to two alternative ways of speaking about God: an Hebraic way or Hellenistic (esp. Philonic) way. It is already becoming clear that Paul cannot be easily categorized.

Before we come to Paul's concluding doxology (vv. 33-36), there is a very striking expression used of God by the apostle in the verse immediately preceding the doxology. This verse summarizes the argument which Paul has been pursuing since 9.6:[3] συνέκλεισεν γὰρ ὁ θεὸς τοὺς πάντας εἰς ἀπείθειαν, ἵνα τοὺς πάντας ἐλεήσῃ (v. 32). Paul's use of the verb συγκλείω here is fascinating. Although the verb is common in secular Greek, there are no instances of God or a god being the subject of this verb.[4] Once again, it is necessary to turn to the Old Testament. Here the verb, although used in a variety of contexts and with a variety of meanings,[5] is often used in parallel with παραδίδωμι, meaning 'deliver up'. Thus in Ps. 78 (LXX 77).48 and 50, the psalmist, recounting the plagues in Egypt, declares that God 'gave up' (παραδίδωμι) their cattle to hail (v. 48), and that he 'consigned' (συνέκλεισεν) their cattle to death (v. 50). Here both verbs translate the same Hebrew verb סגר, a word which is used in the Qumran literature in the hithpael in the same way as in the Old Testament.[6] It also has a legal sense in the Damascus Document (13.6-7 and 15.14-15): a man who violates the commandments of the Torah will be 'closed in' by the existence of the overseer.[7]

1. Von Rad, *Genesis*, p. 114.
2. Kaufman, *God*, p. 80. Kaufman is discussing two 'models of transcendence', an impersonal 'teleological' model, and a personal one.
3. Barrett, *Romans*, p. 227 (cf. p. 185).
4. *TWNT*, VII, p. 744.
5. *TWNT*, VII, p. 744.
6. *TWNT*, VI, p. 745.
7. *TWNT*, VI, p. 745.

Another Old Testament usage which may be relevant here is a military one. The Hebrew סגר and the corresponding συγκλείω are used to describe enclosing or surrounding a city in military action (Josh. 6.1; 1 Macc. 5.5; 6.49 and 15.25). We find an example of this military figure applied to divine action in Irenaeus,[1] but this appears to be the only patristic example, and here the object of the verb is the evil represented by anti-Christ.

In Rom. 11.32, therefore, we are dealing with an Old Testament image applied to God, an image which is almost unique in the New Testament, and probably unique in early Christian literature.[2] The nearest parallel to the use of συγκλείω here is to be found in Galatians 3, a passage which has many theological parallels with Romans 9–11. Here Paul, in response to his question τί οὖν ὁ νόμος (v. 19a) concludes: ἀλλὰ συνέκλεισεν ἡ γραφὴ τὰ πάντα ὑπὸ ἁμαρτίαν, ἵνα ἡ ἐπαγγελία ἐκ πίστεως Ἰησοῦ Χριστοῦ δοθῇ τοῖς πιστεύουσιν (v. 22). Here the subject of συγκλείω is 'Scripture', but the thought closely parallels Rom. 11.32: 'God has imprisoned everyone together in the prison of disobedience'.[3] Significantly, however, although the motif of imprisonment features prominently in Gnostic and Mandean writings, particularly as punishment for fallen angels,[4] the imprisonment here is clearly envisaged by Paul as temporary. Here then, in the concluding sentence of his argument, Paul employs yet another word which would have been familiar to Jews from both their Scriptures and from later writings, and employs it in a startlingly new context. Here and elsewhere[5] Paul does not shy away from using aggressive imagery when speaking of God.

Finally, we examine the doxology of vv. 33-36:

Ὦ βάθος πλούτου
καὶ σοφίας καὶ γνώσεως θεοῦ·
ὡς ἀνεξεραύνητα τὰ κρίματα αὐτοῦ
καὶ ἀνεξιχνίαστοι αἱ ὁδοὶ αὐτοῦ.
τίς γὰρ ἔγνω νοῦν κυρίου;

1. *Haer.* 5.29.2, cited in Lampe, *Lexicon*, p. 1271.

2. *TWNT*, VI, p. 745, compares Mt. 16.19 and Jn 20.23 as parallels to the legal meaning of סגר. Here, however, the parallel is conceptual rather than linguistic, since συγκλείω is not used.

3. Wilckens, *An die Römer*, II, p. 262

4. *TWNT*, VI, p. 745; cf. also Rev. 20.1-3.

5. See Chapter 2, section 4.

ἢ τίς σύμβουλος αὐτοῦ ἐγένετο;
ἢ τίς προέδωκεν αὐτῷ,
καὶ ἀνταποδοθήσεται αὐτῷ;
ὅτι ἐξ αὐτοῦ καὶ δι' αὐτοῦ καὶ εἰς αὐτὸν τὰ πάντα·
αὐτῷ ἡ δόξα εἰς τοὺς αἰῶνας, ἀμήν.

The structure of the doxology is fairly clear: it consists of nine lines comprising three strophes.[1] The first two strophes form a *chiasmus* in which the questions of vv. 34-35 correspond in reverse order to the divine attributes (βάθος πλούτου, σοφίας, γνώσεως) mentioned in v. 33.[2] It is also clear that the doxology 'contains both Old Testament and Greek elements'.[3] The Greek elements comprise the following features:

1. the ὦ and ὡς of v. 33, deriving from Greek rhetoric,[4]
2. the verbal adjectives with alpha privative construction (v. 33b) (of which ἀνεξραύνητα occurs only here in the New Testament, and ἀνεξιχνίαστοι elsewhere only at Eph. 3.8),
3. the phrase 'depth of riches' (v. 33a),[5]
4. the 'all' formula of v. 36a. (The best parallel to this occurs in Marcus Aurelius 4.23: 'From thee are all things, in thee are all things, unto thee are all things' [quoted by Barrett, p. 229 n. 2]).

Of the Old Testament elements, first, v. 34 is almost exactly the LXX version of Isa. 40.13.[6] Verse 35 is more problematical. In meaning it corresponds closely with the Hebrew of Job 41.3.[7] However, as Rowley in his commentary on Job notes,[8] the MT and the LXX differ at Job 41.3.

1. Wilckens, *An die Römer*, II, p. 269; Käsemann, *Romans*, p. 318.
2. G. Bornkamm, *Early Christian Experience* (London: SCM Press, 1969), p. 107.
3. Bornkamm, *Experience*, p. 106; cf. Michel, *An die Römer*, p. 360 n. 20.
4. Wilckens, *An die Römer*, II, p. 269. Käsemann (*Romans*, p. 319), however, notes that there are 'many OT examples' of this use of ως in questioning exclamations.
5. Bornkamm, *Experience*, p. 106.
6. Cranfield, *Romans*, II, p. 590 n. 2, notes minor variations from the LXX. The thought of Job 15.8 and Jer. 23.18 is very similar.
7. προέδωκεν corresponds to הקדימני, the *hiphil* of a verb meaning 'be in front' or 'meet', and here, therefore, 'anticipate'; ἀνταποδοθήσεται corresponds to אשלם from the verb meaning 'be complete' and hence 'make whole' or 'pay compensation'.
8. H.H. Rowley, *Job* (London: Marshall, Morgan & Scott, 1976), pp. 260-61.

We are left wondering, therefore, whether Paul is making his own translation here or is quoting a Greek version otherwise unknown to us.[1] However that may be, the Hebrew of Job 41.3 appears to offer the nearest Old Testament parallel.

In addition to the Old Testament and Hellenistic (perhaps mediated via Hellenistic Judaism) elements of the doxology, we should not overlook the possibility of a third source, mentioned by Käsemann,[2] namely an apocalyptic enthusiastic tradition within Judaism. This is possible. Another possible source is later Jewish Wisdom literature, since as Wilckens notes,[3] the inscrutability of God is an important theme in this literature.

Having identified the composite background of the doxology, I turn now to evaluating the similarities with and differences from Jewish and Hellenistic parallels. The most instructive parallel in Jewish writings is a passage in *2 Baruch*, written probably in the early second century of the Christian era.[4] Here the writer is clearly wrestling with questions of theodicy

> For what is the advantage (of this), or what evil worse than that which we have seen befall us can we expect to see... What have they profited who have knowledge before you, and who did not walk in vanity like the rest of the nations... behold, they have been diligent, and, nevertheless, you had no mercy on Zion on their account (14.3, 5a, 6).

It is in this context that the writer expresses himself in words similar to Paul's doxology:

> O Lord, my Lord who can understand your judgment? Or who can explore the depth of your way? Or who can discern the majesty of your path? Or who can discern your incomprehensible counsel? Or who of those born has ever discovered the beginning and the end of your wisdom? (14.8-9).

The divine reply in the next section counters with the affirmation that the world to come is indeed for the righteous (15.7; cf. 14.13), but also

1. Munck, *Christ and Israel*, p. 142, favours the latter view.
2. Käsemann, *Romans*, p. 320. Cf. Michel, *An die Römer*, p. 360 n. 20.
3. Wilckens, *An die Römer*, II, p. 270.
4. Thus A.F.J. Klijn (*Pseudepigrapha*, I, pp. 616-17), who concludes on the grounds that *2 Baruch* was dependent on a source shared in common with *4 Ezra* and yet was later than (though not dependent on) *4 Ezra*, that *2 Baruch* was written between 100 and 120 CE.

with the assertion that 'man would not have understood my judgment if he had not received the Law and if he were not instructed with understanding'.

The similarities with and differences from Paul are instructive. First, the different contexts give the two passages a very different sense. The tone of *2 Baruch* is that of anguished bewilderment. The writer asks why the righteous are punished along with the rest (vv. 5-7). This, as I observed, immediately precedes the parallel with Paul. The writer goes on to reflect on human transience and frailty (vv. 10-11), although he does affirm a future reward for the righteous (vv. 12-13). God, in his reply (15.1-6 and 17.1-3), declares that man is being punished for trespass (15.6) and that the world to come is for the righteous (14.13;15.7).

Secondly, the very different perspectives on the Law (and therefore on Israel) of the two writers shape what they say about God. Paul develops his distinctive view that the Law, although one of God's χαρίσματα (9.4), became the basis of a misplaced zeal for God (9.31; 10.1-3). Baruch, while acknowledging that Israel has sometimes transgressed (1.2; 77.8-10), still asks:

> What have they profited who have knowledge before you. . . ? (14.5a).

Thus Israel's status as God's chosen nation remains (48.20; 77.5), and 48.23-24 are fundamental to the theological perspective of this writer:

> We shall always be blessed; at least, we did not mingle with the nations.
> For we are all a people of the Name;
> we, who received one Law from the One.
> And that Law that is among us will help us,
> and that excellent wisdom which is in us will support us.

It seems, then, that not only the two writers' sharply contrasting views of the Law and of Israel have significantly shaped what they say about God, but also the contexts in which they say it. But the differences should not be exaggerated. Although neither Käsemann nor Wilckens quotes it, there is another doxology in *2 Baruch* which offers a closer parallel to Paul than the one we have studied:

> Who can equal your goodness, O Lord?
> for it is incomprehensible.
> Or who can fathom your grace
> which is without end?
> Or who can understand your intelligence?
> Or who can narrate the thoughts of your spirit? (75.1-4).

These words occur in a much more positive and joyful context than the anguished questions of ch. 14. But part of the cause for joy, it should be noted, is the destruction of the enemies of Israel (72.6).

There is one further parallel in Jewish literature to be noted here. In Wisdom we find a series of questions similar to those which Paul asks here:

> τίς γὰρ ἄνθρωπος γνώσεται βουλὴν θεοῦ
> ἢ τίς ἐνθυμηθήσεται τί θέλει ὁ κύριος...
> ...τὰ δὲ ἐν οὐρανοῖς τίς ἐξιχνίασεν
> βουλὴν δέ σου τίς ἔγνω... (9.13, 16c, 17a).

Again, the language is similar, but the context different. Here the writer of Wisdom is contrasting human life without wisdom (9.4-5, 14-16), and human life with wisdom (vv. 10-12). But a positive note is struck, as the writer's addition to his question in v.17 indicates: βουλὴν δέ σου τίς ἔγνω, εἰ μὴ σὺ ἔδωκας σοφίαν καὶ ἔπεμψας τὸ ἅγιόν σου πνεῦμα ἀπὸ ὑψίστων. This is significant in the light of Paul's question: 'Who has known the mind of the Lord?' Here in Rom. 11.34, one might expect a negative answer to this rhetorical question, and perhaps that is what Paul implies. But Paul quotes this same question from Isa. 40.13 in 1 Cor. 2.16, and there it is not a question, but a statement: ἡμεῖς δὲ νοῦν Χριστοῦ ἔχομεν. Paul here claims that the πνευματικοί may indeed have the mind of the Lord. These two references to 'the mind of the Lord', when taken together, are a good example of how so much of Paul's God-language appears to function: those in Christ 'share in' not only the righteousness of God, but also 'the mind of the Lord' (and, as Chapter Three will indicate, the 'glory' of the Lord). In conclusion, we find again a by now familiar pattern: the use of language about God which would have been very familiar to Jews or to Greeks or to both. The doxology in itself contains no new words or statements about God which had not been used before and, indeed, would be used again. What is new, and this has been true throughout Romans 9–11, is the context and function of the statements about God.

Summary

The final chapter of this section of Romans has provided further evidence of how Paul combines familiar LXX language (e.g. ἀπώσατο, v. 1) with other language, less frequent in, or even absent from the LXX (e.g. προέγνω, v. 2 and the Hellenistic features of the doxology, vv. 33-36). There is also further evidence here of Paul's re-minting of traditional language about God: in this chapter the objects of God's χρηστότης and his ἀποτομία are reversed (v. 22), although the preceding verses hint that this revolutionary state of affairs is by no means irreversible (vv. 20-21).

There are further examples of 'hardening' language (vv. 7-10), indicating that Paul's theology is a far cry from any form of metaphysical dualism. This reluctance to concede that anything happens apart from or 'outside' God reflects the biblical presupposition that God is not '*a* being', an object beside other objects, but, in a modern phrase, Being itself.

In this connection, Paul's use of συνέκλεισεν (v. 32), in effect, attributes aggressive, military-like activity to God. The fact that in the LXX this word is an alternative translation of סגר to παρέδωκεν indicates that Paul's language here should be linked closely with what he says of God in Rom. 1.18-32, where παρέδωκεν is three times predicated of God.

The most important God-word, however, in ch. 11 of Romans is χάρις (11.6). This is not so much because of its importance here, but because of its frequency and significance in Paul's writings as a whole. But the terseness of v. 6, and the antithesis reflected in it (εἰ δὲ χάριτι, οὐκέτι ἐξ ἔργων, ἐπεὶ ἡ χάρις οὐκέτι γίνεται χάρις), typifies a great deal of Paul's God-language. The action of grace highlights what is not 'of grace', and also what is opposed to grace.

Paul's concluding doxology underlines what has become increasingly clear: Paul, whilst drawing heavily on LXX language, does not restrict himself to it. But, once again, the context determines how this mixture of more traditional Jewish language with Hellenistic formulae actually functions. The nearest parallels (in *2 Baruch*), though similar in language, are quite different in their context and meaning, since the seer speaks first in anguished bewilderment (14.8-9), and secondly in triumph over Israel's enemies (75.1-4).

Finally, Paul's echo of Isa. 40.13 and his addition 'but we have the mind of Christ' (1 Cor. 2.16) appears to give a surprisingly affirmative answer to the question 'Who can discern the mind of the Lord?', illustrating the way in which key components of Paul's God-language were appropriated by the Christian community.

4. *Conclusions*

Romans 9–11 forms an integral part of Romans, and is part of Paul's response first to theological questions arising from both the mission to the Gentiles and the rejection of the gospel by the majority of Jews, and secondly to the specific situation, with its Jew–Gentile tensions, in the church at Rome. In the final section of this chapter I evaluate the evidence I have so far reviewed. Before I do so, it is important to recall Paul's hermeneutical starting-point. Quite simply, it was Christ, and in that Paul differed from all his non-Christian Jewish contemporaries.[1] This is particularly important in view of the fact that Paul's language in these chapters is seldom explicitly Christian. The more explicitly christological section (10.1-13), as we have seen, is sandwiched between more *theo*-centric sections, and may be said to contain, in Paul's view, the heart of the matter (especially vv. 4, 11-13). Undoubtedly, Paul's experience and understanding of Christ is the crucial determining factor in his exposition of the Scriptures. It is this, too, which has revolutionized his perception of the Law, and both Paul's understanding of Christ and his understanding of the Law are vitally related to his understanding of God. But how far have they, in this section of Romans, affected (a) his language about God, and (b) his understanding of God, insofar as that can be deduced from the language he uses and the context in which he uses it?

I begin by reviewing briefly the individual words used by Paul, whilst recognizing that individual words alone do not enable us to 'get at' Paul's God-language.

First, Paul's language about God has been shaped to a considerable extent by the LXX. His entire argument is studded with Old Testament quotations; the section 11.11-24 is the only unit of any significant length without such a quotation. From this Old Testament background Paul draws several leading words and themes:

1. καλέω is used in the very first Old Testament quotation (9.7), occurs again in Paul's own comments at 9.11 and 9.24, and finally in two further quotations in 9.25-6 (the noun κλῆσις occurs at 11.29).
2. Closely related to the 'call' of God is the mercy of God. The verb ἐλέω occurs at 9.15-16, 18 and 11.30-2. The noun ἔλεος

1. Badenas, *Christ*, p. 149.

occurs at 9.23 and 11.31. In fact, it seems that to know the call of God is to know his mercy; this is the logic of Paul's argument in ch. 9, and of the climax in 11.29-32 (NB especially the connecting γὰρ in vv. 30 and 32, and οὕτως in v. 31).

3. The 'righteousness' of God, although it occurs less frequently (only at 10.3), has a pivotal importance, particularly in its close association with the righteousness which Israel pursued but did not attain (9.31), and which the Gentiles, though not pursuing it, did obtain (9.30).
4. The obverse of the call and mercy of God is the divine 'hardening'or 'darkening'. Here Paul uses three verbs from the Old Testament, σκληρύνω (9.18), πωρόω (11.7) and σκότιζομαι (11.10). The verb συγκλείω (11.32) is closely related in meaning. Such an experience or process is the result of God's wrath (ὀργή, 9.22), again, another word firmly rooted in the Old Testament.
5. The word 'power' (δύναμις) is predicated of God only in the Old Testament quotation at 9.17 (δυνατός, however, is used of God at 9.22 and 11.23), but it is a theme which underlies the entire argument. Its infrequency here is due to the fact that the emphasis in these chapters does not fall on God's power. That he is *able* to do what he purposes is not in doubt; what *is* in question is *what* God purposes, and whether this is fair and consistent with what he has done in the past.

These leading words or themes have attracted other words in these chapters, some of which have an Old Testament pedigree, some of which have not. In the first category another verb closely associated in meaning with καλέω and ἐλεέω is θέλω (9.18; cf. v. 22), a word used frequently in the LXX both of human and divine willing. ἐπαγγελία (9.4, 8-9) is also clearly an Old Testament word.[1] But Paul is clearly not restricted to the language of the LXX. He uses ἐκλογή (9.11; 11.5, 28), ἀποτομία (11.22) and ἀμεταμέλητα (11.29), which do not appear at all in the LXX; μέμφομαι and βούλημα (9.19), προετοιμάζω (9.23), προγινώσκω (11.2), and χαρίσματα (11.29), which are very marginal to the LXX. μακροθυμία (9.22), too, is a rare word in the LXX, and

1. Other words such as δόξα (9.23), σοφία (11.33) and γνῶσις (11.33), while they incorporate an important strand of Paul's thought, are not important in themselves in this section of Romans.

even χρηστότης (11.22) is infrequent. What is significant about this list is that all are words employed by Paul himself; none appears in the text because it appears in a quotation used by Paul.

There is, therefore, a significant mixture of old and new words here. Some were long-established in Jewish theological vocabulary; others were relatively new. The leading words and themes are drawn, without exception, from the Old Testament, but Paul, in his comments on them, draws on vocabulary which often has little Old Testament pedigree or none. The word χάρις should be included in the list of those words which, *in the sense in which Paul uses them*, were marginal to the Old Testament. Unlike most of the other words noted in the preceding paragraph, χάρις is used a great deal by Paul elsewhere in his writings. Like the word δύναμις used of God, it underlies passages even where it does not occur.

So far, I have surveyed many of the individual 'God' words which Paul uses, but it is important to recall Barr's dictum that 'it is in sentences that theological thinking is done'. What, then, can be said of Paul's 'theological grammar' in these chapters ?

There can be little doubt that Paul has reworked familiar Jewish traditions, sometimes in a strikingly radical way. My comparison of his use in ch. 9 of Old Testament material with the use of the same traditions by other Jewish writers showed that his argument is deeply theocentric. Indeed, it is this theocentricity which sets Paul apart from most other Jewish writers. Unlike the book of *Jubilees*, the Targums, the Midrash and Philo, Paul excludes all reference to the character, worthiness or unworthiness of Esau, Jacob and Pharaoh. This gives to Paul's argument an emphasis on the initiative, grace, and sovereignty of God more thorough-going and consistent than in the parallels studied here.

The root of this difference lay, it must be emphasized again, in Paul's experience of Christ. In fact, it would almost certainly be correct to detect in Rom. 10.2 an autobiographical echo: writing of his fellow Jews, Paul says: μαρτυρῶ γὰρ αὐτοῖς ὅτι ζῆλον θεοῦ ἔχουσιν ἀλλ' οὐ κατ' ἐπίγνωσιν. With this statement may be compared what Paul says of himself at Gal. 1.14 and Phil. 3.5-6[1] (cf. Rom. 7.12-13[2]). But it must now be asked, in the light of the evidence so far reviewed: what was

1. So also Wilckens, *An die Römer*, II, pp. 219-20.

2. It is not that Rom. 7 is directly autobiographical, but rather that Paul's zeal for the law, having led him to persecute the messiah's followers, led him to see that the law had indeed 'multiplied transgressions'.

wrong with this 'zeal for God', shared by Paul and his fellow-Jews?

Since the work of E.P. Sanders and others, it has become clear that generalizations about the 'legalism' and 'works-righteousness' of Judaism have been caricatures and misrepresentations. But Paul's criticism of his countrymen should not be ignored or minimized. There are two points to be made here. First, as the phrase in 10.2 κατ' ἐπίγνωσιν indicates, their zeal is not based on 'true' knowledge, on how things *really* are.[1] Paul, therefore, is undoubtedly indicating a christological failure here; the majority of Jews failed to accept the messiah. But secondly, in the reference in the following verse to the Jews seeking 'their own righteousness' (τὴν ἰδίαν δικαιοσύνην), there is probably a criticism of Jewish ethnocentricity. In fact, many of the sources I have examined show that it is this *ethnocentricity* which has rendered their treatment of tradition less *theocentric* than Paul's.

It is difficult, however, to exclude entirely the notion of 'merit' at this point, particularly in the light of the evidence reviewed from *Jubilees* and from the Targums.[2] The 'official theology' of Judaism, if I may so put it, was that Israel had been called by grace in mercy. The language of piety, however, seems sometimes at least to have compromised these foundational tenets. (It is not otherwise, of course, in the Christian churches.) It was not that theirs was a 'theology' of 'works-righteousness' (the Jews clearly believed in what Paul was to call the 'grace' of God), but nationalist and moralistic sentiments sometimes threatened, or even displaced the centrality of grace.

My first observation, then, about Paul's 'theological grammar' is that it is more theocentric, less ethnocentric, than many of the parallels so far examined.

The second point to note is the strikingly new way in which 'traditional' language is deployed. What John Barton has written of the impact of the gospel on Old Testament texts could equally well be said of the God-language which Paul inherited: 'It draws them into fresh conjunctions, destroys existing threads of connection, and establishes new ones'.[3] In some respects Paul stands here in the tradition of the

1. Käsemann, *Romans*, p. 280; Cranfield, *Romans*, II, p. 514; Wilckens *An die Römer*, II, p. 220.

2. Sanders excludes the Targums from his survey of Palestinian Judaism in the time of Paul, chiefly on the grounds that early material in them cannot be certainly identified (*Paul and Palestinian Judaism*, pp. 25-26).

3. Barton, *People*, p. 33.

prophets, deploying the God-language of the people of God against the people of God ('Woe to you who desire the day of the Lord!' Amos 5.18a). This pattern was already evident in an earlier section of Romans. Not only does 3.1-8 anticipate the theological agenda of chs. 9–11, but also the function of the language about God in ch. 2 anticipates Paul's use of this language in chs. 9–11. Here, too, Paul has reworked traditional Jewish language about God, using it in startlingly new contexts. Thus the 'patience' (μακροθυμίας) of God, associated in v. 4 with his 'kindness' (χρηστότητος) and 'forbearance' (ἀνοχῆς) is intended to bring 'the one who judges' (vv. 1, 3) to repentance. Since that is not happening, the person's heart is being hardened (σκληρότητα, v. 5) and he is storing up wrath 'on the day of wrath'. This passage, therefore, anticipates the language of ch. 9, which envisages, as it were, a later stage: the 'hardening' process is no longer merely a present possibility, and God's patience now is to unbelieving Israel what it was to unbelieving Gentiles. (Thus God's patience is an ambiguous phenomenon: it may denote his slowness to anger with his own people; it may also denote that he is biding his time with those who have incurred or are incurring his wrath.[1])

This process of redeploying, and sometimes redefining, theological terms is focused particularly in the expression 'the righteousness of God'. As others have observed, this expression plays a role similar to that of 'the Kingdom of God' in the teaching of Jesus (although, I would argue, not as central). Just as Jesus redefined *that* concept,[2] so Paul redefines the traditional Jewish understanding of 'the righteousness of God'. Now, in the light of Christ (Rom. 3.21-6; 10.4) the righteousness of God is seen to embrace *all*.

There is one particularly important strand of Paul's theological vocabulary in these chapters which needs to be discussed further, not least because it occasions most difficulty in the twentieth century. This is the concept of 'wrath' and the process of 'hardening' associated with it.

In my earlier discussion of Rom. 9.14-23, I concluded that Paul does not contrast God's ὀργή with his μακροθυμία, since God's μακροθυμία may be a sign of his wrath. In the context in which Paul uses this language, this is a striking example of language used of Gentiles being applied (implicitly) to Israel. But the context also means that, while

1. On this see Sayler, *Promises*, pp. 42-46 and 56.

2. See especially J.J. Riches's study, *Jesus and the Transformation of Judaism* (Edinburgh: T. & T. Clark, 1980).

none may presume to escape the eschatological wrath, none is predestined to it either. It is crucial to a correct understanding of 'the wrath of God' in these chapters to observe the unity of Paul's argument, and to keep in mind where that argument leads: συνέκλεισεν γὰρ ὁ θεὸς τοὺς πάντας εἰς ἀπείθειαν, ἵνα τοὺς πάντας ἐλεήσῃ (11.32). This suggests that, as I observed earlier, two basic theological convictions underlie Paul's language: (a) nothing happens outside the providence and purpose of God, and everything serves that purpose, and (b) that purpose is finally one of mercy.

This means that Paul is a long way from any kind of metaphysical dualism here. Far more than Philo, he holds together the grace and 'severity' of God (as the parallelism between Rom. 1.16 and 18 also shows).

Closely related to the concept of divine wrath, Paul's understanding of divine 'hardening' is a an example of the essentially prophetic nature of his thought. Like the prophets, he implies that 'the opposite of freedom is not determinism, but hardness of heart. Freedom presupposes openness of heart, of mind, of eye and ear'.[1] Like the prophets, Paul believed that

> hardness of heart is a condition of which the person afflicted is unaware. Not knowing what ails him, he is unable to repent and to recover. However, when hardness is intensified from above, responsibility is assumed by God. He smites and He restores, bringing about a revival of sensitivity.[2]

It is particularly here that modern presuppositions cloud our perception of what Paul is saying. Several 'opposites', common in religious thought, have to be set aside: divine transcendence and immanence, predestination and free will, divine love and wrath. But the problem of interpretation may go deeper still. The widespread tendency to think of God as *a* being, and to regard 'God' as the name of that being, all too easily leads to quasi-pagan interpretations of divine wrath, as if the wrath of God were but the biblical version of the thunderbolts of Zeus. The language Paul uses would, in the light of 11.32, be more appropriately dubbed 'Hound of Heaven' language, rather than the language of vengeance or vindictiveness.

1. D. Tiede, *Prophecy and History in Luke–Acts* (Philadelphia: Fortress Press, 1980), p. 31, quoting F. Heschel.

2. Heschel, *Prophets*, p. 191. The whole of this section on 'Chastisement' in Heschel is noteworthy as a commentary on the 'hardening' language of Rom. 9–11.

Is there, then, anything new or distinctive in Paul's language about God in these chapters? If we examine individual words and phrases in isolation from their context, it is clear that, with one exception, they do not add up to very much. The exception is the word χάρις, which together with the verb καλέω takes us to the heart of Paul's understanding of God in the arguments he develops here. The *word* καλέω is fundamental to the midrash of ch. 9, the *concept* of χάρις is fundamental to the argument (as the repeated ἔργων of 9.12 and 11.6 shows), although the word itself does not appear until 11.5. Both concepts, God's call and God's grace, are integral to Old Testament faith and theology, and therefore to Jewish self-understanding—the whole burden of Paul's argument. But the use to which the language is put is unprecedented, even though there are partial precedents in the Old Testament prophets. The reason for these new configurations of God-language, whether old or new, lies in the terse statement of 10.4: τέλος γὰρ νόμου Χριστός. Already it is clear that one must speak of continuity and discontinuity in Paul's understanding of God as a Christian compared with his understanding of God as a Jew. I shall need to return to this subject in subsequent chapters, and to the relationship between Paul's *theo*logy and his *Christo*logy.

Chapter 2

GOD-LANGUAGE IN 1 CORINTHIANS 1.18–3.23

1. *Structure and Contents*

Although the particular concern of this chapter is the God-language of 1 Cor. 1.18–3.23, it is important to recognize that this section is part of a larger whole. Whatever its own origin and structure, it belongs to a clearly defined section whose beginning and end are marked by the παρακαλῶ of 1.10 and 4.16.[1] From Paul's opening exhortation it is clear that a major theme of this section is the divisions within the Corinthian church, reported by Chloe's people (1.11), and, inseparable from these divisions, the relationship of the church to Paul himself. This is clear from the concluding verses of this section (4.14-16), especially the final command: παρακαλῶ οὖν ὑμᾶς, μιμηταί μου γίνεσθε (v. 16).[2]

The connection of ch. 4 with the preceding chapters is indicated by similarities of theme and language, notably the ministry of Paul and Apollos,[3] the foolishness of the apostles contrasted with the wisdom of the Corinthians (4.10)[4] and the recurrence of key words from ch. 2,

1. Noted, for example, by N.A. Dahl, 'Paul and the Church at Corinth according to 1 Cor.1.10-4.21', in W.R. Farmer, C.F.D. Moule and R. Niebuhr (eds.), *Essays in Christian History and Interpretation* (Cambridge: Cambridge University Press, 1967), pp. 313-35.

2. In favour of the view of C. Senft (*La première épître de Saint-Paul aux Corinthiens* [Neuchâtel: Delachaux & Niestlé, 1979], p. 18), that 1 Corinthians is not a single letter is the fact that 4.14-21 'has the character of the end of a letter'. It is not necessary, however, to investigate this here.

3. Cephas is mentioned at 1.12 and 3.22, but, unlike Paul and Apollos, nowhere else in chs. 3 and 4. Barrett thinks the omission deliberate, since 'Peter was... a more dangerous potential cause of schism in Corinth than either Paul or Apollos' ('Cephas and Corinth', in *Essays*, pp. 28-39). This seems less certain than Barrett's contention that Cephas had visited Corinth in person.

4. Although φρόνιμοι is used here of the Corinthians instead of σοφοί, it is

notably μυστήρια[1] and ἀνακρίνω.[2]

Although the section 1.10 to 4.16 is clearly a unity, I shall focus on 1.18 to 3.23 for reasons already given,[3] particularly the fact that clusters of the word θεός occur in chs. 1, 2 and 3, whereas there is very little explicit God-language in 1.10-17 and 4.1-16. Nevertheless, it will be necessary to refer to this wider context from time to time, and as I hope to show, Paul's self-description in 4.9-13 has an important bearing on our subject.

Despite its close links with the wider context, commentators have long regarded the section 1.18 to 3.23 as having its own particular unity and structure. The strongest evidence for this lies in the Old Testament texts cited at the beginning and the end:

> I will destroy the wisdom of the wise,
> and the cleverness of the clever I will thwart (1.19)[4]

and

> For it is written 'He catches the wise in their craftiness',
> and 'The Lord knows that the thoughts of the wise are futile' (3.19b,20).

The view of Conzelmann[5] and others that this is a circular composition is further strengthened by the contents of 3.18b and 21a: εἴ τις δοκεῖ σοφὸς εἶναι ἐν ὑμῖν ἐν τῷ αἰῶνι τούτῳ, μωρὸς γενέσθω, ἵνα γένηται σοφός and ὥστε μηδεὶς καυχάσθω ἐν ἀνθρώποις, picking up, as they do, key words such as σοφός and καυχῶμαι from 1.18-31. But whether 3.22-23 should be regarded as the end of a section (despite its similarity with Rom. 8.38-39) is another matter. Its connection with 4.1 can easily be overlooked.[6]

It is very difficult, however, to be more precise about the structure of this section. Many of the attempts to identify the structure fail to account satisfactorily for all the material. Thus Branick[7] finds here a midrashic

unlikely that this is anything more than 'rhetorical variation' (H. Conzelmann, *1 Corinthians* [Philadelphia: Fortress Press, 1975], p. 89).

1. 4.1 and 2.1.
2. 4.3 and 2.14-5.
3. See the Introduction, pp. 24-25.
4. Isa. 29.14, Ps. 33.10. For further discussion of these and other Old Testament texts in this passage see section 5 below.
5. Conzelmann, *1 Corinthians*, p. 39.
6. See the conclusion to this section.
7. V.P. Branick, 'Source and Redaction Analysis of 1 Corinthians 1-3', *JBL* 101 (1982), pp. 251-69.

homily, but his conclusion that 1.17, 2.1-5 and 3.1-4 were outside the original homily founders on the fact that 2.1-5 are firmly linked with the preceding verses both in theme and language, and, similarly, 3.1-4 are difficult to detach from both preceding and following verses.

Wuellner is another scholar who finds here a structure derived from the synagogue.[1] Building on Borgen's work on John 6, he finds here the characteristics of an haggadic homily. His analysis, however, runs into difficulties when he identifies the whole of 2.6 to 3.15 as the third treatment of the theme stated in 1.19 ('For it is written "I will destroy..." '). For Wuellner, 3.20 ('"The Lord knows that the thoughts of the wise are futile"') marks the end of the homily, but while this recognizes the 'circularity' referred to earlier, it overlooks the way in which the theme of God's judgment on human wisdom is interwoven with references to the Corinthian situation and to the ministries of Paul and Apollos (esp. in 3.5-21).

Yet another analysis was made by M. Bünker[2] who regards 1.18 to 3.23 as circular in its composition, but distinguishes the following sections, with the help of the technical terms used in ancient rhetoric of the various parts of an orator's speech:[3] 1.18 to 2.16 as the *narratio,* 3.1-17 as the *probatio,* and 3.18-23 as the *peroratio*. It is possible that such a rhetorical structure underlies this section, although it is unlikely that the whole of 1.18 to 2.6 constitutes the *narratio*. It is more likely that 2.6-16 comprises the *propositio*—i.e. a bridge passage, summarizing the issues underlying the *narratio* and anticipating the argument of the *probatio* which follows.[4] Any attempt to analyse the structure and contents of this section of 1 Corinthians must begin by recognizing the framework provided by the twofold παρακαλῶ at 1.10 and 4.16. That is the framework within which Paul proceeds to develop the theological basis for his exhortation to the Corinthians. The section about the divisions at Corinth (1.10-17) ends with a verse which is crucial for understanding vv. 18-25, as the connecting γάρ of v. 18 indicates:

1. W. Wuellner, 'Haggadic Homily Genre in 1 Corinthians 1-3', *JBL* 89 (1970), pp. 201-202.

2. M. Bünker, *Briefformular und rhetorische Disposition im Korintherbrief* (Göttingen: Vandenhoeck & Ruprecht, 1983), pp. 54-55.

3. On this see H.D. Betz's analysis of Galatians in his commentary, *Galatians: A Commentary on Paul's Letter to the Churches in Galatia* (Philadelphia: Fortress Press, 1979), pp.14-25, and subsequent amendments of Betz's approach, Chapter 4, pp. 204-205).

4. Thus Betz, *Galatians*, sees Gal. 2.15-21 as the *propositio* of Galatians.

> οὐ γὰρ ἀπέστειλέν με Χριστὸς βαπτίζειν ἀλλὰ εὐαγγελίζεσθαι, οὐκ ἐν σοφίᾳ λόγου, ἵνα μὴ κενωθῇ ὁ σταυρὸς τοῦ Χριστοῦ. Ὁ λόγος γὰρ ὁ τοῦ σταυροῦ τοῖς μὲν ἀπολλυμένοις μωρία ἐστίν, τοῖς δὲ σῳζομένοις ἡμῖν δύναμις θεοῦ ἐστιν (vv. 17-18).

The meaning of the phrase οὐκ ἐν σοφίᾳ λόγου will concern us later on. But these verses together introduce the basic premiss: the word of the cross stands in flat contradiction to the wisdom of this world. That is not all, since Paul is stating not only a contrast, but *a judgment* and *a defeat*: God's action destroys human wisdom (v. 18), and 'has foolished the wisdom of the world' (v. 20).

Two illustrations now follow. First, the calling of the Corinthians themselves is evidence that God inverts worldly standards, and thereby judges them (vv. 26-31). Secondly, Paul's visit to Corinth is further evidence of the contrast between God's wisdom and human wisdom, since he did not preach 'in lofty words or wisdom' (2.1).[1] The theme of divine judgment is less prominent in this section, but it is still implied in Paul's claim that he preached 'in demonstration of the Spirit and power' (2.4).

Thus far, the unity of 1.18–2.4 is fairly clear. But the next section, 2.6-16, has caused exegetes a great deal of trouble. It has been regarded as a digression,[2] but even more widely as an attempt by Paul to win over his Gnostic opponents by using their language.[3]

1. 'Just as the attitude of the community must accord with the word of the cross, so also must the form of the preaching and the bearer of the preacher' (Conzelmann, *1 Corinthians*, p. 53).

2. So, for example, Bunker, *Briefformular*, pp. 55-56.

3. Thus, for example, Conzelmann, *1 Corinthians*, pp. 59-67; W. Schmithals, *Gnosticism in Corinth: An Investigation of the Letters to the Corinthians* (Nashville: Abingdon, 1971), pp.151-55, although here Schmithals believes that Paul is reproducing 'the genuinely Gnostic concept of knowledge'; D. Lührmann, *Das Offenbarungsverständnis bei Paulus und in Paulinischen Gemeinden* (WMANT, 16; Neukirchen–Vluyn: Neukirchener Verlag, 1965), pp.113-14, believes that Paul is using Gnostic language to correct Gnostic claims about God; B.A. Pearson, *The Pneumatikos-Psychikos Terminology* (Missoula, MT: Scholars Press, 1973), p. 27 argues similarly, comparing 2 Cor. 11.18-23a and Phil. 3.3 as examples of the same technique; J.A. Davis, *Wisdom and Spirit: An Investigation of 1 Corinthians 1.18–3.20 against the Background of Jewish Sapiental Traditions in the Graeco-Roman Period* (Lanham, MD: University Press of America, 1984) thinks Paul is engaging in dialogue with the Corinthians here, but redefining their basic terms. This is probable, although it is unlikely that 'the wisdom of this age' (2.6) is the Torah, as Davis contends (pp. 89) (on this, see the discussion in the next section).

G. Theissen[1] distinguishes between what he calls the 'gradualist' interpretation of 2.6-16 (i.e. 2.6-16 is a surpassing of the λόγος σταυροῦ), and the 'dialectical' interpretation (i.e. 2.6-16 is an 'insider's' interpretation of the λόγος σταυροῦ). In favour of the former he cites the literary form, in his view a λόγος σοφίας, a 'wisdom discourse', and the milk/meat illustration of 3.2. In favour of the dialectical interpretation Theissen cites the contents of 2.6-16. In his view, therefore, the arguments are fairly evenly balanced. But the evidence seems decisively to favour the dialectical interpretation. First, much of 1.18 to 3.20, not just 2.6-16, adopts the language of a wisdom discourse, and the milk/meat illustration of 3.2 is not relevant here, since in Paul's view the λόγος σταυροῦ cannot be surpassed. Secondly, the many points of contact of 2.6-16 with the preceding sections of the epistle should not be overlooked. Verse 6, both in its language and its contents picks up earlier themes:

> Σοφίαν δὲ λαλοῦμεν ἐν τοῖς τελείοις, σοφίαν δὲ οὐ τοῦ αἰῶνος τούτου οὐδὲ τῶν ἀρχόντων τοῦ αἰῶνος τούτου τῶν καταργουμένων (cf. 1.20, 28).

Similarly, the phrase 'wisdom of God' used by Paul in the next verse (v. 7) has already been carefully defined in 1.24, where Paul declares Christ to be 'the wisdom of God'. The transition in 2.7-8 from pre-existent wisdom to the crucified 'Lord of glory'[2] shows that Paul is still working with the same definition of divine wisdom.

The word τελείοις (v. 6) has been one of the main reasons for suggesting that 2.6-16 introduces a different theme, or that Paul is combatting a kind of Gnosticism. It is best understood, however, as a synonym for the σωζομένοις of 1.18. The reason why Paul uses a different word here lies in the perspective from which he is now stating his case. Hitherto he has described how God's wisdom looks 'from the outside'. Now he expresses substantially the same points, but this time from the 'insider's' viewpoint, probably using some of the Corinthians' key words. In fact, the remainder of this section deals with the contrast between those who have received the Spirit of God and those who have not.

The structure of Paul's argument becomes more difficult to trace in ch. 3. Despite the *Stichwort* πνευματικός (3.1; cf. 2.13, 15), Paul's

1. Theissen, *Psychological Aspects*, pp. 346-52.
2. For a discussion of this phrase see section 5 below.

language here recalls the section 1.10-17, with the repetition of ἔρις (3.5; cf.1.11) and of the party slogans (3.4) mentioned in 1.12. Nevertheless, the connection in *thought* is not difficult to follow. A contrast continues to be made between the standards (or wisdom) of the world, and the standards (wisdom) of the gospel. Now, however, the contrast is applied concretely to the life of the community (vv. 1-11).

The theme of divine judgment returns in vv. 12-17, and is repeated in the summarizing section which begins at v. 18:

> Μηδεὶς ἑαυτὸν ἐξαπατάτω. εἴ τις δοκεῖ σοφὸς εἶναι ἐν ὑμῖν ἐν τῷ αἰῶνι τούτῳ, μωρὸς γενέσθω, ἵνα γένηται σοφός.

It is this section which offers the clearest evidence of a circularity in the structure of 1.18–3.23, but it is by no means clear whether Paul has adapted older material to the Corinthian situation. Nor is it possible to be precise about the detailed structure. What *is* clear is (a) the unity of the whole, including the dialectical relationship of 2.6-16 to the preceding verses, and (b) the close connection between three themes. These are

1. Paul's relationship with the church at Corinth
2. The contrast between the wisdom of the world and the wisdom of God, which finds concrete expression in the difference in attitude and conduct between Paul and the Corinthians
3. God's judgment on human wisdom.

Although there is little explicit God-language in ch. 4, and it will not be part of the focus of this chapter, it clearly forms an integral part of the section of 1 Corinthians beginning at 1.10. This is confirmed by the presence of the three themes just noted. First, Paul's relationship with and authority in the Corinthian church remains a major concern (esp. vv. 14-17). Secondly, the contrast between divine and human wisdom is carried through in the contrast between the attitude of the Corinthians implied in Paul's irony in v. 8 (ἤδη κεκορεσμένοι...) and the references to their divisive arrogance (vv. 7, 18-19), and to his own conduct (vv. 9-12, 16-17). Finally, in case the Corinthians should fondly imagine that they had become expert connoisseurs of apostles, Paul reminds them that he is subject not to theirs or anyone else's judgment, but to God's (vv. 1-5).

2. *Background*

In recent years a number of scholars have suggested that the particular problems which Paul is addressing in 1 Corinthians arose out of Jewish influences in the church at Corinth. B.A. Pearson concentrated his attention on the πνευματικός/ψυχικός terminology which Paul uses in ch. 2, contending that this was the terminology of Paul's opponents. Although Pearson acknowledges the later use of these terms by Gnostics, he believes that they developed initially out of Hellenistic-Judaism's exegesis of Gen. 2.7.[1] This, in Pearson's view was the Jewish version of the Hellenistic distinction between νοῦς and ψυχή. Similarly, the terms νηπίοι (3.1) and τελείοι (2.6) derive from Hellenistic Judaism.[2] According to Pearson, the views of Paul's opponents found expression in a *theologia gloriae* (τὸν κύριον τῆς δόξης, 2.8), being taken from their Christology.[3] Paul is clearly prepared to use the same language, but in Pearson's view he reinterprets it in terms of Jewish apocalyptic and primitive Christian eschatology.

It is questionable, however, whether the words πνευματικός and ψυχικός should be singled out for special attention in this way. Although 1 Cor. 12.1 (περὶ δὲ τῶν πνευματικῶν, ἀδελφοί, οὐ θέλω ὑμᾶς ἀγνοεῖν) suggests strongly that the word πνευματικός was in vogue at Corinth, there is little evidence that ψυχικός was its 'partner'.[4] In fact, the occurrence of οἱ πνευματικοί at Gal. 6.1 may indicate that the word was coined by Paul himself.[5] A further problem for Pearson's theory is the appearance at 1 Cor. 3.1 of the word σαρκίνοις[6] and at 3.3 (cf. 9.11) of the word σαρκικοί.

J.A. Davis is another scholar who has recently explored the possibility of a Jewish background for the opposition to Paul at Corinth. Davis, building on the work of Pearson and Horsley,[7] shows how widely held was the view that divine wisdom was embodied in the law, and how closely linked were the gift of wisdom and the gift of the Spirit. He goes on to argue that 1 Cor. 1.19 ('For it is written "I will destroy the wisdom of the wise"') is the 'text' for this whole section[8] and is

1. Pearson, *Pneumatikos*, p.82.

2. Pearson, *Pneumatikos*, p.28, citing Philo (*Migr. Abr.* 28-29 and 46; cf. *Leg.* 1.93-94 and 3.196 and *Agr.* 8-9).

3. Pearson, *Pneumatikos*, pp. 32-34.

4. ψυχικός occurs in 1 Corinthians only at 2.14, 15.44, 46.

5. See Chapter 3, section 3.

6. Some MSS read σαρκίκοις.

7. Davis, *Wisdom and Spirit*, pp. 4-5.

8. Here Davis draws on the work of Borgen and Wuellner (see the previous section of this chapter).

directed specifically against such *Jewish* sapiential traditions.[1]

The burden of Paul's argument, according to Davis, is that Christ's cross and the *kerygma* of the cross 'have replaced *Torah* as the definitive loci of divine wisdom'.[2] Similarly, 'the wisdom of this age' (1 Cor. 2.6) is to be identified with *Torah*.[3]

Although Davis's view would help to explain the surprising reference to 'the Law' at 15.56 ('the power of sin is the Law'), it is doubtful whether 1 Corinthians as a whole sustains his view, since Paul elsewhere quotes the law (9.8-9), and, most striking of all, speaks of the 'keeping of God's commandments' (7.19) in a context which provides a remarkable contrast with the conclusion of his letter to the Galatians.[4] In particular, Davis does not take into account Paul's phrase in 1.17, οὐκ ἐν σοφίᾳ λόγου, which is an important clue to the problem he is dealing with. Davis also appears to ignore the significance of the παρακαλῶ framework (1.10; 4.16) for this section, and the importance of ἔριδες (1.11; cf. 3.3) for its background.

K. Grayston[5] also finds a Jewish background in 1 Corinthians 1–4, arguing that the issue is the word of the cross versus the bearers of the Jesus tradition.[6] On this view, λόγος in 1.17 refers to the remembered instructions of Jesus, giving λόγου here the common biblical meaning of written or oral instruction. This interpretation links up well with 2 Cor. 11.4 ('For if someone comes and preaches another Jesus…') but it does not seem the most obvious meaning of ἐν σοφίᾳ λόγου, and it is perhaps a little strange that 1 Corinthians is the one epistle where Paul *does* refer explicitly to the instructions or teaching of Jesus (7.10; 9.14; 11.23-26).

Wuellner, in the article referred to earlier[7] has argued that the σοφία at Corinth had its *Sitz im Leben* in the school or synagogue exchange between teacher and disciples recommended by *Pirke Aboth* 6.6.[8] In this

1. Davis examines the work of Ben Sirach, the Qumran literature, and Philo.

2. Davis, *Wisdom and Spirit*, p. 74.

3. Davis, *Wisdom and Spirit*, pp. 89-93.

4. 1 Cor. 7.19: 'For neither circumcision counts for anything nor uncircumcision, but keeping the commandments of God'. Cf. Gal. 6.15: 'For neither is circumcision anything, nor uncircumcision, but a new creation'.

5. K. Grayston, 'Not with a Rod', *ExpTim* 78.1 (1976), pp. 13-16.

6. Grayston, 'Not with A Rod', pp. 14-15.

7. Wuellner, 'Haggadic Homily', p. 203.

8. In the list of the 48 'excellences' by which 'learning in the law' is acquired, according to *Pirke Aboth*, the following are included: '(by being) one. . . that asks

context he cites Acts 18.15 and *1 Clem.* 45.1. However, Paul seems to associate σοφία with Greek rather than Jew (1.22), and though the tradition that Paul began his ministry in Corinth by engaging in discussions in the synagogue (Acts 18.4) must be taken seriously,[1] this section of Acts gives the impression that the majority of Paul's converts were in fact Gentiles.[2] The Jewish minority, if such it was, may have styled itself the Cephas party, but there is no firm evidence that the parties to which Paul refers in 1 Cor. 1.12 divided along racial lines.

It would be unwise to rule out Jewish influence altogether in the Corinthian situation. The complex cross-currents of religions, and the frequency of travel would have made important political and trading centres such as Corinth the meeting-point of many religions. But we should probably look to sources other than Jewish for the origin of Paul's conflict with 'the wisdom of this age'.

A quite different explanation of the situation addressed here by Paul is given by L.L. Welborn.[3] Welborn documents very fully the many parallels between Paul's language here and that of many Greek and Roman authors writing on *political* themes. In some respects Welborn's case is impressive. He points out that the words σχίσματα and ἔριδες, used by Paul in 1.10-11, are often used by Graeco-Roman authors in a political sense, and therefore 'what threatened the survival of the community of chosen people was not seductive gnostic theology or infectious Judaistic propaganda, but the possibility that its adherents might 'behave

and makes answer, that hearkens and adds thereto, that... makes his teacher wiser, that retells exactly what he has heard and reports a thing in the name of him who said it' (H. Danby, *The Mishnah* [Oxford: Oxford University Press, 1933], p. 460).

1. Since the more sceptical approach of Haenchen and others to the historicity of Acts in the heyday of redaction-criticism, Luke's work as a historian has been somewhat restored by the researches, in particular, of M. Hengel, *Acts and Early Christianity* (Philadelphia: Fortress Press, 1980) (cf. also C.J. Hemer, *The Book of Acts in the Setting of Hellenistic History* [Tübingen: Mohr, 1989]). Luke mentions Crispus (ἀρχισυνάγωγος, 18.8) at Corinth, as Paul does at 1 Cor. 1.14, which is at least *prima facie* evidence that Luke's account here is not mere fabrication. It is unsatisfactory to argue that Luke used Paul's letters, since if that were so one would expect much more evidence of borrowing than appears to be the case.

2. Acts 18.4 refers to 'Jews and Greeks', but in the face of Jewish opposition Paul declares 'From now on I will go to the Gentiles' (v. 6). The 'many' Corinthians who believed (v. 8) were presumably Gentiles, Crispus being a notable exception.

3. L.L. Welborn, 'On the Discord in Corinth: 1 Corinthians 1–4 and Ancient Politics', *JBL* 106.1 (1987), pp. 85-111.

like ordinary men (3.3)'.[1] He is probably correct, too, in linking the divisions at Corinth with social inequalities.[2] But at a number of points Welborn overstates his case or is on decidedly weak ground. First, if the problem at Corinth was simply a 'power-struggle' (and there is much to be said for the view that this was a factor), exacerbated by social and economic inequality, it is difficult to see why Paul urged the Corinthians to subject themselves to Stephanas and 'such like' (1 Cor. 16.5-6) if, as Welborn argues, these were the very people who were the protagonists in the power struggle.[3] Secondly, Welborn's explanation of 2.6-16 in political terms is decidedly weak. Even though τέλειος can mean 'perfect citizen', it is a feeble argument to say that it 'recalls' the phrase οἱ ἐν τέλει.[4] Neither the language nor the context supports Welborn's view that in 2.6–3.3 Paul is speaking to the leaders of the factions who were seeking to 'gain control of the ἐκκλησία by advancing claims to higher religious knowledge'.[5] Thirdly, although Welborn demonstrates conclusively the similarity of the slogans of 1 Cor. 1.12 to ancient political slogans,[6] his claim that 'the real party leaders are thus local Christians who seek to legitimate their power by appealing to renowned figures in the church'[7] begs the question of the *significance* of each apostle (and of Christ!) for each faction. If there were no theological issues, and the problem were simply a local power-struggle, why use the names of the apostles and of Christ at all? It is true, as Welborn says, that Paul does not single out any one of these factions for separate mention, and always addresses the Corinthian *ecclesia* as a whole, but this does not mean that the factions did not represent particular theological standpoints, however much these theologies were pressed into the

1. Welborn, 'Discord', p. 88.

2. Welborn notes that the words Paul uses in 1.26-27 were euphemisms for rich and poor. The view of Theissen (*Social Setting*) that social and economic distinctions within the church at Corinth were a cause of division and tension has been widely accepted.

3. Welborn is mistaken in comparing Paul's argument in 1 Cor. 1, together with his support for Stephanas and τοιούτοις in 16.15-18, with Cicero's attempt to win over the lower classes in *Pro Sestio* 96-8. 'Paul sought, like a Greek politician of old, to bring the δῆμος into his faction' ('Discord', pp. 99-101).

4. Welborn, 'Discord', pp. 105-106.

5. Welborn, 'Discord', p. 106.

6. Welborn, 'Discord', pp. 90-93. Political parties in the ancient world bore the name of their leader.

7. Welborn, 'Discord', p. 98 n. 64.

service of local politics. It would, to say the least, have been tactically unwise for Paul to attempt to 'pick off' the factions by detailed arguments against each.

In my view, then, Welborn overstates his case although there are some crucially important features of the background to 1 Corinthians 1–4 which his paper illuminates and I shall draw on his work again in this section.

Other views about the background at Corinth may be briefly considered here. Contemporary conventions of friendship and enmity seem to have become an important factor in Paul's dealings with the church at Corinth.[1] Undoubtedly, Paul's refusal of the Corinthian offer of support was a complicating and major factor,[2] but this probably became so only after Paul had written 1 Corinthians 9 (especially vv. 4-5 and 15). It does not seem to have been a significant factor in the argument in chs. 1–4.

Other scholars have taken the view that in 1 Corinthians Paul is combating a kind of Gnostic enthusiasm.[3] 'Gnosticism', however, is an unhelpful and misleading term to use here. It would be more accurate to speak of an 'over-realized eschatology' to which 1 Cor. 4.8-13, 10.1-13, 13 and 15 are especially important correctives. Immorality was clearly an ever-present danger (5.1-5, 9, 11; 6.13 etc), but there is no evidence that it was related to Gnostic thought. There were also ascetic tendencies (7.1 and perhaps vv. 25-40), perhaps anticipating the asceticism criticized in the deutero-Pauline 1 Timothy (4.3), but it is doubtful whether these can be attributed to anything which can be properly called 'Gnostic'.

In any evaluation of the background at Corinth, it is important to distinguish between 'wisdom' and 'knowledge'. Davis[4] contends that these words should be central in any attempt to define the character of Corinthian Christianity. Pearson[5] shows that the two words are quite different, arguing that 'for the opponents and for Paul, γνῶσις is Christian insight into the realities of Christian existence here and now and its practical consequences'. It is noteworthy that Paul, while later

1. This is the thesis of P. Marshall, *Enmity in Corinth: Social Conventions in Paul's Relations with the Corinthians* (Tübingen: Mohr, 1987), esp. pp. 214, 232-33, 247.

2. Thus Marshall, *Enmity*, pp. 232-33.

3. See the earlier discussion of 2.6-16 in section 1.

4. Davis, *Wisdom and Spirit*, p. 3.

5. Davis, *Wisdom and Spirit*, pp. 42-43.

acknowledging the danger of γνῶσις (8.1), gives thanks for the γνῶσις of the Corinthians (1.5), but not for their wisdom, which, in the light of what follows, seems to have been a word that urgently needed to be theologically disinfected.[1] Perhaps by 12.8 (ᾧ μὲν γὰρ διὰ τοῦ πνεύματος δίδοται λόγος σοφίας, ἄλλῳ δὲ λόγος γνώσεως) Paul felt that this had been done. It is σοφία, therefore, not γνῶσις, which offers the clue to the problem Paul is addressing in 1 Corinthians 1–4. I return, then, to the obscure but surely important phrase in 1.17:

> οὐ γὰρ ἀπέστειλέν με Χριστὸς βαπτίζειν ἀλλὰ εὐαγγελίζεσθαι, **οὐκ ἐν σοφίᾳ λόγου**, ἵνα μὴ κενωθῇ ὁ σταυρὸς τοῦ Χριστοῦ.

First, I take λόγου to be a reference to speaking, and therefore to rhetoric. The value which the Corinthians attached to rhetoric can be gauged from Paul's later reference to their view of his preaching (2 Cor. 10.10 and 11.6, where ὁ λόγος and λόγῳ occur), and from what he says about his preaching in 2.1 and 2.4:

> Κἀγὼ ἐλθὼν πρὸς ὑμᾶς, ἀδελφοί, ἦλθον οὐ καθ' ὑπεροχὴν λόγου ἢ σοφίας καταγγέλλων ὑμῖν τὸ μυστήριον τοῦ θεοῦ (v. 1).
> καὶ ὁ λόγος μου καὶ τὸ κήρυγμά μου οὐκ ἐν πειθοῖς σοφίας λόγοις ἀλλ' ἐν ἀποδείξει πνεύματος καὶ δυνάμεως... (v. 4).[2]

Secondly, the occurrence of ἀπόδειξις in 2.4, a technical rhetorical term,[3] should be noted. If Paul wrote ἐν πειθοῖ σοφίας here, then πειθός would constitute another such rhetorical term.[4] It appears, in fact, that rhetoric was enjoying a revival in the ancient world at about this time.[5]

There is thus much to be said for Welborn's rendering of ἐν σοφίᾳ λόγου as 'by cleverness in speaking'.[6] If that is correct, then in 1 Corinthians we have evidence in Paul's critical use of rhetorical

1. Cf. C.K. Barrett, *The First Epistle to the Corinthians* (London: A. & C. Black, 1968), pp. 52-53.
2. Following the readings of MSS B and D. Thus also Conzelmann, *1 Corinthians*, p. 55 and Barrett, *1 Corinthians*, p. 65.
3. Davis, *Wisdom and Spirit*, p. 80.
4. Davis, *Wisdom and Spirit*, p. 80, Conzelmann, *1 Corinthians*, p. 55 n. 23, (cf. H.-D. Betz, 'The Problem of Rhetoric and Theology According to the Apostle Paul', in A. Vanhoye [ed.], *L'apôtre Paul: Personalité, style et conception du ministère* [Leuven: Leuven University Press, 1986], pp. 36-37).
5. K. Grayston, *Dying We Live* (London: Darton, Longman & Todd, 1990), p. 22.
6. Welborn, 'Discord', p. 101.

conventions[1] an example of 'rhetoric against rhetoric'.[2] In addition to this rhetorical background, there is a further dimension to be noted in the phrase ἐν σοφίᾳ λόγου. It is probable that both σοφία and μωρία here have social connotations. Wisdom, in the Greek view, combined theory and practice; it was 'actualized knowledge'.[3] Thus I take ἐν σοφίᾳ λόγου to mean 'in the wisdom of rhetoric', it being understood that rhetoric was socially acceptable and useful, a worthy, constructive adornment of the Greek πόλις. This 'social' interpretation of σοφία finds support in the language of v. 26, where the terms δυνατοί and εὐγενεῖς should be understood as social terms.[4]

In sum, the theories of a Jewish or Gnostic background to the problems behind 1 Corinthians 1–4 should be rejected. The evidence does not support them. It is more probable that 'secular' Greek influences were at work in the Corinthian community, as well as the social and economic tensions to which Theissen has drawn attention. This is especially important for the evaluation of Paul's language about God in these chapters. Yet there is a further dimension to the background at Corinth which seems not to have received the attention it deserves. This may fairly be called a theological dimension, the subject of the next section.

3. *God and Christ in 1 Corinthians 1.18–3.23*

One of the notable features of this passage is the occurrence of 'clusters' of God-language. The first three chapters of 1 Corinthians account for nearly half the occurrences of θεός in the epistle; this word occurs in these chapters more than half the number of times it occurs in 2 Corinthians. This of itself may not be significant, but when we analyse the occurrences more closely we find that θεός is very often an emphatic word. In this section I shall review the most important of these occurrences, before evaluating their significance.

1. On this see W. Wuellner's essay 'Paul as Pastor: The Function of Rhetorical Questions in 1 Corinthians', in Vanhoye (ed.), *L'apôtre Paul*, pp. 49-77.

2. F. Siegert, *Argumentation bei Paulus* (Tübingen: Mohr, 1985), p. 249. In Siegert's view the kind of rhetoric which Paul rejects is that which tries to manipulate its hearers, without regard for the truth.

3. *TWNT*, VII, p. 473.

4. Grayston, *Dying*, pp. 22-23. *Contra* Davis, *Wisdom and Spirit*, p. 76 who follows Horsley and Pearson in seeing these terms and the preceding σοφοί as religious terms.

The first such occurrence comes in 1.21 where θεός is used three times:

> ἐπειδὴ γὰρ ἐν τῇ σοφίᾳ τοῦ θεοῦ οὐκ ἔγνω ὁ κόσμος διὰ τῆς σοφίας τὸν θεόν, εὐδόκησεν ὁ θεὸς διὰ τῆς μωρίας τοῦ κηρύγματος σῶσαι τοὺς πιστεύοντας.

Paul here is writing in a very rhetorical style, but it would not have been difficult to write substantially the same thing and to use the word θεός at the most twice: for example, ἐπειδὴ γὰρ ἐν τῇ σοφίᾳ τοῦ θεοῦ ὁ κόσμος **αὐτὸν** οὐκ ἔγνω...

Three verses later Paul seems to go out of his way again to emphasize θεός, when he writes of Christ as θεοῦ δύναμιν καὶ θεοῦ σοφίαν (v. 24). The double θεοῦ, preceding the accompanying noun, emphasizes that in the crucified Christ there is a revelation of God.[1] Finally, in this opening section (vv. 18-25) the word θεός is used twice in v. 25 in the phrases τὸ μωρὸν τοῦ θεοῦ and τὸ ἀσθενὲς τοῦ θεοῦ. While all due allowance has to be made for the flow of Paul's rhetoric, this verse has the effect of reinforcing the emphasis of vv. 21 and 24 that Paul's message is fundamentally theocentric.

This initial impression is confirmed by vv. 26-31 by his threefold use of the phrase ἐξελέξατο ὁ θεός, and by the inversion of subject and verb:

> ἀλλὰ τὰ μωρὰ τοῦ κόσμου ἐξελέξατο ὁ θεός, ἵνα καταισχύνῃ τοὺς σοφούς, καὶ τὰ ἀσθενῆ τοῦ κόσμου ἐξελέξατο ὁ θεός, ἵνα καταισχύνῃ τὰ ἰσχυρά, καὶ τὰ ἀγενῆ τοῦ κόσμου καὶ τὰ ἐξουθενημένα ἐξελέξατο ὁ θεός, τὰ μὴ ὄντα, ἵνα τὰ ὄντα καταργήσῃ...[2]

In this way Paul succeeds in once again throwing the emphasis upon God.[3] The Hebraic phrase ἐνώπιον τοῦ θεοῦ, used in v. 29, underlines

1. R. Baumann, *Mitte und Norm des Christlichen: Eine Auslegung von 1 Korinther 1.1–3.4* (Münster: Aschendorff, 1968), p. 108.

2. The threefold pattern almost certainly derives fronm its Old Testament paradigm in Jer. 9.23-24, although these verses have a different pattern of God-language, beginning and ending with λέγει Κύριος. The same threefold pattern as here, with a similar inversion of verb and subject, occurs in Rom. 1.24, 26, 28 (παρέδωκεν ὁ θεός).

3. G.R. O'Day, 'Jeremiah 9.22-3 and 1 Corinthians 1.26-31: A Study in Intertextuality', *JBL* 109/2 (1990), p.262, notes the 'theocentric message' at the heart of Jer. 9.22-23. Contending that it is of the essence of biblical texts to be reinterpreted (p. 260), O'Day argues that that is what Paul has done here, replacing Jeremiah's

the point[1] while in v. 30 the placing of ἐξ αὐτοῦ (referring to God) at the beginning of the sentence (and both words before the δέ)[2] and the inclusion of ἀπὸ θεοῦ make clear (a) God is the ultimate source of the Corinthians' being in Christ, and (b) the 'coming' of Christ from God.

Two emphatic uses of θεός occur in the section which firmly links Paul's own mode of preaching with the *kerygma* of the crucified Christ (2.1-5). In both instances (vv. 1 and 5), the word θεοῦ comes at the end of the sentence, and is the weightiest word in the contrast Paul is making:

> κἀγὼ ἐλθὼν πρὸς ὑμᾶς, ἀδελφοί, ἦλθον οὐ καθ' ὑπεροχὴν λόγου ἢ σοφίας καταγγέλλων ὑμῖν τὸ μυστήριον τοῦ θεοῦ[3] (v. 1).
> . . . ἵνα ἡ πίστις ὑμῶν μὴ ᾖ ἐν σοφίᾳ ἀνθρώπων ἀλλ' ἐν δυνάμει θεοῦ (v. 5).

In the next few verses the examples are not so obvious, although we find the inversion of the genitive and its noun in v. 7 (θεοῦ σοφίαν), and the use of θεός once more in the relative clause which follows: σοφίαν...ἣν προώρισεν ὁ θεὸς πρὸ τῶν αἰώνων εἰς δόξαν ἡμῶν.

The recurrence of θεός in v. 9 is more difficult to evaluate since we do not know the source of Paul's quotation,[4] but it is noteworthy that θεός is twice used in the following verse: ἡμῖν δὲ ἀπεκάλυψεν ὁ θεὸς διὰ τοῦ πνεύματος. τὸ γὰρ πνεῦμα πάντα ἐραυνᾷ, καὶ τὰ βάθη τοῦ θεοῦ (v. 10).[5] Here, as in 1.21, it seems that Paul could perfectly well have expressed himself without so heavy a use of θεός. In v. 11b the double use of θεός is necessary for the parallelism of the two parts of the sentence καὶ τὰ τοῦ θεοῦ οὐδεὶς ἔγνωκεν εἰ μὴ τὸ πνεῦμα τοῦ θεοῦ. In v. 12, however, there is surely yet another

'steadfast love, justice and righteousness' by 'righteousness, sanctification and redemption', and thus reflecting Christian soteriology: 'God through Christ to us' (p. 266).

1. Paul uses the same phrase, probably from Ps. 143 (LXX 142).2, in a not dissimilar context in Rom. 3.20.

2. Noted also by Baumann, *Mitte Und Norm*, p. 132.

3. The probable reading of 𝔓46, the original reading of *Codex Sinaiticus* and the reading of *Codex Alexandrinus*. This seems more likely in this context than τὸ μαρτύριον τοῦ θεοῦ (a later corrector of *Codex Sin.*; cf. also *Codices* B and D). See, however, Barrett, *1 Corinthians*, pp. 62-63.

4. Origen thought it came from the Elijah Apocalypse (Conzelmann, *1 Corinthians*, p. 63). There is, however, some similarity with Isa. 64.4-5 (LXX).

5. For a brief discussion of τὰ βάθη τοῦ θεοῦ see section 5 below.

instance of Paul's use of θεός where he would have omitted it unless he had particularly wished to emphasize the origin of the Spirit. The contrast with 'the world' suggests that he did wish to do so: ἡμεῖς δὲ οὐ τὸ πνεῦμα τοῦ κόσμου ελάβομεν ἀλλὰ τὸ πνεῦμα τὸ ἐκ τοῦ θεοῦ, ἵνα εἰδῶμεν τὰ ὑπὸ τοῦ θεοῦ χαρισθέντα ἡμῖν. (The final phrase in this verse τὰ ὑπὸ τοῦ θεοῦ χαρισθέντα ἡμῖν continues the emphasis upon God.)

Lastly in this chapter, v. 14 contains the phrase τὰ τοῦ πνεύματος τοῦ θεοῦ. In the light of the preceding evidence we may reasonably wonder why Paul did not write simply τὰ τοῦ πνεύματος. In fact, most occurrences of πνεῦμα with θεοῦ in Paul's writings occur in 1 and 2 Corinthians.[1]

In ch. 3 the same pattern continues. In a context in which Paul is anxious to correct what might have been excessive veneration for himself and Apollos at Corinth, or, at the very least, the use of his and other apostles' names as party slogans, Paul stresses: ἐγὼ ἐφύτευσα, 'Απολλῶς ἐπότισεν, ἀλλὰ ὁ θεὸς ηὔξανεν· ὥστε οὔτε ὁ φυτεύων ἐστίν τι οὔτε ὁ ποτίζων ἀλλ' ὁ αὐξάνων θεός (vv. 6-7).[2] Once again, the contrast indicates where the emphasis falls; the positioning of θεός as the last word in the sentence in v. 7 underlines the point.

The emphasis of v. 9 is very clear from the threefold θεοῦ, and also the fact that, once again, each θεοῦ precedes the noun which it accompanies:[3] θεοῦ γὰρ ἐσμεν συνεργοί, θεοῦ γεώργιον, θεοῦ οἰκοδομή ἐστε. A final occurrence of θεός occurs in the following verse, where Paul chose to write κατὰ τὴν χάριν **τοῦ θεοῦ** (v. 10), when αὐτοῦ would clearly have referred back to the threefold θεοῦ of v. 9.

The next cluster of God-language occurs in vv. 16 and 17, Here the word θεός is used no less than five times even though, as with 1.21, the same thought could have been communicated using θεός only two or three times. Thus Paul writes:

> οὐκ οἴδατε ὅτι ναὸς θεοῦ ἐστε καὶ τὸ πνεῦμα τοῦ θεοῦ οἰκεῖ ἐν ὑμῖν; εἴ τις τὸν ναὸν τοῦ θεοῦ φθείρει, φθερεῖ τοῦτον ὁ θεός· ὁ γὰρ ναὸς τοῦ θεοῦ ἅγιός ἐστιν, οἵτινές ἐστε ὑμεῖς.

1. See p. 23 n.4 in the Introduction.

2. Conzelmann, *1 Corinthians*, p. 73, notes here the 'eminently critical sense' of the word 'God'.

3. Noted, e.g., by A. Robertson and A. Plummer, *A Critical and Exegetical Commentary on the First Epistle of St Paul to the Corinthians* (Edinburgh: T. & T. Clark, 1914), pp. 58-59.

The temple imagery used by Paul in v.16 is not our immediate concern.[1] The full significance of these verses, however, cannot be evaluated without due attention to the structure, which is unmistakably chiastic, exhibiting an ABCCBA pattern. The most intriguing and difficult bit of God-language within this chiastic structure occurs in v. 17a, with the double use of φθείρω. Such double uses of verbs occur elsewhere in Scripture (e.g. Mt. 7.1), and it is probable that Paul is here drawing on tradition. In a study of this and similar verses in Paul, Käsemann[2] concluded that Holy Scripture provided the primitive Christian prophets with the stylistic form in which to clothe their sentences of 'holy law'. Hence 'in the early days of the Christian religion, Spirit and Law are not separated. At this point the Spirit creates Law'.[3]

This theory of Käsemann has not gone uncriticized, and it may be that he, like others in the Bultmannian school, has exaggerated the role of Christian prophets in the early church.[4] It is probable, too, that Käsemann ignored the debt of the early Christian tradition to 'the genre of sapiential exhortation'[5] in what he calls 'holy law'. But the question remains of the theological presuppositions underlying the language and the structure, and of the implications for Paul's understanding of God.

Conzelmann notes 'the formal correspondence between the offence and God's reaction to it'.[6] Robertson and Plummer call this 'the just working of the *lex talionis*...one destruction is requited by another destruction'.[7] It is questionable, however, whether 'destroy' is the correct translation of φθείρω here. J. Shanor[8] puts forward a persuasive case for translating φθείρω as 'damage' or 'harm', citing ancient inscriptions relating to temple building and public works as the key to

1. For the background of Paul's temple imagery see the commentaries for both Jewish and Hellenistic parallels.

2. E. Käsemann, 'Sentences of Holy Law in the New Testament', in *New Testament Questions for Today* (London: SCM Press, 1969), pp. 66-81.

3. Käsemann, *New Testament Questions*, p. 80.

4. On this, see, for example, the criticisms of Käsemann's position in D. Hill, *New Testament Prophecy* (London: Marshall, Morgan & Scott, 1979), pp. 170-74.

5. Hill, *New Testament Prophecy*, p. 171.

6. Conzelmann, *1 Corinthians*, p. 78.

7. Robertson and Plummer, *Critical Commentary*, p. 67, comparing Romans 1.28 and Rev. 11.18, which includes the phrase καὶ διαφθεῖραι τοὺς διαφθείροντας τὴν γῆν.

8. J. Shanor, 'Paul as Master Builder: Construction Terms in 1 Corinthians', *NTS* 34 (1988), pp. 461-71.

Paul's language in 1 Cor. 3.9-17. (On this view, the illustration merges into the theology, as in Rom. 14.4.)

But even if Shanor is correct[1] this does not entirely remove the theological problem. Had the apostle forgotten what he had written to the church at Thessaly: 'See that none of you repay evil for evil'?[2] Or did Paul see no contradiction here? It would seem that, in spite of the resemblance of Paul's sentence to the *lex talionis*, an alternative view is preferable. Klaus Koch[3] has questioned whether 'retribution' is the appropriate interpretative concept for similarly structured verses in the Old Testament, preferring to speak of human actions with 'built-in' consequences: 'the Psalms teach the same thing as the Wisdom Literature and Hosea; human action takes place in an arena of built-in consequences set in motion, speeded up and finally brought to completion by Yahweh's active involvement'.[4] To support his argument Koch draws on K. Fählgren's study of '*sedaka*', in which Fählgren showed that a whole series of Hebrew roots were used to describe both an action and its consequences—e.g. '*ra*' meaning 'ethically depraved' and 'bringing misfortune'.

In view of this, it is probably nearer the mark to relate 1 Cor. 3.17a to Paul's language about 'hardening' than to the *lex talionis*. Both kinds of language point to the mysterious but inevitable result of human obstinacy or waywardness, a result in which divine and human agency merge.[5] Further language of this kind follows in this chapter, when Paul indicates, by means of Old Testament quotations, the outcome of the wisdom of 'this age': γέγραπται γάρ· ὁ δρασσόμενος τοὺς σοφοὺς ἐν τῇ πανουργίᾳ αὐτῶν (v. 19b) and κύριος γινώσκει τοὺς διαλογισμοὺς τῶν σοφῶν ὅτι εἰσὶν μάταιοι (v. 20).

1. M. Newton, *The Concept of Purity at Qumran and in the Letters of Paul* (Cambridge: Cambridge University Press, 1985), p. 56, also argues that φθείρω here does not mean complete annihilation.

2. 1 Thess. 5.15; cf. Rom. 12.17a, although Paul's quotation from Proverbs later in this chapter should not be overlooked: ἐμοὶ ἐκδίκησις, ἐγὼ ἀνταποδώσω, λέγει κύριος (v. 19b). (On this verse, see the discussion in Chapter 4 below.)

3. K. Koch, 'Is there a Doctrine of Retribution in the Old Testament?', in J.L. Crenshaw (ed.), *Theodicy in the Old Testament* (Philadelphia: Fortress Press, 1983), pp. 57-87.

4. Crenshaw, *Theodicy*, p. 74.

5. Cf. Heschel, *Prophets*, pp. 279-98 for a valuable discussion of 'The Meaning and Mystery of Wrath'.

There is one final occurrence of θεός to be noted in the section 1.18–3.23, and it occurs in the very last verse: ὑμεῖς δὲ Χριστοῦ, Χριστὸς δὲ θεοῦ (v. 23). The rhetorical structure is obvious[1] but little attention seems to have been paid to the final phrase Χριστὸς δὲ θεοῦ. Conzelmann[2] observes that the subordination of Christ here is not just rhetorical but 'essential'. But why is it essential? The same commentator notes other references back to God in Paul,[3] but it is noteworthy that another very 'subordinationist' statement occurs in this same letter:

> When all things are subjected to him, then the Son himself will also be subjected to the one who put all things in subjection under him, that God may be all in all (15.28).[4]

I return to these verses shortly. The survey of the language about God used by Paul in this section of 1 Corinthians has now been completed, and the reasons for the remarkable frequency of the word θεός need to be considered. In the first section of this chapter it was argued that 1.18–3.23, although the main focus of this study, belonged to a wider unit of which the double παρακαλῶ in 1.10 and 4.16 marked the framework. It is not unreasonable, therefore, to look to this wider framework for an explanation of Paul's language about God here. Such an explanation may perhaps lie in the last of the party slogans mentioned by Paul in 1.12, ἐγὼ δὲ Χριστοῦ. While it is true that Paul does not specifically or explicitly address each party individually,[5] it is clear that he is addressing at least the Paul and the Apollos factions in 3.1-10. In two places, as we have seen, he corrects such partisan veneration of apostles by his emphasis upon God (3.7, 9). It is possible that he is performing a parallel task in verses such as 3.23, but this time with a view to correcting the 'Christ' party.

1. Bünker, *Briefformular*, p. 54, regards 3.18-23 as the *peroratio* of which 1.18–2.17 is the *narratio*, and 3.1-17 is the *probatio*. Siegert, *Argumentation*, p. 192, includes 3.23 in his section on '*Klimax, Kette, Enthumem*', describing it as 'the closure and intensification of a series (*Abschluss und Steigerung einer Aufzählung*)'.

2. Conzelmann, *1 Corinthians*, p. 81.

3. Gal. 1.4, Phil. 2.11.

4. L. Goppelt, *Theology of the New Testament* (2 vols.; Grand Rapids, MI: Eerdmans, 1981, 1982), II, p. 79, links 3.23 with 15.23-24 and 28, but without exploring the christological implications.

5. In the previous section I suggested that it would have been tactically unwise for Paul to do so.

Senft is one commentator who has related the first phrase of 3.23, ὑμεῖς δὲ Χριστοῦ, to the ἐγὼ δὲ Χριστοῦ of 1.12. He notes[1] that ὑμεῖς δὲ Χριστοῦ is an acceptable statement in 3.23, whereas the party slogan in 1.12 is not, and wonders whether 3.23 is a revision and correction of the earlier slogan. One could certainly argue that the problem with the slogan ἐγὼ δὲ Χριστοῦ was not the Χριστοῦ, but the ἐγώ, but this leaves unexplained the second half of 3.23. J. Weiss argues that the hymn-like structure of the passage requires Χριστὸς δὲ θεοῦ, and compares 11.3 and 7. 1 Cor. 11.3 offers a striking parallel to 3.23:

> θέλω δὲ ὑμᾶς εἰδέναι ὅτι παντὸς ἀνδρὸς ἡ κεφαλὴ ὁ Χριστός ἐστιν, κεφαλὴ δὲ γυναικὸς ὁ ανήρ, κεφαλὴ δὲ τοῦ Χριστοῦ ὁ θεός.[2]

Weiss goes on to note the christological importance of this verse, since not only is the subordination of Christ to God mentioned but also the moral and religious implications of that subordination are emphasized.[3] This, however, does not answer the question of why this particular christological point is made here.

Not surprisingly, there has been considerable debate about what the 'Christ party' stood for.[4] T.W. Manson took the view[5] that they were a group for whom Christ meant 'God, freedom and immortality'. But this does not really explain why such a group should have the slogan 'I am *Christ's*'. It is also doubtful whether the pneumatic enthusiasm, whether 'Gnostic' or not, which Paul corrects elsewhere in 1 Corinthians, can be identified solely with the 'Christ party'.[6]

It seems preferable in the light of the God-language surveyed in this section to suggest that the Christ party's failure was to regard Christ as

1. Senft, *Aux Corinthiens*, pp. 34-35.

2. Weiss, *Korintherbrief*, also quotes *1 Clem.* 42.2 (also written to Corinth!): ὁ Χριστὸς οὖν ἀπὸ τοῦ θεοῦ καὶ οἱ ἀπόστολοι ἀπὸ τοῦ Χριστοῦ.

3. Weiss, *Korintherbrief*, p. 91.

4. Weiss, *Korintherbrief*, p. 16, is one commentator who has argued that there was no 'Christ party', not least because of the first phrase of 1.13: μεμέρισται ὁ Χριστός. But the parallelism of the four phrases in v. 12 tells decisively against this.

5. T.W. Manson, *Studies in the Gospels and Epistles* (Manchester: Manchester University Press, 1962), p. 207.

6. Schmithals, *Gnosticism*, pp. 203-204, wrongly concludes that it is the Christ party which is destroying the unity of the community built on the foundation of the apostles.

a kind of cult-figure or idol, rather than as the '*eikon*' of God. In this respect their failure was parallel to that of the Paul, Apollos and Cephas parties, who failed to look beyond the apostles to Christ. (Hence Paul's questions in 1.13: Was Paul crucified for you? Or were you baptized in the name of Paul?)

Conzelmann approaches this view when he says

> the main defect of Corinthian conditions... Paul sees to consist in the boldness, assurance and enthusiasm with which they believe, not in God, but in their own belief in God and in particular leaders and heroes.[1]

Conzelmann makes this statement of all the Corinthian parties, and this may well be so, but I am arguing that there was a particular sense in which this was true of the Christ party, precisely because their hero was Christ, and not an apostle. This does not mean that they did not believe in God at all, since it seems likely that in 8.4 Paul is quoting Corinthian slogans, or at the very least formulating statements which he knew very well both he and they assented to: 'Hence, as to the eating of food offered to idols, we know that "no idol in the world really exists," and that "there is no God but one"'. It is quite likely, however, in the light of Paul's earlier emphatic God-language, that such a belief in God was marginal in the Corinthians' belief system.[2]

A similar point may be made with reference to πνεῦμα. Paul's apparent stress on the fact that the Spirit is *God's* Spirit suggests that the Corinthian understanding of πνεῦμα was also divorced from God. While this is unlikely to have been confined to the Christ party, this does not affect the point made here. To such a marginalized belief in God, Paul offers the following corrective.

All things come from God, including the salvation of the Corinthians, (1.30; 8.6; 11.30; the word θεός occurs in all three verses). All things are destined for God (8.6; 15.28). Christ himself comes from God (1.30; 11.3), and owes allegiance to God (3.23; 11.3; 15.28). The Spirit is the Spirit *of God* (2.10-14; 3.16; 6.11; 7.40; 12.3).[3] The Corinthians' own

1. Conzelmann, *1 Corinthians*, p. 34 n.31.

2. Barrett, *1 Corinthians*, pp. 359-60, approaches this view in his remarks on 15.27, when he asks why Paul adds, after quoting Ps. 8.7 ('All things are put in subjection under him [sc. Christ]'), the rider that 'it is plain that he (sc. God) is excepted who put all things under him'. Barrett thinks that it is partly to prepare for v. 28, but 'partly also perhaps because of a Corinthian belief (of which we have no other evidence) that at his exaltation Christ became the one supreme God'.

3. Lührmann, *Offenbarungsverständnis*, p. 135, notes the emphasis on God in

calling comes from God (1.27-28), their continuing nurture as Christians derives ultimately from God (3.6-7), and their present status has to be understood in *theo*centric terms (3.9, 16). What they have received as Christians, they have received from God (2.12; cf. 4.7).

Summary

This section has noted not only the frequency of the word θεός in 1 Cor. 1.18–3.23, but also its often emphatic character. In several verses, notably in 1.21, 2.10-12, and 3.16-17, Paul uses the word θεός more than was strictly necessary; in others, θεός is either repeated (1.25; 3.9), or used emphatically, usually by its position in the sentence (1.26-28; 2.1, 5; 3.6, 7, 9), while τὸ πνεῦμα is ἐκ τοῦ θεοῦ (2.11, 12, 14). The explanation for this may well lie in the defective theology of the 'Christ party'. Several verses in 1 Corinthians, notably 3.23, 11.3 and 15.27 lend support to this view. Thus θεός here has a powerfully critical function, and Paul offers a thoroughly theocentric understanding of both the gospel and the Christian life.

4. *The Power and Weakness of God*

In the previous section it was suggested that the concentration of God-language in 1 Cor. 1.18–3.23 may have been intended as a corrective to what we may call the 'Christomonist' tendencies of the Christ party at Corinth. It is clear, however, that this is not all that was amiss at Corinth. It is possible that the views of the other parties, including those of the 'Paul party', were as defective as those of the 'Christ party'.[1] However that may be, Paul's words are addressed to them all. But it is time now to look at the nature of Paul's language about God in this section of 1 Corinthians in order to discover in what ways, if any, it is distinctive.

Clear as it is, Paul's own starting point ought to be acknowledged. For him the new age has dawned with the coming of Christ. The contrast between the new age and 'this age' or 'the world' (1.20-21, 27-28; 2.6, 8; 3.18-19) is fundamental to Paul's argument, and to his language about God. The contrast is developed by means of two contrasting pairs

2.10-16, but believes that the emphasis is anti-Gnostic.

1. Barrett, in his study 'Christianity at Corinth', suggests that Apollos contributed to the Corinthian development of thought about γνῶσις, λόγος and σοφία, and that the 'Cephas party' adopted a Jewish–Christian 'nomistic' attitude to some of the questions at Corinth (*Essays*, p. 4).

of words and their cognates: wise and foolish/powerful and weak. Thus in the section 1.18-31 Paul states, or implies, that powerful in this age are: 'the wisdom of the wise and the cleverness of the clever' (v. 19), 'the wise man', 'the scribe', 'the debater of this age' (v. 20), the 'powerful' and those 'of noble birth' (v. 26), 'the wise' and 'the strong' (v. 27).

By contrast, weak in this age are: we 'who are being saved' (v. 18), 'those who are called' (v. 24), 'what is foolish in the world' (v. 27) 'what is weak in the world' (v. 27) 'what is low and despised in the world, even things that are not' (v. 28).

It is probable that Paul owed the distinction between 'this age' and 'the new age' (although this latter concept is implied rather than expressed) to Jewish apocalyptic. This is the thesis of F.L. Arrington in the study briefly noted in section 2 of this chapter, *Paul's Aeon Theology in 1 Corinthians*. In Arrington's view the two-age motif is fundamental to Paul's perspective in 1 Corinthians.[1] But since the two ages overlap temporally, the moral and spiritual differences between them stand out all the more sharply. Therefore 'what is power in the old age, in the new age is weakness. What is weakness in the old age is strength in the new age.'[2] The immediate task now, therefore, is to explore these themes in Paul's language about God, with particular reference to 1 Cor. 1.18-25, and to draw out the understanding of God reflected in the language.

The closely knit character of Paul's argument in 1 Cor. 1.18-25 is clearly brought out by the string of connecting words. Thus we have γάρ linking v. 18 with v. 17, and v. 19 with v. 18; ἐπειδὴ γάρ links v. 21 with v. 20; ἐπειδή links v. 22 with v. 21; and, finally, the ὅτι of v. 25 links this verse with the preceding one. Here, then, are vital clues to the sequence of Paul's thought here. The γάρ of v. 18 is particularly important in that it points back to the phrase Paul used in v. 17: οὐ γὰρ ἀπέστειλέν με Χριστὸς βαπτίζειν ἀλλὰ εὐαγγελίζεσθαι, οὐκ ἐν σοφίᾳ λόγου, ἵνα μὴ κενωθῇ ὁ σταυρὸς τοῦ Χριστοῦ. The word σταυρός is again used in v. 18: ὁ λόγος γὰρ τοῦ σταυροῦ τοῖς μὲν ἀπολλυμένοις μωρία ἐστιν, τοῖς δὲ σῳζομένοις ἡμῖν δύναμις θεοῦ ἐστιν.

1. F.L. Arrington, *Paul's Aeon Theology in 1 Corinthians* (Washington, DC: University Press of America, 1978), *passim*.

2. Arrington, *Aeon Theology*, pp. 179-80.

Senft,[1] noting the occurrence of σταυρός in Galatians (esp. 6.12, 14), describes it as 'a word of fracture' ('une parole de rupture'). This is apt. Martin Hengel's study of crucifixion in the Roman world has shown that it would have been difficult to think of a word whose associations were further removed from the power of God or the gods than σταυρός (Latin, *crux*).[2] Paul, however, is saying that 'the word of the cross...is the power of God'. Many commentators have noted Paul's apparent preference for the phrase δύναμις θεοῦ rather than σοφία θεοῦ (not, however, as Baumann argues[3] because δύναμις had wide currency in Corinthian religious language). Here Barrett is probably correct in suggesting that 'for the moment at least the word wisdom is in bad odour'.[4] It could be argued, of course, that the word 'power' had even more potential for distortion and misuse, but Paul is clearly happy to use the word δύναμις (notably in Rom. 1.16).

How, then, is the word of the cross the power of God? Paul's next statements supply the answer. We note particularly the four verbs of which God is the implied or expressed subject:

> γέγραπται γάρ· ἀπολῶ τὴν σοφίαν τῶν σοφῶν
> καὶ τὴν σύνεσιν τῶν συνετῶν ἀθετήσω.
> ...οὐχὶ ἐμώρανεν ὁ θεὸς τὴν σοφίαν τοῦ κόσμου;
> ...εὐδόκησεν ὁ θεὸς διὰ τῆς μωρίας τοῦ κηρύγματος σῶσαι
> τοὺς πιστεύοντας (vv.19-21).

The Old Testament background of these will be discussed in the next section. For the moment we are concerned with Paul's argument in relation to his use of God-language. The aorist ἐμώρανεν in v. 20b indicates the nature of his argument: the future tenses of the Isaiah quotation have now found their fulfilment in the foolishing of 'the wisdom of the world'. But when and where has this foolishing taken place? It has occurred in (ἐπειδὴ γὰρ, v. 21) the saving of those who believe 'through the foolishness of the proclamation'. This means that the 'foolishing' of the wise consists in their *not* being saved. That is far from apparent to them (the kerygma remains an 'offence' or 'foolishness', v. 23), but it is clear to believers for whom Christ is the power and wisdom of God (v. 24). Wilckens rightly finds in vv. 22-24 an *a*

1. Senft, *Aux Corinthiens*, p. 42.
2. M. Hengel, *Crucifixion* (London: SCM Press, 1977) *passim*.
3. Baumann, *Mitte und Norm*, p. 87.
4. Barrett, *1 Corinthians*, p. 52.

posteriori proof based on the believers' experience.[1]

The section which follows (vv. 26-31) continues the same theme, not only by the explicit connection (βλέπετε γάρ...), but also by the use of shaming language: ἀλλὰ τὰ μωρὰ τοῦ κόσμου ἐξελέξατο ὁ θεὸς ἵνα καταισχύνῃ τοὺς σοφούς...(v. 27a; cf. v. 27b). Shame, like honour, has to do with status[2] and the shaming of the wise lies in their not being chosen. But it is important to note here that God is most frequently the subject of αἰσχύνω in the LXX.[3] The point is reinforced by the use of καταργέω in the next verse: καὶ τὰ ἀγενῆ τοῦ κόσμου καὶ τὰ ἐξουθενημένα ἐξελέξατο ὁ θεός, τὰ μὴ ὄντα, ἵνα τὰ ὄντα καταργήσῃ (v. 28). Paul, therefore, uses a number of words here of God which denote power. He 'destroys', 'sets aside' (v. 19), 'foolishes' (v. 20), 'chooses to save' (v. 21), 'chooses' (vv. 27-28), 'shames' (v. 27) and 'brings to nothing' (v. 28).

Running parallel with the contrast of power and weakness is the contrast of wisdom and foolishness. This contrast runs throughout vv. 18-25. Underlying it is the apocalyptic schema of the 'two ages', which is also the key to the datives, not only in v. 18 (τοῖς μὲν ἀπολλυμένοις...τοῖς δὲ σῳζομένοις) but also in vv. 23-24:

> ἡμεῖς δὲ κηρύσσομεν Χριστὸν ἐσταυρωμένον, Ἰουδαίοις μὲν σκάνδαλον, ἔθνεσιν δὲ μωρίαν, αὐτοῖς δὲ τοῖς κλητοῖς, Ἰουδαίοις τε καὶ Ἕλλησιν, Χριστὸν θεοῦ δύναμιν καὶ θεοῦ σοφίαν.

In other words, as v. 18 indicated, a person's perspective or standpoint indicates whether the proclamation of Christ crucified is perceived as power and wisdom, or as weakness and foolishness. Within the framework of the new age it is the former; within the old age, it is the latter. It is this dual perspective, noted earlier, which explains the startling expressions which follow in v. 25: ὅτι τὸ μωρὸν τοῦ θεοῦ σοφώτερον τῶν ἀνθρώπων ἐστὶν καὶ τὸ ἀσθενὲς τοῦ θεοῦ ἰσχυρότερον τῶν ἀνθρώπων. The language used here makes it clear that in Paul's view the fact that two quite different views may be taken of the preaching of the cross does not relativize either. There are no datives such as 'for us' here; Paul is simply stating what he believes to be the truth. But to what

1. Quoted by Baumann, *Mitte und Norm*, pp. 108-109.
2. B.J. Malina, *The New Testament World* (London: SCM Press,1983), pp. 44-47. Malina's comment on 'shame' as a positive symbol (i.e. 'sensitivity for one's own reputation') has to be set alongside the Old Testament theological background.
3. Thus Bultmann in *TWNT*, I, p. 189.

is Paul referring? It seems likely, in view of the context, that the 'foolish' and 'weak thing' of God is the preaching of the cross. First, this would correspond with the statement with which Paul began this section: 'the word of the cross...is the power of God' (cf. Rom. 1.16). Secondly, Paul has already referred (v. 21) to 'the folly of what we preach' (τῆς μωρίας τοῦ κηρύγματος). Thirdly, as the connecting γάρ indicates (v. 26), the Corinthians' own calling is evidence that 'the foolish thing of God is wiser than men'. That is to say, the proclamation of the gospel, and the Corinthians' conversion is the means whereby God shames the wise (ἵνα, v. 27). Fourthly, Paul's description of his own preaching (2.1-5) continues the same theme: that which is weak and foolish in this age conveys *for that very reason* the power of God (cf. 3.18, 19a). The context, therefore, strongly suggests that in v. 25 τὸ μωρὸν τοῦ θεοῦ and τὸ ἀσθενὲς τοῦ θεοῦ refer to the preaching of the cross.[1] In the remainder of this section I shall explore the relationship between power and weakness in the writings of Paul, and the theological significance of that relationship.

H.K. Nielson[2] draws attention to the theme of 'power' in Paul, noting the similarity between δόξα and δύναμις in Pauline usage but contending that δύναμις, unlike δόξα, is used of the period between the resurrection and the parousia. This certainly accounts for many occurrences of δύναμις in Paul,[3] though not Rom. 1.20 and 9.17. Nielson goes on to argue that 'a theology of the cross'—*Kreuzestheologie*—is an inadequate summary of Paul's message, since Paul so often links cross and resurrection. For this view there is much to be said, particularly Nielson's contention that we should speak not of the paradoxical identity of weakness and power, but rather of their dialectical relationship, in that 'ἀσθένεια constitutes, so to speak, a void which the δύναμις of God can fill'.[4] Nielson goes on to argue that a number of passages in Paul 'modify' his *Kreuzestheologie*. The passages he lists are

1. This is preferable to the view of Weiss, *Korintherbrief*, p. 34, who argues that the neuter adjectives denote God's act of foolishness in the cross. (So also Barrett *1 Corinthians*, p. 56.)

2. H.K. Nielson, 'Paulus' Verwendung des Begriffes Δύναμις. Eine Replik zur Kreuzestheologie', in S. Pedersen (ed.), *Die Paulinische Literatur und Theologie*, (Aarhus: Forlaget Aros, 1980), pp. 137-58.

3. For example, δύναμις is used in a resurrection context at Rom. 1.4; 1 Cor. 6.14; 15.43; 2 Cor. 4.7; 12.9 and Phil. 3.10, and of the power of the Holy Spirit at Rom. 15.13, 19; 1 Cor. 2.4-5; Gal. 3.5 and 1 Thess. 1.5.

4. Pedersen, *Paulinische Literatur*, p. 157.

Rom. 15.18-9; 1 Cor. 2.4-5; 4.20; 5.4; 2 Cor. 4.7-12; 6.4-10; 10.1-11; 12.12; 13.3-4; Gal. 3.5; 1 Thess. 1.5.

While it is not possible to examine each of these passages in detail, it must be said that they do not 'modify' Paul's *Kreuzestheologie* (any more than one could say that the resurrection 'modified' the cross). In fact, most of these passages refer to the ministry of Paul. Sometimes, as in 2 Cor. 6.1-10 and 1 Cor. 2.4-5, there are explicit references to Paul's weakness or poverty; in others, such as Rom. 15.18-9, 2 Cor. 12.12 and 1 Thess. 1.5, it is natural to assume that the apostle's weakness and poverty, although not explicitly mentioned, remain the foil for the manifestation of divine power.

But can the relationship between weakness and power be more precisely defined? As Nielson's list indicates, what Paul says about himself is vital to this discussion. It is arguable that 'the catalogues of hardships' in the Corinthian letters take us near the heart of Paul's understanding of God.[1] Two texts in 2 Corinthians are especially important. First, Paul, after summarizing the many deprivations he had experienced in the service of the gospel (12.10a, cf. 11.23-33) goes on to say ὅταν γὰρ ἀσθενῶ, τότε δυνατός εἰμι (12.10b). At first sight this looks to be an example of 'paradoxical identity'. Fitzgerald, although he does not include a full analysis of 2 Cor. 11.23-8 and 12.10 in his study,[2] cites this verse in a concluding remark on 2 Corinthians 4:

> It is in 2 Corinthians 4... that Paul points to the appearance of divine power in his human frailty. As a consequence, the catalogue of his hardships serves both to show the power of God at work in him and to demonstrate at the same time his own weakness.[3]

The word 'identity' must be rejected as confusing and misleading. When Paul talks about power and weakness he is never talking about the same thing. 'Paradox', however, there undoubtedly is. Fitzgerald[4] with reference to 2 Cor. 4.7, refers to the paradox of putting 'valuable treasure in a cheap fragile container'.

Perhaps the most revealing text, however, for enabling us to determine the relationship between weakness and power in Paul's thought is

1. On this see especially J.T. Fitzgerald, *Cracks in an Earthen Vessel: An Examination of the Catalogues of Hardships in the Corinthian Correspondence* (Atlanta: Scholars Press, 1988). See also section 5 below.
2. Fitzgerald, *Earthen Vessels*, p. 3 n. 7.
3. Fitzgerald, *Earthen Vessels*, p. 206.
4. Fitzgerald, *Earthen Vessels*, pp. 167-68.

2 Cor. 13.4. In this concluding section to his letter (probably chs. 10–13, rather than 1–13), Paul announces the imminence of his third visit to Corinth, and of the disciplinary action which he will take when he arrives (vv. 1-2), since in his view the Corinthians are seeking proof (v. 3) that Christ really is speaking through Paul, that Christ ὃς εἰς ὑμᾶς οὐκ ἀσθενεῖ ἐν ὑμῖν. This is further supported, as often in Paul, by a γάρ clause expressing the reason why this is so: καὶ γὰρ ἡμεῖς ἀσθενοῦμεν ἐν αὐτῷ, ἀλλὰ ζήσομεν σὺν αὐτῷ ἐκ δυνάμεως θεοῦ εἰς ὑμᾶς (vv. 3b, 4).

The significant thing here is that different tenses are used in the references to weakness and power in vv. 3b and 4b. This is not so elsewhere in Paul's writings (Rom. 8.36-7; 2 Cor. 4.7-12; 6.4-10; 12.9-10). The difference lies in the fact that these last passages refer to the apostle who remains in this life (cf. 2 Cor. 13.4b), but 2 Cor. 13.4a refers to Christ who now lives wholly, one might say, in the new age.

To speak, then, of Christ crucified as the power of God can be misleading. Paul does not do so. Rather, the crucifixion was the locus or foil for the power of God, for 'the cross itself indicates the relation of Christ to the world'.[1] In fact, when we recall the references to δύναμις in Paul, it is significant that the vast majority refer to the impact of the gospel on those who became believers. Hence the close association of the power of God with resurrection (supremely the resurrection of Christ, but see also Rom. 4.17), and with the Holy Spirit.

But what of 1 Cor. 1.18-25, and particularly vv. 23-24, often regarded as the *locus classicus* of *Kreuzestheologie*? Certainly Paul has usually been understood as saying here that Christ *crucified* is the power of God. Yet this may take insufficient account of the flow of Paul's rhetoric, as well as of the context, which we explored earlier in this section. It will be best to quote vv. 23-24 in full:

> ἡμεῖς δὲ κηρύσσομεν Χριστὸν ἐσταυρωμένον, Ἰουδαίοις μὲν σκάνδαλον ἔθνεσιν δὲ μωρίαν, αὐτοῖς δὲ τοῖς κλητοῖς, Ἰουδαίοις τε καὶ Ἕλλησιν, Χριστὸν θεοῦ δύναμιν καὶ θεοῦ σοφίαν.

This is usually taken to mean that Christ crucified was proclaimed *as* the power and wisdom of God. But, in the light of the context and other Pauline references to power and weakness to which I have drawn attention, it may be better to take the final clause as meaning 'the Christ

1. A.T. Hanson, *The Paradox of the Cross in the Thought of Paul* (Sheffield: JSOT Press, 1987), p. 14, quoting F.J. Ortkemper.

crucified and *so proclaimed* is the power and wisdom of God'.

In Paul's writings, therefore, the categories of weakness and foolishness are applied to the crucifixion, to the preaching of the crucifixion and, thirdly, to the apostle's own manner of life. Christ was crucified ἐξ ἀσθενείας (2 Cor. 13.4); Paul's own preaching was ἐν ἀσθενείᾳ (1 Cor. 2.3; cf. 1.21), and he applies to himself (or to himself and his fellow-apostles)[1] *tout court* the epithets μωροί and ἀσθενεῖς. But the language of power is not applied in an identical way to these three things. The word of the cross is the power of God (1.18), for the cross cannot be proclaimed except in the power of the Holy Spirit, which is the power of resurrection. But Paul never describes his weakness as the power of God and, similarly, he does not apply to the cross itself the language of power.

The key to Paul's language here lies in his eschatology: 'What is power in the old age, in the new age is weakness. What is weakness in the old age, is strength in the new age.'[2] There is undoubtedly a 'through the looking-glass' factor in Paul's thought here. The cross perceived from the standpoint of unbelief is weakness and foolishness, but from the standpoint of faith it is the locus or sphere of divine power and wisdom. But to say that the cross *is* the power of God is misleading shorthand: it is rather like saying 'The cross is the resurrection'.

The next section attempts to discover how distinctive Paul's language about God is here, by exploring first the Old Testament background, and secondly, possible parallels in the wider Hellenistic world.

Summary

Paul's eschatology, reflected in this section in the contrast between 'this age' and the life and power of the new age, is the key to understanding the dialectic of power and weakness, wisdom and foolishness. What is weakness and foolishness in this age is power and wisdom in the new age, and *vice versa*. When careful attention is paid to the logic of Paul's argument here, including the many connecting words, it can be seen that for Paul *the word* of the cross and not the cross itself is the power and wisdom of God. Its power can be seen in (a) its saving effect, and (b) its 'shaming' of the wise (even though that is not yet apparent to them). A wider study of passages where this dialectic occurs confirms the view

1. Weiss, *Korintherbrief*, p. 108, thinks that Apollos is excluded here, but that is not clear from the context. Cf. Conzelmann, *1 Corinthians*, p. 88 n. 34.

2. Arrington, *Aeon Theology*, p. 150.

that it is a fundamental error to speak of the paradoxical identity of weakness and power in Paul.

5. *Old Testament and Pagan Parallels*

This section is concerned with three things: first, the Old Testament and Jewish background of this section of 1 Corinthians; secondly, in the light of this background the distinctiveness (or otherwise) of Paul's language about God in these verses; thirdly and more briefly, whether the wider Graeco-Roman world offers any parallels with Paul's God-language here. The first section of this chapter rejected the views that Jewish influences were a major factor in the Corinthian situation at this stage, and that, despite some similarities, 1.18–3.23 bears the structure of a haggadic homily. But Jewish influence on the content and language of these verses is very clear. Most obvious of all, Paul begins and ends with Old Testament quotations (1.19; 3.20-21), includes others (1.31; 2.16; and possibly 2.9), and, no less important, draws on Old Testament language and motifs as he develops his argument.

In the section 1.18-25, the book of Isaiah seems to have been the main Old Testament source. Isa. 29.14 is quoted in v. 19, with the substitution of Isaiah's κρύψω by ἀθετήσω, taken perhaps from Psalm 33 (LXX 32).10:[1]

> ἀπολῶ τὴν σοφίαν τῶν σοφῶν
> καὶ τὴν σύνεσιν τῶν συνετῶν ἀθετήσω.

The probability that Paul himself has introduced the word ἀθετήσω makes it particularly significant. Davis is probably correct in arguing that ἀθετήσω determines the meaning of ἀπολῶ, and not *vice versa*.[2] Thus, both verbs mean 'set aside' or 'do away with', and comprise the first of several examples in this passage of what might be called divine 'put down' language, drawn from the Old Testament.

The next verse contains a clear echo of a verse from Isaiah, although not a direct quotation.[3] The verb ἐμώρανεν is an important component of biblical God-language. It comes from the same passage in Isaiah,

1. The context in which ἀθετήσω is used here supports this view: 'The Lord frustrates the counsels of the nations; he brings to nought (ἀθετεῖ) also the reasonings of the peoples, and brings to nought (ἀθετεῖ) the counsels of princes'.

2. Davis, *Wisdom and Spirit*, p. 4.

3. The questions of v. 20 seem to be a conscious echo of Isa. 19.11-2 and 33.18.

where it is said that the counsel of the king's 'wise counsellors' will be turned into folly (μωρανθήσεται, cf. Isa. 44.25).[1] This verb, too, must be included in the category of Old Testament 'put down' language.

In the section 1.26-31, the possible Old Testament and later Jewish sources are more varied. Of the many which have been suggested, however, some are more probable than others. Thus the view of von Dobschütz[2] that all the elements of 1 Cor.1.26-29 are to be found in *2 Bar.* 70.3-5 is to be rejected. Apart from the fact that this writing comes from a period later than Paul (even if incorporating earlier traditions), the vision of the writer here includes a state of affairs in which 'the despised will rule over the honourable' (v. 3a), and 'the impious will exalt themselves over the brave' (v. 4b). Equally unconvincing are the attempts to link this section of 1 Corinthians with *Bar.* 3.9–4.4. This theory was first put forward by H.StJ. Thackeray, but the parallels between Baruch and Paul are slight.[3] Thirdly, the view of R.P.C. Hanson, who links 1 Corinthians 1 with Job 12.17-22[4] must be deemed unsuccessful. Hanson's contention that the book of Job should be seen as the Old Testament's 'consummation and furthest point of achievement', and therefore comparable with the epistle to the Romans in the New Testament has much to be said for it, but verbal echoes of Job 12.17-22, the passage which Hanson finds behind 1 Corinthians, are slight. Words in common are σύνεσιν and βάθεα (βάθη), but that is all. As for the common theme that God overthrows the mighty (Job 12.19), this is a widespread motif in the Old Testament (cf. for example 1 Sam. 2.4-8; Isa. 13.9).

In fact, two Old Testament books offer convincing parallels to Paul's thought and language here in 1 Cor. 1.26-31. The more obvious is Jer. 9.22-23, from which Paul quotes, although not exactly, in v. 31:

> Thus says the Lord: 'Do not let the wise boast in their wisdom, do not let the mighty boast in their might, do not let the wealthy boast in their

1. The verb μωραίνω occurs six times in the LXX, at least three times referring to the action of God.

2. Cited by Baumann, *Mitte und Norm*, pp. 139-46, where a full survey of the Old Testament and Jewish background to 1 Cor. 1.18-31 is given.

3. See the table in Baumann, p. 142. The most convincing is the occurrence in *Bar.* 3.27 of the phrase οὐ τούτους ἐξελέξατο ὁ θεός, but this expresses a motif which is widespread in the Old Testament.

4. R.P.C. Hanson, 'St. Paul's Quotations of the Book of Job', *Theology* 53 (1950), pp. 251-52.

> wealth; but let those who boast boast in this, that they understand and know me, that I am the Lord; I act with steadfast love, justice and righteousness in the earth; for in these things I delight', says the Lord.

These verses from Jeremiah have few parallels in their God-language with that used by Paul, but his clear echo of this passage (ὁ καυχώμενος ἐν κυρίῳ καυχάσθω), together with the similarity in content, makes these verses the most certain of Paul's Old Testament sources here.

A second very probable source is the book of Deuteronomy. Here the verbal parallels are less close, but there is a parallel between Paul's understanding of the Church and Israel's self-understanding as it is expressed, for example, in Deut. 7.7:

> It was not because you were more numerous than any other people that the Lord set his heart on you and chose you—for you were the fewest of all peoples (cf. 26.5-9).[1]

Both the Jeremiah and Deuteronomic backgrounds are significant here. Conzelmann, commenting on 1.27-9, writes of these verses as 'a very Pauline way of working out christologically the Jewish idea of the overthrow of the lofty and the exalting of the lowly by God'.[2] Baumann brings out even more strongly the implications for Paul's understanding of God in his use of motifs about Israel's election. Thus the calling and election of the Corinthians and their social make-up are clear evidence for Paul of 'who and how *God* is'.[3] Finally, with reference to Paul's use of Jeremiah in 9.22-23, we should note the observations of a recent study that (a) there is a 'theocentric message' at the heart of Jer. 9.22-23, and (b) they reflect wisdom teaching, with a messenger formula added.[4] This Old Testament citation, therefore, was doubly apt in the Corinthian context.

Before we turn to the Old Testament background of chs. 2 and 3, it may be worth observing that already we have evidence that Paul's use of the Old Testament is probably his own. When he quotes, he quotes from memory, and in so doing combines, condenses or adapts individual passages.[5]

1. Baumann, *Mitte und Norm*, p. 146, who also cites Ezek. 16.3-14.
2. Conzelmann, *1 Corinthians*, p. 50.
3. Baumann, *Mitte und Norm*, p. 146.
4. O'Day, 'Jeremiah 9.22-3 and 1 Corinthians 1.26-31', pp. 262-63.
5. Thus also J. Munck, *Paul and the Salvation of Mankind* (London: SCM

The Old Testament background to chs. 2 and 3 can be dealt with more briefly. There are no certain indications of Old Testament influence in 2.1-5. The next section, however, is more difficult to evaluate. It is possible that Paul is offering here a 'radical reevaluation of traditional Jewish wisdom theology',[1] but clear examples of Old Testament language about God are harder to come by. Neither of the verbs προορίζω (v. 7) and ἐραυνῶ (v. 10) occur in the LXX.[2] The expression τὸν κύριον τῆς δόξης (2.8) has caused a good deal of debate. Barrett[3] and others note the occurrence of the phrase in *1 Enoch* (e.g. 22.14), and several commentators take the view that Paul here is using the language of his opponents.[4] As I argued earlier, however, this whole passage (vv. 6-16) expresses the 'insider's' point of view, and the expression 'Lord of glory', admittedly a ἅπαξ λεγόμενον in the New Testament, is part of that perspective. (The use of δόξα here probably derives from its use in v. 7.)

The quotation in 2.9 cannot be certainly identified[5] although its language about God needs little comment, since ἑτοιμάζω is used frequently in the LXX of divine (as well as human) action. In the next verse ἀπεκάλυψεν is used rarely in the LXX (except in Ezekiel) of divine action, although it is used elsewhere by Paul in this way (Phil. 3.15). The expression τὰ βάθη τοῦ θεοῦ is more obscure. There are no Old Testament parallels; the nearest is Dan. 2.22 which speaks of God as one who ἀποκαλύπτει βαθέα καὶ ἀπόκρυφα.[6] Weiss[7] draws attention to Rev. 2.24, although there the expression is τὰ βαθέα τοῦ Σατανᾶ. The likeliest source of this expression is Jewish apocalyptic[8] or wisdom

Press, 1959), p. 146, against the view of L. Cerfaux, *Recueil Lucien Cerfaux* (Paris: Gembloux, 1954), in his essay 'Vestiges d'un florilège dans 1 Cor.1.18-3.23', pp. 319-32.

1. Thus Theissen, *Psychological Aspects*, pp. 358-67.
2. Hatch and Redpath, *Concordance*, give no references for either verb.
3. Barrett, *1 Corinthians*, p. 72.
4. Thus Pearson, *Pneumatikos*, pp. 32-34 (cf. Davis, *Wisdom and Spirit*, p. 87) and Lührmann, *Offenbarungsverständnis*, p. 136, who finds it significant that Paul uses κύριος in a polemical passage about the cross, comparing Gal. 6.14.
5. See p. 111 n. 4 above.
6. Thus W.F. Orr and J.A. Walther, *1 Corinthians* (New York: Doubleday, 1976), p. 57, and Senft, *Aux Corinthiens*, p. 52. The other parallels cited by Senft (Job 12.22 [cf. 11.8] and Eccl. 7.24) do not throw any light on Paul's language here.
7. Weiss, *Korintherbrief*, pp. 61-62.
8. Thus also Baumann, *Mitte und Norm*, p. 234-35, citing Wilckens.

traditions, although it is very likely that Paul in vv. 9-15 is using God-language which would resonate for Jew and Greek alike.[1]

The only identifiable Old Testament quotation in this section occurs in the concluding verse, where Paul writes: τίς γὰρ ἔγνω νοῦν κυρίου, ὃς συμβιβάσει αὐτόν; ἡμεῖς δὲ νοῦν Χριστοῦ ἔχομεν (v. 16).[2] Paul used the same verse from Isaiah (40.13) in his doxology in Romans 11 (v. 34). There the question implied the answer 'No—no one can know the mind of the Lord'. Here Paul uses it differently, implying from his use of the phrase νοῦν Χριστοῦ that there is a close analogy (or equation?) between the mind of Yahweh and the mind of Christ, but also stating that the τελείοι (v. 6) have that mind.

There are three factors which are vital for understanding v. 16 and indeed the whole of vv. 6-16 correctly. First, 'we' have what we have because it has been given (2.12; cf. 4.7). Secondly, 'Christ' has been defined as Christ crucified (1.23), a definition which is programmatic for the whole argument.[3] Thirdly, and most important for this study, the 'subordinationism' which is discernible in this passage[4] must be set alongside the use of Old Testament texts such as Isa. 40.13 here, and Jer. 9.24 (cf. 2 Cor. 10.16), which appear to be equating Christ with 'the Lord' of the Old Testament. This question will be addressed more fully in Chapter Five, but the evidence so far reviewed suggests that equality and subordination belong together in Paul's thought (as they do in the Fourth Gospel). For this reason Van Roon is not wholly correct in his assertion that Paul 'considers Christ completely equal to God' even though it is true that 'God's thinking and acting are wholly manifested through Christ'.[5]

In ch. 3 there are two Old Testament quotations (vv. 19b, 20). The first appears to be an abstract of Job 5.12-13: ὁ δρασσόμενος τοὺς σοφοὺς ἐν τῇ πανουργίᾳ αὐτῶν. The use of δρασσόμενος here is remarkable, particularly as it does not occur at this point in any known

1. On the latter, see W.L. Knox, *St Paul and the Church of the Gentiles* (Cambridge: Cambridge University Press, 1939), pp. 116-18.

2. Cf. W.L. Willis, 'The Mind of Christ in 1 Corinthians 2.16', *Bib* 70.1 (1989), p. 117, describing this passage (vv. 6-16) as 'a paraenesis in church conduct'.

3. Although, as Conzelmann says (*1 Corinthians*, p. 69), 'It is still an open question how the being of the person with the mind of Christ takes concrete shape'.

4. Section 3 above.

5. A. Van Roon, 'The Relation between Christ and the Wisdom of God according to Paul', *NovT* 16 (1974), p. 238.

versions of the LXX, and particularly as the word which *does* occur in Job (καταλαμβάνω) is, as Conzelmann points out,[1] a Pauline word. δράσσομαι, in fact, is a ἅπαξ λεγόμενον in the New Testament, and is used in the LXX mainly of grasping in the hand, although at Ps. 2.12 it is used of grasping—i.e. accepting—correction from the Lord. In secular Greek it is similarly used, although occasionally it is used metaphorically of grasping hope etc. Whether Paul read this word in a version of the LXX known to him or introduced it into the text of Job himself, we do not know. But it is another remarkable example of 'aggressive' language which Paul is prepared to predicate of God. 'The reference from Job suggests that human craftiness is some kind of handhold by which God catches the wise.'[2] The second of Paul's quotations here, from Ps. 94 (LXX 93).11, draws on the familar Old Testament theme of God knowing the human heart (cf. 1 Thess. 2.4b): κύριος γινώσκει τοὺς διαλογισμοὺς τῶν σοφῶν ὅτι εἰσὶν ματαίοι.[3]

It is clear from this survey that Paul has drawn widely from both the Old Testament and Jewish traditions outside the Old Testament. There were many Jewish precedents for the kind of language which he uses here about God. In particular, the 'put down' language with which he begins and ends this section (1.19 and 3.19b and 20; cf. 1.27-28) had many precedents in both the prophetic and the wisdom traditions. There were also important precedents in Israel's self-understanding in the Old Testament for the kind of language which Paul uses of God's choice of the Corinthians in 1.26-31. Thirdly, as the study of Romans 9–11 in Chapter 1 showed, Paul's language about God, although partly drawn from the LXX, is by no means confined to the LXX.

But what of parallels for the verse which contains perhaps the most remarkable God-language in this section of 1 Corinthians? In 1.25 Paul writes of τὸ μωρὸν τοῦ θεοῦ and τὸ ἀσθενὲς τοῦ θεοῦ. Are there any parallels in Jewish or pagan literature for these phrases?

Robertson and Plummer, commenting on the phrase τὸ μωρὸν τοῦ θεοῦ, write of the phrase as having a 'somewhat rhetorical sense—not to be pressed'.[4] The same may be said of τὸ ἀσθενὲς τοῦ θεοῦ. But

1. Conzelmann, *1 Corinthians*, p. 80 n.13.
2. Orr and Walther, *1 Corinthians*, p. 175 (these commentators suggest that Paul may have translated freely from the Hebrew here, or else knew another translation, p. 170).
3. Paul replaces the Psalmist's ἀνθρώπων by σοφῶν.
4. Robertson and Plummer, *Critical Commentary*, p. 23.

even when due allowance has been made for Paul's rhetoric, it is difficult to find parallels with his language here either in the Old Testament or in subsequent Jewish writings. Reference is sometimes made to Philo's *Life Of Moses* (1.67-69).[1] This passage forms part of Philo's commentary on Exod. 3.1–4.17. Here Philo is commenting on the burning bush as a bramble, 'a very weakly plant, yet it is prickly and will wound if one do but touch it'.[2] Philo concludes from this that the burning bush is a kind of a parable of the suffering nation, proclaiming in effect to the nation 'your weakness is your strength (τὸ ἀσθενὲς ὑμῶν δύναμίς ἐστιν), which can prick and thousands will suffer from its wounds'.[3] Here, however, the phrase 'your weakness is your strength' is used of Israel not God, and it is used in a very different way from that in which Paul uses it. Paul does not write of 'the foolish thing of God' *harming* others, and it would seem that in Philo an ethnocentric perspective has given a very different meaning to a phrase which at first sight looks like a parallel with Paul's rhetoric in 1 Corinthians.

In Jewish intertestamental and pseudepigraphical writings the concept of divine 'weakness' or 'foolishness' seems to be totally absent. The very opposite concept occurs in the *Psalms of Solomon* (17.37), where the Psalmist says of the messiah: 'he will not weaken (ἀσθενήσει) in his days (relying) on his God'.[4] An interesting contrast with the *Psalms of Solomon* is to be found in the *Odes of Solomon*, which are probably to be regarded as Christian, although very Jewish in style and language.[5] Ode 7, in particular, has some affinity with Pauline thought:

> For there is a Helper for me, the Lord.
> He has generously shown himself to me in his simplicity,
> because his kindness has diminished his grandeur.
> He became like me, that I might receive him.
> In form he was considered like me, that I might put him on.

1. Cited, e.g., by A.C. Wire, 'Pauline Theology as an Understanding of God: the Explicit and the Implicit' (unpublished PhD dissertation, Claremont, 1974), p. 55.

2. *Vit. Mos.* 1.68.

3. *Vit. Mos.* 1.69.

4. Quoted by Stählin, *TWNT*, I, p. 492. Stählin, however, gives the reference as *Ps. Sol.* 17.42. Here we quote the translation of R.B. Wright in Charlesworth, *OT Pseudepigrapha*, II, p. 668.

5. Charlesworth, *OT Pseudepigrapha*, II, pp. 726-28.

Here the Odist approximates to the kind of 'interchange'[1] language used by Paul in verses such as 2 Cor. 5.21 and 8.9. But, as I have indicated, most scholars would now regard the *Odes of Solomon* as Christian, rather than Jewish.

G.F. Moore has some interesting things to say about rabbinic teaching on the humility of God.[2] He claims that the idea and word come from Ps. 18.36 (v. 35 in the NRSV and the REB), which Moore translates as 'Thy humility has made me great'. There are a number of problems about this verse, however, not least the very different LXX (Ps. 17.35) version: 'thy correction has upheld me to the end; yea, thy correction itself shall instruct me'. The uncertainty of Moore's interpretation is compounded by the Hebrew version. A.A. Anderson[3] calls the Hebrew ענוה 'problematic', preferring to derive it from ענה meaning 'to answer', and thus translating here 'Your answer has made me great'.[4]

But in spite of this uncertainty about Ps. 18.35 (or 36), Moore amply illustrates the dictum of R. Johanan: 'Wherever in the Scripture you find the almighty power of God, you will find in the context his lowly deeds'[5] (and 'lowly deeds' includes Yahweh's care for the poor etc.). Moore concludes that in Jewish thought about God 'His almighty power and humility go together'. Attractive though this idea is, however, and firmly rooted as it is in the Old Testament, with its emphasis on Yahweh's concern for the poor and needy, it does not provide a parallel with 1 Cor. 1.25, with its language of *weakness* and *foolishness*.

In evaluating Jewish parallels to Paul's language here, it is impossible to avoid speaking of both continuity and discontinuity with Judaism. Continuity can be seen in the use of language and motifs familiar from the Old Testament and/or later Jewish writings. The earlier part of this section has amply demonstrated this. But at the same time there is a new note, implied indeed by Paul himself in 1.22 (Ἰουδαίοις μὲν σκάνδαλον). The discontinuity lies in the fact that a *cross* becomes the centre of the kerygma, and the fact that it is *the messiah* who suffered

1. Morna Hooker's word, as expounded in several articles.

2. G.F. Moore, *Judaism in the First Centuries of the Christian Era: The Age of the Tannaim* (3 vols.; Cambridge, MA: Harvard University Press, 1927–30), I, p. 440.

3. A.A. Anderson, *Psalms* (2 vols.; London: Marshall, Morgan & Scott, 1972), I, p. 163.

4. Ps. 18 also appears, almost in its entirety, in 2 Sam. 22.

5. Moore, *Judaism*, I, p. 440.

on the cross.This radical discontinuity emerges in language about God in 1.25: τὸ μωρὸν τοῦ θεοῦ...καὶ τὸ ἀσθενὲς τοῦ θεοῦ. Whether Paul would have spoken about the 'humility' of God we cannot say; the full force of his 'foolishness' and 'weakness' language derives from the context, and from the Corinthian situation which he is addressing.

When we turn to Graeco-Roman literature, it is difficult to find God-language which can be considered similar to or parallel with Paul's language here. Once again, Paul's own statement ἔθνεσιν δὲ μωρίαν (1.23) suggests that we should not expect to find any.

The nearest parallels to the kind of language we are studying here are probably to be found in the teaching of Stoics such as Seneca and Epictetus about the trials or hardships of the wise man. Fitzgerald, in his discussion of 1 Cor. 4.9-13,[1] notes parallels in Epictetus (*Diss.* 3.24, 113-4 and 22.59), where Epictetus expresses the view that 'it is through poverty, death and hardship that God exhibits the sage's virtue in a more brilliant way than he could otherwise, so that the sage becomes a spectacle'.

In his discussion of 2 Cor. 4.7-12, Fitzgerald goes somewhat further when he says 'The idea that divine power or the divine source of something becomes conspicuous when it is revealed through a weak and lowly instrument is...quite Greek'. There is clearly a basis for this in the examples he cites. In addition to Epictetus and Seneca here, Fitzgerald quotes the second-century rhetorician Aelius Aristides, whose catalogue of illnesses (*Oration* 24) makes more evident 'the healing power of the god' (i.e. Asclepius), and a reference in Plato (*Ion* 534 D-E) to a god singing 'the finest of songs through the meanest of poets', so that the poet could be 'a sign to us that...these fine poems are not human or the work of man, but divine and the work of gods'.[2] Nevertheless, we should note Fitzgerald's conclusion that, despite some clear affinities between Paul's 'catalogues of hardships' and some Graeco-Roman thought, Paul has 'a quite different understanding of God from that found in the various Hellenistic philosophers'.[3] The principal reason for this difference lies in the two sets of parallels: first, between *both* Paul's language about himself as an apostle and about Christ *and* his language about Christ and about God. Thus, although Fitzgerald's examples from Plato find a parallel in 2 Cor. 4.7: ἔχομεν δὲ τὸν θησαυρὸν τοῦτον ἐν

1. Fitzgerald, *Earthen Vessels*, p. 147; cf. p. 171.
2. Fitzgerald, *Earthen Vessels*, pp. 171-72.
3. Fitzgerald, *Earthen Vessels*, p. 205.

ὀστρακίνοις σκεύεσιν, ἵνα ἡ ὑπερβολὴ τῆς δυνάμεως ᾖ τοῦ θεοῦ καὶ μὴ ἐξ ἡμῶν, it is Paul's God-language and Christ-language *together* in these contexts which comprise the main difference between Paul and Hellenistic writers. In this respect it is significant that Paul's writings provide both parallels and differences from the example Fitzgerald quotes from Aelius Aristides: in particular, 2 Corinthians 12.7b-10 (Paul's *apologia* for his thorn in the flesh) is significant precisely because he was *not* healed, unlike Aelius, and his weakness was thus a channel for divine power.[1]

Appendix 3 is devoted to a more general consideration of Graeco-Roman ideas and language about God and the gods. But Paul's startling language about God in 1 Cor. 1.25 appears to have no clear parallels in Graeco-Roman literature. It may reasonably be assumed that Paul was not exaggerating when he asserted that the proclamation of the foolishness and weakness of God was 'foolishness to Gentiles'.

Summary

Paul's indebtedness to the Old Testament in this section of 1 Corinthians is clear. In particular, he has drawn on prophetic and wisdom traditions in developing the theme that through the Gospel of the cross and resurrection of Christ God 'puts down' or shames the wise and powerful. Similarly, Paul has drawn on Deuteronomic traditions in expounding the significance of the Corinthians' own calling.

In so doing, Paul makes use of Old Testament motifs and language about God which were familiar to anyone conversant with the LXX. Hs language, however, is not confined to LXX language. Most significant of all, the contrasts of weakness and power, and of foolishness and wisdom deriving from the cross and resurrection has resulted in the minting of new language about God. The expressions τὸ μωρὸν τοῦ θεοῦ and τὸ ἀσθενὲς τοῦ θεοῦ owe something to Pauline rhetoric, but it is powerful rhetoric and the language used about God appears to have no parallel in either Jewish or pagan literature. Once again a pattern of continuity and discontinuity can be seen, but the apparent uniqueness of Paul's language about God in 1.25, closely linked as it is with the σκάνδαλον of a *kerygma* about a cross, suggests that we have not only new language about God, but also a new understanding of God.

1. A. Thacker, 'Paul's Thorn in the Flesh', *EpwRev* (January 1991), pp. 67-69, convincingly shows that the interpretation of 'the thorn' as a reference to persecution cannot be sustained.

6. *Conclusions*

Sections 1 and 2 of this chapter offered reasons for rejecting the views that Paul was addressing a specifically Jewish problem, and that his discourse in this section of 1 Corinthians took the form of a midrashic homily. But it is clear that he has drawn on a number of Jewish traditions. In the light of this survey of his use of the Old Testament, it would seem that the theme of each sub-section of his argument helped to determine which tradition he chose and reworked. Thus he drew on Wisdom and prophetic traditions (particularly the Old Testament's 'put-down' language) in his struggle with misguided valuations of wisdom at Corinth; he used the election traditions of Israel (particularly as expressed in Deuteronomy) in order to highlight the significance of the Corinthians' own call; it is possible (although this is less clear) that he drew on prophetic traditions in his own self-portrait in 1 Cor. 2.1-5, and it seems probable that Old Testament traditions about God's secret revelation to his people influenced the section 2.6-16. Thus there is much to be said for Wire's contention that 'how Paul speaks throughout a text is taken as the key to why Paul speaks'.[1]

Underlying all these themes, however, is the fundamental conviction that with Christ the age to come has dawned. (It is a weakness of Wire's argument that she takes insufficient account of Paul's eschatology.) The corollary of this conviction is, to quote Arrington once more, 'What is power in the old age in the new age is weakness. What is weakness in the old age is strength in the new age.' The basis and focal point for this conviction is the cross of Christ. Paul's use of σταυρός and σταυρόω is particularly noteworthy here (1.21, 23; 2.2, 8), and since the cross is the basis for Paul's double contrast of power with weakness and wisdom with foolishness, it follows that the cross is the key to Paul's language about God in this section.

This is important, for although the *amount* of God-language which Paul uses here is significant (section 3 above), most of the vocabulary itself is not new. The expressions 'the wisdom of God' and 'the power of God' were firmly rooted in the Old Testament. Similarly, this chapter has shown that the 'put down' verbs have strong Old Testament precedents. The only possible exceptions are the phrases of 1.25: τὸ μωρὸν τοῦ θεοῦ and τὸ ἀσθενὲς τοῦ θεοῦ. In section 4 it was argued that

1. Wire, 'Pauline Theology', p. 10.

there are no clear parallels in either Jewish or pagan writings for either of these.

But what is Paul actually saying about God? Two features of this section of 1 Corinthians have to be brought together, for it seems they belong together in Paul's thought: Paul's use of the word σταυρός as 'une parole de rupture' (Senft), and the function of the word θεός as a 'critical word' (Conzelmann).

First, Paul's use of σταυρός (and σταυρόω) in this context indicates that the cross radicalizes the Jewish traditions which Paul draws upon here. The cross was the catalyst and paradigm for the creation of a new community of rank outsiders (1.26-31). But this is not simply a new Exodus, God repeating what he had done before (despite the echoes of Deuteronomy here, and the use of the Exodus motif in, e.g., 1 Cor. 5.7). Although the application of the election traditions of Israel to the Corinthians *does* mean that Judaism has been universalized (as the description of *Gentiles* as 'the temple of God' [3.16] suggests), Paul's language implies more. The σκάνδαλον of the cross to Jews did not consist in the first place in the fact that it was the means by which Gentiles entered into Israel's heritage. It lay in the fact that it was *God's* messiah who hung there.

The σκάνδαλον was re-enacted in the person of the apostle himself. Although Paul nowhere describes himself as an εἰκὼν τοῦ θεοῦ, it is the clear implication of his self-descriptions, and, of course, of his references to 'imitating' Christ (1 Cor. 11.1; cf. 1 Thess. 1.6) when they are placed alongside his designation of Christ as the εἰκὼν τοῦ θεοῦ (2 Cor. 4.4). This suggests that the language of weakness and foolishness (and poverty, 2 Cor. 6.10; 8.9) is an important key to Paul's understanding of God.

It is here that Paul's eschatological perspective is vital. This is more important than what seems to me Wire's somewhat artifical distinction between Paul's implicit and explicit language about God. What must not be done, however, is to import quasi-docetic notions at this point. It would be alien to Paul's thought to conclude that the weakness and foolishness of the apostle (and of Christ) were not real, but were merely a 'cover' for power and wisdom. It would also be a mistake to import a futurist eschatology which divorced this weakness and power: in effect, weakness now, but in the end power. This would be to ignore the present tenses of Paul's writings: power and wisdom are being revealed precisely in the weakness and foolishness. The theological consequence of this recognition that for Paul divine weakness and power *belong together* has been well-expressed by D.M. Mackinnon: writing of God's self-limitation with particular reference to God's self-limitation in Christ, he says 'the kenosis whose depths we have not begun to plumb, is not strange or alien to His being, but the declaration of its substance and the disclosure of the inwardness and manner of His power'.[1] It is important to note, in the light of the earlier discussion of 1 Cor. 1.18-25, that Mackinnon does not say the kenosis *is* the power, but rather 'the disclosure' of its 'inwardness and manner'.

The power/weakness dialectic, therefore, is fundamental to the way in which God is both perceived and experienced *post eventum Christi*. Bonhoeffer's words 'God allows himself to be edged out of the world and on to a cross'[2] expresses an important part of this perception and experience. The cross, then, is the key to understanding both divine weakness and divine power. It is probable that the Corinthians, or at least some of them, had tended to distance Christ from the cross, or, to put it another way, to marginalize the cross, both in their perception and praxis of the faith. But the critical function of the word σταυρός here must also be put alongside the critical function of the word θεός.

In section 3 of this chapter it was suggested that the 'clusters' of θεός in this section of 1 Corinthians may have been due to the existence of a 'Christ party' which, in effect, made Christ an idol, thereby excluding God. From what we know of contemporary religion, this would not have been a very surprising development. The 'qualitative difference' between God and humans which was part of Hebrew religion was not part of Greek theism, and therefore it would not be surprising if the κύριος Ἰησοῦς filled the whole horizon to the exclusion of 'God'. Paul, therefore, uses θεός here to correct a defective Christology.

The critical function of θεός here, however, is wider than this. Just as in Romans 9–11, 'God' undermines national, religious and moral pretensions, so here the same God undermines cultural and intellectual pretensions. In both situations the use of God-language reflects the conviction of Paul that God himself stands over against human pretensions and arrogance, particularly as these manifest themselves in social exclusivism and divisions. But in 1 Corinthians this critical use of θεός finds its root in the fact that the word σταυρός, symbol of the very margin of

1. Mackinnon, *Themes*, p. 235.

2. D. Bonhoeffer, *Letters and Papers from Prison* (London: Fontana, 1963), p. 122.

human life, has become the indispensable context for what Paul has to say about God.

Paul uses very little 'revelation' language here, or indeed elsewhere. He speaks much more of what God has done in and through Christ.[1] Nevertheless, the language which Paul *does* use here raises the question of whether in passages such as this we have the root of a new understanding of God. This clearly brings us to the heart of the question of the continuity and discontinuity between Old Testament and New Testament, between Judaism and Christianity. It was the unanimous conviction of the New Testament that the God of Jesus, the God worshipped by Christians was the God of Israel. The testimony of the Old Testament, and of Judaism, completely preclude facile contrasts between an Old Testament God of wrath and a New Testament God of love (2 Cor. 4.6 is one among many verses which could be cited). Indeed, as we have seen, the Old Testament shows clearly that God's choice of the weak and lowly did not begin with Gentile Christians. So there is undoubtedly continuity in the Jewish and Christian understanding of God.

On the other hand, the new faith to which Paul's letters give expression was not simply an enlarged or universalized Judaism. The universalized dimension of Paul's understanding of God is extremely important, but it is not all that is new in his understanding of God. The power/weakness dialectic of the Corinthian correspondence is crucial here. It is true that the Old Testament testifies to what Moltmann has called the pathos of God, (notably in Hosea), to the suffering servant of Yahweh (Deutero-Isaiah), and to God's choice of the lowly (e.g. 1 Sam. 2.1-10). Later Judaism also knows the concept of God's humility, (section 5). All of these themes may be regarded as hints and prefigurations of τὸ μωρὸν τοῦ θεοῦ and τὸ ἀσθενὲς τοῦ θεοῦ. But these phrases themselves, whether applied to Christ himself, or, as I have argued, to the Christian proclamation, are something strikingly new in God-language.

At this stage, the relationship between God and Christ is inchoate in many respects. But the foundations are here for a new understanding of God. The eschatology of Paul, based as it is on the Jewish concept of the two ages, offers a bifocal view of reality. What can be seen is not all that there is. Those who are powerful are more vulnerable than they appear. Most important of all, the God who seems to be nowhere is in fact the

1. On this dimension of Paul's language and thought see Chapter 5 below.

ultimate reality which is the great subverter of the status quo. As Chapter 1 showed, language reflecting God the enemy comprises an extremely important strand of Paul's language. In Romans 9–11 we find the concept of the divine 'hardening'; here God 'foolished', 'set at nothing' etc. In both passages this language is the necessary foil for the gospel itself. Yet this is by no means obvious to all. The reason why Paul in 1 Cor. 2.6-16 seems to be more Gnostic than anywhere else in his writings is because the theme of *discernment* is central to his argument. The language from start to finish is strongly experiential: not everyone can see the truth of what Paul is talking about, but τοῖς σωζομένοις ἡμῖν (1.18), the word of the cross is the power of God.

Chapter 3

GOD-LANGUAGE AS POLEMIC: 2 CORINTHIANS 2.14–4.6

This chapter examines the God-language of 2 Cor. 2.14–4.6, looking first at the background, context and argument of these verses, before proceeding to an analysis of the language about God which they contain. I shall argue that an important part of this God-language is Paul's use of the word πνεῦμα. In a third section I explore the context and function of πνεῦμα-language in Paul's writings, before drawing some conclusions.

1. *Background, Context and Argument*

Since there are widely varying views among scholars about the integrity of 2 Corinthians, it will be necessary to set out briefly the view taken here about the relationship of 2.14–4.6 to the canonical 2 Corinthians. First, it will be assumed that 2.14 does not mark the beginning of an interpolation which interrupts the allegedly smooth transition[1] from 2.13 to 7.5. The transition is not, in fact, a smooth one: the phrases in 2.13 and 7.5 (οὐκ ἔσχηκα ἄνεσιν τῷ πνεύματί μου, 2.13, and οὐδεμίαν ἔσχηκεν ἄνεσιν ἡ σὰρξ ἡμῶν, 7.5) are too alike to have been as close to one another as they would have been if the interpolation theory is correct.[2] In any case, 2.12-13 belong closely with the preceding section in which Paul has been explaining to the Corinthians the reasons for the changes in his travel plans.[3] This connection provides a clue, not only to the nature of 2.14–4.6, but to the whole of the section of

1. R. Bultmann, *Der zweite Brief an die Körinther* (Göttingen: Vandenhoeck & Ruprecht, 1976), p. 55 notes that 2.13 and 7.5 are 'perfectly consonant', but that is part of the problem.

2. A second difficulty for supporters of the interpolation theory lies in the switch from the first person singular in 2.13 to the first person plural in 7.5.

3. Thus Furnish, *II Corinthians*, p. 172.

2 Corinthians in which it is set. Fitzgerald[1] calls 2 Corinthians 1–7 a letter of self-commendation, and that is the view taken here.[2] In this letter 2.14 marks the beginning of a new section extending as far as 6.10, its principal theme being the office of an apostle.[3]

One would expect a letter of self-commendation to be apologetic in tone. The circumstances in which it was written, however, resulted in a piece of writing which was polemical as well as apologetic. But in order to substantiate this point it will be necessary to look briefly at another aspect of the debate about the integrity of 2 Corinthians. This is the question of whether chs. 1–9 and 10–13 were originally separate letters, and therefore the relevance of chs. 10–13 to the background of chs. 1–9.

Despite the argument of Ford and Young that the rhetorical norms of the time account for 'the changes in emotional tone within the epistle',[4] the discrepancies between chs. 1–9 and 10–13 seem too great for them to have belonged originally to the same letter. Quite apart from the 'changes in emotional tone' (for example, the difference between the confidence expressed in 7.16 and the extreme anxiety of 11.2-3), there are two weighty arguments for regarding chs. 10–13 as part of a separate and later letter. First, this view makes better sense of the comings and goings of Titus, since the references to Titus's journeys are hard to explain on the theory of only one letter.[5] Secondly, the suspicion which the collection seems to have generated at Corinth is referred to at 12.14-18, but not in the earlier chs. 8 and 9 (whether these chapters were

1. Fitzgerald, *Earthen Vessels*, p. 150.

2. I incline to the view that chs. 8 and 9 were probably part of the same letter, but this is hardly relevant for this study.

3. Thus, e.g., Bultmann, *Zweite Brief*, *ad loc.*

4. Ford and Young, *Meaning and Truth*, pp. 36-40.

5. The crucial verses are 7.13-14, 8.18 and 12.18. The last two seem to refer to the same visit of Titus and his unnamed companion, yet the contexts require different interpretations of the aorists συνεπέμψαμεν (8.18) and παρεκάλεσα... καὶ συναπέστειλα (12.18). συνεπέμψαμεν is an epistolary aorist, as the following verses (particularly vv. 22 and 24) show, whereas the συναπέστειλα of 12.18 must be a genuine aorist, in view of the suspicion which Titus's visit is now said to have generated, a suspicion to which this and the preceding verse refer. Yet 7.13-4 refer to what was clearly Titus's first visit to Corinth. In sum, chs. 1–9 look back on Titus's first visit, and were delivered by him to Corinth on his second visit; chs. 10–13 look back on the second visit. (The details of this argument are given in Furnish, *II Corinthians*, p. 38.)

originally separate letters or not) in which Paul sets out arguments why the Corinthians should support the collection.[1]

This, however, does not mean that the later chapters cannot be used to throw light on the earlier ones. They were written, after all, to the same church, and probably only a short time after the earlier letter. It is clear from 11.22 that Paul's rivals (that, at least, seems to be how Paul perceived them) were Jewish Christian missionaries who were undermining the allegiance of the Corinthian church to Paul and to the Pauline gospel (11.1-4). Thus, while there is a danger that we identify Paul's opponents, if such there were, in 2.14–4.6, and then seek to find evidence for them,[2] it seems reasonable to argue that the painful conflicts evidenced by chs. 10–13 were already brewing when the earlier chapters were written.

The language in 2.14–4.6 seems to support this view. First, some of the language used by Paul has a strongly Jewish background. T.W. Manson, in a study of 2.14 and 2.16,[3] has drawn attention to the strikingly similar statements about the Torah in rabbinical writings, where the Torah is described as giving off a good 'smell' for some, but a deadly 'smell' for others.[4]

1. Furnish, *II Corinthians*, p. 38, who also shows clearly why chs. 10–13 cannot be regarded as having been the 'tearful' letter referred to by Paul in 2.3-4: in particular there is no reference at all in chs. 10–13 to the offender referred to in 2.3-11 and 7.8-12, verses which indicate that he *was* mentioned in the tearful letter.

2. T.E. Provence, '"Who is Sufficient for These Things?" An Exegesis of 2 Corinthians 2.15–3.18', *NovT* 24.1 (1982), p. 55, rightly warns of the dangers of circular arguments but seems not to allow for the evidence of chs. 10–13. J.L. Sumney, *Identifying Paul's Opponents. The Question of Method in 2 Corinthians* (Sheffield: JSOT Press, 1990), p. 179, concludes that Paul's opponents were 'Pneumatics' (p. 179), downplaying their Jewishness (e.g. p. 184). Earlier in his study, however (pp. 77-86), Sumney makes some important points about historical reconstructions, rightly emphasizing the crucial importance of passages within what he calls the 'primary text'.

3. T.W. Manson, '2 Cor. 2.14-17: Suggestions towards an Exegesis', in J.N. Sevenster and W.G. van Unnik (eds.), *Studia Paulina* (Haarlem: Bohn, 1953), pp. 153-62.

4. Cf. Grayston, *Dying*, p. 53. It is less certain that the ὀσμή of v. 14 is Christ himself, as Manson argues, for although the Jewish parallels which he cites might support that interpretation, the context in 2 Corinthians does not. M. Carrez, *La deuxième épître de Saint Paul aux Corinthiens* (Geneva: Labor et Fides 1986), p. 78, notes that ὀσμὴ εὐωδίας is the more common LXX expression (46 times), whereas ὀσμή occurs a mere nine times on its own.

Another example of Paul's use of language with a strongly Jewish background occurs in the 'sufficiency' motif, which is introduced in 2.16b (καὶ πρὸς ταῦτα τίς ἱκανός;) and sets the agenda for the next stage of Paul's argument.[1] It seems probable, in the light of the comparison with Moses and the old covenant which follows in ch. 3, that Paul is consciously comparing himself with Moses who at Exod. 4.10 says, 'I am not sufficient' (ἱκανός), but who was made sufficient by the All-Sufficing (El Shaddai), interpreted as θεὸς ὁ ἱκανός.[2]

One further example of the Jewish background of Paul's language and arguments in this section of 2 Corinthians may be given here. D. Lührmann has drawn attention to the frequency of 'revelation' language in the polemical section of 2 Corinthians, and finds the explanation of their use by Paul in the tradition that the Torah leads to enlightenment.[3]

A second indicator that the conflicts reflected in 2 Corinthians 10–13 were already simmering lies in Paul's earlier references to the nature and authority of his apostleship. Such references occur at 1 Cor. 4.9-13, and in an earlier chapter of this letter. The section beginning at 1.12 paves the way for the argument which now follows from 2.14 onwards. Paul's alteration of his travel plans (1.15-17) had led to criticism of himself at Corinth, and perhaps misunderstanding.[4] There are, therefore, good grounds for saying, in the light of the context of 2.14–4.6 and the language contained in it, that this is a polemical passage directed against continuing criticisms of Paul, criticisms which have been further fuelled by new Jewish Christian influences at Corinth.

Finally, in this section it will be useful to give a summary of the argument of 2 Cor. 2.14–4.6, noting particularly further evidence that this is

1. Thus Provence, '"Who is Sufficient?"', p. 57.

2. Thus S.J. Hafemann, *Suffering and the Spirit* (Tübingen: Mohr, 1986), pp. 98-101, following A. Farrer's arguments in his essay in K.E. Kirk (ed.), *The Apostolic Ministry* (London: Hodder & Stoughton, 1946), pp. 115-82. This seems a more convincing explanation of Paul's language here than that of Georgi, *Opponents*, pp. 232-33, who argues that Paul's opponents were saying ἱκανοί ἐσμεν and who sees a connection with Joel 2.11: 'Who will be sufficient (ἱκανὸς) for it (sc. the day of the Lord)?'

3. Lührmann, *Offenbarungsverständnis*, p. 43.

4. We should not forget also the controversy generated by Paul's refusal of Corinthian offers of material support (1 Cor. 9) (see the earlier reference to P. Marshall's study of friendship conventions, Chapter 2, p. 107 n. 1).

a polemical passage, before offering a detailed examination of the God-language which it contains.

Paul begins with a description of his ministry (vv. 14-17) which, containing as it does clear echoes of Jewish Torah-language (Manson's argument), invites comparison with the old covenant. The question with which these verses end (καὶ πρὸς ταῦτα τίς ἱκανός;) may have been put not only because of its link with the Moses story of Exodus 4, but also because Paul's own ἱκανότης was being disputed at Corinth.[1] The polemical nature of the argument is made more evident in the next verse by Paul's contrast between himself and οἱ πολλοὶ καπηλεύοντες τὸν λόγον τοῦ θεοῦ[2] and by a reference in 3.1 to τινες, a word which normally refers in Paul's letters to Paul's opponents.[3]

Paul's response to his own questions (v. 1), whether he is beginning to commend himself again[4] or whether he needs 'commendatory letters',[5] is to describe the Corinthian Christians as 'our letter of recommendation' (v. 2). This is elaborated in the next verse by means of Old Testament allusions[6] which introduce the contrast now to be developed:

> ὅτι ἐστὲ ἐπιστολὴ Χριστοῦ διακονηθεῖσα ὑφ' ἡμῶν, ἐγγεγραμμένη οὐ μέλανι ἀλλὰ πνεύματι θεοῦ ζῶντος, οὐκ ἐν πλαξὶν λιθίναις ἀλλ' ἐν πλαξὶν καρδίαις σαρκίναις.

This reference to the fruits of Paul's ministry brings Paul back to the theme of the basis of his confidence (v. 4) and of his sufficiency for the task (vv. 5-6a). Verse 6, with its reference to ministers of the new

1. Thus Bultmann, *Zweite Brief*, p. 72. Carrez, *Deuxième épître*, pp. 75-76 finds vv. 14-17 an important summary, anticipating the *apologia* which follows.

2. Here καπηλεύω must mean 'water down' or 'adulterate', as most commentators conclude. Provence ('"Who is Sufficient?"', pp. 58-59) rightly notes the root meaning of the εἰλικρινείας which immediately follows, a point ignored by Hafemann who argues that καπηλεύω here means 'selling... i.e. as a retailer sells... in the market' (Hafemann, *Suffering*, p. 125).

3. Rom. 3.8; Gal. 1.7; Phil. 1.15.

4. R.P. Martin, *2 Corinthians* (WBC, 40; Waco, Texas: Word Books, 1986), p. 50, notes the problem raised by the πάλιν here, but concludes that it is difficult to be sure when was the previous occasion on which Paul 'commended' himself.

5. Furnish, *II Corinthians*, p. 193 notes the observation of Theissen that such letters are only advantageous to itinerant Christian preachers when there are established churches which can receive such letters.

6. Bultmann, *Zweite Brief*, p. 76 lists Exod. 31.18, Jer. 38(31).33 and Ezek. 11.19 and 36.26 as the passages on which this verse is based.

covenant, introduces the contrast which forms the substance of the next stage of the argument (vv. 7-11):

> ὃς (sc. θεὸς) καὶ ἱκάνωσεν ἡμᾶς διακόνους καινῆς διαθήκης, οὐ γράμματος ἀλλὰ πνεύματος· τὸ γὰρ γράμμα ἀποκτέννει, τὸ δὲ πνεῦμα ζῳοποιεῖ.

In vv. 7 to 11 the contrast between the old and new covenants is developed by means of three a fortiori arguments[1] which are part of a midrash based on Exod. 34.29-35, a midrash in fact which comprises the whole of vv. 7-18.[2] First, the old dispensation is described as ἡ διακονία τοῦ θανάτου, but, says Paul, if this had its origin in glory (ἐν δόξῃ), how much more will ἡ διακονία τοῦ πνεύματος be ἐν δόξῃ? The same argument is reinforced by the second comparison and contrast: if there was glory in the dispensation of condemnation, the dispensation of righteousness (ἡ διακονία τῆς δικαιοσύνης) must far exceed it in glory (v. 9). The comment of v. 10 with its introductory καὶ γάρ is, in effect, a gloss on what has been said, but is noteworthy for the oxymoron οὐ δεδόξασται τὸ δεδοξασμένον which epitomizes very well the tension Paul felt in wishing to affirm the validity of the old covenant *as the old covenant*, but at the same time to stress the surpassing (ὑπερβαλλούσης) glory of the new.[3] The third contrast (v. 11) is based on that which is 'fading' (τὸ καταργούμενον) and that which is permanent (τὸ μένον).

Verses 12 to 18 comprise the most obscure part of this section of 2 Corinthians, not least because of Paul's use of the Old Testament here.[4] The function of these verses is twofold. First, Paul moves from a comparison of the two 'dispensations' to a comparison of the ministers of the two dispensations—that is Moses (vv. 13-15) and the apostles (ἡμεῖς) (v. 18). Secondly, he moves from the past (v. 13) to the present,

1. Here, as in Rom. 5.9-10, Paul is using the rabbinical exegetical *middah* of 'the light and the heavy' (*qal-wāhômer*). Thus, e.g. Martin, *2 Corinthians*, p. 59.

2. Thus, for example, Barrett, *Corinthians*, pp. 113-14. The presence of a midrash here, however, is disputed, as Martin's discussion (pp. 58-59) shows.

3. W.D. Davies, 'Paul and the People of Israel', in *Jewish and Pauline Studies* (London: SPCK, 1984), pp. 123-52 concludes that Paul still had not resolved his attitude to his people, and that this confusion has invaded the text here.

4. We noted above the debate about whether these verses are part of a midrash based on Exod. 34.29-35. Whether they are or not, the difficulties here are partly due to the fact that v. 13b introduces an idea quite alien to the text of Exod. 34.29-35, while v. 16 alters the text of Exod. 34.34.

emphasizing the point by the double use of τὸ κάλυμμα (vv. 14, 15). Thus vv. 14 and 15 refer to the contemporary resistance of Israel to the gospel. Verse 16 with its rather free rendering of Exod. 34.34[1] describes the process of conversion. There follows a gloss on this scriptural interpretation (ὁ δὲ κύριος πνεῦμά ἐστιν..., v. 17), a famous *crux interpretum* which I discuss in the next section. Finally, in this part of Paul's argument v. 18 fuses two contrasts: the contrast between Moses and Christian ministers (highlighted in vv. 12 and 13) and the contrast between unbelieving Israel and all Christians.[2] Thus far, then, Paul's argument supplies further evidence of its polemical nature. This is clear from explicit references to others (2.17; 3.1) even though they cannot be certainly identified, and from the sharp contrasts drawn between on the one hand the old covenant, its minister Moses, and contemporary Israel, and on the other the new covenant, its ministers, and all Christian believers.[3] It remains to note the polemical character of the last part of the section we are studying (4.1-6).

There are several indications that these verses are closely linked with what has gone before: διὰ τοῦτο and τὴν διακονίαν ταύτην (v. 1), and the echo in v. 3 ('And even if our gospel is veiled [κεκαλυμμένον]) of the 'veil' theme used in 2.13-18, and deriving from Exodus 34. But if the link with the preceding verses is clear, the meaning of individual phrases in these verses is not so clear. Paul begins by asserting that he does not lose heart (v. 1). Why should he lose heart? Presumably the unbelief of Israel, to which he has just referred, might cause him to lose heart. Instead, however (ἀλλά, v. 2), Paul declares that

> ἀπειπάμεθα τὰ κρυπτὰ τῆς αἰσχύνης, μὴ περιπατοῦντες ἐν πανουργίᾳ μηδὲ δολοῦντες τὸν λόγον τοῦ θεοῦ ἀλλὰ τῇ φανερώσει τῆς ἀληθείας συνιστάνοντες ἑαυτοὺς πρὸς πᾶσαν συνείδησιν ἀνθρώπων ἐνώπιον τοῦ θεοῦ.

It is possible that the somewhat surprising phrase τὰ κρυπτὰ τῆς αἰσχύνης is a reference to circumcision.[4] It is difficult to see how Paul

1. Paul has ἡνίκα δὲ ἐὰν ἐπιστρέψῃ πρὸς κύριον, περιαιρεῖται τὸ κάλυμμα where the LXX has ἡνίκα δ' ἂν εἰσεπορεύετο Μωϋσῆς, ἔναντι κυρίου λαλεῖν αὐτῷ, περιῃρεῖτο τὸ κάλυμμα ἕως τοῦ ἐκπορεύεσθαι (Exod. 34.34a).

2. Although 𝔓46 omits πάντες here, the evidence for its authenticity is strong.

3. The ἡμεῖς of v. 18 could refer to apostles only, but the addition of πάντες probably means that all Christians are intended here (Furnish, *II Corinthians*, p. 213; Barrett, *Second Epistle*, p. 124).

4. This is not a widely accepted interpretation, although E.B. Allo, *Saint Paul:*

can be intending a contrast with the παρρησία to which he referred as far back as 3.12.[1] The contrast more probably lies in the second half of this verse: 'but by the open statement of the truth we would commend ourselves to the conscience of everyone in the sight of God'. Here the NRSV translation does not perhaps do full justice to the emphatic position[2] of πᾶσαν, which in this context probably refers to the universal character of Paul's mission. That is to say, having renounced 'circumcision', he now preaches the gospel to the Gentiles.[3]

But if this interpretation is on the right lines, what would be the point of Paul saying 'we refuse to practise cunning or to tamper (δολοῦντες) with God's word'? It could refer to Paul's opponents or be a more general reference to any who plied their religious wares in the market place. It is more likely a rebuttal of the kind of charge made against Paul because of his preaching a circumcision-free gospel to Gentiles. Galatians 1.10 strongly suggests that Paul was accused of 'trimming' his gospel: 'Am I now seeking the favour of men, or of God?... If I were still pleasing men, I should not be a servant of Christ.' One might wonder whether Paul's own manifesto in 1 Cor. 9.20-23 ('all things to all people') did not lay him open to the charge of 'trimming'. (Rom. 3.8, and perhaps 6.1, are further indications of contemporary misrepresentations of Paul's message—again almost certainly a misrepresentation or misunderstanding by Jewish Christians and/or Jews.)

In v. 4 Paul attributes the blindness to the gospel of unbelievers (τῶν ἀπίστων) to ὁ θεὸς τοῦ αἰῶνος τούτου.[4] The gospel is defined here as 'the gospel of the glory of Christ' (v. 4b). Verse 5 picks up the reference to Christ ('For what we preach is not ourselves, but Jesus Christ as Lord'). This verse in itself does not seem to be polemical, but we should note that it is connected with the following verse by ὅτι. Thus it is v. 6

Seconde épître aux Corinthiens (Paris: Gabalda, 2nd edn, 1956), p. 80, notes that it was the view of Theodoret.

1. The view of Bultmann, *Zweite Brief*, p. 103. Cf. Carrez, *Deuxième épître*, p. 106, who notes Philo *Leg. All.* 1.321.

2. Noted, e.g. by Barrett, *Second Epistle*, p. 129, and Furnish, *II Corinthians*, p. 129.

3. Phil. 3.19 (...καὶ ἡ δόξη ἐν τῇ αἰσχύνη αὐτῶν...) is probably a reference to circumcision, and if so provides further support within the Pauline corpus for the interpretation adopted here.

4. A unique expression in Paul. Thus Carrez, *Deuxième épître*, p. 107. As Carrez notes, Paul's choice of words (elsewhere 'Satan', 2.14, 11.14) derives in large part from those he is addressing, but also from the *purpose* of his assertions.

which provides the rationale, or justification, for what Paul does; significantly this is a verse which firmly identifies the God of the old covenant with the God of the new:

> ὅτι ὁ θεὸς ὁ εἰπών· ἐκ σκότους φῶς λάμψει, ὃς ἔλαμψεν ἐν ταῖς καρδίαις ἡμῶν πρὸς φωτισμὸν τῆς γνώσεως τῆς δόξης τοῦ θεοῦ ἐν προσώπῳ ('Ιησοῦ) Χριστοῦ.

Thus Paul concludes this section of his argument with a ringing declaration that the Christian apostle proclaims the very same God to whom the Jewish Scriptures refer: the God who was active in creation is now active in the gospel.[1]

Summary

It is clear from this survey of the background, context and argument of 2 Cor. 2.14–4.6 that these verses form part of a letter of self-commendation addressed to a church where Paul had already been experiencing challenges to his own authority and standing. This conflict, however, has now been exacerbated by Jewish-Christian influence which, whether intentional or not, is further undermining Paul's position at Corinth. This conflict compels Paul to spell out in a series of sharp contrasts the difference between Judaism and the new Christian faith and, inseparably connected with this, his own 'sufficiency' for his task as apostle to the Gentiles. The passage, therefore, is polemical as well as apologetic, and it will now be necessary to examine the nature and function of the language about God within it.

2. *The God- and* πνεῦμα*-Language of 2 Corinthians 2.14–4.6*

Most of the occurrences of θεός are concentrated in the first and last sections of this passage, that is to say, in 2.14-17 and 4.1-6. θεός occurs five times in the first section, and although this is not as heavy a concentration as in some sections of 1 Corinthians 1–3, four of the five occurrences are particularly noteworthy.

First, in the thanksgiving which introduces this section Paul inverts the usual order of the words, so that τῷ θεῷ is emphasized by virtue of its position:

> τῷ δὲ θεῷ χάρις τῷ πάντοτε θριαμβεύοντι ἡμᾶς ἐν τῷ Χριστῷ καὶ τὴν ὀσμὴν τῆς γνώσεως αὐτοῦ φανεροῦντι δι' ἡμῶν ἐν παντὶ τόπῳ (v. 14).

1. Grayston, *Dying*, p. 53 describes 2 Cor. 4.3-6 as a midrash on Gen. 1.

In all other examples of this kind of thanksgiving except one (1 Cor. 15.57) Paul writes χάρις first.[1] Collange writes: 'This detail is easily explicable on the basis of the polemical perspective we have just analysed'.[2] This detail, therefore, small as it is, is the first indication in this section that *God* (i.e. the one God) will be the principal stay of Paul's defence.[3]

The next verse picks up the metaphor of 'fragrance' (ὀσμήν) as Paul goes on: ὅτι Χριστοῦ εὐωδία ἐσμὲν τῷ θεῷ ἐν τοῖς σωζομένοις καὶ ἐν τοῖς ἀπολλυμένοις...(v. 15). There is no textual basis for regarding τῷ θεῷ as a later addition, as Bultmann wishes to do.[4] He objects on the grounds that τῷ θεῷ introduces a sacrifical image which conflicts with the image of the 'triumphal procession' (θριαμβεύοντι) of v. 14.[5] But this difficulty is removed when we note that vv. 15 and 16 envisage the direction of the 'sweet smell' as the world of human beings (ἐν τοῖς σωζομένοις κτλ.), not God.[6] τῷ θεῷ therefore, cannot be translated 'to' or 'for God' in the LXX sense of a sweet savour 'to the Lord', despite, admittedly, the occurrence of both ὀσμή and εὐωδία in a sacrifical context such as Lev. 6.15.[7]

It is worth noting that Paul's sentence does not actually require τῷ θεῷ, as it would make sense without it. Bultmann may be correct to

1. Rom. 6.17; 7.25; 2 Cor. 8.16; 9.15.

2. J.-.F. Collange, *Enigmes de la deuxième épître aux Corinthiens. Etude exégétique de 2 Cor. 2.14–7.4* (Cambridge: Cambridge University Press, 1972), p. 22. Collange goes on to observe that, although the form of this thanksgiving (as Schubert showed) is Hellenistic, 'Paul has filled this form with the entire contents of his Christian faith, rooted in Judaism' (p. 23). P.T. O'Brien, *Introductory Thanksgivings in the Letters of Paul* (Leiden: Brill, 1977), endorses Schubert's view that the form of the Pauline thanksgiving is Hellenistic, but notes that much of Paul's prayer language is Jewish in both form and content.

3. With reference to the αὐτοῦ of this verse, it is probable that it refers to God rather than to Christ—i.e. the knowledge of God (thus, e.g. Furnish, *II Corinthians*, p. 176, and Collange, *Enigmes*, p. 31; against Allo, *Seconde épître*, p. 45).

4. Bultmann, *Zweite Brief*, p. 70, following Weiss.

5. The meaning of θριαμβεύοντι is much disputed, but the image is probably that of the apostle as Christ's prisoner in his triumphal procession. (See the discussion in Furnish, *II Corinthians*, pp. 174-75).

6. *Contra* also Barrett, *Second Epistle*, p. 99.

7. Carrez, *Deuxième épître*, p. 72, wrongly translates 'for God', arguing that τῷ θεῷ replaces the τῷ κυρίῳ of the LXX (although he allows that it has a new meaning here because of the following reference to τοῖς σωξόμενοις κτλ.).

interpret this as 'in God's service' or 'to the honour of God'.[1] This is Bultmann's view if τῷ θεῷ is retained; as we noted, he excludes the words, although without good textual evidence. More probably, however, τῷ θεῷ here is the equivalent of the expressions κατέναντι θεοῦ and ἐνώπιον τοῦ θεοῦ which Paul uses elsewhere, and which, it will be argued here, carry a polemical function in this passage. Paul probably avoided such a prepositional phrase here as that would certainly have conveyed a sacrifical idea, whereas Paul here wishes to convey a picture of the apostle's responsiblity to and accountability before God: this is what we are and do *before God*.[2]

The emphasis on God continues in Paul's response to his rhetorical question: καὶ πρὸς ταῦτα τίς ἱκανός; (v. 16c). His response consists of a contrast between οἱ πολλοὶ who 'water down' (καπηλεύοντες) the word of God and the apostle[3] who ἐξ εἰλικρινείας, ἀλλ' ὡς ἐκ θεοῦ κατέναντι θεοῦ ἐν Χριστῷ λαλοῦμεν (v. 17b). The position of these phrases, their wording and the repetition of some of the words in 2 Cor. 12.19 (κατέναντι θεοῦ ἐν Χριστῷ λαλοῦμεν), even though in a different letter, all underline their importance. First, we noted in the previous section[4] the probable pun behind the use of εἰλικρινείας here, picking up, as it does, the use of καπηλεύοντες in the preceding verse. The following phrases amplify what Paul means by this pure or unalloyed character of his ministry. Its source is God (ἐκ θεοῦ). Schütz[5] notes this typically Pauline expression, commenting that 'for Paul this characteristically expresses God as the actor'. (He compares Rom. 2.29; 1 Cor. 2.12; 7.17; 11.12 etc.) Schütz interprets εἰλικρινείας here as moral integrity, taking the phrases ἐκ θεοῦ and κατέναντι θεοῦ as

1. Bultmann, *Zweite Brief*, p. 70.

2. There is another occurrence of the dative θεῷ at 5.13 of this epistle: εἴτε γὰρ ἐξέστημεν, θεῷ· εἴτε σωφρονοῦμεν, ὑμῖν. Most commentators takes this to be a reference to Paul's ecstatic experiences—i.e. speaking in tongues is a matter between him and God alone. If that is so, the use of θεῷ here is a fairly close parallel with the use of τῷ θεῷ in 2.15.

3. Collange, *Enigmes*, pp. 25-26, gives a useful summary of the evidence and the various possible interpretations of the first person plural in 2 Corinthians, concluding that 'in the whole of our passage' (here he means 2.14 to 7.4) 'it is Paul—and only Paul—who speaks, and it is his own concept and his own experience of apostleship which he is setting out'.

4. See p. 145 n. 2.

5. J.H. Schütz, *Paul and the Anatomy of Apostolic Authority* (Cambridge: Cambridge University Press, 1975), p. 211 n. 2.

parallel to and clarifying it. This is probably correct, although we note once again that the sentence would have made sense without the two θεός phrases, and that their inclusion is a further instance of Paul's polemical use of this kind of language. The emphasis falls upon God as the source of the apostle's authority, and the one to whom he is responsible.[1]

The polemical edge of the theme that God is the final judge and arbiter of Paul's ministry should not be missed. A.E. Harvey, in a study of Jewish legal concepts notes:

> one consequence of the informality of proceedings... was that it was not always clear who was judging whom: the tables might actually be turned as the case progressed... if either party were prepared to bring God in (so to speak) on his side... then grave consequences followed.[2]

It is true that Paul is not calling God to witness in quite the impassioned way in which he does in Gal. 1.20b (ἰδοὺ ἐνώπιον τοῦ θεοῦ ὅτι οὐ ψεύδομαι), but the implication of κατέναντι θεοῦ is the same. Thus a later comment of Harvey is applicable here:

> In other respects, however, the familiar procedure of the earthly Jewish court does apply to the heavenly. In particular, the defendant... in meeting the accusations of his adversary, may become the accuser: demonstrating the righteous man's innocence may involve convicting the accuser of falsehood.[3]

So Paul's use of κατέναντι θεοῦ here has a double-edged force: it denotes the apostle's accountability, and *pari passu* expresses the idea that God is the final arbiter in the case, with the implied judgment that carries for Paul's opponents.[4]

Paul next formulates his questions about commendation (3.1), declaring that it is the Corinthians themselves who are the fruits of his ministry (3.2-3). He continues πεποίθησιν δὲ τοιαύτην ἔχομεν διὰ

1. Commentators are generally agreed that κατέναντι θεοῦ carries with it the idea of accountability before God: Bultmann, *Zweite Brief*, p. 73; Furnish, *II Corinthians*, p. 179; Barrett, *Second Epistle*, p. 104; cf. Schütz, *Apostolic Authority*, p. 211: 'the phrase... (sc indicates) his awareness that God scrutinizes what he says'. κατέναντι is used in the Synoptics six times, but only in Paul with θεοῦ (Rom. 4.17, in addition to 2 Cor. 2.17 and 12.19).

2. A.E. Harvey, *Jesus on Trial* (London: SPCK, 1976), p. 57.

3. Harvey, *Jesus*, p. 110.

4. Collange, *Enigmes*, p. 39 rightly notes 'the needs of polemics' behind Paul's language here.

τοῦ Χριστοῦ πρὸς τὸν θεόν (v. 4). Again it is necessary to ask: what does the addition of πρὸς τὸν θεόν add to the sentence? It is almost certainly incorrect to link it with πεποίθησιν in the sense of 'confidence in God',[1] since πεποίθησις is normally followed by εἰς or ἐν.[2] One parallel apparently unnoticed by commentators lies in Rom. 4.2, where Paul writes of Abraham: ἔχει καύχημα, ἀλλ' οὐ πρὸς θεόν. Both there and here it is probably best to interpret the phrase with Bultmann 'not "to God"...but "in relation to God, in the sight of God"'.[3] It seems best, therefore, to regard the phrase, as Collange does,[4] as a further example of Paul's polemical language.

There are two examples of the polemical use of θεός in 4.1-6. First, Paul uses the phrase ἐνώπιον τοῦ θεοῦ in v.2 in a way parallel to his use of κατέναντι θεοῦ in 2.17. (See the earlier discussion of v. 2 in the previous section.) Paul uses the phrase several times in situations of conflict or controversy (Rom. 3.20; 14.22; 2 Cor. 4.2; 7.12; 8.21; Gal. 1.20).[5] Secondly, θεός is used polemically in 4.6. We have already noted the place of this verse in Paul's argument. Here we note the emphatic θεός at the beginning of the verse and the second reference to God later in the verse. The textual evidence for τοῦ θεοῦ here is not unanimous, but almost certainly Paul wrote either τοῦ θεοῦ or αὐτοῦ referring to God. Paul often begins and ends sections of his epistles by references to God,[6] and here, as in v. 4 (Χριστοῦ, ὅς ἐστιν εἰκὼν θεοῦ), it seems he did not wish to define the gospel solely in terms of Christ.

Paul's God-language, however, is not confined to phrases in which θεός occurs. So we turn next to his use of πνεῦμα-language in this section of 2 Corinthians, in order to discover its function and

1. *Contra* Allo, *Seconde épître*, p. 83 and Barrett, *Second Epistle*, p. 110, although Barrett prefers the translation 'before God'.

2. Thus Collange, *Enigmes*, p. 58.

3. Bultmann, *Zweite Brief*, p. 78.

4. Collange, *Enigmes*, p. 56.

5. A glance at a concordance shows that ἐνώπιον seems to have become the most favoured preposition of this kind in the later language of Christian piety. It occurs in several of the later New Testament writings, and is particularly common in Luke–Acts and Revelation. ἔμπροσθεν is used in the New Testament in a variety of contexts, but not often with θεοῦ. In Paul all occurrences of this preposition with θεοῦ and κυρίου are in 1 Thess. (1.3; 2.19; 3.9, 13). ἐναντίον and ἔναντι occur only in Luke–Acts, four times with θεοῦ.

6. See the discussion in Chapter 5, section 5.

significance in the contexts in which it is used.

The word πνεῦμα first occurs in the first of a series of contrasts between the old and new covenants. In 3.3 Paul describes the Corinthians as a 'letter of Christ'

> διακονηθεῖσα ὑφ' ἡμῶν, ἐγγεγραμμένη οὐ μέλανι ἀλλὰ πνεύματι θεοῦ ζῶντος, οὐκ ἐν πλαξὶν λιθίναις ἀλλ' ἐν πλαξὶν καρδίαις σαρκίναις.

Bultmann rightly comments that Paul seems to be combining two ideas: (a) written not on stones, but on hearts, and (b) the replacement of hearts of stone by hearts of flesh.[1] The word μέλανι, the first in the double contrast made here, derives not from any of the Old Testament passages which may lie behind this verse[2] but from the metaphor of the letter which Paul has just employed. The phrase πνεύματι θεοῦ ζῶντος is therefore one of many examples in Paul's writings of πνεῦμα used anarthrously in an important contrast.[3]

Perhaps because of its Old Testament background, Paul employs here an Old Testament phrase: θεοῦ ζῶντος. This phrase, however, does not occur in any of the verses in the Old Testament which may be the basis of Paul's thought and language.[4] Paul no doubt felt it necessary to amplify the single word πνεύματι, making clear its *theological* significance.[5] It is noteworthy that in the three other instances where Paul applies the epithet 'living' to God, it is either because he is quoting the Old Testament (Rom. 9.26; cf. 14.11) or because he is using particularly Jewish language (1 Thess. 1.9; cf. 2 Cor. 6.16, if this last verse is to be considered Pauline). The use of θεοῦ ζῶντος here, therefore, is another indication that Paul is using God-language (in this case *their* language) to argue against his rivals.

The contrast between the old and the new resurfaces in Paul's argument in v. 6, where he describes the new covenant as οὐ γράμματος

1. Bultmann, *Zweite Brief*, p. 76.
2. See p. 145 n. 6 above.
3. See, e.g. Rom. 8.4, 9; Gal. 3.3; 4.29 etc.
4. Martin, *2 Corinthians*, p. 52, thinks that θεοῦ ζῶντος replaces the τῷ δακτύλῳ τοῦ θεοῦ of Exod. 31.18.
5. Thus also I. Hermann, *Kyrios und Pneuma: Studien zur Christologie der paulinischen Hauptbriefe* (München: Kösel, 1961), p. 28: 'The genitive θεοῦ ζῶντος characterizes God as the origin and owner of the Spirit through which Christ works.' (Cf. pp. 142-43).We noted in the previous chapter (section 3) a tendency of Paul to make the same theological emphasis in 1 Corinthians.

ἀλλὰ πνεύματος· τὸ γὰρ γράμμα ἀποκτέννει, τὸ δὲ πνεῦμα ζῳοποιεῖ. The same two words γράμμα and πνεῦμα are also used by Paul in Rom. 2.29 and 7.6. It is an antithesis which, as Käsemann says, is 'so significant but hard to interpret'.[1] We approach the task of interpretation by first examining another significant antithesis in Paul's writings, that of σάρξ and πνεῦμα.

It may be an exaggeration to say that the dualism between σάρξ and πνεῦμα underlies the whole of Galatians.[2] The origin of this dualism is still debated, but Jewett has drawn attention to the way in which the LXX often uses σάρξ in a circumcision context, and in two places—Gen. 34.24 and Jer. 9.26—where the Hebrew does not require it.[3] In Galatians the word is first used in a reference to circumcision at 3.3.[4] In the light of the Old Testament background, it was an obvious word to use of a physical rite. By the time we reach Galatians 5 (vv. 16-21) the word has broadened and deepened in its significance, without, however, losing the polemical reference which it acquired earlier in the argument: ἡ γὰρ σὰρξ ἐπιθυμεῖ κατὰ τοῦ πνεύματος, τὸ δὲ πνεῦμα κατὰ τῆς σαρκός...(5.17). It seems, then, that there is much to be said for Jewett's view that Paul's distinctive use of σάρξ originated in the circumcision controversy.[5] Can the same be said of Paul's use of πνεῦμα? We shall return to this question later, but for the moment we should note that the majority of the occurrences of πνεῦμα in Galatians are to be found where a contrast is being made between 'flesh' and 'spirit' (4.29; 5.16-21, 22, 25; 6.8), or where reference is being made to the beginning of the Galatians' life as Christians (3.2, 3, 5, 14; and perhaps 4.6).

But what does Paul mean by πνεῦμα in these contexts? There is some truth in Isaacs' observation that in Gal. 3.3 'flesh' and 'spirit' mean the Jewish and Christian dispensations respectively.[6] Watson

1. Käsemann, *Romans*, p. 76.

2. Thus Betz, *Galatians*, p. 249.

3. R. Jewett, *Paul's Anthropological Terms* (Leiden: Brill, 1971), p. 96. Cf. Grayston, *Dying*, p. 84: '*Flesh* means not corporeality but sociality'.

4. It is used in its more neutral sense in 1.16, 2.16, and 2.20.

5. Davies has drawn attention to the ethical connotations of the word 'flesh' in some late documents in the Old Testament (*Paul*, pp. 18-20), in the *Mishnah* and the Jerusalem Targum, but above all in the Dead Sea Scrolls ('Paul and the Dead Sea Scrolls: Flesh and Spirit', in *idem*, *Christian Origins and Judaism* (London: Darton, Longman & Todd, 1962), pp. 145-77.

6. M.E. Isaacs, *The Concept of the Spirit* (London: Heythrop College, 1976), p. 98.

argues along similar lines when he claims[1] that Paul uses the 'spirit–flesh' antithesis to legitimate the separation of church from synagogue. It seems more likely that Paul is using the antithesis to legitimate the mission to the Gentiles, even though that mission eventually led to the separation, but it is clear that the antithesis itself was deeply rooted in, and probably originated in, the Judaizing controversy.

Nevertheless, it can hardly be denied that πνεῦμα is a 'God' word. Sjöberg, writing of the rabbinic use of the term 'Spirit', argues that for the rabbis the spirit is 'an objective divine reality which encounters and claims man...a reality which comes from God, which in some sense represents the presence of God, and yet which is not identical with God'.[2] In Philo, too, 'spirit' is generally to be regarded as a God-word: J.A. Davis in the study of 'wisdom' and 'spirit' referred to in the last chapter has concluded that 'the spirit in Philo is always connected with the activity of God as divine power and not detached from God'.[3]

There seems, then, little doubt that for Jews the word 'spirit' was a God-word, whereas for Greeks it was more ambiguous. The question of whether by 'spirit' Paul means the human or the divine spirit has been much discussed. It is true that he occasionally distinguishes between the

1. F. Watson, *Paul, Judaism and the Gentiles: A Sociological Approach* (Cambridge: Cambridge University Press, 1986), pp. 46-47.

2. *TWNT*, VI, pp. 387-88. Cf. E. Schweizer, *The Holy Spirit* (Philadelphia: Fortress Press, 1980), p. 17: 'If the Israelite wishes to emphasize the source of life, and to praise him who gives us this life, he speaks of the "spirit" of God'. For a discussion of the relationship between 'spirit' and *shekinah*, see below.

3. Davis, *Wisdom and Spirit*, p. 182 n. 30. This is not always so apparent in the writings of Philo, who sometimes seems to blur the distinction between divine activity in humans and their 'natural' endowment. In *Gig.* 22-23, for example, Philo defines the 'spirit of God' as 'the air which flows up from the land' (ὁ ῥέων ἀὴρ ἀπὸ γῆς), but also as 'the pure knowledge in which every wise man naturally (εἰκότως) shares' (Loeb, Vol II, p. 457). Elsewhere, however, Philo's use of Gen. 2.7 (e.g. *Spec. Leg.* 4.123 and *Her.* 55) shows that πνεῦμα for him is a divine word. This is particularly clear in *Plant.* 18 where Philo contrasts those who claim the human mind gives man kinship with the upper air (αἰθέρα) with Moses, who regards it as 'a genuine coinage of that dread spirit, the Divine and Invisible One' (τοῦ θείου καὶ ἀοράτου πνεύματος). Here Philo differs from some aspects of Greek thought in which πνεῦμα is never wholly outside the realm of sense '. . . a vital, natural force immanent and impersonal' (*TWNT*, VI, p. 358). This last quotation, however, should be balanced against an earlier observation in the same article (pp. 338-39) that 'in virtue of its uncontrollable elemental nature and its direct efficiency, πνεῦμα is often felt to be something divine'.

two (Rom. 8.16; 1 Cor. 2.10-11). But normally in his writings πνεῦμα denotes the Spirit *of God*. Thus Pfister writes that because the Spirit represents God's gift and strength given to humans, it also comes to mean the divine working in them: 'That is to say, it can emphasize the Spirit's sanctifying work in human beings more than its divine origin'.[1] Thus far I have argued that Paul's distinctive use of the word σάρξ and the antithesis σάρξ/πνεῦμα originated in the Judaizing controversy, but that although the word πνεῦμα is often used by him to denote the Christian dispensation, in contrast with the old, it is nevertheless a God-word and must be considered part of his God-language unless there is clear evidence to the contrary. With this discussion of the σάρξ/πνεῦμα dualism in mind, we return to the contrast of γράμμα/ πνεῦμα in 2 Cor. 3.6.

I have already noted Paul's polemical use of God-language in this section of the letter in a situation where he is contending against Jewish or Jewish–Christian opposition. But why is the word γράμμα used here? The Old Testament throws no light on this Pauline antithesis. Where γράμμα occurs in the LXX, it is usually in the plural.[2] There seems to be no parallel to Paul's use of the word. Its use here is due partly to the context: first, to the use he has made of the Old Testament in v. 3 (particularly with his use of the verb ἐγγεγραμμένη), and secondly, to the contrast he is about to make in vv. 7 and 8 between two ministries: ἡ διακονία τοῦ θανάτου and ἡ διακονία τοῦ πνεύματος. The context and the argument, therefore, require a word such as γράμμα, but Paul's use of it may be due simply to its similarity in sound to πνεῦμα.[3] 'Gramma' in this polemical context comes to mean not only the law as a tangible, external phenomenon, but also the law as a phenomenon of the past.[4]

To explore fully the series of contrasts which Paul develops in vv. 7-11 is outside the scope of this particular study, concerned as it is with

1. W. Pfister, *Das Leben im Geist nach Paulus* (Freiburg: Universitätsverlag, 1963), p. 7. Cf. Schweizer, *Holy Spirit*, p. 84 and Whiteley, *Theology of St Paul*, p. 127.

2. Hatch and Redpath, *Concordance*, I, p. 275, list less than 30 occurrences of γράμμα in the LXX, the word occurring in the singular only at *1 Esd.* 3.9, 13, 15 and 4.3, 8.

3. Thus also *TWNT*, I, p. 765.

4. For the γράμμα/πνεῦμα contrast see also the discussion in Provence, '"Who is Sufficient?"', pp. 62-68.

Paul's use of God-language rather than his understanding of the law and the old covenant. But one more use must be noted of the word πνεῦμα in which the polemical contrast between the old and the new is heightened. After declaring that 'the letter kills, but the Spirit gives life' (v. 6) Paul expounds further this life/death contrast by a contrast between ἡ διακονία τοῦ θανάτου (v. 7) and ἡ διακονία τοῦ πνεύματος (v. 8). πνεῦμα, therefore, like θεός, is used by Paul in a polemical way.

There are three further occurrences of πνεῦμα in this section of 2 Corinthians, and since they belong closely together it will be as well to quote the whole passage:

> ἡνίκα δὲ ἐὰν ἐπιστρέψῃ πρὸς κύριον, περιαιρεῖται τὸ κάλυμμα. ὁ δὲ κύριος τὸ πνεῦμα ἐστιν· οὗ δὲ τὸ πνεῦμα κυρίου, ἐλευθερία. ἡμεῖς δὲ πάντες ἀνακεκαλυμμένῳ προσώπῳ τὴν δόξαν κυρίου κατοπτριζόμενοι τὴν αὐτὴν εἰκόνα μεταμορφούμεθα ἀπὸ δόξης εἰς δόξαν καθάπερ ἀπὸ κυρίου πνεύματος (3.16-18).

These verses come at the end of what was observed earlier to be most likely a midrash on Exod. 34.29-35. I noted in the last section of this chapter that Paul's words here in v. 16 depart significantly from Exod. 34.34, notably in his introduction of the word ἐπιστρέψῃ, so that the Old Testament verse is now understood as a reference to Christian conversion. Our chief concern, however, is with Paul's subsequent comment: ὁ δὲ κύριος τὸ πνεῦμα ἐστιν. First, there is a precedent in Paul's writings for his use of δὲ here: in 1 Cor. 10.4 Paul alludes to the 'rock' which accompanied the Israelites on their wilderness wanderings, and adds ἡ πέτρα δὲ ἦν ὁ Χριστός.[1] So here v. 17 seems to be an interpretative gloss on the Old Testament quotation of v. 16: 'The Lord'—that is to whom I have just referred in the Scriptural quotation—*means* the Spirit.[2] Collange rightly notes the unusual

1. Noted by Collange, *Enigmes*, p. 111.

2. So also J.D.G. Dunn, *Christology in the Making* (London: SCM Press, 1980), p. 143, followed by Provence, '"Who is Sufficient?"', p. 80. Theissen objects that if Paul had intended this meaning he would have indicated the quotation by means of τό, but the examples he gives (Mk 9.10, 23) of a quotation introduced by τό are not really parallel, since in neither of these verses does the quotation begin, as it does here (ὁ) with the definite article (*Psychological Aspects*, p. 130). Hermann (*Kyrios und Pneuma*, pp. 39-52) like Theissen believes that the κύριος of v. 17a is Christ, but he does not consider the possibility of a *pesher*-like quotation, and his

retention of the definite article in a predicate, and so rejects the interpretation of 'the Spirit' here as 'a mere spiritual power', preferring to interpret it as 'the one who inaugurates and promotes the new covenant and new ministry'.[1] It would seem to be in line wih this interpretation to regard τὸ πνεῦμα κυρίου (v. 17b) as equivalent to the Old Testament expression 'the Spirit of the Lord'.[2] Finally, as several recent commentators have done,[3] the last problematical phrase of v. 18, ἀπὸ κυρίου πνεύματος should be translated 'from the Lord who is the Spirit'.

What do these verses add to the argument? Or, more precisely, what do the references to 'the Lord' and to 'the Spirit' signify? Paul here and elsewhere has used the term πνεῦμα in polemical contrasts with Judaism. I have also noted the polemical nature of 2 Cor. 4.6, with its reference to the God of creation (or the God proclaimed in the prophecies of Isaiah). Here in 3.17 a similar equation is being made: the Lord of whom the Jewish Scriptures speak is also the Spirit so clearly at work in the new Christian dispensation. The Old Testament expression τὸ πνεῦμα κυρίου confirms the equation.

So far, the examination of Paul's use of θεός and πνεῦμα in this section of 2 Corinthians leads to the conclusion that Paul's use of both words is thoroughly polemical. But it must be acknowledged that Paul's use of θεός and πνεῦμα does not comprise the sum total of God-language in the broader sense. In particular, the word δόξα has a strong claim to be considered a God-word. In the LXX it is used many times to denote the nature of God,[4] a usage which is carried over into the New Testament.[5] We cannot undertake a full study of δόξα in this section of 2 Corinthians, but it is surely significant that it occurs 19 times in chs. 1–8, 15 of which are in chs. 3 and 4.[6] This heavy use of δόξα was no

exegesis seems to be shaped by his overall thesis that 'Christ is experienced as Spirit' (p. 49).

1. Collanges, *Enigmes*, p. 111.

2. Thus, e.g., Furnish, *II Corinthians*, p. 213.

3. Thus Barrett, *Second Epistle*, p. 126; Bultmann, *Zweite Brief*, p. 99 (who notes also the possibility of 'the Lord of the Spirit'). Furnish *II Corinthians*, p. 216 merely lists the possibilities.

4. Thus Kittel in *TWNT*, II, p. 244.

5. *TWNT*, II, pp. 247-48. See also the essay by L.H. Brockington 'The Septuagintal Background to the New Testament Use of ΔΟΞΑ', in D.E. Nineham (ed.), *Studies in the Gospels* (Oxford: Basil Blackwell, 1955), pp. 1-8.

6. Martin, *2 Corinthians*, pp. 61-2.

doubt due partly to the occurrence of δοξάζω in the Exodus passage on which 2 Cor. 3.7-18 is based, but it may also be due to the nature of the theological conflict in which Paul was engaged. D. Lührmann, noting the frequency of φανερόω, φανέρωσις and ἀποκάλυψις in the polemical sections of 2 Corinthians, has argued that revelation was an issue at Corinth.[1] If that were so, then δόξα would have to be included in the panoply of Paul's polemical language.

In the article just cited Brockington lists four uses of δόξα in the New Testament which, in his view, correspond with the usage of the word in the LXX:

1. Conception of brightness
2. Power and wonder-working of God
3. Saving power of God
4. Conception of God-likeness.[2]

At least three of these aspects of δόξα (1, 3 and 4) are implied here; and since 2 and 3 are so intimately related we should probably conclude that all four aspects are present. There are two important points to note here.

1. The divine glory is now defined by reference to Christ: εἰς τὸ μὴ αὐγάσαι τὸν φωτισμὸν τοῦ εὐαγγελίου τῆς δόξης τοῦ Χριστοῦ, ὅς ἐστιν εἰκὼν τοῦ θεοῦ (v. 4). Yet it is clear from the expression εἰκὼν τοῦ θεοῦ and the deliberate echo of the Exodus 34 story in the phrase ἐν προσώπῳ Χριστοῦ (v. 6)[3] that Christ's glory reflects or mediates the glory of God. Thus an important LXX God-word is now redefined christologically.

2. The δόξα is shared. This was implied in 3.7 in the reference to Moses. But now, not only does the δόξα *surpass* that of the old dispensation, which is fading anyway (v. 7)—it is, moreover, *revealed*, not concealed (vv. 13-18)—it is also *shared more widely*, as the πάντες of v. 18 implies. There are possible parallels here with other language in Paul which has been noted in the course of this study, notably 1 Cor. 2.16b: ἡμεῖς δὲ νοῦν Χριστοῦ ἔχομεν. Ford and Young, in their

1. Lührmann, *Offenbarungsverständnis*, p. 45. His contention that the γράμμα/ πνεῦμα antithesis derived from Paul's opponents (p. 47) seems less probable.

2. Nineham, *Studies in the Gospels*, p. 3.

3. The phrase ἐν προσώπῳ Χριστοῦ clearly echoes the references to Moses' face in Exod. 34.29-35.

discussion of 'glory' in 2 Corinthians,[1] suggest that δόξα is the biblical word which approximates most closely to the concept of transcendence. If that is so, it is necessary to speak of a sharing by God of that transcendence.

Summary

Three important God-words have been examined in this section: θεός, πνεῦμα and δόξα, noting the polemical function of θεός and πνεῦμα in particular, but probably of δόξα, too. First Paul uses θεός, drawing on traditional language (θεοῦ ζῶντος, 3.3) and especially on Old Testament traditions drawn from Exodus 34 and elsewhere. He also uses prepositional phrases (2.19; 3.4; 4.2) in order to counter criticisms, probably from a Jewish standpoint, of his ministry and gospel.

Secondly, the evidence of Old Testament and Jewish traditions that πνεῦμα is a God-word is overwhelming. But πνεῦμα, too, is used polemically in a series of sharp antitheses: οὐ μέλανι ἀλλὰ πνεύματι (3.3), οὐ γράμματος ἀλλὰ πνεύματος (3.6), ἡ διακονία τοῦ θανάτου...ἡ διακονία τοῦ θανάτου (3.7-8), finally being equated by means of a *pesher*-like quotation from the Old Testament with 'the Lord'—i.e. with Yahweh himself. Behind these sharp antitheses there probably lay the Judaizing controversy. This was the most likely cause of Paul's polemical use of σάρξ and, therefore, of πνεῦμα as well.[2]

These observations complete this analysis of the God-language of 2 Cor. 2.14–4.6. Before drawing some conclusions in a final section of this chapter, I turn to the exploration of the origin and function of πνεῦμα in Paul's writings: in particular I shall be asking whether his use of πνεῦμα, like his use of σάρξ, arose out of the Judaizing controversy, which itself arose as a response to the mission to the Gentiles.

3. *The Context and Function of Paul's Language about the Spirit*

It has long been a commonplace of New Testament scholarship that Paul understood the Spirit primarily and fundamentally as an eschatological phenomenon, and that this eschatological understanding of the Spirit was deeply rooted in Jewish expectation. But how strong is the evidence for these views? In this section I shall argue that Paul's use of the term

1. Ford and Young, *Meaning and Truth*, pp. 254 and 259.
2. σάρξ and πνεῦμα are often paired antithetically in Galatians and Romans.

'Spirit' is primarily polemical and apologetic, relating this to a strand of Jewish thought about the Spirit.[1]

I begin with the evidence of Paul's own letters. There are four references to the Spirit in the earliest letter, 1 Thessalonians. Two of these occur in the opening thanksgiving:

> εὐχαριστοῦμεν (v. 2)...εἰδότες (v. 4)...ὅτι τὸ εὐαγγέλιον ἡμῶν οὐκ ἐγενήθη εἰς ὑμᾶς ἐν λόγῳ μόνον ἀλλὰ καὶ ἐν δυνάμει καὶ ἐν πνεύματι ἁγίῳ καὶ (ἐν) πληροφορίᾳ πολλῇ...(v. 5), καὶ ὑμεῖς μιμηταὶ ἡμῶν ἐγενήθητε καὶ τοῦ κυρίου, δεξάμενοι τὸν λόγον ἐν θλίψει πολλῇ μετὰ χαρᾶς πνεύματος ἁγίου (v. 6).

Verse 5 may be compared with other verses of the Pauline corpus in which the apostle is speaking of his own ministry (and often, as here, of *his* gospel). At 1 Cor. 2.4 Paul declares,

> καὶ ὁ λόγος μου καὶ τὸ κήρυγμά μου οὐκ ἐν πειθοῖ(ς) σοφίας (λόγοις) ἀλλ' ἐν ἀποδείξει πνεύματος καὶ δυνάμεως.

Similarly, in Paul's description of the apostolic ministry at 2 Cor. 6.3-10, the expression ἐν πνεύματι ἁγίῳ occurs in what is clearly an apologetic and/or polemical context in which Paul juxtaposes the outward deprivations and public estimation of his ministry alongside its spiritual content and power. The most significant example of this use of πνεῦμα, however, occurs in Rom. 15.18-19, where Paul once more links his ministry with the work of the Holy Spirit, defining here that his purpose was the obedience of the Gentiles:

> οὐ γὰρ τολμήσω τι λαλεῖν ὧν οὐ κατειργάσατο Χριστὸς δι' ἐμοῦ εἰς ὑπακοὴν ἐθνῶν, λόγῳ καὶ ἔργῳ, ἐν δυνάμει σημείων καὶ τεράτων, ἐν δυνάμει πνεύματος (θεοῦ) (vv. 18, 19a).[2]

There are therefore several references to the Spirit in Paul's writings, mostly in apologetic or polemical contexts about his own ministry. As usual in Paul, that ministry is closely identified both with 'his' gospel and with the mission to the Gentiles.

There are fewer obvious parallels to 1 Thess. 1.6 elsewhere in Paul's writings, although the link should be noted between the Holy Spirit and joy at Rom. 14.17 and 15.13 and Gal. 5.24. Joy is closely linked in

1. See also Appendix 1.

2. Although I have printed the Nestlé-Aland text here, Cranfield (*Romans*, II, p. 758 n. 5) is probably correct in regarding both θεοῦ and ἁγίου (each found in some MSS) as 'improvements' on the simple πνεύματος found in B.

Paul's experience with suffering (as here and, e.g., 2 Cor. 7.4). Paul's usual word for the suffering of Christians was, as here, θλίψις, a word specifically associated with the sufferings of the messianic age, and so there is certainly an eschatological dimension to Paul's language in 1 Thess. 1.6 (although this dimension is not so clear in Rom. 14.17, 15.13 and Gal. 5.24).

The next occurrence of πνεῦμα in 1 Thessalonians is at 4.8: τοιγαροῦν ὁ ἀθετῶν οὐκ ἄνθρωπον ἀθετεῖ ἀλλὰ τὸν θεὸν τὸν (καὶ) διδόντα τὸ πνεῦμα αὐτοῦ τὸ ἅγιον εἰς ὑμᾶς. Most commentators link this verse with the prophecies of the Spirit in Ezek. 36.27 and 37.14. It is true that this verse and the verses in Ezekiel both contain the word δίδοντα and the phrase εἰς ὑμᾶς, but this is too tenuous a link to indicate a deliberate citation.[1] At the most, Paul's knowledge of the LXX has influenced his choice of words here.[2] But the main significance of πνεῦμα here lies not in an allusion to the eschatological fulfilment of Old Testament prophecy, whether an intended allusion or not, but in the emphasis on holiness. This is indicated not only by the paraenetic context (NB ὁ ἁγιασμὸς ὑμῶν, v. 3) but also by the unusual word order of v. 8: τὸ πνεῦμα αὐτοῦ τὸ ἅγιον.[3] Von Dobschütz, therefore, is probably correct that the emphasis here falls on the Spirit as 'the power of a new moral existence', a powerful reason for discarding all *Gentile* (my emphasis) impurity.[4]

Again, there are several parallels in Paul's writings. The link between the Spirit and purity is made at 1 Cor. 6.19, the addressees again being entirely, or predominantly, Gentile. 1 Cor. 3.16 and 6.11 and Gal. 5.19-23 are other passages which make the connection between the Spirit and purity or holiness.

The final occurrence of πνεῦμα in 1 Thessalonians is too brief to shed much light on the Pauline use of πνεῦμα (τὸ πνεῦμα μὴ σβέννυτε [5.19]). It is probable that the reference is a general one: to all

1. *Contra*, e.g., E. Best, *A Commentary on the First and Second Epistles to the Thessalonians* (London: A. & C. Black, 1972), pp. 169-70.

2. Thus E. von Dobschütz, *Die Thessalonicherbriefe* (Göttigen: Vandenhoeck & Ruprecht, 1909), p. 173. I.H. Marshall, *1 and 2 Thessalonians* (London: Marshall, Morgan & Scott, 1983) leaves open the question of whether Paul consciously or unconsciously echoes Ezekiel here (p. 114).

3. Best, *Commentary*, p. 169 compares Ps. 143 (LXX 142) v. 10 (τὸ πνεῦμά σου τὸ ἀγαθόν) and Isa. 63.10 (τὸ πνεῦμα τὸ ἅγιον αὐτοῦ).

4. Von Dobschütz, *Thessalonicherbriefe*, p. 173.

Christians not to quench the work of the Spirit in themselves.[1]

In Paul's earliest letter, then, Paul's use of the phrase 'Holy Spirit' occurs in a reference to his own ministry (1.5) and in the context of an exhortation to Gentiles to sexual purity (4.8), observing that both uses have several parallels elsewhere in the Pauline corpus. An eschatological note is not entirely absent (1.6) (and there are other verses in other letters which we shall need to examine), but in this letter, at least, it is not the dominant one.

In Galatians we find further evidence that Paul's use of the word πνεῦμα is associated particularly with his mission to the Gentiles. Although J.L. Martyn has convincingly shown that Galatians is more apocalyptic in its language and thought than first meets the eye,[2] it does not seem that the main thrust of Paul's πνεῦμα-language here is eschatological. It is significant that, in a passage where Paul asks the Galatians to look at the roots of and the evidence of their Christian faith, the word 'Spirit' is mentioned no less than three times:

> τοῦτο μόνον θέλω μαθεῖν ἀφ' ὑμῶν· ἐξ ἔργων νόμου τὸ πνεῦμα ἐλάβετε ἢ ἀκοῆς πίστεως; οὕτως ἀνόητοί ἐστε, ἐναρξάμενοι πνεύματι νῦν σαρκὶ ἐπιτελεῖσθε; τοσαῦτα ἐπάθετε εἰκῇ; εἴ γε καὶ εἰκῇ· ὁ οὖν ἐπιχορηγῶν ὑμῖν τὸ πνεῦμα καὶ ἐνεργῶν δυνάμεις ἐν ὑμῖν, ἐξ ἔργων νόμου ἢ ἐξ ἀκοῆς πίστεως; (3.2-4).

F.F. Bruce[3] rightly links the theme of the Spirit here with justification, but, in spite of a reference to Paul's law-free gospel, does not bring out the fact that it is to *Gentiles* that these remarks are addressed. The Galatians really had experienced the Spirit of God, and this was the justification, the divine confirmation of Paul's law-free gospel. (The same note is struck by Luke in his account of the conversion of Cornelius [Acts 10.45,47; cf. 11.15-17]).

It is not possible to survey all the occurrences of πνεῦμα in Galatians here. It is not difficult, however, to show that the function of πνεῦμα in this letter is primarily polemical. The promise to Abraham that in him all the Gentiles would be blessed forms a vital part of Paul's argument (3.8, a conflation of Gen. 12.3 and 18.18).[4] This promise is further defined in

1. Hill (*Prophecy*, pp. 119-20, 150-51) may however be correct in linking 1 Thess. 5.19-21 with charismatic prophecy in worship.

2. J.L. Martyn, 'Apocalyptic Antinomies in Paul's Letter to the Galatians', *NTS* 31.3 (1985), *passim*.

3. Bruce, *1 and 2 Thessalonians*, p. 149.

4. Betz, *Galatians*, p. 128, identifies 3.1–4.31 as the *probatio*, this section

3.14 as 'the promise of the Spirit', to be received διὰ τῆς πίστεως, a further indication of the close link in Paul's theology between the Spirit and his law-free mission to the Gentiles.

In the second half of Paul's letter the σάρξ/πνεῦμα antithesis emerges: Paul concludes his allegorical interpretation of the Genesis story of Hagar and Sarah by calling Ishmael ὁ κατὰ σάρκα γεννηθείς, and Isaac τὸν κατὰ πνεῦμα (4.29). The function of πνεῦμα here is clearly polemical, and the polemical contrast with σάρξ continues in the remaining occurrences of πνεῦμα in Galatians: 5.16, 17, 18, 22; 6.8.[1]

Thus the evidence of the two letters which are probably Paul's earliest[2] shows that the main function of the word πνεῦμα is apologetic and/or polemical, although in 1 Thessalonians the link of the Spirit with suffering and joy (1.6) and with the sexual purity of, significantly, Gentiles (4.8) was also noted. But what of the remaining letters of Paul? While, again, all the references to πνεῦμα cannot be individually examined, I turn first to the evidence of the Corinthian correspondence.[3]

It is very probable that the word πνεῦμα played a prominent part in Corinthian religious vocabulary. It is certain that the word πνευματικός

being 'the most decisive of all, because in it the "proofs" are presented'.

1. D. Lull, *The Spirit in Galatia* (Chico, CA: Scholars Press, 1980), p. 39 also recognizes that polemic was a major factor in Paul's use of πνεῦμα in Galatians, but later over-emphasizes the eschatological content of the πνεῦμα references (pp. 169-78). To say, for example, that 'the presence and activity of the Spirit were experienced by Christians in Galatia as evidence of the coming of the last age' (p. 169) may be true, but it is not the primary emphasis of what Paul was actually writing.

2. Galatians is notoriously difficult to date; almost certainly it preceded Romans, but we cannot be certain that it preceded the letters to Corinth. The precise dating of Galatians, however, does not affect the argument here.

3. Philippians will not figure prominently in this enquiry, chiefly because most of the references to the Spirit in this letter are obscure in one way or another. In 1.19 we have the unusual reference to 'the Spirit of Jesus Christ'; 1.27 (στήκετε ἐν ἑνὶ πνεύματι) and 2.1 (εἴ τις κοινωνία πνεύματος) are probably references to the Spirit of God rather than to the human spirit, in paraenetic contexts; 3.3 (οἱ πνεύματι θεοῦ λατρεύοντες) is another example of πνεῦμα occurring in a polemical context. The possibility that Phil. 4.2-8 comprise the fragment of a letter (see Chapter 4, section 3 below) weakens the objection of Lull that Philippians is an example of polemic against Jewish-Christian nomists, yet does not have πνεῦμα as a key term. (There are no references to the Spirit of God in the letter to Philemon.)

did so,[1] but the origin of this word is debatable. It is a word rarely used of people.[2] D. Lull believes that the word was coined by the Galatians,[3] but there is no evidence that there was any 'spiritual' enthusiasm in Galatia of the kind which was probably prevalent at Corinth. It is not impossible, therefore, that Paul himself introduced the word both at Galatia and at Corinth. At Corinth it caused considerable problems, as 1 Corinthians 12–14 indicate.

In the previous chapter it was argued that the Corinthian situation was shaped by first an over-emphasis by the Christian community there on rhetoric, and secondly by what might be called a 'simmering' Jewish dimension. But, thirdly, it is probable that the Corinthians' understanding of the Spirit had been significantly influenced by Hellenistic categories of thought. In Greek thought πνεῦμα is never wholly outside the realm of sense: 'it is a vital, natural force, immanent and impersonal'.[4] Kleinecht goes on to argue that πνεῦμα in the religious sphere has an enthusiastic or ecstatic character, and concludes by suggesting that the crucial difference between the Hellenistic πνεῦμα and πνεῦμα in the New Testament lies *in God*.[5] That is to say, πνεῦμα is fundamentally a *theological* word. (Occasionally in Paul's writings πνεῦμα refers to the human spirit; Rom. 8.16 and 1 Cor. 2.11 make clear both the correlation and the difference between the human and the divine spirit, Phil. 2.1 being one of the rare instances where it is not clear whether the referent of πνεῦμα is human or divine.) But most of the occurrences of πνεῦμα with θεοῦ occur in 1 and 2 Corinthians. This feature has already been noted in the passages studied so far.[6] Since the use of θεοῦ with πνεῦμα otherwise occurs in Paul only at Phil. 3.3 and Rom. 8.9 and 14, there seems some justification for concluding that the stress on the Spirit as the Spirit *of God* was a distinctive feature of Paul's πνεῦμα-language in the Corinthian correspondence.

1. The main evidence for this is 1 Cor. 12.1 (περὶ δὲ τῶν πνευματικῶν...), where περί, as in 7.1, 8.1 and 16.1, almost certainly picks up questions raised by the Corinthians in their letter to Paul. (The classic study here is J.C. Hurd, *The Origin of 1 Corinthians* [London: SPCK, 1965].)

2. BAGD, p. 685, although, interestingly, Liddell and Scott note references in the 2nd century CE to a school of physicians called οἱ πνευματικοί.

3. Lull, *Spirit*, p. 32.

4. Thus Kleinecht in *TWNT*, VI, p. 357.

5. *TWNT*, VI, p. 360.

6. See pp. 111-12.

The second distinctive feature of Paul's πνεῦμα-language in the Corinthian correspondence lies in Paul's response to the enthusiasm which seems to have been current at Corinth. Paul's use of the figure ἀρραβών, used at 2 Cor. 1.22 and 5.5, is especially important. These texts, together with Rom. 8.23 (where Paul uses ἀπαρχή with a similar meaning) are often cited as paradigmatic for Paul's primarily eschatological understanding of the Spirit. Yet it seems significant that these figures appear relatively late in the Pauline correspondence, and significant that ἀρραβών first makes its appearance in 2 Corinthians. Admittedly, neither ἀρραβών nor ἀπαρχή are used by Paul in 1 Corinthians, where Paul responds at length to the inquiry περὶ δὲ τῶν πνευματικῶν.[1] The situation faced by Paul in 2 Corinthians (both 1–9 and 10–13) is not entirely different from that which he faced in writing 1 Corinthians. Throughout, Corinthian enthusiasm was inseparable from criticism of Paul's own ministry, and a defence of the pattern of his ministry (1 Cor. 4.9-13; 2 Cor. 4.7-15; 6.3-10; 12.7-10) runs throughout this correspondence. The point here which is crucial for this argument is that the pattern of power-in-weakness, expressed in these passages,[2] is inseparable from Paul's eschatological understanding of the faith, classically expressed in yet another polemical passage, 1 Corinthians 13:

> βλέπομεν γὰρ ἄρτι δι' ἐσόπτρου ἐν αἰνίγματι, τότε δὲ πρόσωπον πρὸς πρόσωπον· ἄρτι γινώσκω ἐκ μέρους, τότε δὲ ἐπιγνώσομαι καθὼς καὶ ἐπεγνώσθην (v. 12).

It seems, therefore, that Paul's twofold use of ἀρραβών with πνεῦμα in 2 Corinthians is to be regarded as part of his response to Corinthian enthusiasm, rather than illustrative of a more general eschatological understanding of the Spirit. His polemical/apologetic use of πνεῦμα, particularly in vindicating the Gentile mission and in his conflicts with the Judaizers, is primary; the eschatological emphasis is secondary.[3]

1. The use of περί once again (1 Cor. 12.1) indicates that Paul is addressing one of *their* concerns. (Cf. the use of πνευματικός in 1 Cor. 2.13-15.) It is impossible to be certain whether πνευματικῶν at 12.1 is masculine or neuter, but that does not affect the argument here.

2. Not so much in 1 Cor. 4.9-13, where the emphasis falls on the weakness and foolishness of the apostle.

3. Strack–Billerbeck offer precedents in the Old Testament for the use of ἀρραβών, and also examples of later Jewish usage, but give no examples with 'spirit'.

The evidence of the letter to the Romans need not detain us long. This is obviously not because πνεῦμα is unimportant, but because some sections of Romans comprise 'recycled' material which Paul had used in earlier letters ('emotion recollected in tranquillity'?). Thus Romans also provides evidence of Paul's apologetic use of πνεῦμα (15.18-19), the polemical contrast between γράμμα and πνεῦμα (2.29 and 7.6), between σάρξ and πνεῦμα (8.2, 4, 5, 6, 9, 13), the link of the Spirit with 'adoption' (8.14-16; cf Gal. 4.4-6), the categorizing of the Spirit as τὴν ἀπαρχήν (8.23;[1] cf. 2 Cor. 1.22; 5.5), and finally, the reference to the Spirit's help in prayer (8.26-27; here v. 27 seems to have some affinity with 1 Cor. 2.10).[2] If Käsemann[3] and others are correct in seeing this section of Romans as dealing with misunderstandings arising from glossolalia, then the eschatological understanding of the Spirit, expressed particularly in 8.23, is once again part of Paul's response to some of the problems engendered by Christian enthusiasm. Even if enthusiasm of the Corinthian kind were not a problem at Rome, Rom. 8.18-27, which include several themes found in the Corinthian letters[4] have fewer references to the Spirit (vv. 23, 26 [twice] 27) than the earlier section of the chapter (vv. 1-17), with its recycling of the polemical σάρξ/πνεῦμα contrast first developed in Galatians.

In sum, I suggest that Paul's use of the word πνεῦμα is predominantly polemical and/or apologetic, and that the eschatological emphasis of the Spirit as 'seal' (ἀρραβών) and 'firstfruits' (ἀπαρχή) was a relatively late development in Paul's thought, constituting part of his considered response to the excesses of Christian enthusiasm at Corinth and, perhaps, at Rome.

But what of Jewish traditions about the Spirit?[5] Here we note the conclusions of Marie Isaacs in her book *The Concept of the Spirit.* In a section of her study entitled 'πνεῦμα as an Eschatological Category in Contemporary Judaism' she writes that Jewish Diaspora writers 'were not primarily orientated towards eschatological thinking, arguing that the

1. Strack–Billerbeck, *Kommentar*, III, p. 255, list no entries under this verse.

2. The use of ἐραυνῶ in both letters here is noteworthy.

3. Käsemann, *Romans*, pp. 239-42.

4. In addition to 8.23 (2 Cor. 1.22 and 5.5), we note also the themes of 'image' and 'glory' (8.29-30; cf. 2 Cor. 4.4 and 3.18) and of the sufferings of the apostle (8.35-39; cf. the 'power-in-weakness' passages cited above, and 2 Cor. 12.10, which is the closest parallel with Rom. 8.35).

5. See also Appendix 1.

Spirit was more often associated with the past rather than the future activity of God',[1] although Isaacs goes on to note that Philo still thought of the Spirit as 'a permanent principle at work in the present, both in man and in the universe'. For Diaspora writers this is not very surprising. Isaacs, however, draws a similar conclusion about the place of the Spirit in the thought of Palestinian Judaism: 'What is striking...is the minor role played by "*ruach*" in the eschatological thinking of Palestinian Judaism'.[2] A full discussion of this question cannot be given here. Yet there *is* a dimension of Jewish thinking about the Spirit which is very significant for our understanding of the function of πνεῦμα in the thought of Paul, and to that I now turn.

W.D. Davies, over a number of years, has drawn attention to the place of 'The Land' in the theology of Judaism. In his classic study *Paul and Rabbinic Judaism* Davies, commenting on rabbinic references to the absence of the Spirit from Israel, writes: 'A sinful nation is no longer a suitable environment for the Holy Spirit'.[3] Davies goes on to comment on rabbinic passages where 'the geographical incidence of the Holy Spirit' is discussed. Quoting the work of H. Parzen, Davies writes 'we must bear in mind that Palestine is the Holy Land. Therefore it is the proper place for Revelation. Foreign lands are from the Rabbinic viewpoint "impure"; consequently not suitable for Divine Revelation.'[4] The broader question of 'the Land' in Jewish theology was a subject to which Davies returned in his book *The Gospel and the Land*. Here he links the emphasis on the land in Acts with this particular strand of Jewish thought, arguing that 'geographic limits to "the Spirit" are transcended' (i.e. from Acts onwards).[5] Jn 3.8 and 4.19-24 are, thinks Davies, to be explained in the same way.[6]

Other scholars have also noted this strand of Jewish thought. Sjöberg writes, 'The Spirit cannot work in unclean localities' and hence not outside Israel.[7] Similarly, Strack–Billerbeck[8] in their comment on the

1. Isaacs, *Concept*, p. 82.
2. Isaacs, *Concept*, p. 84.
3. Davies, *Paul*, p. 206.
4. Davies, *Paul*, p. 206.
5. W.D. Davies, *The Gospel and the Land* (Berkeley: University of California Press, 1974), pp. 273-75.
6. Davies, *Gospel*, p. 302, and especially n. 23.
7. Sjöberg, 'The Spirit in Palestinian Judaism', *TWNT*, VI, p. 383 cites

astonishment of the Jews present at the giving of the Spirit to Gentiles (Acts 10.45) write that their surprise was due to two prevailing maxims *(Sätze)*: (a) God dwelt in, and revealed Himself in only Israel, and, if in a foreign land, only in and to the Israelites living there, (b) in the days of the messiah no proselyte will be adopted.

The rabbinic text most frequently cited or quoted in this context is *Mekilta Exodus* 12.1:

> God spoke to Moses in Egypt, outside the city: and why did he not speak to him in the city? Because it was full of abominations and idols. Though God spoke to some of the prophets outside Palestine, He spoke only in a clean place near water, as in Daniel 8.2: 'And I was in the stream Ulai'; and in 10.4: 'And I was by the side of the great river which is Tigris'; and Ezekiel 1.3: 'The word of the Lord came expressly unto Ezekiel the priest, the son of Buzi, in the land of the Chaldeans by the river Chebar'.[1]

The same thought occurs elsewhere, in *Mekilta Pisha* 1:

> You can learn from the following that the *Shekinah* does not reveal itself outside of the land. It is said: 'But Jonah rose up to flee unto Tarshish from the presence of the Lord' (Jonah 1.3)... But Jonah thought 'I will go outside of the land, where the *shekinah* does not reveal itself'.[2]

(It seems that the terms 'Holy Spirit' and *shekinah*, while not identical, had much in common: 'Both are frequently used as synonyms for God, and are to be so interpreted in Tannaitic texts'[3].)

W.D. Davies, in a third contribution to this theme,[4] argues that the geographical extent of the Spirit's operations was a particular concern in the *Mekilta*, wondering whether this was a response to the spread of

M.Exod. 12.1, Strack–Billerbeck, *Kommentar*, I, p. 643 and the article by Parzen referred to above.

8. Strack–Billerbeck, *Kommentar*, II, p. 705.

1. The translation here is that given in Davies, *Paul*, pp. 206-207 n. 6, quoting from A. Büchler.

2. J.Z. Lauterbach (trans.), *Mekilta* (Philadelphia: Jewish Publication Society of America, 1933–35), pp. 6-7.

3. A. Marmorstein, *Studies in Jewish Theology* (Oxford: Oxford University Press, 1950), p. 130. Cf. Davies, *Paul*, p. 214. See also, however, Davies's brief comments on the *shekinah* and the Spirit in the article on the *Mekilta* referred to below. Here Davies quotes *Mekilta Pisha* 14, which refers to the *shekinah* going into exile with Israel (pp. 77-78).

4. 'Reflections on the Spirit in the Mekilta', reprinted in Davies, *Studies*, pp. 72-83.

Christianity. (He recognizes that the *Mekilta* is one of the oldest of the Tannaitic *Midrashim*, and for that reason particularly important for the understanding of the New Testament.) Several passages, for example, seem to reflect the view that '*where* a person prays or God speaks is important'.[1] Davies goes on to quote extensively from *Pisha* 1 (from which I quoted two passages in the paragraph above) and comments: 'In this section the fact of prophecy outside the land is squarely faced and its seriousness as a problem recognized'.[2] Davies goes on to contrast what he calls the 'almost complete absence' of references to the Spirit in the *Midrash Rabbah* on the very Exodus passages which are commented on in the *Mekilta*.[3] Davies's own suggestion for this striking difference is that the older materials preserved in the *Mekilta* were 'more directly influenced by the spread of Christianity than those preserved in later *Midrasim*'.[4] In short, 'early Christianity radically challenged the view that the Spirit was inextricably related to the land of Israel'.[5]

In the light of this rabbinic evidence, and the arguments of Davies based upon it, I suggest that the polemical function of πνεῦμα at so many points in Paul's letters was due to Jewish (and perhaps Jewish-Christian) scepticism about whether the Spirit of God normally (or to any great extent) operated outside Palestine. References to the Spirit as a gift of the End Time are not lacking in Jewish sources (although in Appendix 1 it will be argued that they are not as plentiful as has often been assumed), but it is the debate about the geographical extent of the Spirit's operations, expressed especially clearly in the *Mekilta*, which fits the Pauline evidence better.

This explanation of the function of πνεῦμα in Paul's writings also coheres with the paucity of pre-Pauline references to the Spirit. (A fuller discussion of this question must be sought in the Appendix.) Here, however, it may be pointed out by way of example that if the quotation from Joel about the outpouring of the Spirit 'in the last days'

1. Davies, *Studies*, p. 73.
2. Davies, *Studies*, p. 75.
3. Davies, *Studies*, p. 80. Cf. S. Sandmel, *Judaism and Christian Beginnings* (Oxford: Oxford University Press, 1978), pp. 174-75, who comments on the frequency of 'the Holy Spirit' in the Old Testament (presumably finding 'the Holy Spirit' in the Old Testament when the precise phrase does not occur).
4. Davies, *Studies*, p. 82.
5. Davies, *Studies*, quoted p. 160.

(Acts 2.17-21) is basically Lucan rather than pre-Pauline,[1] then the Gentile mission spearheaded by Paul may well have been the reason why 'the Spirit' became an issue in Christian theology.

It may be correct to see the incident at Antioch, referred to by Paul in Gal. 2.11-14, as a turning point. Of course, Syrian Antioch was outside the land of Israel, but in the earliest period of the Church the framework of reference was still entirely Jewish. The nickname 'Christian' (Acts 11.26) may indicate that at this stage they were still regarded as a Jewish sect. (Was this possibly why Paul never uses the term?) Paul's confrontation with Peter, however, may have been a turning point, not so much in the life and practice of the Antiochene church, since on this occasion Paul lost, if not the argument, the support of the other Jewish Christians including Barnabas (Gal. 2.13), but rather a turning point in his own thought and ministry. From this time onwards Paul's stance became more radical, and his attitude towards Judaism more polemical. It is from this period onwards, and for these polemical reasons, that 'the Spirit' began to play a larger part in his language and in his arguments. As we saw in the survey of references to the Spirit in Paul's earliest letter, 1 Thess. 1.6 and 4.8 already anticipate the conflicts which were to come. But the antitheses of 'flesh' and 'spirit', and of 'letter' and 'spirit' were the product of the Judaizing controversy.[2]

A similar argument to that developed here has been put forward by H. Räisänen.[3] Räisänen argues that Paul at first espoused the 'liberal' Hellenist interpretation of the Law, but after the incident at Antioch his statements about the Law became more and more radical; his

1. 'In the last days', however, is Luke's own addition to the words quoted from Joel.

2. J. Jervell, 'Das Volk des Geistes', in J. Jervell and W.A. Meeks (eds.), *God's Christ and his People* (Oslo: Universitetsforlaget, 1977), pp. 87-106, makes a similar point, but emphasizes more strongly that the γράμμα/πνεῦμα antithesis belonged to one phase of his activity (pp. 88-90). Jervell here (pp. 90-91) and elsewhere in his writings develops the view that Jewish influence in the Church increased, rather than decreased after the Jerusalem council. That is possible, but more questionable is his view that the different pictures of Paul in the New Testament go back to Paul himself. ('Der unbekannte Paulus', pp. 34-35, in Pederson, *Paulinische Literatur*). Although we may concede the point that Paul's personality was undoubtedly complex, this view probably underestimates Paul's increasingly radical stance *vis-à-vis* the law.

3. H. Räisänen, 'Paul's Conversion and the Development of his View of the Law', *NTS* 33.3 (1987), pp. 404-19.

'justification' language, too, belongs to this later stage.[1]

Paul's use of the word πνεῦμα in 2 Corinthians 3, therefore, is not unusual. Here, as elsewhere in Paul's writings, it reflects his response to Jewish and/or Jewish-Christian doubts as to whether his Gentile mission was 'of God'. The polemical emphasis is more common than the eschatological. The two emphases, of course, are not mutually exclusive, but if we are asking what the function of πνεῦμα is, the evidence indicates clearly that a polemical function is the predominantly Pauline usage.

4. *Conclusions*

A substantial part of the Pauline corpus is polemical or apologetic or both. (The two terms clearly overlap, since attacking his opponents often involved defending his apostleship, and *vice versa*.) We should therefore expect to find that God-language in Paul sometimes has a polemical function.[2] This chapter has suggested that 2 Cor. 2.14–4.6 is a section of Paul's *apologia* to Corinth (chs. 1–9) in which language both about God and about the Spirit are used in a polemical way.

The survey of Paul's use of θεός (section 2) concluded that Paul's self-defence involved stressing both his accountability before God, and God as arbiter and judge of Paul's ministry. Various expressions were used in this way: τῷ θεῷ (2.15), ἐκ θεοῦ and κατέναντι θεοῦ (2.17), πρὸς τὸν θεόν (3.4), ἐκ τοῦ θεοῦ (3.5) and ἐνώπιον τοῦ θεοῦ (4.2), as well as the emphatic use of θεός in the thanksgiving of 2.14 and in the conclusion to this section (4.6). It would take us too far afield to survey all such occurrences of God-language in Paul's writings, but they are to be found in other letters (for example 1 Thess. 2.4; 3.9; Gal. 1.20).

Secondly, Paul's use of the word πνεῦμα in this section of 2 Corinthians was analysed, in the recognition that πνεῦμα in Jewish tradition must be considered a God-word, and therefore an extension of Paul's God-language. It might be asked why, if 'Spirit' was a God-word, did Paul not simply use the one word θεός rather than θεός and πνεῦμα? The same question, of course, could be put to other New Testament writers, and indeed to many Jewish writers. In fact, several Jewish concepts such as 'Wisdom', 'the *Shekinah*' and 'glory' belong in

1. Räisänen, 'Paul's Conversion', pp. 414-15. Cf. Jervell's observation of the link between justification and the Spirit in Paul's thought (Jervell and Meeks, *God's Christ*, p. 88). *Contra* Seifrid, *Justification*.

2. Cf. the work of Moxnes, *Theology*, referred to in the Introduction, p. 19.

the same category as 'Spirit'. Of them also it could be said that they denote 'a reality which comes from God, which in some sense represents the presence of God, and yet which is not identical with God'.[1]

The experiential roots of this diversification in God-language are clearly important. If God is not experienced or perceived as an undifferentiated monad, or if the creed behind the language is not a vague kind of deism, then a development of words denoting God's presence and activity is both natural and necessary. (The variety of Philo's God-language provides an interesting contrast here.) What is important for the purposes of this study is that in the Old Testament and Judaism, the concept of the *ruaḥ*, or πνεῦμα of God denoted the divine energy or power, and sometimes the divine presence.[2]

πνεῦμα, then, in Paul's writings, is clearly a God-word, but the survey in this chapter has shown that πνεῦμα, like θεός in this section of 2 Corinthians has a polemical function. Section 3 of this chapter showed that this polemical use of πνεῦμα is typical and distinctive of Paul. The gift of the Spirit was no doubt perceived and understood as an eschatological phenomenon, but it acquired its distinctively Pauline meaning in the context of the mission to the Gentiles. As such, it signifies God's mission to 'the unclean'. Thus, according to Paul what is most characteristic of the Spirit—that is, the outflowing energy and activity of God—is his going out to and living in 'the unclean', not thereby acquiescing in or leaving untransformed their uncleanness,[3] but changing them 'from glory into glory' (2 Cor. 3.18).

No representation of Paul's understanding of God would be complete without this polemical dimension, inseparable as it is from its origin in the mission to the Gentiles. It is not difficult to see here a connection with the ministry of Jesus himself. AJ.M. Wedderburn[4] rightly says that both Jesus and Paul showed 'an openness to the outsider...in the name

1. See p. 156 above. The writer of Jn 1.1 wrestled with the same theological problem.

2. Thus Hermann, *Kyrios und Pneuma*, p. 128: 'The Spirit is the indication of God's activity... It can be used simply as an expression for God himself and for his presence.' (Hermann goes on to quote Ps. 139.7.)

3. This point was contested by the Judaizers on the grounds that to be uncircumcised was to be unclean.

4. A.J.M. Wedderburn, 'Paul and Jesus: Similarity and Continuity', *NTS* 34.2 (1988).

of their God'.[1] Wedderburn's own conclusions are very similar to the point made here: the Spirit is to Gentiles as Jesus' presence was to outcasts.[2]

It is important, once again, not to lapse into facile and inaccurate contrasts between Judaism and Christianity, but the Judaizing controversy itself and the ethnocentric tendencies in Jewish religion (not least the emphasis on the land) indicate that some kind of contrast must be made. The kind of monotheism which Paul preached was an *inclusive* kind (Rom. 3.29-30) and by its very inclusive character it generated controversy and conflict, challenging, as it did, the Israel-centred character of the faith from which it sprang.

If the arguments of this chapter are sound, a number of important consequences for our understanding of early Christian theology, and indeed of Christian theology in general, follow. First, the *theological* connection between Jesus and Paul is a close one. There is a close relationship between Jesus' mission to Jewish outcasts and Paul's mission to the Gentiles. Secondly, the Christian understanding and experience of the Holy Spirit were inextricably related from the very beginning to mission. It is significant that the resurrection, the giving of the Spirit and a commission to take the gospel to the Gentiles are closely associated in Matthew 28 and Luke 24 . It would not be going too far to suggest that 'mission' is *the* characteristic of the God proclaimed by Jesus and by Paul. And if it is correct that 'the Spirit' became a vital part of Christian self-understanding and self-expression in the Judaizing controversy, it would seem that an authentically *Christian* understanding of the Spirit really develops only in the context of a mission to the outcast and the unclean.

It seems clear that the life and death of Jesus were foundational to this understanding of God and the Spirit. In the passage studied here, two

1. Wedderburn, 'Paul and Jesus', p. 167.

2. Wedderburn, 'Paul and Jesus', pp. 171-72. Wedderburn shares Räisänen's view that the language of justification was 'a relatively late development in a particular polemical context'. (He also notes the function of 'the Spirit' in Paul's defence of his mission to the Gentiles.) Seifrid (*Justification*, pp. 141-46) has challenged this view, arguing that there is no evidence that Paul ever preached the Law after his conversion, and that the message of the crucified messiah itself constituted an intrinsic challenge to Torah and the social order. It seems likely, however, that the encounter at Antioch (Gal. 2.11-14) was the spur which led Paul to work out *the full implications* of the cross.

verses in particular, 4.4 and 4.6, make clear both the *christological* basis of the gospel and the way in which the Old Testament concept of the divine δόξα is redefined *christologically*. Thus there is further evidence here of a new understanding of God deriving from the cross and resurrection. The interaction between Paul's language about God and his language about Christ will be examined in Chapter 5. But first, another use of God-language in his letters must be explored.

Chapter 4

GOD-LANGUAGE IN PAULINE PARAENESIS

1. *The Background, Sources and Form of Pauline Paraenesis*

In recent years a good deal of work has been done on the form and structure of Paul's letters. The view of Deissmann that Paul was an undisciplined, spontaneous letter-writer has now been discredited.[1] Instead it has become clear that Paul adapted and used the epistolary conventions of his day. J.L. White, in particular, building upon and refining the work of earlier scholars such as Koskenniemi and Schubert, has shown how Paul's letters, especially their opening and closing sections, share with contemporary papyri many of the formulaic or quasi-formulaic constructions which featured in the tightly-structured epistolary framework of the time.[2] Other scholars, and White himself, have demonstrated how Paul appropriated and adapted particular epistolary forms. Thus the apostolic greeting in Paul's letters is expressed in more scriptural language instead of the standard Greek χαίρειν.[3] Similarly, T.Y. Mullins has shown that the language of official petitions is used but at the same time modified by Paul.[4]

1. J.L. White, *The Form and Function of the Body of the Greek Letter* (Columbia, MO: SBL, 1972), pp. 43-46, building on the work of R.W. Funk and others.

2. J.L. White, *The Form and Structure of the Official Petition: A Study in Greek Epistolography* (Columbia, MO: SBL, 1972), pp. 93-94. Cf. W.G. Doty, *Letters in Primitive Christianity* (Philadelphia: Fortress Press, 1973), pp. 11-12 and 22-23.

3. J. Lieu, '"Grace to you and Peace": The Apostolic Greeting', *BJRL* 68.1 (1985), pp. 161-78. Thus also M. Dibelius, *A Fresh Approach to the New Testament and Early Christian Literature* (Westport, CT: Greenwood, 1979 [1936]), p. 142. Doty , *Letters*, pp. 22-23, argues that the *shalom* greeting is the only clear evidence of direct borrowing by Paul from Jewish epistolary materials.

4. T.Y. Mullins, 'Petition as a Literary Form', *NovT* 5 (1962), pp. 46-54. See also White, *Form and Structure*, for an analysis of many letters of petition from the

A rather different kind of adaptation seems to lie behind the paraenetic sections of the epistles. Here at least two (perhaps more) streams converge. First, there can be little doubt that Christian paraenesis originated in a non-epistolary framework;[1] the heavy borrowing by Christians from Jewish paraenesis[2] confirms the point. Secondly, paraenesis in the wider Hellenistic world seems to have been a technical term in rhetoric: it denoted the 'moral or application' of either hortatory or epideictic speeches.[3] There is evidence that such rhetorical techniques were being studied and taught in Pharisaic schools in Palestine.[4] In addition to these two traditions, we should note the argument of J.M. Robinson[5] should be noted that Paul in his letters created a hybrid form by grafting liturgical materials on to the traditional epistolary form, and the view of Doty[6] that 'the Jewish sermonic tradition' and the popular 'street preaching' of the Hellenistic world were two contributory factors to Paul's paraenesis. Finally, it is relevant to observe that letters in the Graeco-Roman world had become a frequent means of moral teaching and advice.[7]

There is thus an impressive consensus among scholars that Paul used and adapted existing epistolary conventions. Roetzel goes so far as to argue that the alterations Paul made to the traditional epistolary forms 'tell us most' about Paul's self-understanding, intentions and theology.[8]

papyri; White argues that such letters have a common structure, and suggests that there is the basis here of a methodology for understanding the New Testament letters.

1. White, *Form and Function*, p. 44, citing Dibelius.

2. Examples are given below, although the *caveat* of V.P. Furnish, *Theology and Ethics in Paul* (Nashville: Abingdon, 1968), p. 27, should be noted, that parallels do not necessarily indicate 'genetic relationships'.

3. G. Lyons, *Pauline Autobiography—Towards a New Understanding* (Atlanta: Scholars Press, 1985), p. 220.

4. Lyons, *Pauline Autobiography*, p. 6, citing the work of H. Fischel.

5. Cited in C.J. Roetzel, *The Letters of Paul—Conversations in Context* (London: SCM Press, 1983), p. 34. Cf. also in this context the study of O'Brien, *Introductory Thanksgivings*, who endorses Schubert's earlier finding that the form of the Pauline thanksgiving is Hellenistic, but differs from Schubert's view that Paul was Ἑλληνιστὴς ἐξ Ἑλληνιστῶν, and the implication that the thanksgivings were merely formal and epistolary.

6. Doty, *Letters*, pp. 22-24.

7. A.J. Malherbe, *Moral Exhortation: A Graeco-Roman Source-Book* (Philadelphia: Westminster Press, 1986), pp. 68, 79.

8. Roetzel, *Letters of Paul*, p. 29. Roetzel goes on to illustrate this with reference to the salutation, arguing that in Romans 'we see Paul's most original

Paul's creativity in this area is an important pointer towards his use of paraenetic material. Is it possible that Paul showed the same freedom here as in his use of epistolary conventions? This has an important bearing on this investigation of God-language in Pauline paraenesis. In particular, I am concerned with the question of whether much of this teaching is Paul's own creation *ex nihilo* as it were, or whether he is simply quoting catechetical traditions, or whether the truth lies somewhere in between.

There has been a tendency in New Testament scholarship to stress the traditional character of Paul's paraenetical material. Dibelius was a leading exponent of this view.[1] E.G. Selwyn has been a notable advocate of the view that Paul, like other New Testament letter-writers, was drawing on a primitive Christian catechesis.[2] Other scholars have suggested that behind individual passages an original source may sometimes be discerned. Thus Daube, followed by W.D. Davies, argued for a Semitic original behind the imperatival participles in Rom. 12.6-19.[3] This view however is rendered questionable by Furnish's argument that Greek examples of imperatival participles are nearer Pauline usage than the Tannaitic parallels quoted by Daube.[4] A similar argument has been put forward by O.L. Yarborough, who points to the close similarity between 1 Thess. 4.3b-5, on the one hand, and *T. Levi* 9.9-10 and Tob. 4.12 on the other.[5] Apart from the occurrence of πορνεία in all three passages, there are no verbal similarities between them; although the teaching is similar in substance, the evidence falls far short of

adaptation of the conventional letter opening'. Cf. J.C. Beker, *Paul the Apostle* (Edinburgh: T. & T. Clark, 1980), pp. 23-24. An interesting contrast with Paul is provided in J.G. Winter's study of later Christian Letters (J.G. Winter, *Life and Letters in the Papyri* [University of Michigan Press, 1933], especially pp. 136-91). Winter shows that many letters by Christians in the early centuries of the Christian era were 'Christianized' at only a very superficial level.

1. See, for example, the introduction in M. Dibelius and H. Greeven, *James* (Philadelphia: FortressPress, 1976 [1964]).

2. E.G. Selwyn, *1 Peter* (London: Macmillan, 1949), pp. 18-23, pp. 363-466. Selwyn was drawing on the earlier work of P. Carrington, *The Primitive Christian Catachism* (Cambridge: Cambridge University Press, 1940).

3. Most recently in D. Daube, *Ancient Jewish Law* (Leiden: Brill, 1981), pp. 82-86.

4. Furnish, *Theology and Ethics*, p. 39.

5. O.L. Yarborough, *Not Like the Gentiles: Marriage Rules in the Letters of Paul* (Atlanta: Scholars Press, 1985), pp. 69-70.

indicating, let alone proving, a common catachetical tradition.

In the light of these views, a number of points can be made. First, it is probable that there are four sources behind or contributing to Pauline paraenesis: the logia of Jesus, Jewish paraenesis, early Christian paraenesis, and Hellenistic paraenesis. The extent of the influence of the teaching of Jesus on Pauline paraenesis has been much discussed[1] and cannot be explored in detail here. Despite a few explicit allusions[2] and a few striking similarities with the teaching in the Synoptics,[3] the evidence as a whole suggests either that Paul has drawn on the teaching of Jesus very little, or that he has used it in a very free way, adapting it to his own purposes.

The possibility that Paul drew on early Christian paraenesis is, of course, a strong one. Since he quotes or uses early credal formulations (e.g. 1 Cor. 15.3-7), it is likely that he used early paraenetic traditions as well. The reference to διδαχή in Rom. 6.17 is another indication that this is so. To discern pre-Pauline Christian paraenetic tradition is difficult, however, since Jewish and Christian paraenesis clearly overlapped a good deal.[4] My particular concern here is *how* Paul used the traditions from which he drew, but here, in anticipation of more detailed exegesis below, it may be said that none of the alleged parallels in Jewish or Christian paraenesis suggests that Paul was simply quoting fixed traditions. The tables of parallels given by Selwyn[5] point to a common fund of motifs and even of language, but *verbatim* parallels are few.[6]

As for Paul drawing on Hellenistic paraenesis, this clearly cannot be ruled out. The work of A. Malherbe has drawn attention to similarities

1. See the brief discussion in J.M.G. Barclay, *Obeying the Truth: A Study of Paul's Ethics in Galatians* (Edinburgh: T. & T. Clark, 1988), pp. 129-30, especially n. 72.

2. 1 Cor. 7.10; 9.14; 11.23-26.

3. E.g. Rom. 12.14 and Mt. 5.44.

4. See the discussion in section 4 on *The Testaments of the Twelve Patriarchs*.

5. Selwyn, *1 Peter*, pp. 370-449.

6. The kind of *verbatim* parallels which exist between the *Didache* (1-6) and the *Epistle of Barnabas* (18-20) are not to be found in the New Testament, except in the *Haustafeln* and the Synoptic Gospels, but it is worth noting that even in the *Didache* and *Barnabas*, where the two writers are probably drawing on a common source, whether originally Jewish or Christian, the differences between them are still very great, suggesting that the authors have adapted this source freely for their own purpose.

between Christians and their pagan neighbours.[1] In a study of paraenesis in 1 Thessalonians, Malherbe suggests this epistle may be illuminated not only by parallels with Jewish advice to converts, but also by parallels with Graeco-Roman traditions of moral exhortation.[2] Here again, however, we need to be on our guard against 'parallelomania'. Malherbe himself, in the article just cited, draws attention to ways in which Paul modifies the Graeco-Roman hortatory tradition.[3]

Some recent studies, in fact, have suggested that Paul, while sometimes drawing on earlier traditions, adapted them and integrated them thoroughly into a new context. Thus H. Boers, while following Dibelius in regarding 1 Thess. 4.1-8, and probably 5.16-22 as traditional, concludes that 4.9-10a, 10b-12, 13-18 and 5.1-11 are probably Pauline.[4] B.H. Brinsmead, in a study of Galatians, reached a similar conclusion about Gal. 5.19-23, claiming that even the lists of virtues and vices have been modified to fit the Galatian context.[5] Another recent study of Galatians makes a similar point: the really interesting question is 'how Paul uses the traditions he inherits and what meaning they acquire within his social and theological context'.[6]

Researches, therefore, into the background of Paul's letter-writing, (particularly the epistolary conventions of the time) and into the possible sources from which he drew his paraenetic teaching have shown that Paul, while using contemporary literary conventions and drawing freely on the traditions of moral teaching available to him, adapted both to suit his particular purposes. The task of this chapter will be to investigate how he used language about God in these contexts, but first some final points may be made about the form of Pauline paraenesis.

David Daube, in his lectures on ancient Jewish law to which reference has already been made, devoted the third of his lectures to the theme 'The Form is the Message'.[7] Daube argued that the form of law reveals

1. Malherbe, *Moral Exhortation.*

2. A.J. Malherbe, 'Exhortation in 1 Thessalonians', *NovT* 25.3 (1983), *passim.*

3. Malherbe, 'Exhortation', e.g. pp. 248-49.

4. H. Boers, 'The Form-Critical Study of Paul's Letters. 1 Thessalonians as a Case-Study', *NTS* 22 (1976), pp. 140-58, p. 154.

5. B.H. Brinsmead, *Galatians: Dialogical Response to Opponents* (Chico, CA: Scholars Press, 1982), pp. 165 and 167.

6. Barclay, *Obeying the Truth*, p. 176.

7. Daube, *Law*, pp. 71-116.

something about its setting and presuppositions. Thus the direct address 'Thou shalt not' of some of the ten commandments reflected an absolute obligation, with sanctions only occasionally mentioned. It is not the details of Daube's argument which matter here, but the thesis itself: the form is the message. I shall be investigating in more detail what might be called the theological grammar of Paul's paraenesis, but here I note two more general but basic points. First, Paul's paraenesis is conveyed by means of letters and, except in one instance, letters to *communities*. This in itself is a reflection of the theological presuppositions behind the writing. As will be shown in section 5 (in the comparison of Pauline with Hellenistic paraenesis) the latter is much more individualistic and autonomous. Secondly, as Furnish argued in his study of Pauline ethics, theology and paraenesis are intricately bound up together: in this respect, too, the form is the message. Furnish concludes his study by singling out what he considers to to be the three basic motifs of Paul's ethic: his eschatology, Christology, and what he calls Paul's 'radical theocentrism'.[1] The last of these will be the concern of the sections that follow.

2. *God-Language in Romans 12.1–15.13*

Opinions differ among scholars about the extent to which Paul is drawing on traditional material in Romans 12. In the previous section we noted the view of Daube about the imperatival participles in vv. 9-19, and although there seemed grounds for questioning his view that Paul was using a Semitic source here, it is still possible that vv. 9-13 are basically traditional material, lightly redacted by Paul. This may be true, in fact, of most of the chapter. The verses which have strongest claim to be Paul's own composition are vv. 1-2, which constitute a kind of headline for the whole of the paraenesis as far as 15.13.[2] It is noteworthy, therefore, that in these opening verses θεός is used three times:

> παρακαλῶ οὖν ὑμᾶς, ἀδελφοί, διὰ τῶν οἰκτιρμῶν **τοῦ θεοῦ** παραστῆσαι τὰ σώματα ὑμῶν θυσίαν ζῶσαν ἁγιάν εὐάρεστον **τῷ θεῷ**, τὴν λογικὴν λατρείαν ὑμῶν· καὶ μη συσχηματίζεσθε τῷ αἰῶνι τούτῳ, ἀλλὰ μεταμορφοῦσθε τῇ ἀνακαινώσει τοῦ νοὸς εἰς τὸ δοκιμάζειν ὑμᾶς τί τὸ θέλημα **τοῦ θεοῦ**, τὸ ἀγαθὸν καὶ εὐάρεστον καὶ τέλειον.

1. Furnish, *Theology and Ethics*, p. 214.
2. Michel, *An Die Römer*, p. 365, describes vv. 1-2 as 'a kind of headline for, and definition of the Christian life'.

The οὖν of v. 1 indicates a connection with what has gone before, although it is difficult to be sure whether Paul is linking this paraenesis with the whole of the epistle thus far or merely with chs. 9–11. The same question applies to the phrase διὰ τῶν οἰκτιρμῶν τοῦ θεοῦ: some scholars believe that this refers back to the argument of the preceding three chapters,[1] others to chs. 1–11.[2] Most commentators recognize the importance of the phrase, but differ in their interpretation of it. Käsemann compares Rom. 15.30, and translates διὰ by 'in the name of'.[3] Furnish interprets διὰ as instrumental, explaining this, rather oddly, as Paul the instrument 'by which God exhorts'.[4] A survey of the occurrences of παρακαλῶ or παρακαλοῦμεν in Paul suggests that the use of παρακαλῶ here is an example of the official petition language found in the papyri. Here, in the διὰ clause, Paul has added what Mullins calls a 'divine authority phrase'. (The use of παρακαλοῦμεν in 2 Cor. 6.1 makes this particularly clear, since Paul has just referred to God's own *paraklesis*: ὡς τοῦ θεοῦ παρακαλοῦντος δι' ἡμῶν (2 Cor. 5.20).[5]

In Rom. 12.1 the divine authority phrase is emphatic.[6] As Wilckens says, by virtue of this phrase Rom. 12.1 is a statement about the basis and nature of authority in the church:

1. Thus, for example, Barrett, *Romans*, pp. 230-31.
2. Thus, for example, Cranfield, *Romans*, II pp. 595-96.
3. Käsemann, *Romans*, p. 326.
4. Furnish, *Theology and Ethics*, pp. 101-102.
5. Elsewhere Paul urges the Roman Christians 'through our Lord Jesus Christ' and 'through the love of the Spirit' to 'struggle' with him in prayer before God that he might be rescued from 'the unbelievers in Judaea' (Rom. 15.30); at 1 Cor. 1.10 he urges harmony upon the Corinthians 'through the name of our Lord Jesus Christ' that they should all speak the same. In 2 Cor. 10.1 Paul urges the Corinthians 'through the meekness and gentleness of Christ' that he 'might not have to show boldness' when he is with them. In 1 Thess. 4.1 Paul urges the Thessalonians 'in the Lord Jesus' (ἐν κυρίῳ Ἰησοῦ) to advance still further in the kind of living they had learned from Paul. By contrast, Paul uses the same verb without any 'divine authority' phrase at Rom. 16.17, 1 Cor. 4.16 and 16.15, 2 Cor. 2.8 and 6.1, Phil. 4.2 and 1 Thess. 4.10 and 5.14. What these verses show is that when Paul is introducing an extended *topos* or a difficult subject, he uses a 'divine authority' phrase (Rom. 12.1 [cf. v. 3]; 15.30; 1 Cor. 1.10, 2 Cor.10.1; 1 Thess. 4.1). But he does not use such a phrase when he is summarizing or concluding such a discussion (1 Cor. 4.16), rounding off a letter (1 Cor. 16.15 and 1 Thess. 5.14, and Rom. 16.17, if this is Pauline), when he is in the middle of a *topos* (2 Cor. 2.8 and 1 Thess. 4.10) or, finally, when he addresses individuals (Phil. 4.2).
6. Käsemann, *Romans*, pp. 326-27.

> in that God's authority, in the strength of which the apostle makes his exhortation, finds its substantial definition in his mercy. Thus the ways and means by which authority in the Church should be maintained are precisely laid down.[1]

This is the only instance in Paul's writings of his use of such a phrase referring to God, rather than to Jesus, and is in keeping with the markedly theocentric character of Romans which was noted in the introductory chapter. Not only does Paul appeal through *God*, but does so by using the Hebraism οἰκτιρμῶν.[2] The stress, therefore, falls on the *continuity* between the old and the new: the connection between the two lies in 'the mercies of God'.

The phrase εὐάρεστον τῷ θεῷ also has a biblical ring about it. The word εὐάρεστον only rarely occurs in secular Greek, and in the LXX only at Wis. 4.10 and 9.10. The verb εὐαρεστῶ, although again rare in secular Greek, occurs 14 times in the LXX, almost always in the religious sense of living a life 'well-pleasing' to God. It is used twice of Enoch (Gen. 5.22, 24), once of Noah (Gen. 6.9) and once of Abraham: καὶ ὤφθη κύριος τῷ Ἄβραμ καὶ εἶπεν αὐτῷ, ἐγώ εἰμι ὁ θεός σου· εὐαρέστει ἐναντίον ἐμοῦ καὶ γίνου ἄμεμπτος (Gen. 17.1). Förster[3] notes that εὐάρεστος is used only once in the New Testament of acceptance by human beings (Tit. 2.9), and only once 'retrospectively' (i.e. the word normally indicates the present or future direction of one's life). Here in Rom. 12.1 the phrase might seem superfluous, coming as it does after ἁγίαν, but the use of εὐάρεστος here and the recurrence of θεός are yet other instances of the 'radical theocentrism' of Paul's thought.

The theocentric character of this opening exhortation is enhanced by a third use of θεός in the phrase τὸ θέλημα τοῦ θεοῦ. The commentators differ over whether the accompanying adjectives are epithets or appositional. Black[4] takes them to be predicates of θέλημα—without, however, explaining what εὐάρεστον might mean. Cranfield, more probably, regards them as appositional, εὐάρεστον being added to correct any possible anthropocentric misunderstanding of τὸ ἀγαθόν.[5] Rom. 12.1-2, with its threefold reference to God, gives Paul's

1. Wilckens, *An die Römer*, III, pp. 2-3.
2. The plural of this word occurs in Ps. 119 (LXX 118).156 (Sanday and Headlam, *Romans*, p. 352).
3. *TWNT*, II, p. 457.
4. Black, *Romans*, p. 151.
5. Cranfield, *Romans*, II, p. 610. Paul does not use the phrase 'the will of God'

introduction to his paraenesis a very theocentric emphasis. The 'mercies of God' are the basis of Paul's appeal and authority; the objective is to please God and to 'prove' his will.

What Paul has done, in fact, is to lay the theological foundations for the rest of the chapter, and probably for the rest of this paraenetical section of Romans. Verse 3 continues:

> Λέγω γὰρ διὰ τῆς χάριτος τῆς δοθείσης μοι παντὶ τῷ ὄντι ἐν ὑμῖν μὴ ὑπερφρονεῖν παρ' ὃ δεῖ φρονεῖν ἀλλὰ φρονεῖν εἰς τὸ σωφρονεῖν, ἑκάστῳ ὡς ὁ θεὸς ἐμέρισεν μέτρον πίστεως.

The connecting γάρ links this sentence, and subsequent verses, firmly with what has gone before, and the διά clause serves as a kind of divine authority phrase in a lower key than that of v. 1: διὰ τῆς χάριτος τῆς δοθείσης μοι (cf. a similar phrase applied in v. 6 to the whole community). The reference to grace, and the phrase ὡς ὁ θεὸς ἐμέρισεν, make divine grace both the reason for the exhortation and the means of fulfilling it.

There is, therefore, no mistaking the very theocentric beginning of Paul's paraenesis here. But in the various units which make up this section of Romans (12.1–15.13) the incidence of God-language (and of κύριος-language) varies. In the remainder of ch. 12 there are few references to God. We have noted the δοθεῖσαν of v. 6, but apart from a possible reference to 'the Lord' in v. 11,[1] the next clear example of God-language occurs in vv. 19-21:

> μὴ ἑαυτοὺς ἐκδικοῦντες, ἀγαπητοί, ἀλλὰ δότε τόπον τῇ ὀργῇ, γέγραπται γάρ· ἐμοὶ ἐκδίκησις, ἐγὼ ἀνταποδώσω, λέγει κύριος. ἀλλὰ ἐὰν πεινᾷ ὁ ἐχθρός σου, ψώμιζε αὐτόν· ἐὰν διψᾷ, πότιζε αυτόν· τοῦτο γὰρ ποιῶν ἄνθρακας πυρὸς σωρεύσεις ἐπὶ τὴν κεφαλὴν αὐτοῦ. μὴ νικῶ ὑπὸ τοῦ κακοῦ ἀλλὰ νίκα ἐν τῷ ἀγαθῷ τὸ κακόν.

very frequently in his letters, and quite seldom in paraenetic contexts. It is used in two opening preambles with reference to Paul's apostleship (significantly, no doubt, in the Corinthian letters, 1 Cor. 1.1 and 2 Cor. 1.1; cf Gal. 1.1 and Col. 1.1); it is used twice with reference to Paul's travel plans (Rom.1.10; 15.32, and, perhaps, with reference to Apollos' travels, 1 Cor. 16.12); it is also used in 2 Cor. 8.5 of the Macedonians giving themselves to the Lord and to Paul (διὰ θελήματος θεοῦ); finally, it is used twice in a paraenetic context in 1 Thessalonians (4.3 and 5.18).

1. Here some important Western MSS have καιρῷ instead of τῷ κυρίῳ. See the discussion in Käsemann, *Romans*, p. 346, who inclines to καιρῶ, translating 'be ready at any moment for service'.

There are two points to be addressed here. First, it seems clear that the words λέγει κύριος are Paul's own addition. They were probably added in order to make the quotation from Deuteronomy (32.35) 'a direct word of God', Paul using the formula 'to accentuate the decree of God'.[1] The second and more difficult question is the meaning of both the Deuteronomy and the Proverbs (25.21-2) quotations in this context. The contents of vv. 19-21 find close parallels in Jewish sources.[2] My concern, however, is the function and meaning of the God-language used here.

Much depends on the meaning of ἀλλά at the beginning of v. 20. Clearly some kind of contrast with the preceding verse is intended. Wilckens[3] writes: 'Whereas in v. 19 the vengeance of divine judgment against the enemy is envisaged, in v. 20 there appears a possibility for the enemy to escape this judgment'. Wilckens concludes that the Christian is thus being exhorted to respond to evil in the way that God in Christ responded to sin (Rom. 5.8). He rightly notes that only this interpretation makes sense of v. 21. This interpretation is also supported by the Targum of Prov. 25.21-2, to which Dunn draws attention.[4] The Targum adds 'on his head, and God will hand him over to you' or 'will make him your friend'.[5]

But if the general thrust and motivation of these verses is clear, what is not so clear is the reference to ὀργή, and to divine ἐκδίκησις. A tension remains between v. 19 and vv. 20-21. It must be said, however, that this tension runs throughout this epistle. An earlier chapter noted

1. Michel, *An die Römer*, pp. 390-91 n. 43.

2. There is a particularly close parallel in *T. Gad*: 'But even if he is devoid of shame and persists in his wickedness, forgive him from the heart and leave vengeance to God' (trans. from Charlesworth, *OT Pseudepigrapha*, I, p. 816. Compare also 1 QS10.17-18 and CD 9.2-5 for the concept of leaving vengeance to God). The Testaments of the Twelve Patriarchs also provide quite a close parallel with v. 21: 'And even if persons plot against him for evil ends, by doing good this man conquers evil' (*T. Benj.* 4.3, trans. Charlesworth, *OT Pseudepigrapha*, I, p. 826).

3. Wilckens, *An die Römer*, III, p. 26.

4. Dunn, *Romans*, II, p. 751.

5. Both translations are given in Strack–Billerbeck, *Kommentar*, III, p. 302. A positive meaning here is made still more probable if, as several commentators suggest (e.g. Dunn, *Romans*, II, p. 751; Michel, p. 392), the image of 'coals of fire' came originally from an Egyptian ritual, symbolizing genuine repentance on the part of the person bearing such coals in a dish on his head. (But, as Michel notes, this may not have been readily comprehensible to the Christians at Rome.)

the parallelism of Rom. 1.17-18. Similarly here, it cannot be concluded that either human or divine 'overcoming evil with good' (and human behaviour here is surely founded on the divine example) renders unnecessary or abolishes the reality of ὀργή. But though that ὀργή remains the inescapable backcloth to all human action, the emphasis here clearly falls on the possibility of the redemption of evil.

In these verses, therefore, traditional God-language is deployed in the context of an ethical command which, though not entirely without Jewish precedents and parallels,[1] has a specific *theological* precedent in the action of God in Christ (Rom. 5.9). It is interesting, however, that Paul uses as a warrant here the familiar Jewish idea of letting God exact punishment, rather than using a theological or christological paradigm, as he does later on in this section (14.3; 15.7).

The views of commentators on Rom. 13.1-7 differ. Michel considers these verses an insertion ('Einlage') in the style of Jewish-Hellenistic wisdom teaching, with no distinctively early Christian motif.[2] Wilckens, however, rejects the view that they have been left unchristianized, arguing that stylistically and in terms of content they fit into the context.[3] The view taken here is that these verses are essentially Pauline. There are notable differences from alleged Jewish parallels, as I shall observe later, and the differences between this passage and 1 Pet. 2.13-17, the closest early Christian parallel, preclude a common source.[4]

Whether they are Pauline or not, these verses are remarkable for the high incidence of God-language. In v. 1 the command to submit to the authorities is followed by the explanation: οὐ γὰρ ἔστιν ἐξουσία εἰ μὴ ὑπὸ θεοῦ, αἱ δὲ οὖσαι ὑπὸ θεοῦ τεταγμέναι εἰσίν. The consequences of resisting the authorities are spelled out in the next sentence: anyone resisting the (secular) authority resists τῇ τοῦ θεοῦ διαταγῇ, and such people will receive judgment.[5] The next imperative ('Do

1. See the discussion in E.P. Sanders and M. Davies, *Studies in the Synoptic Gospels* (London: SCM Press, 1989), pp. 317-23, on the New Testament teaching on 'love enemies; pray for persecutors', and the references to Old Testament and Jewish parallels.

2. Michel, *An die Römer*, p. 366.

3. Wilckens, *An die Römer*, III, p. 30.

4. Thus Wilckens, *An die Römer*, III, p. 31, who argues that the many typically Pauline words in Rom. 13.1-7 mark it out as Paul's own. Cf. E. Best, *1 Peter* (London: Marshall, Morgan & Scott 1971), p. 31, although Best perhaps makes too much of the absence here of imperatival participles.

5. It is uncertain whether κρῖμα here refers to divine or human judgment;

good', v. 3c) is followed by another warranting statement containing the word θεός: καὶ ἕξεις ἔπαινον ἐξ αὐτῆς· θεοῦ γὰρ διάκονός ἐστιν σοὶ εἰς τὸ ἀγαθόν (3d, 4a). Here, and in a closely parallel statement in v. 4d (θεοῦ γὰρ διάκονός ἐστιν...), θεοῦ is placed in an emphatic position. There is yet another example of this use of θεός in a warranting statement: the command to pay taxes is followed by the statement λειτουργοὶ γὰρ θεοῦ εἰσιν εἰς αὐτὸ τοῦτο προσκαρτεροῦντες (v. 6b).

1 Pet. 2.13-17 provides both similarities and contrasts with these details of Paul's God-language here. In 1 Peter the reason given for the submission by Christians πάσῃ ἀνθρωπίνῃ κτίσει is 'for the Lord's sake' (διὰ τὸν κύριον). A further reason is given that 'it is God's will that by doing right you should put to silence the ignorance of foolish men' (v. 15). Two further instances of God-language follow: the writer's addressees are urged to live ὡς θεοῦ δοῦλοι (v. 16), and to fear God (θεὸν φοβεῖσθε) (v. 17). Thus, although there is an unmistakable similarity in theme, 1 Peter differs from Paul in (a) its more distinctively Christian language (διὰ τὸν κύριον and θεοῦ δοῦλοι) and (b) the fact that the word θεός is not used in the emphatic way in which it is used in Romans 13.[1]

There are also differences in similar teaching in Jewish sources. A similar theology can be found in several passages, but the context is different. Thus the writer of Enoch writes of God as 'the source of kingship', but this is stated in the context of a threat against kings, since they do not acknowledge God.[2] More positive parallels to Paul's thought come from the Old Testament:

> By me (sc. divine wisdom) kings reign, and rulers decree what is just,
> By me rulers rule, and nobles, all who govern rightly (Prov. 8.15-6; cf. Dan. 2.37).

In the light of these parallels, one feature of Rom. 13.1-7 stands out: the emphatic and frequent use of θεός. It is impossible to be sure of the occasion or situation to which these verses are addressed,[3] but the

perhaps, as with ὀργή in v. 4, Paul himself did not clearly distinguish.

1. This contrast between the two writers at this point is particularly noteworthy in that 1 Peter in general is notably theocentric (cf. Selwyn, *1 Peter*, pp. 75-76).

2. *1 Enoch* 46.5. Cf. Wis. 6.3 and *2 Bar.* 82.9.

3. Wilckens, *An die Römer*, III, p. 34, rightly rejects the view of Michel and Käsemann that these verses are directed against enthusiasts in the church, and argues that we just do not know the reason for the inclusion of this teaching. Later on,

emphasis on God is unmistakable. Two references, not one, to God are made in the first warranting statement (v. 1). Verse 2a underlines the point, although not strictly necessary to the argument. Thirdly, as I have noted, θεοῦ twice stands in an emphatic position in v. 4. It is possible that the frequency of theological warrants increases in proportion to the resistance which Paul anticipates to any particular teaching. But whether that is so or not, these verses provide further evidence of the crucial role of God-language in Paul's paraenesis, and in particular in his warranting statements.

There is a marked contrast in this respect with the section which follows, vv. 8-14, where there is no God-language at all.[1] Paul may be drawing on traditional material here (there are parallels both in 1 Thess. 4.12 and 5.6, in Gal. 5.14 and possibly in 1 Peter[2]), but this does not rule out the likelihood that Paul is freely adapting tradition in his own words. And if there is, as I suggested earlier, a correlation between the frequency of God-language and the controversial nature of the commands for which such God-language provides the warrants, we may perhaps conclude that in Rom. 13.8-14 Paul was assuming that the church at Rome would readily endorse this teaching.

Commentators are generally agreed that the long section which begins at 14.1 and extends to 15.13 is substantially Paul's own, addressed to a particular problem at Rome.[3] It begins with a command to the strong

however (p. 36), he notes that by the time this letter was written, Jewish-Christians expelled by Claudius's edict, might have returned to Rome. It is tempting to make a connection between Rom. 13.1-7 and the admittedly enigmatic statement of Suetonius (*De Vita Caesarum* 25.4): 'since the Jews constantly made disturbances at the instigation of Chrestus, he expelled them from Rome' (trans. Loeb Library, quoted in J. Stevenson [ed.], *A New Eusebius* [London: SCM Press, 1968], p. 1). J.I.H. McDonald, 'Romans 13.1-7: A Test Case for New Testament Interpretation', *NTS* 35 (1989), pp. 544-47, while rejecting the anti-enthusiast interpretation, takes the view that Paul's teaching is dealing with agitation about taxation—something to which Tacitus (*Annales 13.50)* testifies.

1. There is no Christ-language either, except in v. 14.

2. Although Selwyn, *1 Peter*, pp. 375-82, tends to exaggerate the parallels.

3. R.J. Karris, 'Romans 14.1-15.13: The Occasion of Romans', in Donfried, *Debate*, pp. 75-99, argues (pp. 83-90), that this section of Romans is a 'generalized adaptation' of what Paul had earlier worked out in 1 Corinthians. This may be so. It is possible that Paul had some knowledge of what the problems were in the Roman church, but the evidence of this section makes it difficult to determine what they were. (Cf. W. Meeks, 'Judgment and the Brother: Romans 14.1–15.13', in G.F. Hawthorne and O. Betz (eds.), *Tradition and Interpretation in the New*

(v. 1a), a parenthetical explanation or recognition of the differences in the community (v. 2), and a double command to the strong and to the weak (v. 3a). There follows a theological *paradigm* (v. 3b), and then an illustration of master and slave, although as Käsemann notes 'the reality [i.e. the theology] invades the image' very quickly.[1] With a further recognition of the differences at Rome, Paul proceeds to the verses (vv. 7-9) which have good claim to be the heart of the argument.[2] (I examine them in detail below.) A final appeal to both groups is followed by a reference to the future judgment (vv. 10 and 12), and the sub-section reaches its climax in the scriptural quotation from Isaiah.

A further sub-section (14.13-23) develops the understanding of food behind the preceding argument. Once again the argument includes a theological *paradigm* (v. 17). The phrase 'pleasing to God' reappears (v. 18), and other references to God and to Christ (vv. 15, 20 and 22) underline the importance of responsibility for fellow-Christians. In 15.1 Paul unequivocally idenitifes himself with 'the strong', and the argument that we should not 'please ourselves' is supported by a christological paradigm (v. 3). A benediction (vv. 5-6) is the prelude to the summarizing exhortation (v. 7) which, echoing as it does 14.1 and 3, provides a chiastic structure to the whole. A final reference to Christ brings out the fruits of his 'servanthood' (v. 8) for both Jew and Gentile, the reference to the Gentiles serving to introduce a catena of Old Testament quotations before a final benediction (v. 13) rounds off this long section.

An investigation of the God-language of this section must begin with the theological *paradigm* of 14.3c. The double injunction 'Let not him who eats despise him who abstains, and let not him who abstains pass judgment on him who eats', ὁ θεὸς γὰρ αὐτὸν προσελάβετο. The paradigmatic force of this phrase is considerably heightened by the fact that προσελάβετο picks up the προσλαμβάνεσθε of v. 1: the 'welcoming' character of God is to be reflected in the life of the community.

The word 'paradigm' in this context is drawn from L.R. Donelson's book *Pseudepigraphy and Ethical Argument in the Pastoral Epistles*. Donelson shows how the Aristotelian categories of the *enthymeme*—a rhetorical syllogism[3]—and the *paradigm* had become commonplaces in

Testament (Grand Rapids, MI: Eerdsmans, 1987), pp. 290-98.

1. Käsemann, *Romans*, p. 369.

2. Michel, *An die Römer*, p. 427, describes vv. 7-9 as 'the truly essential part'.

3. L.R. Donelson, *Pseudepigraphy and Ethical Argument in the Pastoral Epistles* ((Tübingen: Mohr [Paul Siebeck], 1986), p. 75.

Graeco-Roman paraenesis. This was especially true of the paradigm, of which Aristotle distinguished two kinds: (1) a *paradigm* used without an *enthymeme* as a form of inductive argument, and (2) a *paradigm* used as an 'illustration of the argument contained in an existing *enthymeme*'.[1] Despite Aristotle's view that the first kind were not suitable to rhetorical speeches, the inductive *paradigm* became 'one of the leading forms of paraenesis'.[2] Donelson goes on to illustrate this with reference to the writings of Epictetus and Seneca, citing Cancik's observation on Seneca that 'the letter is the ideal genre for the kind of paraenesis which depends heavily on *paradigms*'. Turning to the Pastorals, Donelson shows how the author presents Paul as an 'inductive *paradigm* of ethical conduct, but not only Paul; God and Jesus are also *paradigms*. With reference to 2 Timothy, Donelson comments 'his *paradigms* also show how God behaves'.[3]

To return to Romans 14, the paradigmatic character of 14.3c is clear, and part of the task of this chapter is to investigate the frequency of this use of God-language in Pauline paraenesis.[4] At this point, however, Paul's language broadens to include not only God-language but also 'Lord'-language. As we saw, the lord–slave analogy of v. 4a and 4b is quickly superseded by a reference to the reality to which the analogy points: (sc. ὁ οἰκέτης) σταθήσεται δέ, δυνατεῖ γὰρ ὁ κύριος στῆσαι αὐτόν.[5] The subsequent verses are dominated by the use of κύριος in the dative singular:

> ὁ φρονῶν τὴν ἡμέραν κυρίῳ φρονεῖ καὶ ἐσθίων κυρίῳ ἐσθίει, εὐχαριστεῖ γὰρ τῷ θεῷ καὶ ὁ μὴ ἐσθίων κυρίῳ οὐκ ἐσθίει καὶ εὐχαριστεῖ τῷ θεῷ. οὐδεὶς γὰρ ἡμῶν ἑαυτῷ ζῇ καὶ οὐδεὶς ἑαυτῷ

1. Donelson, *Pseudepigraphy*, p. 91.
2. Donelson, *Pseudepigraphy*, p. 93.
3. Donelson, *Pseudepigraphy*, p. 106.
4. Although the general sense of προσελάβετο is clear, its precise reference is not. Wilckens, *An die Römer*, III, p. 82, sees here a reference to the death of Christ, citing Rom. 5.8; Black, *Romans*, p. 165, and Barrett, *Romans*, p. 258, take προσελάβετο in the sense of 'taking into one's household', so that the phrase thus anticipates v. 4. Michel, *An die Römer*, p. 423, sees here an echo of Ps.26.10: ὁ δὲ κύριος προσελάβετό με. Käsemann, *Romans*, p. 369, finds here a reference to baptism.
5. It is probably correct to read ὁ κύριος here, rather than ὁ θεὸς (the reading of the uncials D, F and G). (Thus also Dunn, *Romans*, II, p. 796.)

> ἀποθνῄσκει. ἐάν τε γὰρ ζῶμεν, τῷ κυρίῳ ζῶμεν, ἐάν τε ἀποθνῄσκωμεν τῷ κυρίῳ ἀποθνῄσκομεν, ἐάν τε οὖν ζῶμεν ἐάν τε ἀποθνῄσκωμεν, τοῦ κυρίου ἐσμέν (vv. 6-8).

The use of κυρίω here is clearly significant. There are three occurrences of this dative in v. 6 and two more in v. 8. Commentators interpret them in one of two ways: either they are datives 'of advantage' to be translated by 'for the Lord' or some such phrase,[1] or they are the equivalent of the phrase ἐνώπιον τοῦ θεοῦ.[2] There are two reasons for preferring the latter alternative. First, as Dunn points out,[3] the master's advantage does not appear to be in view in v. 4, where κύριος is first used in the dative. Secondly, as the survey of 2 Cor. 2.14–4.6 in the previous chapter showed, there are many examples in Paul of God-language used in this way. Sometimes Paul uses a prepositional phrase such as ἐνώπιον τοῦ θεοῦ, sometimes the simple dative θεῷ or τῷ θεῷ.[4] Paul's use of θεῷ elsewhere with the verb 'to live' suggests that we have here a parallel use of κυρίῳ. Thus, for example, he writes in Rom. 6.10-11 of how the person who has died 'to sin' ζῇ τῷ θεῷ, and therefore Paul commands the Christians at Rome to consider themselves dead to sin ζῶντας δὲ τῷ θεῷ ἐν Χριστῷ Ἰησοῦ. Wilckens comments: 'The datives τῇ ἁμαρτίᾳ and τῷ θεῷ indicate the respective owners'.[5] We find a similar thought in Gal. 2.19: ἐγὼ γὰρ διὰ νόμου νόμῳ ἀπέθανον, ἵνα θεῷ ζήσω. Bruce considers θεῷ here to be used 'in a relational sense'.[6] It is probably correct, therefore, particularly in view of the genitive of v. 8, to see in the use of κυρίῳ in Rom. 14.6 and 8 the implication both of ownership and of relationship.

What is particularly relevant for this inquiry is the parallel use by Paul of κυρίῳ and θεῷ. This does not mean, of course, that Paul's use of κύριος here permits us to say that the κύριος is God. But it certainly suggests that the κύριος is, in some sense, *in loco Dei*; as v. 9 will make clear, he exercises, as God's vice-gerent, the authority of God himself.

1. Thus, e.g., H. Schlier, *Der Römerbrief* (Freiburg: Herder 1977), pp. 408-409.

2. Thus, e.g., Michel, *An die Römer*, p. 427: 'In life and death the believer is accountable to his Lord: he lives and dies in the sight of Christ'.

3. Dunn, *Romans*, p. 804.

4. See the discussion in Chapter 3, section 2, and especially p. 153, n. 5.

5. Wilckens, *An die Römer*, II, p. 19.

6. F.F. Bruce, *The Epistle to the Galatians* (Exeter: Paternoster, 1982), p. 143.

The probability that Paul is thinking in this way is strengthened by a passage in the *Pirke Aboth* (4.22) to which Michel has drawn attention:[1]

> They that have been born (are destined) to die, and they that are dead (are destined) to be made alive, and they that live (after death are destined) to be judged, that men may know and make known and understand that he is God... he is the Judge... and it is he that shall judge... despite thyself shalt thou hereafter give account and reckoning before the king of kings, the Holy One, blessed is he.[2]

While the *Pirke Aboth* in its final form in the *Mishnah* comes from a later period, it is possible that Paul was familiar with earlier forms of teaching of this kind. If that is so, it is significant that Paul has used κύριος in the kind of context where Judaism used God-language.

The justification for this κύριος-language is now given in v. 9: εἰς τοῦτο γὰρ Χριστὸς ἀπέθανεν καὶ ἔζησεν, ἵνα καὶ νεκρῶν καὶ ζώντων κυριεύσῃ. This statement probably comes within the Aristotelian category of an enthymeme. The reasoning behind it is fairly simple:

1. Christ died and lived and so became κύριος,
2. As κύριος he is κύριος of the dead and the living,
3. Therefore we live and die as the Lord's.

The 'interplay' (Dunn's word) between κύριος and θεός in these verses has led to more textual variants in v. 10. Some witnesses, perhaps influenced by the reference in 2 Cor. 5.10 to 'the judgment-seat *of Christ*', have the same phrase here, but the weight of evidence supports the reading of θεοῦ:[3] πάντες γὰρ παραστησόμεθα τῷ βήματι τοῦ θεοῦ (v. 10c). Another interesting contrast with another Pauline epistle emerges in Paul's use of Isa. 45.23 (preceded by an introductory formula common in the Old Testament) in v. 11:

> γέγραπται γάρ·
> ζῶ ἐγώ, λέγει κύριος, ὅτι ἐμοὶ κάμψει πᾶν γόνυ
> καὶ πᾶσα γλῶσσα ἐξομολογήσεται τῷ θεῷ.

1. Michel, *An die Römer*, p. 427.
2. Danby, *Mishnah*, p. 455.
3. So Michel, *An die Römer*, p. 428 n.27. Michel also notes the observation of Origen on the difference between 2 Cor. 5.10 and Rom. 14.10 in this respect. (Black, *Romans*, p. 167; Cranfield, *Romans*, II, p. 709 n.4; also note Origen's observation). While Origen's testimony is not conclusive, it reinforces the view that Χριστοῦ here is a later alteration.

If θεοῦ is read in v. 10, the κύριος referred to here must be God, not Christ. Yet in Phil. 2.11 Paul uses the same Old Testament quotation with reference to Christ, adding εἰς δόξαν θεοῦ πατρός. Thus in two consecutive verses in Romans 14 Paul has used, with reference to God, material which elsewhere he uses of Christ. The theological emphasis here is heightened still further if in v. 12 Paul wrote 'So each of us shall give account of himself *to God*', but not all manuscripts have τῷ θεῷ. On balance, however, it seems likely that Paul wrote τῷ θεῷ here.[1] Thus the alternation in these verses between God-language and κύριος- or Christ-language occurs within a strongly *theological* framework: Paul begins (v. 3) and ends (vv. 10-12) with references to God. (I shall return to this pattern in Paul's theological 'grammar' in Chapter 5 below.)

The next section (vv. 13-23) also makes use of material which Paul has already used in 1 Corinthians.[2] The God-language used here, however, is quite different from that employed in the similar arguments of 1 Corinthians. The reference to Christ in v. 15 (μὴ τῷ βρώματί σου ἐκεῖνον ἀπόλλυε ὑπὲρ οὗ Χριστὸς ἀπέθανεν) corresponds closely with 1 Cor. 8.11, but the God-language which follows in vv. 17-20 is unique to Romans:[3]

> οὐ γάρ ἐστιν ἡ βασιλεία τοῦ θεοῦ βρῶσις καὶ πόσις ἀλλὰ δικαιοσύνη καὶ εἰρήνη καὶ χαρὰ ἐν πνεύματι ἁγίῳ. ὁ γὰρ ἐν τούτῳ δουλεύων τῷ Χριστῷ εὐάρεστος τῷ θεῷ καὶ δόκιμος τοῖς ἀνθρώποις. Ἄρα οὖν τὰ τῆς εἰρήνης διώκωμεν καὶ τὰ τῆς οἰκοδομῆς τῆς εἰς ἀλλήλους. μὴ ἕνεκεν βρώματος κατάλυε τὸ ἔργον τοῦ θεοῦ.

There is no need to dwell at length on the scarcity of the phrase 'the Kingdom of God' in the letters of Paul.[4] More important is the *function*

1. Thus also Cranfield, *Romans*, II, p. 711 n. 3, and Dunn, *Romans*, II, p. 796, against Käsemann, *Romans*, p. 373.

2. Parallels with 1 Cor. 8 are particularly close: the verb σκανδαλίζω, for example, occurs here in v. 21 and in 1 Cor. 8.13, and v. 15 corresponds closely with the substance of 1 Cor. 8.1, and 11.1-13.

3. There is a similarly structured saying about the Kingdom of God in 1 Cor. 4.20, εὐάρεστος is used with reference to God at Rom. 12.1-2, 2 Cor. 5.9 and Phil. 4.18, but that is all.

4. Two references, 1 Cor. 6.9-10 and Gal. 5.21, almost certainly belong in the context of catachetical instruction; two others, 1 Cor. 15.50 and 1 Thess. 2.12 may well be Pauline adaptations of traditional formulations; the reference here, and 1 Cor. 4.20, are probably his own (polemical) statements.

of the God-language here, and its interaction with Christ-language. The verses belong closely together, as the connecting particles (γάρ, vv. 17-18; ἄρα οὖν, v. 19) show. Yet the trend of thought is not easy to follow. The command of v. 16 is followed by a theological warranting statement (v. 17), which in its turn is followed by a statement of the consequences of the conduct commanded in v. 16. (The NRSV is probably right in not translating the γάρ of v. 18). The key to Paul's thought here lies in recognizing the implicit identification of the Kingdom of God with the Lordship of Christ: 'When Paul speaks of service to Christ in the expression of v. 17, he thereby shows how he can self-evidently make one the kingdoms of God and of Christ'.[1] Thus the *enthymeme*, or syllogism, which lies behind these verses seems to be this:

1. The Lordship of Christ represents the Kingdom of God
2. The Kingdom of God is not a matter of food and drink
3. The person who serves Christ will not make food and drink causes of division.

The interaction of God- and Christ-language will be the concern of Chapter 5. Here I note further examples of the warranting function of God-language (and, in v. 15, of Christ-language) in Pauline paraenesis. The γάρ of v. 17 makes the warrant explicit, but in v. 20 the warrant (or more correctly, perhaps, the sanction) is implied in the expression τὸ ἔργον τοῦ θεοῦ.This is the only occurrence in Paul's writings of ἔργον with the genitive θεοῦ.[2] The nearest parallel in meaning is probably 1 Cor. 3.17 ('If anyone destroys the temple of God…'), although that verse envisages the whole Christian community, whereas here Paul has the individual in mind.[3]

There is one further instance of God-language in this section. Despite textual variants,[4] ἐνώπιον τοῦ θεοῦ should be read in v. 22a. A full exegesis of this difficult verse need not be undertaken here; but we note the by now familiar Pauline idea of accountability before God in this prepositional phrase. This accountability, together with the 'brother' for whom Christ died (v. 15), and who is 'the work of God' (v. 20) (here

1. Wilckens, *An die Römer*, III, p. 94.
2. The phrase ἔργον τοῦ κυρίου (e.g. 1 Cor. 15.58 and 16.10) has a quite different meaning.
3. So also Cranfield, *Romans*, II, p. 723.
4. Notably the original hand in Codex Sinaiticus; the weight of evidence, however, favours reading ἐνώπιον τοῦ θεοῦ here.

again there is a correlation of God- and Christ-language), provides the framework within which Paul works through the problem before him.

As Paul nears the end of this long paraenetical section, the God-language he uses acquires the character of prayer (15.5-6, 13) and, at the same time, a doxological character (vv. 6-7, 9). The first explicit God-language is the prayer-wish of vv. 5-6:

> ὁ δὲ θεὸς τῆς ὑπομονῆς καὶ τῆς παρακλήσεως δῴη ὑμῖν τὸ αὐτὸ φρονεῖν ἐν ἀλλήλοις κατὰ Χριστὸν Ἰησοῦν, ἵνα ὁμοθυμαδὸν ἐν ἑνὶ στόματι δοξάζητε τὸν θεὸν καὶ πατέρα τοῦ κυρίου ἡμῶν Ἰησοῦ Χριστοῦ.

There is general agreement among the commentators that we are dealing here with liturgical language. The genitives ὑπομονῆς and παρακλήσεως derive from the preceding verse (διὰ τῆς ὑπομονῆς καὶ διὰ τῆς παρακλήσεως τῶν γραφῶν), which in its turn rests on the paradigmatic behaviour of Christ described in v. 3. Once again, therefore, there is a clear connection between God and Christ: the ὑπομονή of Christ, which is witnessed to by the Scriptures, is the gift of God.[1] (The somewhat vague prepositional phrase κατὰ Χριστὸν Ἰησοῦν further indicates the close connection in Paul's thought between God and Christ). The connection is made still more plain by the final phrase of the prayer: τὸν θεὸν καὶ πατέρα τοῦ κυρίου ἡμῶν Ἰησοῦ Χριστοῦ. (A fuller discussion of the word πατήρ applied to God properly belongs in Chapter 5. It occurs here in a paraenetical section because Paul is now moving to its doxological climax.)

In the summarizing command which follows this prayer-wish, Paul uses the verb (προσλαμβάνεσθε) which he had used with God as subject back in 14.3. This time the command is followed by a christological *paradigm*: Διὸ προσλαμβάνεσθε ἀλλήλους, καθὼς καὶ ὁ Χριστὸς προσελάβετο ὑμᾶς εἰς δόξαν τοῦ θεοῦ (v. 7). Thus we have another correlation between Paul's God- and Christ-language: what God has done (14.3), Christ has done. Such an obvious parallel, however, is not very common in Paul's language.[2] The repeated reference to 'the glory of God' is now explained in a twofold way: God is glorified by the confirmation of his promise to the fathers, and by the praise which the Gentiles are now bringing to him for his mercy (ἐλέους).

1. It is unnecessary to distinguish sharply between the gifts and attributes of God; it is unlikely that Paul did so here.

2. *Pace* Black, *Romans*, p. 171 ('Paul frequently uses the same expressions of God and Christ'). See Chapter 5 below.

(Here is one of the rare occurrences in Paul of ἔλεος outside Romans 9–11: as Käsemann notes, the word indicates that God's 'covenant faithfulness is cosmically extended'.[1])

In the final prayer wish (v. 13) the language is again liturgical. (The letter would almost certainly have been read in the context of worship.) As in v. 6, the prayer ends with a resounding theological reference—here to 'Holy Spirit':

> ὁ δὲ θεὸς τῆς ἐλπίδος πληρώσαι ὑμᾶς πάσης χαρᾶς καὶ εἰρήνης ἐν τῷ πιστεύειν, εἰς τὸ περισσεύειν ὑμᾶς ἐν τῇ ἐλπίδι ἐν δυνάμει πνεύματος ἁγίου (v. 13).

The genitive ἐλπίδος is regarded by Barrett as attributive ('May the God who is thus the ground of hope'),[2] whereas Cranfield interprets it as 'God the giver of hope'.[3] Again, as with the genitives of vv. 5-6 it is unnecessary to distinguish sharply between these two senses of ἐλπίδος, since it is probable that Paul intended both.

The section vv. 7-13 is rightly called by Michel 'the obvious highpoint and goal of the entire section'.[4] The God-language is noteworthy for its doxological character. The context, as usual, is vital. The God-language of vv. 7-9a and 13 encompasses four scriptural references to 'Gentiles' (the word ἔθνη actually occurs five times in vv. 9b-12). There can be little doubt, therefore, that Jew–Gentile unity is the practical, ecclesiological basis from which and in which God is glorified. It reflects, in fact, what is one of the most important statements Paul makes about God in this letter: ἢ Ἰουδαίων ὁ θεὸς μόνον; οὐχὶ καὶ ἐθνῶν; ναὶ καὶ ἐθνῶν (Rom. 3.29).

Summary

The God-language of this long paraenetical section presents a very varied pattern, and it will be useful to summarize the evidence and the conclusions to be drawn from it.

1. Most of the God-language here has a *warranting* function, answering in effect the question 'why should we (do this)?' Thus the reasons for conduct time and again are *theocentric* in character: (because of) what God has done (12.1, 3; 14.3c, 20—cf. similar

1. Käsemann, *Romans*, p. 386.
2. Barrett, *Romans*, p. 272.
3. Cranfield, *Romans*, II, p. 747.
4. Michel, *An die Römer*, p. 367.

statements of Christ at 14.9; 15.3, 7-8), what God will do (12.19), what God wants (12.2; cf. 14.17), or (because) we shall be judged before God (12.19; 13.2; 14.10-12; cf. 14.22) or (because) the authorities have been ordained by God (13.1-7). Thus God is both the supreme authorizer and the ultimate judge.

2. Three sections stand out by virtue of the frequency and/or emphatic character of their language about God. These are: 12.1-2, 13.1-7, and 15.7-13. The first serves as a theological summary of the entire section, and the last as a doxological climax of it. The teaching in 13.1-7 contains repeated and emphatic theocentric warrants (1b and c, 2, 4a and d, 6b), prompting the thought that theological warrants increase in proportion to the controversial character of (or estimated resistance to) the teaching given.

3. Much of the God-language reflects again Paul's redeployment in a new Christian context of traditional or LXX language about God ('the mercies of God' [12.1], 'well-pleasing to God' [12.1-2 and 14.18], the language of 'wrath' and 'revenge' [12.19-21]. This may well be true also, in the light of *Pirke Aboth* 4.22, of Paul's κύριος-language in 14.7-10. In particular we noted that the phrase 'the mercies of God' (12.1), and the command to overcome evil with good (12.21), derived their meaning from what Paul has already said in this epistle about what God has done through Christ.

4. The interplay between and juxtaposition of θεός- and κύριος-language (14.1-12) and of θεός/Χριστός-language (14.3c, 17-18; 15.5, 7) constitute a very significant development of God-language, suggesting not only that action predicated of God can be predicated of Christ too (14.3c; 15.7), but also that the lordship of Christ somehow represents the sovereignty of God or 'the kingdom of God' (14.8-12, 17-8). Yet the *theo*centric character of the argument throughout is sustained, 14.10-11 in particular providing two examples of *theo*logical expressions which have christological parallels elsewhere (2 Cor. 5.10; Phil. 2.11).

5. The prayer wishes of 15.5-6 and 15.13 are almost certainly liturgical expressions, or Pauline adaptations of them. By employing them in this context Paul finishes, as he began this long section back in 12.1, in a very theocentric way. Here the description of God as πατέρα τοῦ κυρίου ἡμῶν Ἰησοῦ Χριστοῦ, and the emphasis on the place of both Jew and Gentile in the purposes of God (15.8-9) reflect central and crucial characteristics of Paul's language about God.

There is thus further evidence here of both similarity with and differences from traditional Jewish language about God. There is also further evidence that language about Christ was not simply inserted into pre-existing dogmas about God. Instead, there is an interplay between language about God and language about Christ which has far-reaching implications for our understanding both of God and Christ. In the following sections I shall widen the scope of my inquiry, first by examining other paraenetical sections in Paul's letters, and secondly by comparing and contrasting Paul's language about God in these contexts with that found in Jewish and Graeco-Roman paraenesis.

3. *God-Language in the Paraenesis of Other Pauline Letters*

I shall be concerned in this section with patterns of God-language in the paraenesis of other Pauline letters, in order to compare and contrast them with the findings of the previous section. Following Aune's observation that paraenesis is woven throughout Philippians and 1 and 2 Corinthians,[1] I shall treat those letters together in a second sub-section, looking first at 1 Thessalonians and Galatians.[2]

a. *1 Thessalonians*

The word θεός occurs 35 times in 1 Thessalonians, compared with 10 occurrences of Χριστός (five times with κύριος Ἰησοῦς); κύριος is used 24 times, in addition to its five occurrences with Ἰησοῦς. There are several notable uses of God-language in this letter, some of which are paralleled in other letters—for example, Paul's swearing by God (2.5 and 10)[3]—and others not paralleled elsewhere—for example, the use by Paul in the opening greeting of ἐν θεῷ πατρί. Here, however, we are concerned with the letter's paraenesis.

Following a widely held view of the structure of 1 Thessalonians,[4] I

1. D.E. Aune, *The New Testament in its Literary Environment* (Cambridge: J. Clark, 1988), p. 191. Aune also compares James and Hebrews.

2. Surprisingly, Aune does not cite 1 Thessalonians and Galatians as examples of those letters where 'epistolary paraenesis' is found in 'defined concluding sections', but as letters where 'paraenetic styles' permeate the whole. Although I do not deny the element of truth in this last point, clearly defined paraenetic sections can be discerned in both letters.

3. 'Unlike the Pharisaic Rabbis with whom he had formerly been associated, Paul does not hesitate to swear by God' (Collins, *Thessalonians*, p. 242).

4. One widely held view of the structure of 1 Thessalonians is that 1.2–3.10 consists of the thanksgiving, or 'body' of the letter, and that 4.1ff onwards consists

shall concentrate my inquiry on chs. 4 and 5, while acknowledging that the earlier chapters are not entirely devoid of paraenesis.[1] The occurrence of παρακαλοῦμεν in 4.1 strengthens the view that an extended section of paraenesis begins here.[2]

The section begins (4.1-2) with a general exhortation whose function seems to correspond with that of Rom. 12.1-2. Here, however, the language is not quite so theocentric, although we note the important definition of the objective of the Christian's conduct: περιπατεῖν καὶ ἀρέσκειν θεῷ. (There is an important parallel here with Paul's description of his own conduct in 2.1-12, especially v. 4.[3]) The 'Christ' language used in vv. 1-2 is something of a puzzle. The expression ἐν Χριστῷ Ἰησοῦ (v. 1), used with ἐρωτῶμεν καὶ παρακαλοῦμεν is similar to phrases used elsewhere by Paul (e.g. 1 Cor. 1.10). The expression διὰ τοῦ κυρίου Ἰησοῦ (v. 2) is more difficult. The most probable explanation is that it is a literary variant for the phrase ἐν Χριστῷ Ἰησοῦ.[4]

This general introduction paves the way for the treatment of four topics in the section 4.3 to 5.11. Of these the first and third (4.3-8 and 4.13-18), sexual morality and the fate of those who have died in Christ,

of 'exhortation', 3.11-13 being a prayer-wish which provides a transition from one to the other. (See, for example, von Dobschütz, *Thessalonicherbriefe*, p. 23, who notes that the thanksgiving makes up most of chs. 1–3, citing 1.3, 2.3 and 3.9). It is probably unwise, as Marshall notes (*1 and 2 Thessalonians*, p. 9), to look for too formal a structure in this part of the letter, but Marshall himself notes the 'clear break' at the end of ch. 3. R. Jewett, *The Thessalonian Correspondence* (Philadelphia: Fortress Press, 1986), p. 71, considers that 1 Thessalonians falls into the rhetorical genre which he terms 'demonstrative /epideictic', identifying 4.1–5.22 as the *probatio* (p. 75).

1. Thus Collins, *Studies*, p. 64. Cf. Marshall, *1 and 2 Thessalonians*, p. 9.

2. Despite the view of Bjeerkelund, cited by Boers ('Form-Critical Study', pp. 154-55), that παρακαλῶ is not a technical term for paraenesis, the contexts in which Paul uses the word (see the earlier discussion on p. 183 above), justify us in associating it with paraenesis.

3. Thus W. Meeks, *The Moral World of the First Christians* (London: SPCK, 1987), pp. 127-28.

4. Thus Marshall, *1 and 2 Thessalonians*, pp. 105-106. We may reject the view that it refers to the historical Jesus, since not only do vv. 3-8 not introduce any distinctively Christian teaching, but also they have no clear parallels in the Gospels. To say that the expression is used here in a mystical sense (Best, *Commentary*, p. 158, cf. von Dobschütz, *Thessalonicherbriefe*, p. 159) seems a rather vague expedient.

are topics on which the apostle says, or implies, they need teaching. The second and last topics (4.9-12 and 5.1-11) Paul says the Thessalonians do not need to be reminded about (4.9 and 5.1), although he immediately proceeds to do that.

The first topic (4.3-8) has the greatest number of Jewish and pagan parallels, although Yarborough's comment is worth noting: 'When one compares the precepts he rehearses with those of the Graeco-Roman moralists and discovers just how similar they were, the theological element in his treatment stands out sharply'.[1] Paul begins his treatment of this topic, in fact, by an emphatic theological declaration: τοῦτο γάρ ἐστιν θέλημα τοῦ θεοῦ, ὁ ἁγιασμὸς ὑμῶν, ἀπέχεσθαι ὑμᾶς ἀπὸ τῆς πορνείας (v. 3). This, however, does not comprise all the God-language of this short section by any means. By their morality the Thessalonians are to be distinguished from τὰ ἔθνη τὰ μὴ εἰδότα τὸν θεόν, although, as Meeks points out,[2] much of the moral content of 1 Thessalonians, including this particular topos, is common to 'decent' Graeco-Roman society. It seems likely that this particular strand of teaching was meeting with some resistance at Thessaly,[3] since the strong theological language continues with the warning (v. 6b) ἔκδικος κύριος περὶ πάντων τούτων. The κύριος here is probably God rather than Christ.[4] (It is possible that the influence of the LXX has determined Paul's language at this point: Ps. 94 [93 in the LXX] has θεὸς ἐκδικήσεων κύριος [v. 1].) Finally, the section ends with yet further theological warrants:

> οὐ γὰρ ἐκάλεσεν ἡμᾶς ὁ θεὸς ἐπὶ ἀκαθαρσίᾳ ἀλλ' ἐν ἁγιασμῷ. τοιγαροῦν ὁ ἀθετῶν οὐκ ἄνθρωπον ἀθετεῖ ἀλλὰ τὸν θεὸν τὸν (καὶ) διδόντα τὸ πνεῦμα αὐτοῦ τὸ ἅγιον εἰς ὑμᾶς (vv. 7-8).

The fact that Paul felt it necessary to end his treatment of this theme with such a stern warning strengthens the probability that sexual immorality among the Thessalonians was a major problem. It is possible that some at Thessaly had not made the connection between the Spirit of God and moral conduct,[5] hence the emphatic τὸ ἅγιον in v. 8.

1. Yarborough, *Not like the Gentiles*, p. 123.
2. Meeks, *Moral World*, pp. 128-29.
3. Thus also Marshall, *1 and 2 Thessalonians*, p. 115; cf. Jewett, *Correspondence*, pp. 105-106.
4. Thus Collins, *Studies*, pp. 319-20, against Marshall, *1 and 2 Thessalonians*, p. 112.
5. Similarly, Jewett, *Correspondence*, p. 106.

In the section 4.3-8, then, we have a passage which deals with a traditional theme, but the resistance to it obliges Paul to spell out, as he does in Rom. 13.1-7, theological warrants in no uncertain fashion.

There is far less God-language in 4.9-13, perhaps because the emphasis is different: Περὶ δὲ τῆς φιλαδελφίας οὐ χρείαν ἔχετε γράφειν ὑμῖν, αὐτοὶ γὰρ ὑμεῖς θεοδίδακτοί ἐστε εἰς τὸ ἀγαπᾶν ἀλλήλους (v. 9). Malherbe thinks that θεοδιδακτοί is 'a Pauline coinage'.[1] Whether that is so or not, the word carries a theological warrant for the conduct which is being encouraged here.[2] There is a similar pattern in the unit 5.1-11, which begins in an almost identical way: Περὶ δὲ τῶν χρόνων καὶ τῶν καιρῶν, ἀδελφοί, οὐ χρείαν ἔχετε ὑμῖν γράφεσθαι (v. 1; cf. 4.9). Here, too, there is little God-language: the sole instance occurs in v. 9, where the emphasis falls, as in 4.7 with its reference to the *call* of God, on what God has done: ὅτι οὐκ ἔθετο ἡμᾶς ὁ θεὸς εἰς ὀργὴν ἀλλὰ εἰς περιποίησιν σωτηρίας διὰ τοῦ κυρίου Ἰησοῦ Χριστοῦ.

The intervening unit, 4.13-18, is rather different from 4.3-8 and 4.9-12 in that it deals with a distinctively Christian problem, the question of the fate or destiny of those who have died before the Parousia.[3] Here Paul uses both God-language and Christ-language to a degree not found elsewhere in chs. 4 and 5. If Malherbe is correct in seeing in 4.13–5.11 some similarities with the 'letter of consolation' familiar in Graeco-Roman literature,[4] then these verses provide yet another instance of how Paul Christianized current literary conventions.

The basis of the argument in these verses is an *enthymeme* which can be expressed in the form of three simple propositions:

1. Jesus died and was raised by God
2. God will raise us when we die
3. Therefore we have hope.

This syllogism is followed by κύριος-language, combined with traditional apocalyptic imagery, including the theological image σάλπιγγι θεοῦ (v. 16).

Although it is impossible to be certain, I suggest that this unit, like

1. Malherbe, 'Exhortation', p. 253.
2. Malherbe, 'Exhortation', pp. 252-54, finds an anti-Epicurean motif here.
3. This seems the likeliest explanation. But see Marshall, *1 and 2 Thessalonians*, pp. 120-22 for other possibilities.
4. Malherbe, 'Exhortation', pp. 254-56.

4.3-8 and Rom. 13.1-7, is one in which Paul felt he had to argue his case. For this reason we have, in effect, a double warrant, εἰ γὰρ πιστεύομεν ὅτι Ἰησοῦς ἀπέθανεν καὶ ἀνέστη (v. 14a) and τοῦτο γὰρ ὑμῖν λέγομεν ἐν λόγῳ κυρίου (v. 15a). Here, however, unlike 4.3-8 and Rom. 13.1-7 where the issues were ethical and not distinctively Christian, there is a further example of the interplay between God- and κύριος-language.

The final section of the letter before the closing greetings (5.12-24) is more general in character. Commentators are generally agreed that it was not related to a specific situation at Thessalonika, although the tables of parallels in Selwyn[1] show that there is sufficient variation between the 'parallels' to justify the view that Paul is composing freely as, in the view taken here, he normally does in his paraenetic sections.[2] As in Rom. 12.3-21, the God-language is not plentiful; the only explicit reference to God occurs in v. 18b, following three briefly expressed injunctions to rejoice, to pray and to give thanks: τοῦτο γὰρ θέλημα θεοῦ ἐν Χριστῷ Ἰησοῦ εἰς ὑμᾶς.[3] It is probable that Paul has added this phrase here, but why he has done so is not immediately obvious. Von Dobschütz believes that the addition was made not because the commands were difficult, but because they were so important.[4] Holtz[5] compares and contrasts the reference here to the will of God with the reference in 4.3, the latter referring to the conduct of Christians in the world and 5.18 referring to the conduct of Christians 'before themselves and before God'. Whatever the reason for Paul's addition here, the theological warrant has the effect of underlining the importance of the preceding commands before the staccato-like list of commands is resumed in vv. 19-22. Here, however, it is important to note that the reference is not simply to 'the will of God', but to 'the will of God *in Christ Jesus*'. This does not mean that the commands to rejoice, to pray

1. Selwyn, *1 Peter*, pp. 371, 408-409 and 416.

2. Marshall, *1 and 2 Thessalonians*, pp. 145-46, notes the parallels between this section and Romans 12, observing that the themes broadly occur in reverse order, and comments: 'A common basis in tradition exists, but Paul handles it quite freely'.

3. Most commentators take the view that this explanatory clause goes with all three of the preceding commands; thus, e.g., Marshall, *1 and 2 Thessalonians*, pp. 145-46, von Dobschütz, *Thessalonicherbriefe*, p. 224, and T. Holtz, *Der erste Briefe an die Thessalonicher* (Zürich: Benzinger Verlag, 1986), p. 258.

4. Von Dobschütz, *Thessalonicherbriefe*, p. 224.

5. Holtz, *Erste Briefe*, p. 258.

and to give thanks were distinctively Christian, but rather that the *grounds* for so doing were.[1]

Verses 23-24 are probably to be regarded as the conclusion of the section beginning at v. 12:[2]

> Αὐτὸς δὲ ὁ θεὸς τῆς εἰρήνης ἁγιάσαι ὑμᾶς ὁλοτελεῖς, καὶ ὁλόκληρον ὑμῶν τὸ πνεῦμα καὶ ἡ ψυχὴ καὶ τὸ σῶμα ἀμέμπτως ἐν τῇ παρουσίᾳ τοῦ κυρίου ἡμῶν Ἰησοῦ Χριστοῦ τηρηθείη. πιστὸς ὁ καλῶν ὑμᾶς, ὃς καὶ ποιήσει.

There are several parallels elsewhere in Paul's writings, notably in Rom. 15.5, 13, where prayer-wishes occur near or at the end of a long paraenetical section. There is also a close parallel in 1 Thessalonians itself, in 3.11-13 which also begins with αὐτὸς δέ. (The αὐτός both in 3.11 and in 5.23 replaces the direct 'you' or 'thou' of prayer-language[3].) Here in 5.23-24 the Jewish roots of Paul's language are unmistakable: 'God of peace' is 'an expression of Jewish prayer-language',[4] while the phrase πιστὸς ὁ καλούμενος is reminiscent of one of the benedictions after the *Haftarah* in the synagogue,[5] and has several close parallels in Paul's letters (1 Cor. 1.9; 10.13; 2 Cor. 1.18). What is significant here is not the change in God-language—that remains substantially the same—but the change in context: the prayer-wish looks forward to 'the parousia of our Lord Jesus Christ', and the 'call' of v. 24, addressed as it is to Gentiles, is clearly a call in and through Jesus Christ.

Summary. The paraenesis of 1 Thessalonians thus presents us with varying patterns of God-language. In this respect it is like the paraenesis of Rom. 12.1–15.13. The theocentric nature of the paraenesis is stressed in a 'headline' (4.1-2; cf. Rom. 12.1-2), and an injunction which probably anticipates some resistance is underlined with particularly strong theological warrants and sanctions (4.3-8; cf. Rom. 13.1-7). In the remaining paranaesis theological warrants are given in 4.9, 5.9 and 5.18, and the whole rounded off with a prayer-wish and benediction-like language (5.23-24) which again serve to accentuate the theocentric

1. Holtz, *Erste Briefe*, p. 258, notes the absence of the definite article with θεοῦ, rightly attributing this to the style of the context with its repeated asyndeton.

2. Thus Marshall, *1 and 2 Thessalonians*, pp. 160-61, and Best, *Commentary*, p. 242.

3, Thus Holtz, *Erste Breife*, pp. 141-42 and 263.

4. Von Dobschütz, *Thessalonicherbriefe*, p. 228.

5. Thus Van Unnik, quoted in O'Brien, *Introductory Thanksgivings*, p. 130.

character of the teaching (cf. Rom. 15.6, 13). Much of the God-language used in these chapters, however, is 'glossed' by a reference to Christ (4.1-2; 5.9, 18, 23), providing further evidence of the interplay of God- and Christ-language. Finally, the distinctively Christian problem of 4.13-18 is answered by, in effect, a christological enthymeme. (Compare Rom. 14.1–15.7, and especially 14.8-9 and 15.7, where Paul is also addressing a distinctively Christian problem.)

b. *Galatians*[1]

In the study of the structure of Galatians, new ground was broken in the article by H.D. Betz, 'The Literary Composition and function of Paul's Letter to the Galatians'.[2] In this article, and subsequently in his commentary on Galatians, Betz argues that the structure of Galatians conforms to the pattern of judicial rhetoric: 'The apologetic letter, such as Galatians, presupposes the real or fictitious situation of the court of law, with jury, accuser, and defendant'.[3] There is, however, a problem about the section which Betz designates the paraenesis (5.1-6.10), as Betz himself acknowledges, noting 'the marginal role' of paraenesis in ancient rhetorical handbooks.[4] The solution to the problem, as other scholars have noted, probably lies in recognizing that Galatians is not 'judicial rhetoric' as Betz claimed, but 'deliberative rhetoric'. Kennedy, for example, notes that paraenesis is part of the latter, but not part of the former.[5] Within the genre of deliberative rhetoric, then, there are good grounds for recognizing Gal. 5.1–6.10 as paraenesis.

1. It is neither possible nor necessary to enter into a full discussion of the date of Galatians. It is assumed here that Gal. 2.1-10 is Paul's version of the event described in Acts 15, although there is no view which is without its difficulties. Even if one espouses the view that Gal. 2.1-10 is the equivalent of Acts 18.22 (as, for example, R. Jewett, *Dating Paul's Life* [London: SCM Press, 1979], pp. 78-80, following Knox and Lüdemann, is inclined to do), Galatians would still have been written later than 1 Thessalonians (thus Jewett, *Paul's Life*, p. 103).

2. H.D. Betz, 'The Literary Composition and Function of Paul's Letter to the Galatians', *NTS* 21 (1975), pp. 353-79.

3. Betz, *Galatians*, p. 24.

4. Betz, 'Literary Composition', p. 375; cf. *idem*, *Galatians*, pp. 253ff.

5. G.A. Kennedy, *New Testament Interpretation through Rhetorical Criticism* (Chapel Hill: University of North Carolina Press, 1984), pp. 144-45; cf. J. Smit, 'The Letter of Paul to the Galatians: A Deliberative Speech', *NTS* 35.1 (1989), *passim*, and F. Vouga, 'Zur rhetorischen Gattung des Galaterbriefes', *ZNW* 9.3-4 (1988), pp. 291-92.

The structure of this section of Galatians, and its place in the letter as a whole, has often seemed puzzling. In his recent study of this section of Galatians, however, John Barclay has shown that 5.25–6.10 does not comprise so unsystematic a series of exhortations as has often been thought. Rather, 5.25-26 provide the 'headline' for what follows, with its emphasis on the dual theme of accountability before God and responsiblity for others in the context of community strife at Galatia.[1] Secondly, there are good grounds for regarding 5.13–6.10 as an integral part of Paul's letter: the σάρξ/πνεῦμα antithesis of this section relates closely to what has gone before (e.g. 4.29), as the references to the law in 5.14 and 18 also indicate.[2]

In this paraenetic section of Galatians it is at once apparent that πνεῦμα-language and Χριστός-language are more common than θεός-language. πνεῦμα-language occurs at 5.5, 17-18, 22, 25; 6.1, 8; Χριστός-language occurs at 5.1, 2, 4, 6, 24 and 6.2, while θεός-language occurs only at 5.8 (ἐκ τοῦ καλοῦντος), 5.21 and 6.7. In order to appreciate why this is so, it is necessary to look briefly at the language of the earlier sections of the letter.

In the earlier chapters of Galatians, there are none of the 'clusters' of God-language observable elsewhere in Paul's writings, unless we except 4.8-9a: ἀλλὰ τότε μὲν οὐκ εἰδότες θεὸν ἐδουλεύσατε τοῖς φύσει μὴ οὖσιν θεοῖς· νῦν δὲ γνόντες θεόν, μᾶλλον δὲ γνωσθέντες ὑπὸ θεοῦ. What we *do* have is a steady, but for the most part infrequent use of θεός.[3] In these earlier chapters the most significant function of θεός is that it designates 'author' and 'authorizer'. Thus the salvific work of Christ was κατὰ τὸ θέλημα τοῦ θεοῦ καὶ πατρὸς ἡμῶν (1.4); Paul's own apostleship originated in the initiative of God (1.15); it is God himself who legitimates the mission to the Gentiles (3.8); it was God who

1. Barclay, *Obeying the Truth*, especially p. 149.

2. In an earlier chapter (ch. 4) Barclay convincingly demonstrates the connection of 5.13–6.10 with the preceding sections of Galatians, arguing that these verses are 'a continuation and completion of the argument' (p. 143). Smit, 'Letter', pp. 8-9, cf. p. 25, argues that there is an 'unmistakable connection' between Gal. 5.7-12 and 6.11-18, suggesting that 5.13–6.10, a 'coherent unit' in itself, may have been added later.

3. Following Smit's structural analysis of Galatians, we note the following occurrences of θεός: in the opening salutation 1.1-5, at vv. 1 and 3, 4; in the *exordium* (1.6-12) at v. 10; in the *'narratio'* at 1.13, 15, 20, 24 and 2.6, 19, 20 and 21 (although the passive forms of δικαιόω in vv. 16-17 should not be overlooked); in the *'confirmatio'* (3.1–4.11) at 3.6, 8, 11, 17-18, 20-21, 26; 4.4, 6-7.

ratified the earlier covenant (3.17), granted (κεχάρισται) the inheritance to Abraham (3.18) and 'in the fulness of time' engaged in a twofold action, sending his Son Jesus (4.4) and his Spirit (4.6).[1]

Finally, there is the emphatic διὰ θεοῦ at the end of 4.7: ὥστε οὐκέτι εἶ δοῦλος ἀλλὰ υἱός· εἰ δὲ υἱός, καὶ κληρονόμος διὰ θεοῦ.[2] Mussner in his commentary compares 1 Cor. 1.9 (πιστὸς ὁ θεός, δι' οὗ ἐκλήθητε εἰς κοινωνίαν τοῦ υἱοῦ αὐτοῦ...), commenting, 'God is the author of the whole salvation-event, and therefore God is emphasized in the conclusion (cf. also 3.18) which has gradually led to a theme which will be dealt with at greater length later in the epistle: the theme of freedom'.[3]

Turning to the word Χριστός in Galatians, we find that it occurs 37 times.[4] Why is this so?[5] It seems natural to link the frequency of Christ-language with the Judaizing controversy which gave rise to this letter. In fact, the emphatic Χριστός at the beginning of 3.13 (an emphasis made all the greater by asyndeton) and the equally emphatic Χριστός at the end of 3.16 together with the 'clusters' of Christ-language in 2.16-17 and 3.26-29 suggest that Paul's Christ-language has an *identifying* function. That is to say, it is employed in order to differentiate the community of Christ from the community of Moses.

Finally, and briefly (since Paul's use of πνεῦμα was examined in the previous chapter), πνεῦμα-language has a primarily polemical function, legitimating the mission to the Gentiles against Jewish opposition (3.2, 4; 4.29).

In the light of this admittedly brief survey of the earlier sections of Galatians, the predominance of Christ- and Spirit-language over God-

1. It is possible that 4.6 is Paul's own amplification of a pre-Pauline credal statement which forms the basis of 4.4 (Bruce, *Galatians*, pp. 194-95).

2. The unexpectedness of διὰ θεοῦ here has given rise to a number of manuscript variants, but as Bruce points out (*Galatians*, pp. 200-1), an original διὰ θεοῦ would explain the variants, but none of the other readings can satisfactorily account for the occurrence of διὰ θεοῦ.

3. F. Mussner, *Der Galaterbrief* (Freiburg: Herder, 1977), p. 277.

4. Apart from the opening and closing greetings (1.3 and 6.18), and the analogy of 4.1, κύριος is used of Christ only at 1.19 ('the brother of the Lord'), 5.10 ('in the Lord') and 6.14 ('in the cross of our Lord Jesus Christ').

5. Philippians is the only other Pauline letter which has a comparable amount of Christ-language. The letter to Philemon is too short for a significant comparison to be made; the word Χριστός occurs eight times within its 25 verses.

language in the paraenetical section is less surprising. The word πνεῦμα is used mainly in contrasts with σάρξ (5.16-25; 6.8). Even 5.5 (ἡμεῖς γὰρ πνεύματι ἐκ πίστεως ἐλπίδα δικαιοσύνης ἀπεκδεχόμεθα) is given a polemical edge by the reference to the Law in the preceding verse.[1] Secondly, the word Χριστός, as in the earlier chapters, is used to denote the Galatians' roots and identity as Christians (5.1, 2, 4, 6). The phrase οἱ δὲ τοῦ Χριστοῦ ('Ιησοῦ) at 5.24 has the same identifying and differentiating function. Most clearly of all, the unusual τὸν νόμον τοῦ Χριστοῦ (6.2) serves to differentiate the 'law' under which Christians stand from the Torah.[2]

I conclude, then, that the Judaizing controversy has resulted in the diversification of Paul's language in the paraenesis of Galatians. The polemical use of πνεῦμα and the differentiating function of Χριστός are both more plentiful than the occurrences of θεός.

God-language occurs three times in the section 5.1–6.10. The traditional (i.e. traditional in Paul) expression 'the Kingdom of God' at 5.21 need not detain us, since this was discussed in an earlier chapter and, as I have already noted here, the key word in this context is not θεός but πνεῦμα. A more significant use of God-language occurs at 5.7-8, where Paul writes: ἐτρέχετε καλῶς· τίς ὑμᾶς ἐνέκοψεν (τῇ) ἀληθείᾳ μὴ πείθεσθαι; ἡ πεισμονὴ οὐκ ἐκ τοῦ καλοῦντος ὑμᾶς.[3] The participle τοῦ καλοῦντος (cf. ἐκλήθητε, v. 13) refers as always in Paul[4] to God, the ἐκ phrase here replacing a *Genitivus Auctoris*.[5] This expression, taken in conjunction with v. 13a (ὑμεῖς γὰρ ἐπ' ἐλευθερίᾳ ἐκλήθητε), seems to underpin Paul's argument with the following *enthymeme*:

1. In this context Barclay's work confirms what we concluded in the previous chapter: Paul uses πνεῦμα (in keeping with Jewish tradition) with reference to *God's* activity (Barclay, *Obeying the Truth*, p. 228).

2. Thus also Bruce, *Galatians*, p. 261, and U. Borse, *Der Brief an Die Galater* (Regensburg: Pustet, 1984), p. 210, who compares Paul's appropriation of the terms 'Israel' at 6.16 and 'circumcision' at Phil. 3.3 (cf. Col. 2.11).

3. The Western reading in v. 7 μηδενὶ πείθεσθαι, with the consequent omission by some Western MSS of οὐ in v. 8 should be rejected. With the RSV I translate 'this persuasion is not from him who called you'.

4. J.B. Lightfoot, *Saint Paul's Epistle to the Galatians* (London: Macmillan, 1896), p. 206.

5. Thus Mussner, *Galaterbrief*, p. 356.

1. You have been enticed (lit. persuaded) back into slavery
2. God called you into freedom
3. the call to obey the law is not the call of God.

Thus the participial phrase ἐκ τοῦ καλοῦντος, employing as it does the verb Paul uses more than any other of God's activity, serves as a theological warrant for the whole of this section 5.7-12, verses which focus sharply on the Judaizers at Galatia.

The last occurrence of God-language in this section of Galatians is the most difficult: Μὴ πλανᾶσθε, θεὸς οὐ μυκτηρίζεται (6.7a). The relevance of this terse warning to the preceding command ('Let him who is taught the word share all good things with him who teaches') is not immediately obvious. If, however, we regard this as a parenthetical statement which suggested itself to Paul because of φορτίον in v. 5, then the sequence of thought becomes more clear. The emphasis falls upon self-examination (v. 4), accountability (v. 5) and judgment (vv. 7-8). Verse 7a, therefore, seems best understood as a warranting statement which links vv. 1-5 and vv. 7b-8.

But what of the theological language used here? There is no exact parallel in the LXX for the use of μυκτηρίζεται here, although the word is used, for example, at Jer. 20.7, of the mocking of God's prophet. Lührmann[1] calls v. 7 'a kind of "peasant-maxim" ("Bauernregel")' which occurs in both Greek and Jewish texts. It should not, however, be abstracted from its broader context here. Betz tends to do this when he assumes that v. 7a is a proverb widespread in the Hellenistic world, concluding,

> The idea of God expressed in the 'proverb' was common in antiquity; he was thought of as the inescapable and dangerous deity who relentlessly destroys those who rebel against him. Any cynical attempt to reject his redemption in Christ will bring down God's wrath upon the rebels.[2]

This, however, will not do. It has become increasingly clear in the course of this study into Paul's language about God that words and phrases borrowed from other contexts acquire new and different meanings in new contexts. So the statement here, for all its *apparent* parallels in paganism, is expressing a thoroughly biblical understanding of wrath and judgment.[3]

1. D. Lührmann, *Der Brief an Die Galater* (Zürich: Theologischer Verlag, 1978), pp. 97-98.
2. Betz, *Galatians*, p. 307.
3. Barclay, *Obeying the Truth*, pp. 170-77, subjects Betz's work on Gal. 5–6 to

Summary. In Galatians, then, we find a pattern different from that of Rom. 12.1–15.13 and 1 Thess. 4.1–5.24. Here the σάρξ/πνεῦμα antithesis has invaded the paraenesis, and Christ-language has a sharp, differentiating function to an extent not found in the other two letters.[1] This, I conclude, is the result of the Judaizing controversy which compelled Paul to use Christ-language in the polemical way I have indicated, and to use πνεῦμα-language (also polemically) to vindicate both the mission to the Gentiles and the new-found status of Gentile Christian converts. θεός-language is infrequent. In the body of the letter it has the by now familiar function of indicating God as the ultimate author and authorizer. In the paraenesis it is used in a minatory way (5.8, 21; 6.7a), but in this respect there are parallels in Rom. 12.19c and 13.2 and 4, and in 1 Thess. 4.6b.

c. *Philippians*

It is not easy to decide whether *Philippians* as it now stands was originally one letter or not. On balance there seem to be fewer difficulties in the view that it was one letter, not least because so many questions about the nature and purpose of a later editor's work are raised by the composite theory.[2] I approach the paraenesis of Philippians, therefore,

severe criticism in a section of his book called 'The Significance of Parallels'. Barclay urges the importance of taking into account the broader context in which apparently similar statements occur (p. 175). So, 'the Stoic Epictetus examines himself in order to discern his essential rational nature and to measure his behaviour by it. . . ' (here Barclay cites Betz' commentary p. 302 n. 91) '. . . whilst Paul tests his work to see if it is of value before God and will stand his scrutiny at the judgment (6.3-5)'.

1. In Rom. 12.1–15.13 the nearest parallel is 12.5 (οἱ πολλοὶ ἓν σῶμά ἐσμεν ἐν Χριστῷ) but the language does not have the sharpness of the Christ-language of Galatians. In the Romans paraenesis 'Christ' has a paradigmatic function at 15.3, 7, and 8, appears in quasi-liturgical phrases at 13.14 and 15.6, and has a warranting function at 14.9, 15 and perhaps 15.5. Similarly, in 1 Thessalonians, the Christ-language (4.16, 5.9, 18, 23) does not have the differentiating function we have found in Galatians.

2. Thus G.F. Hawthorne, *Philippians* (Waco, TX: Word Books, 1983), p. xxxii. Hawthorne (pp. xxix-xxxii) offers a useful summary of the arguments for and against the epistle's unity.

Arguments against the integrity of Philippians tend to focus on two problems: first, what is perceived to be a rift between 3.1 and 3.2 ('the evident break', J.-F. Collange, *The Epistle of Saint Paul to the Philippians* [London: Epworth, 1979], p. 22) and the thanks expressed by Paul to the Philippians in 4.10-20, thanks

on the assumption that the epistle was written as one whole.

To a far greater degree than the other three letters examined so far, Philippians exhibits a 'tightly conceived unity of theological body and paraenesis'.[1] Nevertheless it is possible to distinguish those passages in which Paul turns to explicit exhortation. The first of these begins at 1.27. Paul encourages the Philippians to let their common life (πολιτεύεσθε) be worthy of the gospel, to be united, and not to be frightened (μὴ πτυρόμενοι) by their opponents; their lack of fear, Paul goes on, is αὐτοῖς ἔνδειξις ἀπωλείας, ὑμῶν δὲ σωτηρίας, καὶ τοῦτο ἀπὸ θεοῦ (v. 28b).

This is a different kind of exhortation from any that we have so far encountered in Paul's letters. 1 Thessalonians 1–2 represent the nearest parallel to the situation envisaged here. The Thessalonian Christians stood firm in the face of opposition (1.6; 2.14; 3.6-8), as, it would seem, they had been urged to do (3.4). The Philippians are now being urged to do the same. The question for both communities was: Can our sufferings

which, some scholars argue, would hardly have been deferred to the very end of the letter. Thus many scholars take the view that Philippians in its present form consists of three letters put together by a later editor. Details of the hypothesis vary, as does the chronology of the letters, but Collange is not untypical in his conclusion that 4.10-20 or 23 comprises the first letter, 1.1–3.1 and 4.2-7 (and possibly 4.21-3) the second, and 3.1–4.1 and 4.8-9 the third. W. Schenk, *Die Philipperbriefe des Paulus* (Stuttgart: Kohlhammer, 1984) identifies 4.10-23 as the first letter, 1.1-3.1 and 4.4-7 as the second, and 3.2–4.3, 8-9 as the third. Proponents of a composite theory of Philippians usually cite Polycarp who, writing to the Philippians c. 135 CE, referred to the 'letters' which Paul had written. (This is discussed in some detail by R.P. Martin, *The Epistle of Paul to the Philippians* [London: Marshall, Morgan & Scott, 1976], pp. 11-13).

On the other hand, a number of arguments are put forward in favour of the epistle's unity. First Kümmel, followed by Martin, asks how a later editor felt able to make these 'arbitrary combinations', including the excision of introductions and conclusions (Kümmel, *New Testament*, p. 236; cf. Martin, *Philippians*, p. 19). Secondly, proponents of the epistle's unity point out the recurrence in ch. 3 of words and themes used in chs. 1 and 2 (D.E. Garland, 'The Composition and Unity of Philippians: Some Neglected Factors', *NovT* 27.2, pp. 141-73, esp. pp. 159-62; and, more tentatively and generally, J.L. Houlden, *Paul's Letters from Prison* [London: Pelican, 1970], p. 41).

1. R. W. Funk, quoted by D.C. Verner, *The Household of God* (Atlanta: Scholars Press, 1983), pp. 124-25. Cf. the view of Aune, *New Testament*, noted at the beginning of section 3 of this chapter.

be *theologically* explained? Is the persecution we face confirmation of our faith, or the contrary?

In Phil. 1.28b the emphatic prepositional phrase ἀπὸ τοῦ θεοῦ is used as always in Paul to refer to the effects of the grace of God,[1] a point emphasized by the following ἐχαρίσθη (v. 29). So even their *sufferings* are the gift of grace.[2]

The next explicit use of God-language in a paraenetic context occurs in 2.12-13. (I reserve for Chapter 5 a discussion of the hymn in 2.6-11.) Paul exhorts the Philippians to work out their own salvation μετὰ φόβου καὶ τρόμου (v. 12b), and goes on θεὸς γάρ ἐστιν ὁ ἐνεργῶν ἐν ὑμῖν καὶ τὸ θέλειν καὶ τὸ ἐνεργεῖν ὑπὲρ τῆς εὐδοκίας (v. 13). The force of the connection between vv. 12 and 13 seems to be missed by several commentators. Schenk is an exception, finding here an oxymoron which he summarizes as: 'God has accomplished everything, therefore they have to do everything!'[3] Schenk rightly notes the emphatic use of θεός here, and also the periphrastic tense which 'emphasizes the personal element once more'. Collange sees the connection rather differently, linking v. 13 with the preceding reference to Paul's presence and absence: 'it is God himself (and not me) who presides at this' [i.e. at the communal life of the Philippians]. This is not incompatible with the interpretation offered by Schenk, and the two interpretations together show that vv. 12-13 are intended as encouragement rather than as a warning: here God is not only the warrant for their conduct, but also the author of it. (The obscure ὑπὲρ τῆς εὐδοκίας is probably best understood as a reference to the purpose of God, rather than to human goodwill.)[4]

1. Thus Schenk, *Philipperbriefe*, p. 170, citing 1 Cor. 1.30; 4.5; 6.19 and Rom.15.15 (in this last instance, reading ἀπὸ rather than ὑπὸ).

2. The meaning of 1.28b as a whole is not easy to determine. If, however, ὑμῶν rather than ὑμῖν is read, as the more difficult reading (in that there is no parallel with the preceding αὐτοῖς), the meaning becomes clearer: the ἔνδειξις is for the opponents only, who interpret the Philippians' perseverance in suffering as a sign of their (i.e. the Philippians') ruin, whereas (in reality) it is a sign of the Philippians' salvation (thus, e.g., Hawthorne, *Philippians*, pp. 58-60; and Collange, *Philippians*, p. 75).

3. Schenk, *Philipperbriefe*, p. 217. Schenk's attempt to link v. 12a with v. 1, v. 12b with vv. 2-5, and vv. 6-11 with v. 13, however, is too schematized.

4. Thus Schenk, *Philipperbriefe*, p. 219, who paraphrases 'for the sake of his freely-given love (εὐδοκία), flowing from his innermost being', against, e.g., Hawthorne, *Philippians*, pp. 100-101, who interprets the phrase as referring to the

It is likely that the next instance of God-language was also intended by Paul to be emphatic. Paul urges the Philippians to do everything 'without grumbling or questioning' (v. 14): ἵνα γένησθε ἄμεμπτοι καὶ ἀκέραιοι, τέκνα θεοῦ ἄμωμα μέσον γενεᾶς σκολιᾶς καὶ διεστραμμένης...(v. 15). Schenk refers to the phrase τέκνα θεοῦ as 'the newly introduced, and therefore emphatic concept'.[1] There can be little doubt that the ἵνα clause consists largely of a conscious or unconscious echo of Deut. 32.5, where Moses in his farewell address to the people of Israel describes them as τέκνα μωμητά, γενεὰ σκολιὰ καὶ διεστραμμένη. There seems, therefore, to be a hint of polemic here.[2] The effect of the τέκνα θεοῦ phrase is to provide a warrant for the conduct advocated: this is how children of God should behave.

In the following sections of Philippians, as indeed in the letter as a whole, God-language is fairly infrequent. The phrase ἐν κυρίῳ, however, occurs often,[3] belonging probably to the category of early Christian language of piety.[4] The command to 'rejoice in the Lord' (3.1) is followed by a section of polemic against, in all probability, Judaizers (3.2-4, 17-18).[5] If that is so, it is not surprising that we now have a preponderance of Christ-language, functioning (as in Galatians) as the language of identity and differentiation,[6] and one example of polemical σάρξ/πνεῦμα-language (3.3).[7] The only instance of God-language in this polemical section occurs in 3.9, where Paul contrasts the righteousness originating in the law (ἐκ νόμου) with that which originates with God (ἐκ θεοῦ). This looks like a close parallel with Paul's polemical use

goodwill which Paul wishes the Philippians to attain.

1. Schenk, *Philiperbriefe*, p. 221.

2. Thus Collange, *Philippians*, p. 100. The Old Testament allusion was anticipated by the use of γογγυσμῶν in the preceding verse (see, e.g., Exod. 16.2 and 1 Cor. 10.10).

3. 2.14, 2.19 (ἐν κυρίῳ Ἰησοῦ) 2.24; 2.29; 3.1; 4.1, 2, 4, 10.

4. The phrase ἐν κυρίῳ means, in effect, ' as a Christian'. (See also Appendix 5.) It is interesting to speculate whether Paul knew of, but rejected the use of, the word Χριστιανός, a term which, according to Luke, was first given to Christians at Antioch (Acts 11.26). (It occurs elsewhere in the New Testament only at Acts 26.28 and 1 Pet. 4.16, and may have had a very localized use in the earliest years.)

5. E.g. Collange, *Philippians*, p. 122.

6. Thus 3.3, 7, 8, 9, and 14.

7. The reading θεοῦ is to be preferred in 3.3, rather than θεῷ, since as Hawthorne (*Philippians*, p. 122), points out, λατρεύειν necessarily means to worship *God* (his italics), and therefore the phrase πνεύματι θεοῦ is instrumental.

of πνεῦμα, and in one sense it is. Here, however, the emphasis falls on the *origin* and *authority* behind the righteousness which he now advocates over against δικαιοσύνην τὴν ἐκ νόμου, and for this purpose the word θεός is needed.

Two more occurrences of the word θεός deserve mention in ch. 3. Although the reference to 'Christ Jesus' in v. 14 is an example of the language of differentiation, Paul's use of the noun κλήσεως attracts to itself the word θεός, since in Paul's writings it is always God who calls. Similarly, the verb 'reveal' (ἀποκαλύψει) in v. 15, although quite rare in Paul, never has 'the Lord' 'Christ' or 'the Spirit' as the subject.[1]

In the remaining verses of Philippians there are a few expressions which must briefly concern us. First the terse expression ὁ κύριος ἐγγύς (4.5) is probably a reference to the Parousia.[2] The next two verses contain expressions which are unique in the New Testament. In v. 6b Paul urges the Philippians τὰ αἰτήματα ὑμῶν γνωριζέσθω πρὸς τὸν θεόν. Lightfoot[3] notes the significance of πρὸς τὸν θεόν rather than τῷ θεῷ. This is all the more striking in view of the apparent play on words[4] with the verb to know in v. 5, where the dative πᾶσιν ἀνθρώποις is used. Paul's language, therefore, does not imply *informing* God of what he did not previously know. A promise now follows: Paul assures the Philippians: καὶ ἡ εἰρήνη τοῦ θεοῦ ἡ ὑπερέχουσα πάντα νοῦν φρουρήσει τὰς καρδίας ὑμῶν καὶ τὰ νοήματα ὑμῶν ἐν Χριστῷ Ἰησοῦ (v. 7). This verse contains another ἅπαξ λεγόμενον in the New Testament: ἡ εἰρήνη τοῦ θεοῦ. (It is also absent from the LXX.) Here the most probable interpretation of θεοῦ is that it is subjective: that is the peace which God *gives*.

Summary. The evidence of Philippians is difficult to evaluate. But there are a few examples (1.28b; 2.13, 15) of the emphatic use of God-language which we observed in Romans and, to a lesser extent, in 1 Thessalonians. The reason for Paul's less frequent use of theological warrants probably lies in the fact that he appears to have anticipated no resistance from the Philippians to his teaching; indeed, his relationship

1. 1 Cor. 2.16 and Gal. 1.16; cf. the 'divine passives' of Rom. 8.18; 1 Cor. 14.30; and Gal. 3.23.

2. So most commentators, comparing 1 Cor.16.23.

3. J.B. Lightfoot, *St Paul's Epistle to the Philippians* (London: Macmillan, 1885), p. 161.

4. Thus Schenk, *Philipperbriefe*, p. 246.

with them seems to have been very warm and cordial. Secondly, the Judaizing crisis is reflected in this letter, notably in 3.2-19—and this may explain the prevalence of Christ-language, as in Galatians.

d. *1 and 2 Corinthians*

1 Corinthians 5.1-13. The picture is even more complicated when we turn to 1 Corinthians, not only because of its length but also because of the variety of the material and the interweaving of paraenesis and theological argument. I examine first the passage dealing with a case of gross immorality in the Corinthians community, 5.1-13.[1]

At first sight this passage might seem similar to 1 Thess. 4.3-8. The circumstances, however, are very different. At Corinth the problem was not persuading the Corinthians that wrong had been done (5.1),[2] but rather persuading them to take action against the offender. Because it is a matter of congregational discipline, κύριος-language predominates in the earlier verses (vv. 4-5). But the origin and the very identity of the community are brought into question by this flagrant immorality—hence the reference to 'Christ our Passover' (v. 7).[3] Finally (v. 13a), Paul refers to the future[4] judgment of 'those outside'.

In this discussion God-language plays only a small part and there are no instances of its warranting function which we have seen elsewhere. But this is an extended discussion of a specific internal matter, as in Rom. 14.1–15.7. Yet, unlike that situation at Rome, Old Testament *halakah* is relevant to this issue, which was far more clear-cut than the Roman situation.

1. 4.1-21 must be considered as the practical conclusion to the extended theological argument (i.e. 1.18—3.23) examined in Chapter 2, rather than as paraenesis of the kind this chapter is concerned with. Although these verses bear some resemblance to the conclusions of other letters, there are no breaks in the thought or structure of 1 Corinthians to warrant the view that it consists of more than one letter. (Thus Barrett, *1 Corinthians*, p. 15; and Conzelmann, *1 Corinthians*, p. 3 n. 21 and p. 298 n. 9).

2. 5.2a (καὶ ὑμεῖς πεφυσιωμένοι ἐστέ. . .) might suggest that the Corinthians were not as aware as they should have been of the seriousness of this particular case of immorality. It would probably be more accurate to say that their particular kind of Christian 'individualism' made them blind to the damaging effects of such conduct by one individual on the *whole* community.

3. See Grayston (*Dying We Live*, pp. 29-30), who refers to the importance of maintaining a 'well-recognized boundary'.

4. Thus Conzelmann, *1 Corinthians*, p. 102 n. 84; Barrett, *1 Corinthians*, p. 133.

1 Corinthians 6.1-11. These verses deal with the question of Christians engaging in litigation against each other in pagan lawcourts. So this is a distinctively Christian problem, and an 'intra-mural' one (or at least one which Paul felt *should* be intra-mural). The words κύριος, πνεῦμα, and χριστός do not occur until v. 11, and θεός only in v. 11 and in the traditional phrase 'kingdom of God' (vv. 9-10).[1] In contrast with the infrequency of God-language, Paul three times uses the expression οὐκ οἴδατε in rhetorical questions (vv. 2, 3 and 9).[2] In the first two instances this must mean that these points were the substance of earlier teaching. (Who else but Christians would have known or believed that they would judge the world?)[3] Similarly, vv. 9-10 seem to be a reminder of the traditional paraenesis which also occurs in Gal. 5.19-21.[4]

Verse 11, however, is probably Paul's own composition, and for our purpose the most interesting in this particular paraenetic unit: καὶ ταῦτά τινες ἦτε· ἀλλὰ ἀπελούσασθε, ἀλλὰ ἡγιάσθητε, ἀλλὰ ἐδικαιώθητε ἐν τῷ ὀνόματι τοῦ κυρίου Ἰησοῦ Χριστοῦ καὶ ἐν τῷ πνεύματι τοῦ θεοῦ ἡμῶν. Here the three passive verbs presuppose God as the subject of the action, the threefold ἀλλά giving added emphasis to the verbs. The reference to 'the name of the Lord Jesus Christ' makes clear the focus of God's action, the final reference to 'the Spirit of our God' reflecting Paul's tendency to trace everything back to God.[5]

1 Corinthians 6.12-20. Here Paul offers his own theological commentary on the Corinthians watchword 'All things are lawful for me',[6] with

1. Here in v. 9 Paul has inverted the word order, perhaps to throw the emphasis upon θεοῦ: θεοῦ βασιλείαν.

2. Elsewhere in Paul at 1 Cor. 6.15, 16, 19; 9.13, 24; Rom. 6.16; 11.2.

3. Conzelmann, *1 Corinthians*, p. 104.

4. It may seem surpising that Paul does not back up his argument at the end of v. 7 (διὰ τί οὐχὶ μᾶλλον ἀδικεῖσθε;) with a quotation from the teaching of Jesus, or a paradigm based on his life or death (as he does in Rom. 15.3), particularly as this is the only Pauline letter with explicit quotations of Jesus' teaching (7.10; 9.14; 11.23-26; cf. 11.1). Perhaps Paul thought that the conduct of the Corinthians was so bad that something minatory was required (vv. 9-10). On the other hand, the foundational character of 1.23 ('Christ crucified') is never far from the surface in this letter.

5. Thus Conzelmann, *1 Corinthians*, p. 107. This verse may be a further example of Paul's apologetic use of πνεῦμα—i.e. the Corinthians, Gentiles though they were, had actually received the Spirit of 'our God'.

6. Cf. 10.23a. For a detailed study of what the Corinthians probably wrote to

particular reference to πορνεία. Here Paul combines an appeal to what was, or should have been self-evident to the Corinthians (οὐκ οἴδατε, vv. 15, 16, 19) with powerful theological warrants (vv. 13-14, 19-20). We note, first, the parallelism of structure in vv. 13-14:

> τὰ βρώματα τῇ κοιλίᾳ καὶ ἡ κοιλία τοῖς βρώμασιν, ὁ δὲ θεὸς καὶ ταύτην καὶ ταῦτα καταργήσει. τὸ δὲ σῶμα οὐ τῇ πορνείᾳ ἀλλὰ τῷ κυρίῳ, καὶ ὁ κύριος τῷ σώματι· ὁ δὲ θεὸς καὶ τὸν κύριον ἤγειρεν καὶ ἡμᾶς ἐξεγερεῖ διὰ τῆς δυνάμεως αὐτοῦ.

In the first half of the statement the relationship between the stomach and food is followed by an emphatic ὁ δὲ θεός, and a future verb καταργήσει. In the first half of the second statement the relationship between the body and the Lord is mentioned, and followed again by an emphatic ὁ δὲ θεός (this time with two verbs ἤγειρεν and ἐξεγερεῖ). The two verses, therefore, comprise a striking example of the warranting function of θεός-language, and of the subordination of 'the Lord' to God.

The following rhetorical questions imply that the substance of these verses has been the content of earlier teaching (vv. 15, 16, 19). The Christ-language of v. 15 indicates, as in 5.7, that the community's very identity and boundaries are under threat. In the third of the rhetorical questions ('Do you not know that your body is a temple of the Holy Spirit?') Paul repeats again the emphasis which we noted in 1 Corinthians 2 and 3,[1] that the Spirit is *from God* (ἀπὸ θεοῦ), indicating once again the theocentric concern of this epistle. Finally, this discussion ends with a passive verb again implying the action of God, and with a command to glorify God: ἠγοράσθητε γὰρ τιμῆς· δοξάσατε δὴ τὸν θεὸν ἐν τῷ σώματι ὑμῶν (v. 20). We should probably be correct in classing 6.12-20 with 1 Thess. 4.3-8 (and Rom. 13.1-7) as examples of teaching to which Paul expected some resistance. In all three instances the theological warrants are powerfully emphatic. This particular unit has additional references to 'Christ' (v. 15), perhaps because Paul felt that the attitudes implied in the Corinthian watchword 'All things are permitted *to me*' (v. 12a) were especially destructive of community.

1 Corinthians 7.1-40. It is clear that from 7.1 onwards that the Corinthians themselves supplied much of the agenda for the remainder

Paul, Hurd's study (*1 Corinthians*) is still important.

1. See Chapter 2, section 3.

of the letter.[1] Chapter 7 itself is in some ways unique in Pauline paraenesis. There are more explicit references to the apostle's personal opinions[2] than anywhere else in Paul's writings. This is largely, perhaps, because Paul was facing some new problems here for which traditional paraenesis, whether Jewish or Christian, did not have the answer. This may help to explain the relative paucity of God-language in this chapter. Nevertheless, the Pauline tendency to 'trace everything back to God' may still be discerned (vv. 7b, 15c, 17, 18-24, with the frequent recurrence of the passive of καλέω). God's call, therefore, is the fundamental theological *datum*.

But that is not all. What matters supremely is τήρησις ἐντολῶν θεοῦ (v. 19b).[3] And not only is God the instigator and authorizer, he is also the goal: the summarizing command of v. 24 makes clear that all Christian life is lived 'before God':[4] ἕκαστος ἐν ᾧ ἐκλήθη, ἀδελφοί, ἐν τούτῳ μενέτω παρὰ θεῷ.[5]

The remainder of the chapter (vv. 25-40) contains practically no God-language, (only πνεῦμα θεοῦ at v. 40), but several instances of κύριος-language (vv. 25, 32 [twice], and vv. 34, 35, 39). This is in keeping with the matters under discussion, namely allegiances and relationships. The strongly eschatological character of the passage, however, especially v. 26a and vv. 29-31, reflects the underlying theology.

1 Corinthians 11.2-16.[6] It is not possible or directly relevant to this inquiry to explore here all the obscurities of this passage. First, v. 3

1. Cf. 7.25; 8.1; 12.1; 16.1, 12.

2. Verses 6, 12, 25, 40.

3. This extraordinary statement by Paul was almost certainly due to antinomian tendencies at Corinth. (See J. Drane *Paul—Libertine or Legalist?* (London: SPCK, 1975). When this verse is set side by side with Gal. 6.15, the versatility and flexibility of Paul's teaching is even more striking.

4. This translation of παρὰ θεῷ is to be preferred to 'with God'. (Thus Conzelmann, *1 Corinthians*, p. 129, against Barrett, *1 Corinthians*, p. 172). παρὰ θεῷ occurs in Paul at Rom. 2.11, 13; 9.14; 1 Cor. 3.19 and Gal. 3.11. In each instance ἐνώπιον would seem to fit in place of παρά.

5. This section also includes κύριος-language, not surprisingly, since the word δοῦλος tends to 'attract' κύριος.

6. Chapters 8–10 form an extended discussion of whether Christians should eat meat which had been offered to idols. The important verse 8.6 will be considered in Chapter 5 section 5, where the theological emphasis of these chapters as a whole will also be considered.

provides what Conzelmann calls the 'fundamental ground' on which Paul bases his argument: θέλω δὲ ὑμᾶς εἰδέναι ὅτι παντὸς ἀνδρὸς ἡ κεφαλὴ ὁ Χριστός ἐστιν, κεφαλὴ δὲ γυναικὸς ὁ ἀνήρ, κεφαλὴ δὲ τοῦ Χριστοῦ ὁ θεός. The sequence of the argument here is surprising: it is not clear why the headship of Christ is mentioned before the headship of the husband. But the addition of the third phrase is interesting, particularly as it does not seem relevant to the argument. It is yet further evidence of Paul's concern to stress that *God* is the source of everything. The same emphasis is repeated in the middle of the following jumble[1] of warrants: τὰ δὲ πάντα ἐκ τοῦ θεοῦ (v. 12c). Thus, although in this section Paul seems less sure of his ground than perhaps anywhere else in his writings (with the possible exception of some sections of 1 Cor. 7), he does seem to go out of his way to appeal to God as the *ultimate* warrant.

1 Corinthians 12–14. It is possible that in much of this extended discussion, περὶ...τῶν πνευματικῶν,[2] Paul is being 'a Greek to Greeks'.[3] That he does so here may be due not only to his addressees, but also to the nature of the subject, particularly 'the body' of the community (vv. 12-27).[4]

It may be partly for this reason that references to God in this extended paraenesis are fewer than in many other of the sections of Pauline paraenesis which we have studied here. Nevertheless, there are important references to God at 12.24 and 28, and not least in a concluding warrant in 14.33: οὐ γάρ ἐστιν ἀκαταστασίας θεὸς ἀλλὰ εἰρήνης. In 12.4-6, however, we encounter the only place in Paul's writings where πνεῦμα, Χριστός and θεός occur in consecutive and closely parallel statements:

> Διαιρέσεις δὲ χαρισμάτων εἰσίν, τὸ δὲ αὐτὸ πνεῦμα· καὶ διαιρέσεις διακονιῶν εἰσιν, καὶ ὁ αὐτὸς κύριος· καὶ διαιρέσεις ἐνεργημάτων εἰσίν, ὁ δὲ αὐτὸς θεὸς ὁ ἐνεργῶν· τὰ πάντα ἐν πᾶσιν.

1. Most commentators note the contrast, if not contradiction, between vv. 11-12 and earlier verses, especially v. 8.

2. It is not clear whether the Greek πνευματικῶν refers to people or gifts.

3. Siegert, *Argumentation*, has argued that Paul's methods of argument were those which were widely employed in his time, and that, in employing them, Paul took the presuppositions of his addressees seriously.

4. See Conzelmann, *1 Corinthians*, p. 211 nn. 7 and 8 for the many parallels in Greek and Roman literature.

Although repeated references to the Spirit now follow (v. 7, v. 8 [twice], v. 9 [twice] and v. 11), the *theo*centric character of the Spirit is underlined by the use in v. 11, with the Spirit as subject, of the same verb used in v. 6 with ὁ θεός as subject: πάντα δὲ ταῦτα ἐνεργεῖ τὸ ἓν καὶ τὸ αὐτὸ πνεῦμα διαιροῦν ἰδίᾳ ἑκάστῳ καθὼς βούλεται.

Paul's argument, therefore, for all its undoubted and probably intentional similarities with Graeco-Roman paraenesis, is different from them in its *theological* emphasis.[1]

2 Corinthians. There is little material in 2 Corinthians relevant to this study. Whatever view is taken of the integrity of 2 Corinthians, much of it is concerned with personal issues such as Paul's own status as an apostle at Corinth. This is the main theme of both chs. 10–13 and chs. 1–7, while the Collection is the subject of chs. 8 and 9. Thus there are no identifiable paraenetical sections such as we have been able to identify in the other letters (although Philippians comes closest to 2 Corinthians in this respect).[2] Yet even here we find an occasional *enthymeme* or *paradigm* (e.g. 8.9, '*For* you know the grace of our Lord Jesus Christ...', or at 9.7b '*for* God loves a cheerful giver').

Summary

This section has reviewed the paraenesis of those letters in which paraenesis is more interspersed throughout the body of the letter. It has become increasingly clear that there is no single pattern in Pauline paraenesis, although in every letter there are examples of God-language used to provide a theological warrant for the teaching being given. In Philippians the warrants are less frequent, perhaps because of Paul's positive estimate of the church at Philippi. In 1 Corinthians the pattern varies. Most frequently, however, Paul's arguments either begin or end with an appeal to God. Thus weighty theological affirmations are made at an early stage of the argument in 6.12-20 (vv. 14-15), 8-10 (8.6[3]),

1. The stylistically unique (in Paul) ch. 13 is not strictly speaking paraenesis, although it clearly has a paraenetic function (12.28). Here the perspective is deeply eschatological, the passive verbs (vv. 8, 10, 12) tending to disguise its theological character.

2. 6.14–7.1 is not certainly Pauline, although it contains a theological warrant (v. 16b) of the kind we have been studying in this chapter. (See Furnish, *2 Corinthians*, pp. 375-83, on the origin of these verses, though Furnish ends by acknowledging the lack of hard evidence [p. 382]).

3. See Chapter 5, section 5 for 8.6.

11.2-16 (v. 3) and 12-14 (12.4-6). Similarly, discussions end with an appeal to God as judge (5.13), an assertion of what God has done in Christ (6.11, 20), a reference to God's gifts or call (7.7, 15, 24), or an appeal to the character of God (14.33).

The warranting function of God-language is thus very clear. In much Pauline paraenesis God-language is far from marginal: God is supremely the *alpha* and *omega* of the Christian's existence, and the one before whom the Christian life is lived out. That much is clear. Similarly, the identifying or differentiating function of much Christ-language is clear. But can we speak here of a *new* God-language, or even of a new understanding of God?

First, we have encountered more familiar language used in a quite revolutionary way (τέκνα θεοῦ, Phil. 2.15), and a new (?) expression (εἰρήνη τοῦ θεοῦ, Phil. 4.7, although it must be stressed that this concept is far from new). Secondly, these letters provide further evidence of an extraordinary emphasis on God's grace (e.g. Phil. 1.28-29) and God's call (e.g. 1 Cor. 7). But, thirdly, we have encountered many examples of the juxtaposition or interplay of God-language with both Christ- and κύριος-language. There is thus emerging an important paradox: Paul's writings are utterly theocentric, and yet Paul's God-language, by itself, is not the centre of gravity. Much of it relates grammatically—and therefore, I suggest, points *theologically*—to language about Christ. This will concern us later on in this study, but first it is necessary to see Pauline paraenesis in sharper focus by a brief examination of Jewish and Graeco-Roman paraenesis.

4. *God-Language in Jewish Paraenesis*

The use of God-language to provide warrants for ethical action is so widespread in the Old Testament as hardly to need documentation. Kennedy notes that the first five commandments of the Decalogue 'are all accompanied by some kind of reason why the commandment should be accepted'.[1] The first four reasons are, in fact, theological. It is not necessary here to enter into the long debate about the history of traditions behind the Decalogue; it is clear that, whatever traditions lie behind the form of the Decalogue in which we now have it, there can be no doubt about their 'highly distinctive form'.[2] Thus, the first

1. Kennedy, *New Testament Interpretation*, p. 7.
2. Thus, most recently, R.E. Clements, 'The Ten Commandments: Law and

commandments 'You shall have no other gods before me' is preceded by the proclamation 'I am the Lord your God, who brought you out of the house of bondage' (Exod. 20.2-3). The second, prohibiting the making of graven images, rests on the statement 'For I the Lord your God am a jealous God...' (v. 5). The third, 'You shall not take the name of the Lord your God in vain', then goes on 'for the Lord will not hold him guiltless who takes his name in vain' (v. 7). In the fourth we have what seems to be a *paradigm*: the Israelites are forbidden to work on the sabbath 'for in six days the Lord made heaven and earth, the sea and all that is in them, and rested the seventh day; therefore the Lord blessed the sabbath day and hallowed it' (vv. 8-11).

Kennedy contends that 'such a statement with a supporting reason' is what classical rhetoric called an *enthymeme*[1] (a term we encountered in our earlier discussion of theological warrants in Paul's paraenesis). Here as in many other Old Testament passages, the Decalogue reflects the understanding that 'the speaker is a vehicle of God's will'.[2] Both these features are found elsewhere in the Pentateuch, Leviticus 19 being a notable example. This chapter begins with the paradigm quoted in 1 Peter (1.16): 'You shall be holy; for I the Lord your God am holy'. Thereafter the commands are punctuated frequently by the terse 'I am the Lord your God' (vv. 3, 4, 10, 12, 14, 16, 18, 25, 28, 30, 31, 32, 34, 36, 37).

A similar pattern is found in the prophetic literature, although here direct commands are not so common and are not usually found in tersely expressed series as in the Pentateuch and some sections of New Testament epistles. Nevertheless, there are instances of commands followed by *theological* reasons for the command. At Amos 5.6, for example, we have the command 'Seek the Lord and live', and the supporting reason 'or he will break out against the house of Joseph like fire'. J.L. Mays notes the 'marginal' character of exhortation in Amos,[3] but another example of command and supporting theological reason occurs at 5.14:

> Seek good, and not evil,
> that you may live;
> and so the Lord, the God of hosts, will be with you,
> just as you have said.

Social Ethic', *EpwRev* 16.3 (1989), pp. 71-81, p. 74, cf. p. 72.

1. Kennedy, *New Testament Interpretation*, p. 7.
2. Kennedy, *New Testament Interpretation*, p. 7.
3. J.L. Mays, *Amos* (London: SCM Press, 1969), p. 89.

A similar pattern may be discerned in other prophets where direct commands occur: 'Do not fear, *for* I have redeemed you' (Isa. 43.1c; cf. 55.6-8), and 'Maintain justice, and do what is right, *for* soon my salvation will come, and my deliverance be revealed' (Isa. 56.1b,c; cf 60.1).

The Wisdom Literature also offers clear examples of *enthymemes* in the form of theological warrants, although here too direct paraenesis in the forms we have been studying, is not always prominent.[1] Von Rad, for example, in his discussion of the 'literary proverb' writes

> Even if the sentences were also used in the schools, neverthless their style is not directly didactic. Far and away the majority of them are statements which make assertions in thetical form quite neutrally, that is without any direct appeal to the listeners. They are not imperative in character.[2]

This is especially true of Proverbs, although a theological *enthymeme* occasionally occurs, as in 3.11-12:

> My child, do not despise the Lord's discipline
> or be weary of his reproof,
> for the Lord reproves the one he loves,
> as a father the son in whom he delights.

This is so also of Ecclesiastes, part of which is autobiographical reflection (e.g.1.12–2.20) or gnomic sayings or 'adages' (e.g. 3.1-8). Direct exhortations do occur, however, and though not all are followed by a theological warrant (e.g. 8.2-4), they frequently are:

> Never be rash with your mouth nor let your heart be quick to utter a word before God, *for* God is in heaven, and you upon earth; therefore let your words be few (5.2; cf. 7.17-18; 9.7; 12.13-14).

It is possible that some of the references to God were added by a later editor anxious to give a more 'orthodox' tone to this writing. This view is widely held[3] of the final enthymeme: 'Fear God, and keep his

1. J.L. Crenshaw, *Old Testament Wisdom* (London: SCM Press, 1982), pp. 36-39, briefly lists the literary forms of Old Testament wisdom, noting eight categories: proverb, riddle, allegory, hymn, dialogue, autobiographical narrative, noun lists, and didactive narrative (poetry and prose).

2. G. Von Rad, *Old Testament Wisdom* (London: SCM Press, 1972), p. 31. Cf. R.N. Whybray, *The Intellectual Tradition in the Old Testament* (Berlin: de Gruyter, 1974), p. 73, who notes the case against the view that the admonition (*Mahnung*) was characteristic of wisdom literature.

3. E.g. Crenshaw, *Old Testament Wisdom*, p. 146; M. Hengel, *Judaism and Hellenism* (London: SCM Press, 1974), I, p. 127.

commandments: for this is the whole duty of man. *For* God will bring every deed into judgment, with every secret thing, whether good or evil' (12.13b, 14). (Elsewhere, in the view of Hengel[1] the writer comes close to equating 'God' with whatever happens, and his will with simply what befalls everyone.)

Like Qoheleth, the Wisdom of Ben Sirach reflects the influence of Hellenistic ideas and language.[2] His concept of God, however, is not so impersonal as that of Qoheleth; much more central to his thought, and perhaps central to his theology,[3] is a doctrine of retribution: 'For the Lord always repays' (35.11). There are many examples of 'negative retribution', as when the advice to refuse bread to the man who never gives alms (12.4-5) is followed by the warrant 'The Most High also hates sinners and will inflict punishment on the ungodly'. Not surprisingly, we find many examples in Sirach's work of theological statements used as warrants, both positive and negative. (Examples of positive warrants include 1.26; 2.6, 8; 3.18; 4.10, 28; examples of negative warrants are 1.30; 3.16; 5.3, 7; 26.28; 28.1.)

Alongside such theological statements we find secular, or prudential warrants. In the long section of ethical precepts beginning at 6.23 and concluding at 9.16, theological warrants are few (7.11 is an exception). More frequent is advice such as 'Do not desert an old friend', the reason for this being 'a new one is not worth as much' (9.10). Here, perhaps, we find an example of the eudaimonism of Hellenistic thought which has influenced Sirach, without determining his theology.[4] It is important,

1. Hengel, *Judaism*, I, p. 121; cf. Crenshaw, *Old Testament Wisdom*, pp. 137-39.

2. Hengel, *Judaism*, I, pp. 147-50, although he emphasizes the differences between Sirach and the ideas of the Stoa. Cf. Crenshaw, *Old Testament Wisdom*, p. 159, who speaks both of Sirach's 'complete' Hellenization and of the thorough Hebraizing of the expressions and ideas which he borrowed.

3. This is certainly the view of Hengel, *Judaism*, I, pp. 138-44.

4. Hengel, *Judaism*, I, pp. 142-43. The importance of Ben Sirach's theological warrants are enhanced if, as Crenshaw (*Old Testament Wisdom*, p. 172) and Hengel (*Judaism*, I, pp. 143-48) believe, there were contemporary challenges to the very notion of the justice and righteousness of God. Ben Sirach's response is far from simplistic; he recognizes that mystery remains: '. . . for the power of the Lord is wonderful and his power is hidden from men' (11.4, quoted by Von Rad, *Old Testament Wisdom*, p. 249) and secondly, that everything has its appointed time (Von Rad, *Old Testament Wisdom*, pp. 251-54; Crenshaw, *Old Testament Wisdom* pp. 167-68).

however, not to define 'Judaism' and 'Hellenism' too rigidly. One recent survey of the traditions utilized by Sirach concludes that while he attempted to *Judaize* all his sources (including Hellenistic and Egyptian ones), the Judaic traditions on which he drew included the Proverbial wisdom tradition, with which Sirach shared a pronounced 'eudaimonism'.[1] What is relevant for our purpose, however, is that the tradition of grounding commandments in statements about God, found in both the *Torah* and the prophetic literature, is carried on by this writer of the early second century BCE.[2]

In the book of Tobit, 'a wisdom novel'[3] written probably in the Dispersion in the post-exilic period[4] there are three sections of paraenesis, the longest of which is 4.4-21. Not all the commands here have an explicit theological warrant (e.g. vv. 5-6 and 12, although it would probably be true to say that a theological warrant is implicit in both these passages). There are, however, clear examples of such warrants at v. 7: 'Do not turn your face away from anyone who is poor, and the face of God will not be turned away from you.'[5]

This sentence is an example of what S. Schechter calls 'Measure for Measure',[6] in which the same verb is used in both the command and warrant (Cf. Mt. 7.1; 1 Cor. 3.17). A further example of a theological warrant occurs in v. 11 where Tobit supports his exhortation to give alms (v. 8) by stressing that 'Almsgiving for all who practise it, is an excellent offering in the presence of the Most High' (v. 11).[7]

Thus far we have seen how deeply embedded in Jewish moral teaching is the use of God-language. The earliest traditions, it would seem, have theological warrants undergirding the commandments. The same pattern can be discerned in the prophetic literature and the

1. Thus J.T. Sanders, *Ben Sira and Demotic Wisdom* (Chico, CA: Scholars Press, 1983), *passim*; on the 'eudaimonism' of Sirach, see pp. 9-11.

2. Hengel, *Judaism*, I, p. 131, dates Ben Sira between 190 and 175 BCE.

3. Nickelsburg's description (*Jewish Literature*, p. 35).

4. Nickelsburg, *Jewish Literature*, notes that Tob. 14.1-7 almost certainly implies a date before the persecution of the Jews by Antiochus Epiphanes in 168 BCE, but it is difficult to establish much more than this.

5. REB translation (the translators here note that vv. 7-19 are not found in all MSS, although this is not discussed in Nickelsburg).

6. S. Schechter, *Studies in Judaism* (New York: Meridian Books Inc. and the Jewish Publication Society of America, 1958), p. 106.

7. Compare also 12.8-10, where almsgiving is similarly extolled with implicit theological warrants.

Wisdom literature. Finally in this section I turn to a document the precise origins and nature of which continue to be hotly debated, but which I include here because of the correspondence of some of its paraenesis with that of the New Testament. This is the *Testaments of the Twelve Patriarchs*. Although the evidence is complex and by no means conclusive, the view taken here is that *Testament XII* is a Jewish document with later Christian interpolations, and not, in the first instance, a Christian document.[1]

1. Until the work of F. Schnapp and R.H. Charles in the late nineteenth and early twentieth centuries, the consensus was that the Testaments were Christian (H.D. Slingerland, *The Testaments of the Twelve Patriarchs* [Missoula, MT: Scholars Press, 1977], pp. 5-15). From Charles's work until the publication of de Jonge's dissertation *The Testaments of the Twelve Patriarchs* (Leiden: Brill, 1953), the majority of scholars subscribed to the view of Charles that the Testaments were basically a Jewish writing which had been interpolated by a Christian editor. De Jonge challenged this consensus. First, drawing on the earlier work of Hunkin and Messel, de Jonge argued that the MSS evidence did not prove that there ever was a pre-Christian version of the Testaments (de Jonge, *Testaments*, pp. 10-11, pp. 15-16. Cf. Slingerland, *Testaments*, p. 47, and now the commentary by H.W. Hollander and M. de Jonge, *The Testaments of the Twelve Patriarchs: A Commentary* (Leiden: Brill, 1985). This view is now generally accepted (cf. de Jonge, *Studies in the Testaments of the Twelve Patriarchs* [Leiden: Brill 1975], p. 184), in an article 'The Interpretation of the Twelve Patriarchs in Recent Years' (pp. 183-92). Conversely, however, textual criticism cannot establish that there was *not* a pre-Christian Testaments. Slingerland, *Testaments*, p. 95, points out that the oldest extant textual tradition may reflect only a late or Christian stage of the tradition. Textual criticism, therefore, cannot solve the question of the origin of this work.

Source-criticism, similarly, has a limited value. Motif-criticism has more interesting possibilities. Slingerland points out the major drawback here, namely the overlap between Judaism and Christianity. He himself criticizes the work of P.W. Macky for what he calls an uncontrolled use of motif-criticism (Slingerland, *Testaments*, pp. 98-103), and in particular for never raising the question of what is distinctive to Judaism or Christianity. This seems to constitute the greatest obstacle to resolving the question of the origins of the Testaments. There is so much which is neither distinctively Jewish nor Christian (Hollander and de Jonge, *Commentary*, pp. 83-84). Consequently, Slingerland himself is pessimistic about what can be achieved by the method of motif-criticism (p. 106), although in later studies he contends for a Jewish origin for the Testaments on precisely these grounds (Slingerland, 'The Nature of *Nomos* [Law] within the Testaments of the Twelve Patriarchs', *JBL* 105 [1986], pp. 39-48, in which he contends that νόμος for the authors of the Patriarchs was Israel's traditional legal corpus understood in its wholeness. Cf. also his article 'The Levitical Hallmark within the Testaments of the

If, then, what we have is an essentially Jewish document, what material does it provide for this study of Jewish paraenetical traditions? It seems probable that paraenesis is the most important element, but what are its forms and origins? Nickelsburg observes that most Testaments have a common structure, including two sections of exhortation.[1] What places does God-language have in these sections?

There is a variety of warrants and motivations for ethical conduct in the Testaments. As one might expect in a document which has a considerable amount of narrative material, the patriarchs' lives are paradigmatic. In the case of Reuben and Judah the patriarchs' lives are a kind of negative *paradigm* (*T. Reub.* 4.1 etc., *T. Jud.* 13.1-8, 17.1-2). There are also occasional examples of prudential warrants, such as we found in the Wisdom Literature[2] (e.g. *T. Benj.* 5.1). Where God-language is used in a warrant, however, the warrant normally takes the form of a promise or a threat (as is usual in the Wisdom traditions). Thus the warning against the sons of Levi in *T. Reub.* 6.1-5 is followed by the warning ὁ γὰρ θεὸς ποιήσει τὴν ἐκδίκησιν αὐτῶν, καὶ ἀποθανεῖσθε θανάτῳ πονηρῷ (6.6). A more extended threat is made in *T. Naph.* 8.6 where it is said that 'the one who does not do the good, men and angels will curse, and ὁ θεὸς ἀδοξήσει ἐν τοῖς ἔθνεσι δι' αὐτοῦ...καὶ ὁ κύριος μισήσει αὐτόν'. But promises also abound in the Testaments. In *T. Iss.* 5.1-4 the advice is given 'Keep the law of God my children... love the Lord and your neighbour...ὅτι ἐν πρωτογενήμασι καρπῶν γῆς εὐλογήσει σε κύριος.'[3]

There are very few exceptions to the pattern of promise or threat when God-language is used with this warranting function. Only rarely is the character of God the warrant for action. An example occurs at

Twelve Patriarchs', *JBL* 103 [1984], pp. 531-37, in which he argues for Levitical authorship).

It is not possible to discuss in detail here all the arguments marshalled by de Jonge in his earlier writings for a Christian origin for the Patriarchs, or the arguments in the commentary by Hollander and de Jonge. But, on balance, the evidence for regarding the Testaments as primarily a Jewish document with later Christian interpolations outweighs the arguments for regarding them as a primarily Christian document.

1. Nickelsburg, *Jewish Literature*, p. 232.

2. H.W. Hallender, *Joseph as an Ethical Model in the Testaments of the Twelve Patriarchs* (Leiden: Brill, 1981), pp. 94-95, observes that the exhortatory sections 'often employ themes, language and forms typical of wisdom literature'.

3. Hollander and de Jonge prefer to read the aorist εὐλόγησε here, arguing that this would correspond with the δέδοται of v. 5 (*Commentary*, p. 246).

T. Zeb. 7.2: 'You therefore, my children, on the basis of God's caring for you (ἐξ ὧν παρέχει ὑμῖν ὁ θεός)[1] without discrimination be compassionate and merciful to all'.

The 'measure for measure' formula which we encountered both in Paul (1 Cor. 3.17) and in Tobit (4.7) occurs also in the Patriarchs. Thus in *T. Zebulon* we have 'Have mercy in your inner being, my children, because whatever anyone does to his neighbour, the Lord will do to him (οὕτως καὶ ὁ κύριος ποιήσει αὐτῷ)' (5.3; cf: 8.1 and 8.3). Other uses of God-language in the paraenetical sections of the Patriarchs are quite close to some of Paul's language. Thus in *T. Gad* 6.7, in teaching on how to behave towards a potential enemy, the advice is given, 'But even if he is devoid of shame and persists in his wickedness, forgive him from the heart and leave vengeance to God (δὸς τῷ θεῷ τὴν ἐκδίκησιν)'. A similar thought is expressed a little later when the reader is urged not to be jealous if someone becomes rich by evil means, but rather ὅρον γὰρ κυρίου ἐκδέξασθε.[2]

An Old Testament phrase which Paul and the Testaments share in common is the phrase ἔναντι or ἐναντίον κυρίου. Hollander and de Jonge note the frequency of this LXX expression in the Patriarchs.[3] The same idea occurs with a warranting function at *T. Jud.* 13.2: 'do not boast the exploits and strength of your youth because this too is evil ἐν ὀφθαλμοῖς κυρίου'.

In the *Testaments of the Twelve Patriarchs*, therefore, we have further evidence that the practice of sanctioning ethical conduct by reference to God continued in the Jewish tradition.

Summary

This study of Jewish paraenesis both in biblical and post-biblical writers has shown that by far the most common warrants for good conduct, and the most common sanctions for bad conduct, were theological ones.

1. Hollander and de Jonge, *Commentary*, p. 265, translate this phrase 'from that which God gives to you', citing as parallels Jas 1.5 and *Herm. Mand.* 2.4 (p. 267).

2. 'wait for the Lord to set the limits' (Kee's translation, Charlesworth, *OT Pseudepigrapha*, I, p. 816). Hollander and de Jonge, *Commentary*, p. 332, translate 'wait for the decision of the Lord'.

3. In a note on *T. Reub.* 1.8 (Hollander and de Jonge, *Commentary*, p. 90).

Paul stands in this strongly *theocentric* ethical tradition. There is a strong element of continuity here between Jewish and Christian moral traditions, and their *underlying theology*. This is particularly clear in units of Pauline paraenesis which are not distinctively Christian in character, and share much the same God-language as Jewish traditions (notably Rom. 13.1-7 and 1 Thess. 4.3-8).

Nevertheless, within this fundamental continuity some differences can be discerned. The most common form of theological warrant in Jewish tradition is a promise of divine blessing, or a threat of divine punishment. The motifs of promise and punishment are less frequent in Paul, although undoubtedly present (e.g. 1 Thess. 4.6; Rom. 13.4; 2 Cor. 9.7-10). On the whole, the future tense figures less prominently in Pauline warrants; instead, aorist tenses are quite common (Rom. 12.3; 14.3; 1 Thess. 4.7; 5.8 etc.)

Of course, the difference between Christian and Jewish God-language in this respect must not be exaggerated. (The very distinction 'Christian' and 'Jewish' is misleadingly anachronistic when we are speaking of Paul's generation.) The warrant which undergirds the Ten Commandments (Exod. 20.1) refers to God's past action. But Paul's aorists show that the focus has shifted. This is evident from the aorists which are used in christological warrants. There is a particularity about the προσελάβετο of Rom. 15.7 (where the subject is Christ) which lends a retrospective, as it were, particularity to the προσελάβετο of 14.3, where ὁ θεός is the subject. The same particularity can be seen even more clearly in the references to Christ's death in the warrant of Rom. 14.9, and in the implied warrant of Rom. 14.15. (For other christological aorists of this kind, compare Rom. 15.3, Gal. 5.1 and 2 Cor. 8.9.)

This shift in the focus of the divine action which provides the warrant for conduct in Pauline paraenesis means that other theological language used by Paul is implicitly christological. This is true of all the Pauline uses of the verb καλῶ (e.g. 1 Thess. 4.7; Gal. 5.13). Similarly, whether the διὰ τῶν οἰκτιρμῶν τοῦ θεοῦ of Rom. 12.1 refers back to chs. 9–11 or to chs. 1–11, it does not allude to God's mercies in a general way, but to the 'mercies' as they have been narrated in the preceding chapters. This implicit Christology sometimes becomes explicit, when traditional Jewish language is sometimes 'glossed' by a reference to Christ: τοῦτο γὰρ θέλημα θεοῦ ἐν Χριστῷ Ἰησοῦ εἰς ὑμᾶς (1 Thess. 5.18 b).

5. *God-Language in Graeco-Roman Paraenesis*

It is clearly impossible within the scope of this study to offer a full survey of this subject. Instead, this section will focus on examples of the place of God-language, and the nature of warrants for moral action, in the writings of Epictetus, Plutarch and Seneca, all of whom were contemporaries or near-contemporaries of Paul. There is good reason to suppose that such a sample will provide a typical cross-section of Graeco-Roman paraenesis from the time of Paul himself, or from a period soon after he was writing. First, however, some general observations about the relationship of God-language to moral teaching in Hellenistic traditions will be made.

It is important to appreciate the enduring influence of Plato and Aristotle on religious and philosophical thought if we are to understand the place of God-language and the nature of the warrants used in Graeco-Roman paraenesis. In earlier centuries the influence of the gods on human conduct was understood to be greater than in the periods we are considering here. J.M. Rist in his book *A Study in Ancient Philosophical Ethics*[1] notes that human beings in the older 'pre-philosophical way of thought' do what is right simply because that is what the gods want.[2] The reaction against more traditional ways of thought was provoked not so much by polytheism, but by anthropomorphism in religion.[3] This finds expression in the drama of Euripides, and philosophical expression in Plato, for whom 'Forms' or, more precisely, 'the Form of the Good' are the supreme source of value, not the gods,[4] even though human beings are to aim at likeness to God.[5] In Aristotle the gods themselves are 'superior' to moral virtue, and have no concern for virtue in others.[6] Thus Aristotle, and later the Epicureans, 'have almost

1. J.M. Rist, *A Study in Ancient Philosophical Ethics* (Leiden: Brill, 1982).

2. Rist, *Ethics*, pp. 7-8. Cf. W. Den Boer, *Private Morality in Greece and Rome* (Leiden: Brill, 1979), pp. 15, 19-23. L. Schmidt, *Der Ethik der alten Griechen* (Berlin: Hertz, 1882), I, p. 165, finds a greater stress in the Homeric period on 'the social foundations of ethics', but in the period from Homer to the Persian Wars a powerful religious influence on morality.

3. Thus Schmidt, *Ethik*, pp. 135-38.

4. Rist, *Ethics*, pp. 23-26 and 29 (cf. pp. 7 and 73, and Schmidt, *Ethik*, I, p. 282).

5. Rist, *Ethics*, pp. 29 and 42.

6. Rist, *Ethics*, p. 8.

entirely banished the gods from ethics'.[1] What is lacking, in Rist's view, among the philosphers is 'the sense of a personal and, above all, a reciprocal relationship between man and the divine'.[2] A.J. Malherbe sums up the diversity of the Greek tradition, and at the same time a major difference from the Judaeo-Christian tradition, when he observes that the relationship between the traditional Greek gods and morality was ambiguous.[3]

This ambiguity is particularly significant in the light of A.D. Nock's discussion of conversion in the ancient world. Nock finds that philosophy is the only context in which there is anything corresponding to the Judaeo-Christian concept of conversion, that is of 'two types of life, a higher and a lower', and a context in which people were exhorted 'to turn from one to the other'.[4] This is a further reason for concentrating our attention on Epictetus, Plutarch and Seneca, to whose work I now turn.

The Discourses (Διατριβαί) of Epictetus belong to the late first or early second century.[5] As such, they provide an important example of Stoic moral exhortation from a period not much later than that of Paul. The Discourses, as the name suggests, are quite different in style from most Pauline paraenesis; they are much longer and consist of anecdotes, illustrations, the common question and answer form of the *diatribe*, and to a lesser extent moral teaching in the form of direct commands. Compared with the Pauline epistles (apart from the more extended discussions of 1 Cor. 12 and 14), God-language is much less common in the Discourses, although there are occasional passages which are strongly religious in content and style.[6]

Not surprisingly in view of the relative infrequency of God-language, the number of theological warrants in the Discourses are few. In a passage on the supply by God of human wants, Epictetus appears to

1. Rist, *Ethics*, p. 9.
2. Rist, *Ethics*, p. 10.
3. Malherbe, 'Exhortation', p. 11.
4. A.D. Nock, *Conversion: The Old and the New in Religion from Alexander the Great to Augustine of Hippo* (Oxford: Oxford University Press, 1933), p. 14.
5. Epictetus lived from approximately 60 CE to 140 CE. His *Discourses* were recorded by Arrian (c. 95–175 CE), four of the original eight books being extant.
6. E.g. *Discourses* 3.5.7-11 (Loeb, II, pp. 40-43), where Epictetus outlines the questions he might put to God on his death. (Cf. 4.10, 14-17, Loeb, II, pp. 400-403).

suggest that it is man's duty to praise because God has given us the faculty 'to comprehend these gifts and to use the way of reason'.[1] On closer examination, however, it becomes clear that the most pervasive warrant for ethical conduct is 'the law of nature', which Epictetus several times equates with the law of God: 'For the law of nature and of God is this: "Let the better always come out victor over the worse"'.[2] Given this identification of 'God' with nature,[3] God-language rarely has the warranting function which it has in Jewish and Christian paraenesis. One reason for this undoubtedly lies in Epictetus's understanding of God, and of the relationship of humans with God. The nature of God is defined as 'intelligence, knowledge, right reason' (νοῦς, ἐπιστήμη, λόγος ὀρθός).[4] Human beings are correspondingly defined as a fragment (ἀπόσπασμα) of God himself.[5] For this reason the implicit question which lies behind much of the moral teaching of Epictetus is: What kind of conduct enables a human being to function most satisfactorily? Thus, in a passage on the preparation of oneself to lose loved ones, the implied warrant is: so that you may spare yourself suffering and unhappiness.[6] There is an underlying theology here, and it finds expression near the beginning of this section: ὁ γὰρ θεὸς πάντας ἀνθρώπους ἐπὶ τὸ εὐδαιμονεῖν, ἐπὶ τὸ εὐσταθεῖν ἐποίησεν.[7] Once again, however, it is important to remember the close equation in Epictetus's mind between God and nature. A human being thus fulfils the divine intention of happiness in this area of human life by not forgetting a loved one's mortality; to do otherwise is to reach out for the impossible, and thus to fight God.[8] Implicit in all this is the Stoic ideal of αὐτάρκεια: 'This law God has ordained, and says, "If you wish any

1. 1.16.18 (Loeb, I, pp. 112-13).
2. 1.29 19 (Loeb, I, pp. 190-91). See also the sentiment at I 26.1: 'But how much more important is the law of life that we must do what nature demands' (Loeb, I, pp. 164-67; cf. 2.6.9.)
3. For other examples of the close assocation of God-language with nature see *Discourses* 1.1.18, 12.24-25, 20.16, 2.23.42, 3.3.5.
4. 2.8.2 (Loeb, I, pp. 258-59).
5. 1.8.11; cf. 1.14. 6, and 17.27.
6. 3.24.1ff; compare also 3.25.3, where the argument runs: those who are entering on the greatest of all struggles 'ought not to flinch...' because this struggle is actually 'a contest for good fortune and happiness itself' (3.25.3, Loeb, II, pp. 222-23).
7. 3.24.2 (cf. 7 and 63, Loeb, II, p. 184).
8. 3.24.20-24, Loeb, II, pp. 190-93.

thing good, get it from yourself"'.[1] Thus, when Epictetus advises 'will nothing but what God wills',[2] it is very different from what Paul would have meant by such language. Epictetus identifies 'God' closely not only with nature, but also with destiny; the task of humans therefore is to accept their lot, their response to their lot being the primary moral task. It is significant that the prayer which Epictetus seems particularly fond of quoting focuses on the need to accept one's destiny (i.e. what God has ordained): 'Lead me , O Zeus, and Thou my Destiny'.[3]

It is clear, then, that Epictetus's use of God-language in the context of moral instruction is very different from that of Paul. In Pauline paraenesis, as we saw, God-language is usually prominent and frequent, particularly in a warranting function. In the Discourses it is much more marginal, and it rarely has a warranting function. In view of the close association of 'God' and nature in Epictetus's thought, it is difficult to see how it could be otherwise. Two final observations about the theology of Epictetus will serve to reinforce the distinction between Epictetus and Paul. First there is Epictetus's view, already noted, that a human being is a 'fragment' of God. This is an idea which emerges many times in the Discourses, as for example in the first Discourse: 'we are all, before anything else, children of God'.[4] Perhaps the most remarkable expression of all of this kind comes in the second Discourse, where Epictetus seems to equate being 'at one with God' with changing from a man into a god (θεὸν ἐξ ἀνθρώπου...γενέσθαι).[5]

A second point, related to the first, concerns Epictetus's language about God. The amorphous nature of God here can be seen in the way that the singular θεός and plural θεοί are interchangeable.[6] Often the plural is used in set formulae, as in the title of Zeus, 'father of men and gods',[7] but it is surely significant that the singular and plural can be, and sometimes are, interchangeable, as at II 14.11-13, where not only θεός and θεοί but also τὸ θεῖον are used in this way.[8]

1. 1.29.4 (Loeb, I, p. 187); cf. 2.16.28.
2. 2.17.22 (Loeb, I, p. 343); cf. 3.24.95ff, 4.1.89-90 and 99-100, and 4.4.29.
3. 2.23.42, 4.1.131 and 4.34.
4. 1.3.1 (Loeb, I, pp. 24-25; cf. 1.9.1, 5, 13, 22, 25; 14.6; 2.8.13.
5. 2.19.26-7 (Loeb, I, pp. 366-69).
6. Examples of the plural occur at 1.7.32, 16.7, 18.18, 2.20.9.
7. E.g. 1.19.12.
8. Cf. 3.22.53 where τὸ δαιμόνιον and θεός are used interchangeably.

The picture derived from the writings of Plutarch, a near-contemporary of Epictetus,[1] is somewhat similar. The style of his *Moralia* is very similar to that of the Discourses. Anecdotes, paradigms, quotations abound. Here the God-language is even more marginal than in the Discourses. References to 'God', even when they do occur, sometimes seem more decorative than substantial. For example, towards the end of his treatise 'On the Control of Anger'[2] Plutarch refers to God's help (θεοῦ τι συλλαμβάνοντες) in keeping his vow, but the context shows that the primary thought is of his own efforts and perseverance.[3]

As in Epictetus's Discourses, the style is discursive; imperatives are very few. Nevertheless, three kinds of warrants for moral conduct may be discerned. First, Plutarch's arguments are often prudential and utilitarian: act thus because it is in your own interests to do so. Thus, in the same treatise on anger Plutarch suggests that 'we allow no place to anger even in jest', the reason being given that 'that brings in enmity where friendliness was'.[4] A similar argument appears in the treatise 'How to Profit by one's Enemies' (the title itself is significant!), where Plutarch advises:

> So look at your enemy, and see whether, in spite of his being in most respects harmful and difficult to manage, he does not in some way or other afford you means of getting hold of him and of using him as you can use no one else, and so can be of profit to you.[5]

A neat summary of Plutarch's prudential ethic occurs in the short treatise 'Virtue and Vice' where Plutarch's argument is, in effect: 'Vice is bad for you'.[6]

1. Plutarch lived c. 46–120 CE.
2. W.C. Helmbold, *Plutarch's Moralia*, IV (Loeb translation, London: Heinemann, 1939), pp. 89-159.
3. Helmbold, *Moralia*, pp. 158-59.
4. *De cohibenda Ira* 462B (F.C. Babbit, *Plutarch's Moralia*, II [Loeb translation; London: Heinemann, 1928], pp. 146-47).
5. *De Capienda Ex Inimicis Utilitate* 87B (Babbit, *Moralia*, p. 9). Compare the argument later in the same discourse (91B), where giving praise or honour to an enemy when it is due to him 'must' be done, because the one who does so wins 'greater commendation', and because people will have greater confidence in him at a later date if he criticizes his enemy.
6. *De Virtute et Vitio* (Babbit, *Moralia*, pp. 91-101); see especially 100F and 101B, ('Where, then is the pleasure in vice, if in no part of it is to be found freedom from care and grief... ?').

A second kind of warrant is one which we found frequently in the discourses of Epictetus, namely the law of nature. Thus, in the treatise 'On Moral Virtue'[1] Plutarch argues, 'For, in accordance with Nature, it is proper (προσῆκον) that reason, which is divine, should lead and rule the irrational'.[2] It is worth noting that in this treatise, and in the treatise 'Can Virtue Be Taught?' (Loeb, VI, pp. 4ff.) there is no God-language at all, except in 'On Moral Virtue', 'a divinely-sent evil (θεῖον κακόν)'.[3] In keeping with this emphasis on nature, we find that Plutarch sometimes illustrates or supports a piece of moral advice by an example from the world of nature. Thus, in his treatise 'On Brotherly Love'[4] Plutarch argues that the 'increase' of one brother should result in the increase of the other, for the fingers 'all contrive to move together and assist each other'.[5] (1 Cor. 12 and 14 are clearly the closest in style and argument to Plutarch.) Similarly, Plutarch will reinforce a point by an anecdote or observation which simply states what is the case.[6]

A third kind of warrant in Plutarch is best described as moralistic. Here Plutarch tends to resort to a simple 'it is fitting' or 'it is not fitting'. Thus, in his treatise 'On Having many Friends', after arguing that it is inadvisable to have many friends, he goes on 'For these reasons it is not a fit (οὐ προσῆκον) thing to be thus unsparing of our virtue'.[7] Other moralizing expressions occur frequently, such as 'There is nothing more disgraceful or painful',[8] or the use of δεῖ, as in the advice in 'On Having many Friends': 'We ought not to accept readily chance acquaintances'.[9] Frequently such moralizing takes the form of an observation about life, as in 'Virtue and Vice': 'a pleasant and happy life comes not from external things, but...man draws on his own character as a source from which to add the element of leisure and joy to the things which surround him'.[10]

1. *De Virtute Morali* (Helmbold, *Moralia*, pp. 15-87).
2. *De Virtute Morali* 450 E (Helmbold, *Moralia*, pp. 74-75).
3. *De Virtute Morali* 446B (Helmbold, *Moralia*, pp. 48-49).
4. *De Fraterno Amore* (Helmbold, *Moralia*, pp. 243-325).
5. *De Fraterno Amore* 485 F (Helmbold, *Moralia*, p. 291).
6. Thus, for example, *De Fraterno Amore* 490B and C (Helmbold, *Moralia*, pp. 312-13.
7. *De Amicorum Multitudine* 96 D (Babbit, *Moralia*, p. 65).
8. *De Capienda Ex Inimicis Utilitate* 88D (Babbit, *Moralia*, p. 17).
9. 94 E (Babbit, *Moralia*, p. 55. Cf. a similar use of δεῖ in *De Fraterno Amore* 490B, Hembold, *Moralia*, p. 313).
10. 100C (Babbit, *Moralia*, p. 95).

In this mixture of prudential advice with shrewd observations about life and human conduct, some affinity with Jewish wisdom literature can be seen. What is totally lacking, however, are the divine warrants which are also a notable feature of that literature. As we have noted, God-language in Plutarch is rare, and in its rare occurrences there seem no instances of its warranting function so common in Jewish and Christian literature.

The third writer in this section is Seneca, the Roman moralist and philosopher of the first century of the Christian era.[1] As one would expect with a Stoic writer, Seneca like Epictetus equates the will of God with the laws of nature. 'For Seneca acceptance of and acquiescence to God's will are the same as submission to the laws of nature'.[2] Thus, in his essay *De Ira* the starting-point is similar to that of Epictetus and Plutarch: Seneca is responding to Novatus's request to write *quemadmodum posset ira leniri.*[3] After inquiring what anger is, and whether it is peculiar to humans (he argues that it is), Seneca goes on to ask whether anger is *secundum naturam* and whether it is useful (*utilis*). The ensuing argument is based on human nature, and on observations, and concludes that anger *is* contrary to nature.[4] This thesis is supported by further arguments, prudential and moralistic. Thus, 'What need is there of anger when the same end may be accomplished by reason?'[5] What is more, anger is wrong because it does not contribute to 'greatness of soul',[6] and this it cannot do because 'virtue alone is lofty and sublime, and nothing is not great which is not at the same time tranquil'.[7]

As in Plutarch, God-language is almost entirely absent from the three books of this treatise. One reference to the 'immortal gods' may help to indicate why:

> But there are certain agents which are unable to harm us and have no power that is not beneficial and salutary as, for example, the immortal

1. Born in 4 BCE and dying (by suicide) in 65 CE, Seneca will have been an almost exact contemporary of Paul.
2. J.M. Sevenster, *Paul and Seneca* (Leiden: Brill, 1961), p. 39.
3. *De Ira* 1.1.1 (J.W. Basore, *Seneca's Moral Essays I* [Loeb translation; London: Heinemann, 1928], p. 107), 1.1.
4. *De Ira* 1.6.1-5 (Basore, *Moral Essays*, pp. 118-23).
5. *Deinde quid opus est ira, cum idem proficiat ratio? (De Ira* 1.11.2) (Basore, *Moral Essays*, p. 132).
6. *De Ira* 1.20.1 (Basore, *Moral Essays*, p. 161).
7. *De Ira* 1.21.4 (Basore, *Moral Essays*, p. 165).

> gods, who neither wish nor are able to hurt; for they are by nature mild and gentle, as incapable of injuring others as of injuring themselves.[1]

A similar pattern can be seen in Seneca's *Epistulae Morales*. The most frequent warrant for the advice offered by the writer is 'nature'. Thus in Epistle 1 'On Saving Time' Seneca writes 'we were entrusted by nature with the ownership of this single thing' (i.e. time),[2] and again in Epistle V, 'Our motto, as you know, is "Live according to Nature"'.[3]

Seneca has more imperatives and hortatory subjunctives than Plutarch uses in his *Moralia*, a stylistic difference one would expect in a different literary genre. The same mixture of prudential, rational and moralistic warrants can, however, be found. The power of reason is invoked in the Epistle 'On Allegiance to Virtue', when Seneca responds to the inquiry 'How can I free myself?' by proffering the advice 'Betake yourself therefore to philosophy', but he goes on: *si vis omnia tibi subiicere, te subiice rationi; multos reges si ratio te rexerit*.[4] We find, too, expressions corresponding to the Greek δεῖ and προσῆκον, in Seneca's use of the verb *debeo* and the gerundive.[5]

Summary

It is clear that we are moving in a different frame of reference in the world of the three authors whose moral teaching has been sampled in this section. In all three writers, particularly Plutarch and Seneca, language about God or the gods is marginal to their purpose. The gods are not models for ethical behaviour (sometimes quite the opposite, as in Plutarch's 'On the Control of Anger'[6]) and seldom provide the warrants for ethical conduct. When that is the case, as occasionally in Epictetus, the writer is using the word 'god' as virtually a synonym of 'nature'.

Secondly, and this is a corollary of the first point, warrants in these

1. *De Ira* 1.27.1 (Basore, *Moral Essays*, pp. 222-23).
2. *Ad Lucilium Epistulae Morales* (Basore, *Moral Essays*, p. 5).
3. *Nempe propositium nostrum est secundum naturam vivere* (Basore, *Moral Essays*, p. 23).
4. *Epistulae Morales* (Basore, *Moral Essays*, p. 255).
5. Examples of *debeo* occur in Ep. 42 (Basore, *Moral Essays*, p. 281). Gerunds occur at Epp. 3.4, 14.9, 11; 16.1; 17.5, 7; 21.9; 22.3.
6. In this treatise Plutarch quotes Euripides, who writes of how God 'lets pass small things and leaves them to Fate' (τὰ μικρὰ δ' εἰς τυχὴν ἄφεις ἐᾷ) but advises the 'man of sense' (τὸν νοῦν ἔχοντα) to leave nothing to Fate (*De Cohibenda Ira* 464B, Hembold, *Moralia*, p. 157).

Graeco-Roman authors are frequently prudential or moralistic. These kinds of arguments are rare in Paul. He is not so other-worldly as to forgo them altogether, as 2 Cor. 9.7-11 shows, but even here the argument from self-interest is based on theology.

Thirdly, the prominence of references to 'nature' in Graeco-Roman paraenesis has been noted. Again, this is not entirely absent from Paul's writings (Rom. 1.26; 1 Cor. 11.14), but it is rare. In fact, the tendency of Graeco-Roman authors to use the words 'nature' and 'god' or 'gods' interchangeably brings us to the heart of the matter. This is the very different theology, and consequently anthropology, which underlies Pauline paraenesis on the one hand and Graeco-Roman paraenesis on the other. For the Greek, as Kleinknecht has pointed out, θεός is a basic form of reality; hence a Greek would say 'Love is God', but not 'God is Love'. Not surprisingly, in view of this understanding of θεός the distinction between human and divine tended to be blurred. Since, moreover, the Greeks believed that the divine could be apprehended through the human mind or reason (νοῦς), it was natural that people were encouraged to look within themselves for moral guidance, and to act *secundum naturam*. In biblical writers, not only is there a deep sense of the distinction between God and humans (even though, or even perhaps because humans are made in the image of God), but in Paul, especially, the centrality of ἁμαρτία in human life means that there is no natural progression from human beings to God.

Finally, the significance of the *form* of Pauline paraenesis should not be overlooked: he writes to *communities*, not individuals, and that reflects a further difference in his understanding of both God and the nature of the life God requires.

6. *Conclusions*

There is clearly a varied use of language about God in Pauline paraenesis. This section summarizes the findings of this chapter, and draws some conclusions.

1. The *form* of Pauline paraenesis is significant. Paul took over existing epistolary conventions, and Christianized them. His letters (with one exception) are to communities, and this together with the content of his ethical teaching contrasts with the individualistic ethical teaching of the Graeco-Roman authors examined in section 5. Thirdly, patterns of paraenesis varied: although in some letters paraenetical sections could be

clearly distinguished (Romans, 1 Thessalonians, Galatians), in others (notably Philippians) they could not. In all cases, however, paraenesis was intimately related to theology (Rom. 12.1, etc.). In this respect the form reflects the thorough integration of faith and life. (Compare Lev. 19.9-18!)

2. Despite varying patterns, there is a marked continuity with the Old Testament and Jewish tradition in the deployment of God-language in a warranting function. Paul repeatedly emphasizes that God is author, authorizer, destiny and judge. Several units begin with weighty theological affirmations (Rom. 12.1-2; 13.1-4; 1 Thess. 4.3), or such affirmations are made at an early stage in the, sometimes extended, argument (1 Cor. 6.13-4; 8.6; 11.3; 12.4-6). 1 Corinthians 7, in particular, shows the Pauline tendency to 'trace everything back to God'.

3. Pauline paraenesis provides further evidence of how traditional God-language has been drawn into new configurations, and given new content. Examples include: 'the mercies of God' (Rom. 12.1—especially if 'mercies' refers back to chs. 1–11, and not just chs. 9–11), 'the Kingdom of God' (Rom. 14.17-8), what is 'well-pleasing' to God (Rom. 12.1-2; 14.18), 'the will of God' (1 Thess. 5.18; cf. Phil. 2.15; 4.7). Even when the God-language is unchanged, as in Rom. 12.19, the total context derives its content from what has been previously said about God and Christ (v. 21; 5.8-9).

4. The difference between 'the old' and 'the new' must not be exaggerated, however. The God-language of Rom. 13.1-7, and of most if not all of 1 Thess. 4.3-8 is not explicitly or distinctively Christian. These two units, and perhaps 1 Cor. 6.12-20, in their 'heavy' use of God-language may indicate that God-language increases in proportion to the amount of controversy or opposition anticipated.

5. The juxtaposition of God- and Christ- or πνεῦμα-language, and the alternation of God- and κύριος-language (notably in Rom. 14.1–15.13) is the single most significant factor in this redeployment and redefining of traditional theological terms. The title κύριος indicates that the exalted Lord now exercises divine authority. The juxtapositions and alternations of these terms show that, while Paul's ethical teaching is wholly theocentric, much of his God-language is *organized around* statements about Christ, indicating a crucial interdependence.

6. In the body of Galatians Christ- and πνεῦμα-language have a polemical function; Christ-language, in particular, has a sharp differentiating role. (Philippians, to a lesser extent, reflects the same features.)

This has shaped the paraenesis, where, however, God-language still plays an emphatic, warranting role (Gal. 5.8, 21; 6.7a; cf. Phil. 2.13,15).

7. A comparison of Jewish and Pauline paraenesis showed the same pattern of continuity and discontinuity which we have seen elsewhere. Both are theocentric, but Paul has fewer future tenses, and the aorists of his warrants and paradigms (e.g. 2 Cor. 8.9) show a new focus.

8. Graeco-Roman paraenesis, in its emphasis on *secundum naturam*, its prudential, moralistic warrants, and the interchangeability of 'God' and 'gods', reflects both a different concept of θεός and of human beings.

The underlying question behind these patterns of continuity and discontinuity, similarities and differences, is whether there is a new understanding of God. This investigation needs to be continued with particular reference to Paul's language about Christ, to which I turn in the next chapter. But a concluding comment at this point may be appropriate.

The *function* and *effect* of God-language are important. Thus not only the God-language itself, but *the conduct which it is used to reinforce*, may reflect the understanding of God which lies behind both, (e.g. Rom. 12.21; 2 Cor. 8.9). The prominence of the word ἀγάπη in this respect (Rom. 12.9; 13.10; 14.15; 1 Cor. 13, etc.) is especially important. (On this, see Chapter 5.)

The effect of God-language on the community is also clearly important. Here there is undoubted discontinuity with Jewish tradition in the pluralism explicitly urged in 1 Corinthians 8–10, and Rom. 14.1–15.7. Moxnes has noted how Paul uses statements about God in a way 'directly related to his defence for a religiously and socially integrated community of Christians'.[1] To speak about God is to speak about his people. But we might also add: *the way in which God's people are spoken about* reflects the understanding of God who is their *raison d'être* as a religious and social entity.

The distinctiveness of Paul's language, especially in comparison with Jewish paraenesis, should not be exaggerated. Yet a *partly new* language is emerging, not only in christological paradigms, in the greater prominence of ἀγάπη, but also in the language of Romans 6: the whole of life is to be interpreted and lived ὑπὸ χάριν (v. 14) and τῇ δικαιοσύνῃ (e.g. vv. 18-19). (These two words are virtually synonyms for God in this context.) This vision of life is *not* at odds with the Old

1. Moxnes, *Theology*, p. 99.

Testament, which contains, as T.W. Manson once wrote, 'God's demands in the context of God's gifts'. But old words are being used in new ways, new words are being coined, and the texture of the language reflects both a new understanding and a new experience.

Finally, the way in which the apostle sometimes presents himself as a *paradigm* of the conduct he is urging his converts to adopt should not be overlooked (e.g. 1 Cor. 9; cf.11.1; Gal. 4.12; Phil. 3.17; 4.9). The theology behind this encouragement to imitate him is not always clear. When, however, he writes of the pattern of his apostolic ministry, as he does for example in 1 Cor. 4.9-13, 2 Cor. 4.7-12 and 6.2-10, important correlations between his language about himself as an apostle and his language about God and Christ begin to appear. (This was briefly noted in the conclusions to Chapter 2.) Thus it is clear that his ministry is patterned on the cross and resurrection of Jesus.

In conclusion, the patterns of God-language in Pauline paraenesis, especially the interaction of language about God and Christ, together with the function and effect of this language on both the community and the apostle himself, suggest that there is here a new understanding of God.

Chapter 5

The Relationship between Paul's Language about God and his Language about Christ

Thus far this investigation has taken samples of the kind of language which Paul uses about God. In the study of Romans 9–11 in Chapter 1 it became clear that much of the language, when taken out of context and examined in small units, appears very similar to language about God used in the Jewish Scriptures and by other Jewish writers. In the Pauline context it is used quite differently. Paul's conviction, first that the fundamental distinction between Jew and Gentile has been abolished by the coming of Christ, and secondly his experience of (a) Jewish rejection and (b) Gentile acceptance of the Gospel, means that his language about God acquires a context which is new and even revolutionary. In particular, his language about God's gracious choice of the patriarchs was more radically theocentric than many statements on the same theme in Jewish writings. Crucial to the argument are the call of God and the undeserved choice or grace of God, and, in response to the Judaizing crisis, a redefinition of God's δικαιοσύνη to include the Gentiles χωρὶς νόμου (Rom. 3.21).

Chapter 2 provided further evidence that most of the language which Paul used about God had precedents in the Old Testament and elsewhere. But his conviction that the new age had dawned in Christ, and that the cross was the meeting-point of the new age and the old, gave to his God-language, particularly in the paradoxical language about power and weakness, a character which has no clear precedents or parallels. This, together with the very marked, emphatic use of θεός, constituted Paul's critical response to the pretensions of human wisdom, particularly the 'wisdom of rhetoric' (ἐν σοφίᾳ λόγου, 1 Cor. 1.17), and to the defective theology of the 'Christ party' at Corinth.

Chapter 3 examined Paul's language about the Spirit, with particular reference to 2 Cor. 2.14–4.6, maintaining that πνεῦμα-language must be seen as God-language. More particularly, this context is polemical and provides the key to the basic meaning and function of πνεῦμα-language in Paul's writings. Its primary meaning lies in the fact that God has given his Spirit to *Gentiles*, against all Jewish expectations and assumptions about where the Spirit of God was believed to operate. Paul's God-language thus acquires an important missiological dimension. This passage also contains polemical θεός-language, in the form of Paul's appeals to God as the authorizer and arbiter of his ministry.

Chapter 4 explored the function of God-language in Pauline paraenesis, with particular reference to Rom. 12.1–15.13. Although patterns varied, the continuity between Paul and other Jewish writers was clear: Jewish and Christian ethical teaching find their warrants in language about God to a far greater degree than contemporary Greek or Roman paraenesis. Nevertheless, here too differences were noted, particularly in the interaction of language about Christ (including κύριος-language) with more traditional God-language. But while Paul's language always reflects the fact that for him God is the ultimate frame of reference, his response to the Judaizing crisis, notably in Galatians and to a lesser extent in Philippians, includes the deployment of Christ-language with a polemical, differentiating function.

There is thus something of a paradox. Paul's writings are deeply theocentric; time and again God is emphatically the ultimate reference-point. Yet much of his God-language alternates with, and is even dependent on, language about Christ.

But it is precisely here that there is a marked difference of opinion among scholars. On the one hand it is often assumed without question that Paul's christological kerygma was simply 'inserted' into the traditional Jewish understanding of God.[1] On the other hand it is sometimes suggested that in Paul's writings we find a new understanding of God.[2] The major question to be pursued in this chapter, therefore, will be the question of how far Paul's understanding of God has been affected by his experience and understanding of Christ.[3]

1. Hurtado, *One God, One Lord*, pp. 8, 134, rightly warns, however, that Jewish monotheism is more complex than is often realized .

2. Thus, for example, Hanson, *Paradox of the Cross*, p. 184, writes of how Paul's theology of the cross 'implied a startlingly new conception of God'.

3. Cf. the question with which Thüsing begins his study: 'the combination of Paul's intense Christocentrism with his no less "stark" monotheism' (W. Thüsing, *Per Christum in Deum: Studien zum Verhältnis von Christozentrik und Theozentrik*

In fact, it has becoming increasingly clear as this study has proceeded that Paul's language about God is *organized around* another kind of language, namely his language about Christ. This chapter, then, explores the 'christological grammar' of Paul,[1] and particularly how his Christ-language relates to his language about God. In a good deal of New Testament work, the Christology of New Testament authors is all too often studied in isolation from other aspects of their thought and language. This approach, however, is likely to lead to distorted results, unless careful attention is paid to how christological expressions are integrated with other kinds of language, particularly language about God.

Thus the approach in this chapter will be primarily a linguistic one. P. Keifert[2] has argued that the christological debate now has what he calls two 'paradigms': a historical one and, more recently, a linguistic one. The former can be seen in the work of scholars who 'organize their interpretation of the text and authorize their christological claims either in reference to the events behind the text or to the intention of the author and community'. Those scholars who adopt the linguistic paradigm approach the narrative as a whole. Here Kaufert cites the work of Boring on Mark's Christology:

> A study of Mark's Christology forces the issue of whether Christology should not shift its emphasis from the nature(s) of Jesus to the nature of language, without thereby relaxing its interest in and commitment to the person of Jesus of Nazareth. . . Could two natures in one person become 'one person mediated by two kinds of language'?[3]

In this chapter, therefore, I shall begin by examining the nature of Paul's Christ-language, and the contexts in which he uses it.[4] It will be

in den paulinischen Hauptbriefen [Münster: 1965], p. 3) Compare also N.T. Wright, *The Climax of the Covenant: Christ and the Law in Pauline Theology* (Edinburgh: T. & T. Clark, 1991), and his useful phrase 'Christological monotheism'. (This study was largely completed before the publication of Wright's work—an important contribution to our understanding of Paul's teaching about Christ.)

1. The expression of Keck, 'New Testament Christology', noted in the Introduction (p. 21).

2. In a paper 'Interpretative Paradigms: A Proposal concerning NT Christology' (R. Jewett [ed.], *Semeia: Christology and Exegesis: New Approaches* [Atlanta: Scholars Press, 1985], pp. 203-15).

3. Jewett, *Christology and Exegesis*, p. 208.

4. It may be useful to repeat the definition made earlier in this study that the phrase 'Christ-language' is used here of passages in which the word Χριστός occurs.

shown that this language is nearly always dependent upon his language about God.

1. *Paul's Christ-Language*

Paul's language about Christ is not, of course, confined to those contexts where he uses the word 'Christ'. His κύριος-language constitutes a large sub-group of his Christ-language. The occurrence of κύριος-language in paraenetic contexts has already been briefly discussed in Chapter 4, and I shall return to this language in section three of this chapter.[1]

It is clearly impossible to explore the whole of Paul's Christ-language here in detail. The primary concern is its relationship to Paul's language about God. It will be useful, however, to map out the broad contours of this language in order to see the linguistic patterns within it.

First, there is an interesting grammatical contrast with θεός-language.

1. κύριος references occupy about four and a half columns, although a considerable number of these include (a) references to the 'Lord Jesus Christ' and (b) LXX references, most of which are allusions to God, not to Jesus. There is thus considerable overlap between Paul's Christ- and κύριος-language, the expression 'the Lord Jesus Christ' occurring some 35 times in the Pauline corpus (MSS variants occur at Rom. 16.20 and 24, and κύριος is used predicatively at 2 Cor. 4.5). Clearly, however, this expression is relevant to our inquiry in this section.

Paul's Christ-language is not as extensive as his God-language. References to θεός in Paul occupy about nine columns in Moulton and Geden, references to Χριστός about six and a half columns. Moreover, the spread of Christ-language in Paul's letters is quite uneven. There are relatively few references to 'Christ' in 1 Thessalonians (1.1, 3; 2.6, 14; 3.2; 4.16; 5.9, 18, 23, 28), contrasted with Galatians and Philippians (and references respectively (Morgenthaler, *Statistik*, p. 156). Within the major Epistles, too, the spread is uneven. In Romans, for example, there are only three occurrences of Χριστός in chs. 2–4 (2.16; 3.22, 24), two in ch. 7 (vv. 4 and 25), three in ch. 9 (vv. 1, 3 and 5) and only one each in chs. 12 and 13 (12.5 and 13.14). A similar unevenness can be seen in 1 Corinthians, chs. 1 and 15 accounting for more than half (31) the occurrences of Χριστός, while in 2 Cor. 6–9, there are only four occurrences (6.15; 8.9, 23; 9.13).

When we explore the reasons for this uneven spread, it is clear that 'clusters' of Christ-language tend to occur in two kinds of contexts: soteriological (Rom. 5, 6 and 8, 1 Cor.1 and 15, 2 Cor. 5) and ecclesiological (notably the opening and closing sections of Paul's letters). There is thus much to be said for the suggestion which I made earlier that Paul's Christ-language is primarily the language of identity and differentiation.

Whereas θεός is rarely used by Paul in the accusative,[1] Χριστός—i.e. the nominative—tends to be used in a very limited way. The vast majority of occurrences of Χριστός in the nominative are those in which it is the subject of (a) a verb referring to death, sacrifice, etc.,[2] (b) a verb referring to resurrection, exaltation, etc.[3] and (c) other verbs in the passive voice.[4] This leaves a small number of occurrences of Χριστός in the nominative: Gal. 3.13, 5.1, 2 (all of which are polemical in character), Rom. 15.7 and 18 (the latter occurring in a passage where, unusually, Christ-language predominates), and 1 Cor. 1.17 (referring to Paul's apostolic commission from Christ).

The overall preponderance of passive verbs is significant. It has often been pointed out that in Paul's theology it is *God* who raises Jesus, ἐγείρω in the passive voice being Paul's favoured expression. Thus there can be no doubt about the *theocentric* character of almost all Paul's references to the resurrection. (The unusual expression in Rom. 6.4, ἠγέρθη Χριστὸς...διὰ τῆς δόξης τοῦ πατρός makes explicit what is implicit in the many passive verbs.)

Paul's language with reference to the death of Christ is more varied. Several nominatives (notably Rom. 5.6; 2 Cor. 8.9; Gal. 2.21; Phil. 2.6-8) imply that Christ was not the unwitting or unwilling victim of God.[5] But the use of παραδίδωμι (Rom. 4.25; 8.32), together with the *theological* character of Rom. 15.3, 8 and, most of all, the reference to God in Rom. 5.8 (συνίστησιν δὲ τὴν ἑαυτοῦ ἀγάπην εἰς ἡμᾶς ὁ θεός)[6] shows that the death of Christ is understood theocentrically. Similarly, the preceding ἡ χάρις τοῦ θεοῦ in Gal. 2.21 shows that here, too, the death of Christ is interpreted with reference to the grace *of God* .

Thus, in the majority of instances where Χριστός is used as the subject of a verb either the implied subject is God, or there is reference,

1. Rom. 1.21 and Gal. 4.9 are very rare exceptions.

2. Rom. 5.6, 8; 8.34; 14.9, 15; 15.3, 8; 1 Cor. 5.7; 8.11; 15.3; 2 Cor. 8.9; 13.4; Gal. 2.21; Phil. 2.6-8; 1 Thess. 4.14 (cf. Rom. 4.25; 6.10; 2 Cor. 5.14).

3. Rom. 6.4, 9 (cf.10); 8.34; 1 Cor. 15.4, 12-22; 2 Cor.13.4; 1 Thess. 4.14 (cf. Rom. 4.25).

4. Rom. 15.20; 1 Cor. 1.13; 15.12; Gal. 3.1; 4.19; Phil. 1.18, 20. The majority of these refer to the *proclamation* of Christ (Rom. 15.20; 1 Cor. 15.12; Gal. 3.1; Phil. 1.18).

5. M.D. Hooker (cited by Bruce, *Galatians*, p. 146) notes the active role of Christ in his sacrifice, as in Gal. 2.20. This, of course, is correct, but the number of contexts where the agency of *God* is stressed is still striking.

6. The position of θεός here, as in Rom. 8.3, is emphatic.

implicit or explicit, in the context to the will and purpose of God.

Thus far, then, it is clear that Paul's Christ-language is, for the most part, *grammatically subordinate* to his God-language. As usual, the grammar reflects theology: Christ's dependence on and obedience to God. This, however, is not the whole picture. It must be observed that it is possible to turn this evidence around, as it were, and ask an antithetical question: to what extent does Paul's θεός-language *need* Christ-language, in order for it to be fully explicated? Are the two kinds of language *inter-dependent*? Although it is clear that Paul's Christ-language is, in most contexts, grammatically subordinate to his God-language, the linguistic evidence invites us also to consider the extent to which the word θεός receives its content and meaning from its relation to Paul's language about Christ. It will be important to bear these questions in mind.

A second category of Christ-language consists of two prepositional phrases, frequently found in Paul's writings: ἐν (Ἰησοῦ) Χριστῷ or ἐν Χριστῷ (Ἰησοῦ).[1] First, the relationship of the phrase 'in Christ' to Paul's language about God must be examined.

It is impossible to survey all the occurrences of εν Χριστω κτλ. in Paul's writings. But it will be useful to delineate the main functions and the contexts in which the phrase occurs. First, ἐν Χριστῷ[2] occurs in contexts which suggest that it denotes the place ('field of force'),[3] focus, or means of God's action. (The word ἐν merits a separate study, but the question of whether it is locative or instrumental in meaning does not directly affect the thrust of the argument here.) Thus, God's grace is given to the Corinthians 'in Christ Jesus' (1 Cor. 1.4); God's call is actualized 'in Christ Jesus' (Phil. 3.14; cf. Gal. 5.1, 8); God's consolation is to be found 'in Christ' (Phil. 2.1), for it was in him that God's act of liberation (ἀπολυτρώσεως) took place (Rom. 3.24); God's love is experienced 'in Christ Jesus our Lord' (Rom. 8.39); 'Christ Jesus' is the focus of the operation of God's Spirit of life (Rom. 8.2; cf. 6.23); the old dispensation is being abolished 'in Christ' (2 Cor. 3.14)[4] (cf. Gal. 3.14).

1. I also include here those expressions where κύριος is used with Χριστός in such prepositional phrases—e.g. Rom. 6.23 and 7.25.

2. I use this phrase as a comprehensive term to denote all such christological expressions in which Χριστός is governed by ἐν.

3. Grundmann's phrase in *TWNT*, IX, p. 550.

4. It is far from clear what the subject of καταργεῖται is, but the above rendering conveys the sense.

The future, too, is shaped by Christ, since the glory of God will be found or received 'in Christ Jesus' (Phil. 4.19). In a word, 'God was in Christ' (2 Cor. 5.19).[1]

So there are good grounds for the contention of Kramer that God is often explicitly named as the agent in sentences where the formula ἐν Χριστῷ Ἰησοῦ occurs.[2] This is true also of the relatively few occurrences of ἐν Χριστῷ in paraenetic contexts. Thus we have τοῦτο γὰρ θέλημα θεοῦ ἐν Χριστῷ Ἰησοῦ ὑμᾶς (1 Thess. 5.18b), and ἡ εἰρήνη τοῦ θεοῦ...φρουρήσει τὰς καρδίας ὑμῶν καὶ τὰ νοήματα ὑμῶν ἐν Χριστῷ Ἰησοῦ (Phil. 4.7).

God-language is not so frequent in contexts where ἐν Χριστῷ is used by Paul of himself or his circumstances. Nevertheless, we still find several references where Paul explicitly states that what he does ἐν Χριστῷ he does 'before God'. This is true, for example, of the very theocentric passage discussed in Chapter 3 (2 Cor. 2.14-17, especially vv. 14 and 17; cf. 2 Cor. 12.19), and of his 'boast' ἐν Χριστῷ Ἰησοῦ which is τὰ πρὸς τὸν θεόν (Rom. 15.17).

The verb καυχάομαι, in fact, and its cognate nouns tend, in Paul's writings, to 'attract' christological language. Several references to boasting 'in Christ Jesus' occur, however, without explicit God-language—Phil. 1.26, 1 Cor. 15.31, as also in the twice-used citation from Jeremiah in 1 Cor. 1.31 and 2 Cor. 10.17: ὁ καυχώμενος ἐν κυρίῳ καυχάσθω. There is a particular reason why this particular group of words should attract christological language. As Käsemann says,

> In good Semitic fashion it is presupposed that 'boasting' is an existential factor in human existence... If as Paul sees it existence is defined by its lord, the basic understanding of existence comes to expression in boasting. In this a person tells to whom he belongs.[3]

1. For a fuller discussion of this difficult verse see section 4 below.

2. W. Kramer, *Christ, Lord, Son of God* (London: SCM Press, 1966 [1963]), p. 143.

3. Commentators vary in their comments on this phrase. Käsemann, *Romans*, p. 69, thinks no criticism is intended here ('The attack is yet to come'). Barrett, *Romans*, p. 55, while noting that there is a sense in which 'glorying in God' is a proper thing to do, believes that here the Jew's confidence is misplaced. Cf. Ziesler, *Romans*, p. 90, who writes of the Jews' 'over-confidence in being the people of God'.

The distinctiveness of Paul's language becomes apparent by a comparison of two verses in Romans. In his address to 'the Jew' in 2.17 Paul says καυχᾶσαι ἐν θεῷ.[1] The contrast with this created by the gospel emerges in ch. 5 of the epistle (though cf. 3.27 and 4.2 for further uses of this word-group), particularly in v.11, where Paul concludes this unit in an almost doxological style:[2] οὐ μόνον δέ, ἀλλὰ καὶ καυχώμενοι ἐν τῷ θεῷ διὰ τοῦ κυρίου ἡμῶν Ἰησοῦ Χριστοῦ δι' οὗ νῦν τὴν καταλλαγὴν ἐλάβομεν. Another group of texts in which ἐν Χριστῷ expressions occur may be generally described as ecclesiological. That is to say, they refer to the life of a community 'in Christ'. Here, again, we find a number of texts with a 'governing' θεός. Chapter 2 focused on the strongly theocentric language of 1 Cor. 1.18-31, with its description of 'where' the Corinthians now are in v. 30: ἐξ αὐτοῦ (sc. θεοῦ) δὲ ὑμεῖς ἐστε ἐν Χριστῷ Ἰησοῦ, ὃς ἐγενήθη σοφία ἡμῖν ἀπὸ θεοῦ. Similarly, the claim that 'If anyone is in Christ, he is a new creation', is followed by the acknowledgment that τὰ δὲ πάντα ἐκ τοῦ θεοῦ (2 Cor. 5.17-18). The church at Corinth is described not only as those ἡγιασμένοις ἐν Χριστῷ Ἰησοῦ, but also as κλητοῖς ἁγίοις[3] and as τῇ ἐκκλησίᾳ τοῦ θεοῦ (1 Cor. 1.1; cf. 1 Thess. 1.1, 2.14, and the context of Rom. 12.5, where the claim that 'we are one body in Christ' is preceded by a good deal of God-language[4]). In Galatians we find a reference to 'being justified' (δικαιωθῆναι) 'in Christ', where, again, the passive form of the verb implies divine agency, and, secondly, the affirmation in 3.26 that πάντες γὰρ υἱοὶ θεοῦ ἐστε διὰ πίστεως ἐν Χριστῷ Ἰησοῦ. Finally, in 1 Thessalonians Paul affirms that 'the dead in Christ will rise' (1 Thess. 4.16). But this will happen at the divine behest: ἐν σάλπιγγι θεοῦ (cf., in a similar eschatological context, the passive ζῳοποιηθήσονται in 1 Cor. 15.22). There are thus several texts referring to the 'foundation' or 'place' of the church which imply, either by means of the preposition ἐκ, by the use of verbs in the passive, or by adjacent nouns governed by θεοῦ, divine agency or origin. One of the most significant of these, however, Rom. 6.11, has yet to be discussed.

Rom. 6.11 serves as a concluding exhortation to the section 6.1-11, in which Paul has been responding to the question 'Shall we continue in

1. Käsemann, *Romans*, p. 133; cf. pp. 69-70.
2. Thus Michel, *An die Römer*, p. 184.
3. The implied subject of κλητοῖς is, as always in Paul, God.
4. See the discussion of this passage in Chapter 4.

sin, that grace may abound?' by reminding the Roman Christians of the significance of their baptism, through which they were baptized into Christ's death (v. 3). The outcome of that must be οὕτως καὶ ὑμεῖς λογίζεσθε ἑαυτοὺς (εἶναι) νεκροὺς μὲν τῇ ἁμαρτίᾳ ζῶντας δὲ τῷ θεῷ ἐν Χριστῷ Ἰησοῦ (v.11). W. Thüsing discusses this verse at some length, arguing that τῷ θεῷ is emphatic. He rightly stresses the connection between vv. 10 and 11, noting the statement of the earlier verse that Christ ζῇ τῷ θεῷ. This can only mean that being in Christ is thoroughly theocentric.[1] Similar verses in Paul's writings point in the same direction. Thüsing notes the adjacent verse 7.4 with its ἐγερθέντι, denoting, as always, divine agency, and the purpose of the new life ἵνα καρποφορήσωμεν τῷ θεῷ.

The same kind of language is found in 2 Cor. 5.11-21. Thüsing notes the θεῷ of vv. 11 and 13, suggesting that, in view of the γάρ of v. 14, the love of Christ directs the apostle both to the Church and to God.[2] The theocentric language continues with the ἐγερθέντι of v. 15, and God's reconciling work (vv. 18-19). The theocentricity of the passage is concluded in the expression δικαιοσύνη θεοῦ, denoting life given by God and life lived for God: τὸν μὴ γνόντα ἁμαρτίαν ὑπὲρ ἡμῶν ἁμαρτίαν ἐποίησεν, ἵνα ἡμεῖς γενώμεθα δικαιοσύνη θεοῦ ἐν αὐτῷ (v. 21).[3]

There remain a number of passages where the expression 'in Christ' is used, and where there is no apparent 'governing' God-language. Although quite numerous, they fall into three distinct categories. First, in Galatians this expression is used polemically: in the reference to 'the freedom which we have in Christ Jesus' (2.4) and in the assertion that 'in Christ Jesus neither circumcision nor uncircumcision is of any avail' (5.6). Secondly, Paul uses 'in Christ' expressions in personal contexts where such expressions seem to be the equivalent of 'as a Christian' or 'as Christians'. This group includes Rom. 9.1, 2 Cor. 12.2, Phil. 1.13, Phlm. 8, 20, and perhaps also 1 Cor. 3.1, 4.10 and 15. Finally, this particular christological expression tends to occur in closing greetings (Rom. 16.3-23; 1 Cor. 16.24; Phil. 4.21; Phlm. 23).

From this survey of Paul's use of the expression 'in Christ', it is clear that Paul's christocentricity and theocentricity belong together. Except in personal or polemical contexts, ἐν Χριστῷ tends to be used

1. Thüsing, *Per Christum*, pp. 67-78 and esp. p. 78.
2. Thüsing, *Per Christum*, pp. 101-105.
3. Thüsing, *Per Christum*, pp. 105-108.

by Paul in contexts where God is the explicit or implicit subject, origin or instigator.[1] This much is clear. But to what extent does this close interaction of God- and Christ-language give to the word 'God' new content and meaning? How far has Paul's God-language been affected by this interaction?

One might say that for Paul, being 'in Christ' lies in between, as it were, ἀπὸ or ἐκ θεοῦ and εἰς θεόν, not that to be in Christ is to be outside God, since ἀπό and ἐκ denote origin and, as many contexts imply, generosity, not distance. This last point is confirmed by the close correlation in Paul's theology between 'Christ' and 'Spirit'.[2] But if, as I argued earlier, 'in Christ' denotes the 'field of force', or focus of the divine action, can more specific content be given to it? A number of scholars in discussing the formula 'in Christ' draw attention to the work of Neugebauer, who interprets ἐν Χριστῷ 'Ιησοῦ as 'determined by the fact that Jesus Christ died and rose'.[3] (The occurrence of ἐν Χριστῷ 'Ιησοῦ in Phil. 2.5, in Paul's introductory exhortation to the Christ hymn which follows, strongly supports Neugebauer's interpretation, even though the absence of a verb in the relative clause ['Let this mind be in you which was also in Christ Jesus' (ὁ καὶ ἐν Χριστῷ 'Ιησοῦ)] makes the precise meaning uncertain.) But if Neugebauer is correct, it brings into sharper focus our fundamental question about God: if the death and resurrection of Jesus are central to Paul's use and understanding of a major component of his Christ-language—i.e. ἐν Χριστῷ—the question then becomes whether this implies a new understanding of the God whose action is so closely identified with, or discerned in, those events.

To return to an analysis of the linguistic evidence, within the wide Pauline usage of 'in Christ' expressions, differences may be discerned.

1. So also Beker, *Paul*, p. 177, and F.C. Grant, *Roman Hellenism and the New Testament* (Edinburgh: Oliver & Boyd, 1962), p. 144.

2. Thüsing, *Per Christum*, p. 66.

3. Thus, for example, W. Kramer, *Christ, Lord, Son of God* (London: SCM Press, 1966), p. 143. See also Grayston, *Dying We Live*, Appendix C, p. 382. Grayston's own study of the ἐν Χριστῷ formula (pp. 382-89, and esp. pp. 386-89) proceeds by categorizing ἐν Χριστῳ in a way different from that adopted here, but it is noteworthy that, of the texts he lists referring to Paul's actions, seven of the 14 (Rom. 9.1; 15.17; 2 Cor. 2.17; 12.19; 13.4; Phil.1.8; 3.3) have a reference to God or the Spirit. The texts which Grayston lists under the category of the community 'being in Christ' bear out the conclusion reached here: Paul tends to use ἐν Χριστῷ in a less explicitly theistic way in personal and polemical contexts.

When the emphasis falls upon Christian origins, θεός-language tends to appear, or to be implied. In view of their subject matter—i.e. their reference to origins—it seems fair to regard them as normative for other contexts where 'in Christ' expressions occur without God-language. Nevertheless, it is clear that the struggle with the Judaizers, and the need to develop a distinctively Christian vocabulary and identity, has led Paul to (a) a polemical use of such expressions without explicit θεός-language, and (b) the use (Paul perhaps resisted, or was not familiar with, the name Χριστιανός) of these expressions in contexts where they seem to mean, in effect, 'Christian'.

The theocentric character of Paul's other main prepositional phrase with the noun Χριστός is even more explicit. διὰ Χριστοῦ[1] expressions are numerous in Paul, although far fewer than ἐν Χριστῷ and related expressions. If we discount the expressions where 'Christ' or 'Jesus Christ' is dependent on a noun which is itself dependent on διά with the genitive,[2] there are 17 such phrases. A glance at the concordance shows that these account for by far the greatest number of such phrases in the New Testament. There are a few examples in the deutero-Paulines (notably Eph. 1.5 [cf. 2.18] and Tit. 3.6) but not many.[3] There are also a few examples in Acts.[4] We are dealing therefore, with a phrase employed by Paul with a frequency unique among New Testament writers.

A survey of these expressions shows very clearly the theocentric character of Paul's thought. There is always a governing θεός in the

1. Again, I use this expression as an 'umbrella' term for all expressions involving διά with the genitive of Χριστός. The majority, in fact, comprise the fuller, more liturgical-sounding expression διὰ τοῦ κυρίου ἡμῶν Ἰησοῦ Χριστοῦ. The occurrence of δι' αὐτοῦ referring to Christ (Rom. 5.9; 1 Cor. 8.6; 2 Cor. 1.20) must also be noted. The contexts of all three verses are strongly theistic, and 1 Cor. 8.6 and 2 Cor. 1.20 will be discussed more fully below.

2. As in Rom. 3.22 διὰ πίστεως Ἰησοῦ Χριστοῦ.

3. Noted also by Thüsing (*Per Christum*, p. 5) who observes that the theocentricity and Christocentricity of the *Hauptbriefe* are expressed somewhat differently in Ephesians and Colossians ('in a theological world-view which in many respects has changed').

4. 10.36 and 15.11. Occurrences elsewhere are also very few (1 Pet. 2.5; 4.11; Heb. 13.21; Jude 25). It should be noted, however, that although expressions such as 'through (Jesus) Christ' are infrequent in Hebrews, the preposition διά with the genitive is extremely significant in the argument of the letter (e.g. 1.2; 2.10; 7.25).

context. Thus thanks are given to God through Christ.[1] Paul's own apostleship is given through God and Christ (Gal. 1.1). Thüsing notes that the juxtaposition in this verse of 'God' and 'Christ' implies that the work of both are interfused ('ein Ineinander des Wirkens'):[2]

> Paul is an apostle by the agency of the exalted Christ—and precisely for that reason by the agency of God—because God, through the resurrection, made Christ the Lord who was to choose him as his apostle.

(I might add that this is yet another polemical use of Christ-language in Galatians.)

The last chapter noted the use of this phrase in paraenetical contexts.[3] In the remaining instances the 'controlling' θεός is clear. In fact, there is a striking similarity about many of the occurrences of the phrase 'through Jesus Christ our Lord'. Many of the contexts are doxological in character, and Wilckens and Michel are probably correct in positing a liturgical origin for the phrase.[4] This view finds some support in the fact that διὰ christological phrases tend to occur at the end or climax of a section or argument.[5] Our main concern, as always, however, is the relationship of such expressions to Paul's language about God. And here the presence of a 'controlling' θεός is particularly evident. It would be tedious to examine each instance in detail. Instead, the main patterns which can be seen will be briefly surveyed.

διά with Χριστός tends to occur when God is the subject, whether explicit or implied, of the action. Thus in 1 Thess. 5.9 οὐκ ἔθετο ὁ θεὸς εἰς ὀργὴν ἀλλὰ εἰς περιποίησιν σωτηρίας διὰ τοῦ κυρίου ἡμῶν Ἰησοῦ Χριστοῦ.[6] In his commentary on 1 Corinthians, C.K. Barrett, referring to the salutation of 1.3 with its juxtaposition of God and Christ, says, 'the Father is the source, Christ the means or agent'. This is the conclusion to be drawn from the interaction and juxtaposition of God- and Christ-language.[7]

1. Rom. 1.8; cf. 7.25 and 16.27.
2. Thüsing, *Per Christum*, p. 169.
3. Chapter 4, section 2.
4. Wilckens, *An die Römer*, I, p. 289 (cf. p. 300 n. 992); Michel, *An die Römer*, pp. 177 and 184.
5. Thus Rom. 5.11, 21; 7.25; 16.27; 1 Cor. 15.57; 1 Thess. 5.9.
6. Cf. 1 Cor. 15.57, Rom. 2.16; 3.22; 5.9 (where God is clearly the implied subject of both δικαιωθέντες and σωθησόμεθα); Gal. 2.16; 2 Cor. 1.5 and 5.18.
7. Over against the view of B. Rigaux (*Saint Paul: Les épîtres aux Thessaloniciens* [Paris: Gembloux 1956], p. 571), commenting on 1 Thess. 5.9,

Barrett's statement, however, must be amplified when it is applied more widely to Paul's use of διά with Χριστός. For God is not only the source, but the *goal*. A second category of διά phrases with Χριστός, therefore, reflects access to God or movement back to God, often in prayer and thanksgiving. Here the opening of Romans 5 is characteristic: δικαιωθέντες οὖν ἐκ πίστεως εἰρήνην ἔχομεν πρὸς θεὸν διὰ τοῦ κυρίου ἡμῶν Ἰησοῦ Χριστοῦ (v. 1) (cf. 1.8; 5.11; 7.25; 16.27; 2 Cor. 3.4.). To this group of texts should probably be added Phil. 1.11, in which Paul ends his prayer by referring to the Philippians as πεπληρωμένοι καρπὸν δικαιοσύνης τὸν διὰ Ἰησοῦ Χριστοῦ εἰς δόξαν καὶ ἔπαινον θεοῦ (v. 11). There are two more instances of διά used in this way which deserve attention. In Rom. 5.17, in his comparison and contrast of Adam and Christ, Paul writes that 'those who receive the abundance of grace and the free gift of righteousness' will 'reign in life διὰ τοῦ ἑνὸς Ἰησοῦ Χριστοῦ' (v. 17), and concludes the argument (v. 21) with a reference to 'grace abounding all the more' (ὑπερεπερίσσευσεν ἡ χάρις) so that ἡ χάρις βασιλεύσῃ διὰ δικαιοσύνης εἰς ζωὴν αἰώνιον διὰ Ἰησοῦ Χριστοῦ τοῦ κυρίου ἡμῶν. Here the theocentric character of the argument is less obvious. This is partly due to the exigencies of rhetoric, since Paul is struggling to present his argument by pairs of words, contrasting in meaning but similar in sound.[1] The expression in v. 15 should be noted, however: ἡ χάρις τοῦ θεοῦ. As Wilckens observes, there is not an exact correspondence between the words which Paul has chosen for 'in the deed of another "One" (i.e. Christ) the grace of God was at work'. This, however, makes doubtful Wilckens's later contention that 'Christ' and 'grace' are virtually synonyms.[2] It would be more correct to say of Paul's argument here and elsewhere in Romans that Christ is the instrument or vehicle of God's grace.[3] What this means, therefore, is that God is the implied subject of the verb βασιλεύσῃ in v. 21.

One final observation may be made about the διά phrases examined here. It is clear that they vary in form. Sometimes Paul has simply διὰ τοῦ Χριστοῦ (e.g. 2 Cor. 1.5), sometimes διὰ Ἰησοῦ Χριστοῦ

when he speaks of the salvation which comes from Christ and by Christ and of Christ as 'the cause and distributor of salvation'.

1. Wilckens, *An die Römer*, I, p. 322, suggests, for example, that Paul may have used χάρισμα because of its similarity to παράπτωμα.

2. Wilckens, *An die Römer*, I, p. 330.

3. Rom. 1.7; 3.24; 5.2; cf. 1 Cor. 1.4.

(e.g. Rom. 5.17). Here, as in the preceding v. 15, the emphasis falls on the one *man*, in contrast with Adam—hence the διά phrase lacks κυρίου ἡμῶν.[1] The more weighty διὰ τοῦ κυρίου ἡμῶν 'Ιησοῦ Χριστοῦ seems to be used for stylistic reasons.

Thus, like the phrase 'in Christ', Paul's use of the phrase 'through Christ' is deeply theocentric. Thüsing concludes that διὰ Χριστοῦ passages are places where the relationship of the chosen (or even the world) to God are expressed.[2] This corresponds closely with the results of this survey, although I have noted a sub-division in these texts between those which refer to God's action, and those which refer to the human response to that action.[3]

But if the grammatical subordination of Christ-language to God-language is again clear, what of the effect of this connection on Paul's God-language? Here the picture is not quite so clear. Many of the texts in which the διά formula occurs denote a change in the believer: πολλῷ οὖν μᾶλλον δικαιωθέντες νῦν ἐν τῷ αἵματι αὐτοῦ σωθησόμεθα δι' αὐτοῦ ἀπὸ τῆς ὀργῆς (Rom. 5.9; cf. vv. 1, 2, 11). But what kind of God-language is deployed in such statements? Can it be said to be scriptural, or at least part of traditional Jewish language about God? The following observations seem in order.

1. Paul does not rely on divine titles which serve as alternatives to the simple ὁ θεός, nor does he use adjectives qualifying θεός. To get at the nature of his God-language, therefore, in contexts where the phrases ἐν Χριστῷ and διὰ Χριστοῦ are used, it is necessary to explore the total context and, more specifically, the God-words, whether nouns or verbs, which are used in these contexts.

2. The nouns are a mixture of the old and the new. The

1. Similarly Rom. 2.16, where the context requires simply 'Ιησοῦ Χριστοῦ, rather than κυρίου ἡμῶν Ιησοῦ Χριστοῦ.

2. I differ, however, from Thüsing in his stress on the exalted Christ. Although Thüsing insists that the cross and resurrection are fundamental for Paul, he also insists that 'the agent' is the exalted Christ, in that only the living, sovereign Lord can communicate salvation. Thüsing, for example (*Per Christum*, pp. 233-34), thus identifies the Χριστός of 2 Cor. 5.18 as the exalted Christ (p. 197), but to support this on the grounds that v. 16 (εἰ καὶ ἐγνώκαμεν κατὰ σάρκα Χριστόν) refers to the earthly Christ seems questionable to say the least.

3. Cf. Grayston, *Dying We Live*, pp. 383-86. Grayston's list of texts 'qualifying actions by other persons' does not fully bring out their predominantly theocentric character: in 2 Cor. 3.4, Paul's confidence is 'through Christ πρὸς τὸν θεόν'.

'righteousness' of God is demonstrated in the death of Jesus Christ in a new way, and it is appropriated διὰ πίστεως Ἰησοῦ Χριστοῦ.[1] Similarly the scope of God's ὀργή is redefined. It is now unrelated to whether one is a Jew or a Gentile; escape from it is 'through Jesus Christ'.[2]

But while old, familiar words are deployed in new contexts and given new meaning, new, or certainly less familiar words are also employed. Here two may be singled out for mention, both because of their frequency, and the frequency of words related to them or with similar meaning.

The first is the word χάρις. Its frequency in Paul's writings has already been observed.[3] But often it appears in contexts where the phrase (or a related expression) 'through Christ' occurs, as for example in Rom. 5.2:

> δι' οὗ (sc. Χριστοῦ) καὶ τὴν προσαγωγὴν ἐσχήκαμεν (τῇ πίστει) εἰς τὴν χάριν ταύτην ἐν ᾗ ἑστήκαμεν (cf. 5.21, 8.32 for the related verb χαρίζομαι).

First, the word χάρις is almost entirely absent *as a God-word* from the Old Testament. (I noted in Chapter 1, p. 75, Doughty's claim that χάρις is almost totally unknown in Jewish literature.[4]) Secondly, it needs to be said that the absence of the word χάρις must not, of course, be taken to mean that ancient Israel had no experience of grace. But Doughty is surely right in claiming that Paul was the first theologian to use χάρις 'in a technical way' to interpret the salvation activity of God.

Then, there is the word ἀγάπη. The verb ἀγαπάω is used in the Old Testament in a variety of ways. It is used not only of human love, but also of the divine love (e.g. Hos. 3.1; Isa. 41.8). It is also, in the LXX, 'theologically equivocal'; it may denote 'good love' or 'bad love'.[5] In

1. The question of whether Χριστοῦ is a subjective or objective genitive need not concern us here. On this see M.D. Hooker, 'ΠΙΣΤΙΣ ΧΡΙΣΤΟΥ', *NTS* 35.3 (1989), pp. 321-42. For the traditional view see, for example, Ziesler, *Romans* (p. 109), and Dunn, *Romans*, I, p. 166.

2. 1 Thess. 1.10; 5.9; Rom. 5.9.

3. Chapter 1, section 3 a, on Rom. 11.5-6.

4. Doughty, 'ΧΑΡΙΣ'. Certainly the word itself is scarce. I can find no evidence for the claim (*TWNT*, IX, p. 381) that 'the later translators with increasing firmness connect חסד and χάρις'. חסד is normally translated by ἔλεος in the LXX. (See the earlier discussion in Chapter 1, pp. 74-75.)

5. James Barr's essay 'Words for Love in Biblical Greek', in L.D. Hurst and

the New Testament, however, there are two developments. First, the word ἀγάπη appears frequently, and secondly, it is 'theologically unequivocal'—i.e. it is always 'good' love.[1] Barr, in the same article, describes the appearance of ἀγάπη in the New Testament as 'important and significant'. Particularly relevant to this study are (a) its rarity and lateness in the LXX,[2] and (b) its appearance in Paul with specific reference to the death of Christ (Rom. 5.8; 8.31-39; Gal. 2.20).

It would be a grave mistake to equate the rarity of a word in the Old Testament, or its absence from it, and its frequency in the New Testament as, in itself, indicative of a profound theological change. The linguistic situation is more complicated than that, and the words cannot be simply equated with that which they denote. Nevertheless, I suggest that there *is* significance in the appearance of χάρις and ἀγάπη in Paul's language about God, and I shall return to this subject later in this inquiry.

Summary

1. Paul's Christ-language is *grammatically subordinate* to his God-language. This is apparent in several ways. Χριστός is used very rarely in the nominative case, except (a) as the subject of a verb indicating sacrifice or death, and (b) as the subject of (usually) the passive ἠγέρθη, indicating the powerful action of God. Similarly, Paul's use of ἐν Χριστῷ and διὰ Χριστοῦ-language is thoroughly theocentric. Except where ἐν Χριστῷ is used, in effect, to mean 'a Christian' or 'as a Christian', the contexts imply that 'the field of force' indicated by 'in Christ' lies, as it were, between ἀπὸ/ἐκ θεου and εἰς θεόν, but being, at the same time, ἐν τῷ θεῷ. Similarly, διὰ Χριστοῦ expresses the instrument or means, first of God's initiative or action, and secondly of the resulting thanksgiving or praise being returned to God.

2. Yet if Paul's Christ-language is grammatically subordinate to his God-language—and I suggest that this feature of his letters is *theologically* significant—nevertheless, Paul's θεός-language is dependent on Χριστός-language for its full explication. The two kinds of language

N.T. Wright (eds.), *The Glory of Christ in the New Testament* (Oxford: Oxford University Press, 1987), pp. 3-18, dispels some of the widely held misconceptions about biblical words for love. The reference here is taken from p. 12.

1. Barr, in Hurst and Wright (eds.), *Glory of Christ*, pp. 3-18, who points out, however, that the verb ἀγαπᾶν remains equivocal (e.g. Lk. 11.43).

2. See Hatch and Redpath, *Concordance*, *ad loc.*

are frequently inter-dependent. Two features seem particularly important and are closely related. (a) Several factors point to the death and resurrection of Christ as the focus or origin of a new understanding and experience of God. The death and resurrection of Christ are frequently referred to as a particular locus of divine action, and life 'in Christ' is understood as life 'determined by the fact that Christ died and rose'. (b) Two particularly important words, χάρις and ἀγάπη, are associated closely with the death of Christ: this event is the means by which both are experienced or revealed.

2. *Juxtapositions of God- and Christ-Language in Paul*

The previous section of this chapter examined some important components of Paul's Christ-language. But this, of course, is far from comprising the whole. God- and Christ-language alternate, or are juxtaposed, in ways other than the ones we have so far examined. The *interrelation* of these two kinds of language has, I submit, not been sufficiently examined, and so the task of this section is to examine these alternations and juxtapositions and to attempt to discover the presuppositions which they reflect. It will be necessary to make some preliminary definitions, and to determine in view of the amount of the material the criteria for the selection of texts. First, however, the subject needs to be put in a wider perspective by means of a brief survey of the God-language which Paul uses *without* Christ-language in the immediate vicinity. These are the passages where Christ-language does not exert any direct influence on the language Paul uses about God.

First, there is God-language used with reference to Gentiles apart from Christ. They are twice described as 'not knowing God' (Gal. 4.8; 1 Thess. 4.5). Elsewhere there are references to their idolatry, or worship of demons, in contrast with the worship of the one, living God (1 Thess. 1.9; 1 Cor. 8.4-5; 10.20; 12.2; 2 Cor. 6.16). Here the God-language reflects traditional Jewish beliefs both about God and about Gentiles, although at 1 Thess. 1.9-10 and 1 Cor. 8.6 traditional God-language has been supplemented by language about Christ.

Not all God-language about pagans is negative, however. In Rom. 1.21 Paul clearly states that Gentiles *did* know God (cf. v. 32) for

> διότι τὸ γνωστὸν τοῦ θεοῦ φανερόν ἐστιν ἐν αὐτοῖς· ὁ θεὸς γὰρ αὐτοῖς ἐφανέρωσεν. τὰ γὰρ ἀόρατα αὐτοῦ ἀπὸ κτίσεως κόσμου τοῖς ποιήμασιν νοούμενα καθορᾶται, ἥ τε ἀΐδιος αὐτοῦ δύναμις καὶ θειότης, εἰς τὸ εἶναι αὐτοὺς ἀναπολογήτους (1.19-20).

These verses, closely resembling the arguments of the Wisdom of Solomon,[1] represent the most positive God-language Paul uses about Gentiles who are not Christians.[2] Not surprisingly—since Paul nowhere else in his writings deals with this theme—there are several *hapaxes* in the God-language he employs here.[3] But, overall, the picture is negative (Rom. 1.18-32). The characteristic human activity in this passage is described as *exchanging* (ἤλλαξαν, v. 23; μετήλλαξαν, vv. 25 and 27) what was good and true for what was bad and false. The corresponding activity of God was to 'hand them over' (παρέδωκεν, vv. 24, 26, 28) to the consequences of their wrongdoing, for 'they did not honour him as God or give thanks to him' (v. 21) nor did they 'see fit to acknowledge God' (οὐκ ἐδοκίμασαν τὸν θεὸν ἔχειν ἐν ἐπιγνώσει, v. 28). Of Paul's God-language here, some is biblical (ὀργή, ἀληθεία, δύναμις, δόξα, παραδίδωμι), some is not (ἀΐδιος, θειότης); some, as God-language, is very rare in the LXX (φανερόω, only at Jer. 40.6),[4] γνωστός (with θεός as accompanying nominative only at Ps. 75 [76].1).

The God-language which Paul uses about Jews can be divided similarly into positive and negative statements. Chapter 1 noted the frequency of ἔλεος and its cognates in Romans 9–11 (where much of the positive language occurs), contrasted with its infrequency elsewhere in Paul's writngs. Attention must now be drawn to Paul's language of criticism and judgment. The Jews do not 'please' (ἀρεσκόντων) God (1 Thess. 2.15); they have 'a zeal for God' ἀλλ' οὐ κατ' ἐπίγνωσιν (Rom. 10.2); indeed, they boast in God (Rom. 2.17), yet 'dishonour' (ἀτιμάζεις) God (Rom. 2.23). Consequently, they too, like the Gentiles, incur the judgment of God (2.3, 5, 9, 12; cf. 3.5, 19).

Most of these expressions reflect traditional language about God, yet it is used with surprising qualifications or in extraordinary contexts. The

1. See especially Wis.13.1-9. The God-language, however, is not as similar as the arguments.

2. Cf. Rom. 2.14-15, for a parallel statement about the relationship of Gentiles to the Law (cf. Wis.17.11).

3. These include τὸ γνωστὸν τοῦ θεοῦ (v. 19) ἀΐδιος, θειότης (contrast θεότης at Col. 2.9) (v. 20); cf. ἄφθαρτος in v. 23 (elsewhere in the New Testament only at 1 Tim.1.17 as an epithet for God).

4. Dunn, *Romans*, I, p. 63, points out that φανερόω occurs 49 times in the New Testament, but while it is used quite frequently in later New Testament writings of the revelation of Christ, its use by Paul is more varied (compare, for example, Rom. 3.21; 1 Cor.4.5; 2 Cor. 3.8).

negatives are all the more remarkable and, in Paul's view, tragic in view of the privileges which the Jews had received. Twice Paul refers to or enumerates those privileges (Rom. 3.2 ; cf. 9.4-5). But a number of important God expressions occur: the faithfulness of God (τὴν πίστιν τοῦ θεοῦ, v. 3) 'the truth of God' (ἡ ἀλήθεια τοῦ θεοῦ, v. 7) and 'the righteousness of God' (θεοῦ δικαιοσύνην, v. 5). Here Paul is articulating traditional and fundamental covenant theology in thoroughly biblical language.

But the most important feature for our purpose of much of the language reviewed here is its reappearance in christological contexts. This applies to the language Paul uses of both Jew and Gentile. It is true of God's power (1.20; cf. 1.16, etc.), God's glory (1.23; cf. 2 Cor. 3.7-4.6), God's truth (3.2; cf. 15.8); God's righteousness (contrast 10.3 with 3.21, etc.). Most remarkable of all, God's 'wrathful' action in allowing humankind to 'freewheel' into the consequences of their own folly (παρέδωκεν, 1.24, 26, 28) has its counterpart in God 'handing over' (παρέδωκεν) his Son (8.32; cf. 4.25). (Another notable example of a christological counterpart to a theologoumenon occurs in the parallelism of Gal. 3.28 with Romans 2.11.[1])

This is further evidence of how Paul's God-language, already used in a prophetic, iconoclastic way (Rom. 2.11 etc), is re-minted and redeployed in a Christian context. The most important examples are (a) the redefining of God's righteousness[2] and (b) the 'replacement' (if that is the correct evaluation of the apparent change) of τὸ ὄνομα τοῦ θεοῦ (Rom. 2.24) by τὸ ὄνομα τοῦ κυρίου ἡμῶν 'Ιησου Χριστοῦ (e.g. 1 Cor. 1.2), a phrase which will be considered in the next section of this chapter.

Yet this 'Christianizing' of God-language in Paul's writings extends much further, even though parallels of the kind I have just cited do not occur. In fact, by far the largest category of God-language without any juxtaposed or immediately adjacent christological language is applied neither to Jews nor pagans, but to Christians, including Paul himself. But precisely for this reason it is implicitly christological. Here I can only

1. The list could be extended with other, non-theological words: the verb συμμαρτυρῶ (2.15) reappears at 8.16; compare also the language of 2.15 with 2 Cor. 3.3.

2. See Chapter 1, section 2. The near contemporary writings, the Wisdom of Solomon and the Psalms of Solomon, provide further evidence that 'the righteousness of God' has been redefined by Paul.

outline the main areas in which this kind of God-language is used, giving, as far as possible, typical examples of it.

1. God's 'call' is his most characteristic activity, according to Paul. In 1 Thessalonians Paul urges the Christians at Thessalonika to live a life worthy of God, 'who calls (τοῦ καλοῦντος) you into his own kingdom and glory' (2.12). Other occurrences of καλέω, however (e.g. Gal. 1.6), make clear that this 'call' of God is focused in, or channelled through Christ. Many other God expressions in Paul belong in this category: ἐκκλησία τοῦ θεοῦ (1 Cor. 10.32, etc.), τέκνα τοῦ θεοῦ (Phil. 2.15), ναὸς θεοῦ (1 Cor. 3.16-17; 2 Cor. 6.16; cf. 1 Cor. 3.9), Paul's use of ἐκλέγομαι at 1 Cor. 1.27-29, and the occurrence of 'Ισραὴλ τοῦ θεοῦ at Gal. 6.16.

2. When Paul speaks of 'the word of God', he normally means the gospel. (Thus 1 Thess. 2.13; 1 Cor. 14.36; 2 Cor. 4.2). At Rom. 9.6, however, 'the word of God' embraces both the old and the new covenants.

3. God is always the object of Pauline thanksgivings, but the content is always explicitly or implicitly christological. Thus at 1 Thess. 2.13 and 3.9 Paul gives thanks for the Thessalonians' Christian faith and life (cf. Phil. 1.3; 2 Cor. 8.16).

4. Christian faith is born through and in the power and grace of God (1 Cor. 2.5; 2 Cor. 6.1); God 'energizes' Christian life (Phil. 2.13; cf. 2 Cor. 9.8); it is lived out before him (παρὰ θεῷ) (1 Cor. 7.24, cf Rom. 14.22); it is lived out 'in the fear of God' (2 Cor. 7.1), and to the glory of God (1 Cor. 10.31); prayer is directed to God (1 Cor. 11.13; 14.2), and all this 'through Christ' and 'in Christ', as the contexts make clear.

5. Paul makes many 'God statements' with reference to his own life and ministry. The grace of God was foundational to both his call and his work (1 Cor. 15.10; 3.10); God was responsible for the humiliations and frailties of the apostle (1 Cor. 4.9; 2 Cor. 12.21; cf. 12.7),[1] and God, too, in the apostle's humiliations and weakness empowers him (2 Cor. 1.9; 4.7; 6.7). Other God expressions occur: Paul has 'the Spirit of God' (1 Cor. 7.40) is the 'servant of God' (2 Cor. 6.4) courts the Corinthians with the 'zeal of God' (2 Cor. 11.2), defends his ministry with passionate appeals to God as witness (Gal. 1.20; 2 Cor. 1.23; 11.11; 12.2-3;

1. Here the ἔδοθη is almost certainly a divine passive: i.e. 'the thorn in the flesh' was given to Paul by God (So also Furnish, *2 Corinthians*, p. 528; Martin, *2 Corinthians*, p. 412).

cf. Rom. 1.9; 1 Thess. 2.5, 10);[1] even his journeys are determined by 'the will of God' (Rom. 1.10; 15.32).[2]

Again, we have here God-language much of which is traditional—that is, it is firmly rooted in Scripture and Jewish tradition. God's temple, children, 'church', word—all find new definitions. Similarly, the call of God finds a new channel and focus. Even a Christian version of a familiar Jewish oath (2 Cor. 11.31) emerges. In other words, a great deal of Paul's God-language is implicitly christological by virtue of the contexts in which it is used. All of this means that, just as Paul's Christ-language is deeply theocentric in the ways and in the contexts in which he uses it, so much of his language about God is implicitly christological. Our task now is to explore more deeply the relationship between Paul's language about God and about Christ, by examining those contexts in which Paul's God-language and Christ-language are juxtaposed, or alternate. What linguistic patterns can be seen in the many juxtapositions of language about God and Christ, and what are the theological presuppositions behind these patterns? In what follows I have attempted to set out what seem to be the main categories, even though there are variations within some of them.

Pattern 1: θεός *and* Χριστός *Share the Same Preposition*

I begin with this particular pattern because it occurs in the first juxtaposition of God- and Christ-language in all the epistles. Most of the examples, in fact, occur in the opening salutations of Paul's letters. It will be useful to list them at the beginning of this analysis, as several are identical: Παῦλος...τῇ ἐκκλησίᾳ Θεσσαλονικέων ἐν θεῷ πατρὶ καὶ κυρίῳ Ἰησοῦ Χριστῷ, χάρις ὑμῖν καὶ εἰρήνη (1 Thess. 1.1; cf. 2 Thess. 1.1); χάρις ἡμῖν καὶ εἰρήνη απὸ θεοῦ πατρὸς ἡμῶν καὶ κυρίου Ἰησοῦ Χριστοῦ (Gal. 1.3; so also 1 Cor. 1.1; 2 Cor. 1.2; Rom. 1.7b; Phlm. 3).[3]

1. 2 Cor. 11.31 (ὁ θεὸς καὶ πατὴρ τοῦ κυρίου Ἰησοῦ οἶδεν, ὁ ὢν εὐλογητὸς εἰς τοὺς αἰῶνας, ὅτι οὐ ψεύδομαι) is the only explicitly Christian oath in the Pauline letters. The particular expressions used here give Paul's oath added weight and impressiveness (Martin, *2 Corinthians*, p. 383).

2. Dunn, *Romans*, I, p. 30, and Käsemann, *Romans*, p. 18, note the frequency of this pious phrase in the ancient world (cf. 1 Cor. 4.19 and 16.7, discussed in the next section).

3. First, a brief comment is necessary about the form and origin of these greetings. The most probable antecedent of this kind of greeting lies in the formula

Opinions vary about the significance of the juxtaposition of God- and Christ-language in this formula. Some scholars believe that it shows that Paul's attitude to Christ is in effect 'the attitude of man toward God'.[1] Weiss comments as follows: 'The dispenser of grace and peace is Christ just as much as it is God. In the piety of the early Christian both stand side by side: he looks to both in prayer, and thanks both for their blessings.'[2] These observations or deductions seem to oversimplify the situation. First, the large amount of 'subordinationist' Christ-language in Paul must not be lost sight of, and secondly, with reference to Weiss's comment it is possible that the expression should be understood as implying that Christ *mediates God's* grace and peace. Holtz,[3] commenting on 1 Thess. 1.1, writes, 'Here the constituent actions of God and of Christ stand side by side (*nebeneinander*)', assuming the influence of early Christian liturgy here. Barrett comments, '"Each (sc. grace and peace) comes from God the Father and the Lord Jesus Christ; the Father is the source, Christ the means or agent"'. That, in the light of other evidence reviewed here, seems the likeliest explanation of this

'Mercy and peace be with you', found in Jewish letters (e.g. *2 Bar.* 78.2) (Thus, for example, Käsemann, *Romans*, p. 16, Furnish, *2 Corinthians*, p. 107). It seems significant, however, that Paul prefers the word χάρις. (Rigaux, *Epîtres*, p. 353, *contra* Furnish, who appears to treat χάρις and ἔλεος as synonyms in this context, is correct in recognizing that 'ἔλεος has a more Jewish sound...' and that Paul prefers χάρις because 'for him, the divine grace has been abundantly expressed in the universality of the salvation granted to Gentiles'. Although we are not primarily concerned here with the origin of Paul's language, it may be that we have here a Pauline adaptation of a formula used by Jewish Christians. Kramer (*Christ*, pp. 151-53) overestimates the Pauline contribution, but some Pauline influence cannot be ruled out.

The greetings, however, also have a liturgical ring, noted, e.g., by Weiss, *Körintherbrief*, p. 5. Kramer, however (*Christ*, p. 152), contends that there is nothing to indicate that the salutation was used in worship during the pre-Pauline period. He cites Friedrich's criticisms of Lohmeyer's thesis that the language used here is liturgical and pre-Pauline, noting Friedrich's examples of letters where 'grace' and 'peace' are used in the opening salutation. This may explain the omission of the definite article with ἔλεος, πατήρ and κύριος. Collins (*Studies*, pp. 231-32) finds no significant difference in Paul's alternation between θεός with and θεός without the definite article, although we note Rigaux's observation that it tends to be omitted before θεός and κύριος 'before stereotyped formulae'.

1. Martin, *2 Corinthians*, p. 4, quoting J.G. Machen.
2. Weiss, *Körintherbrief*, p. 5.
3. Holtz, *An die Thessalonicher*, p. 39.

juxtaposition. But Barrett goes on: 'It is worth noting that Paul places the two persons side by side without any suggestion that one belongs to a different order of being from the other'.[1]

Clearly the juxtaposition is theologically very significant. The reference to 'the Lord Jesus Christ' cannot be regarded as an addition to distinguish the church from the Hellenistic ἐκκλησία or the Jewish synagogue.[2] With the possible exception of 1 Thessalonians, there are other distinctively Christian terms in the opening sentences of Paul's letter to make this unnecessary, if that were its sole purpose.

What conclusions, then, can be drawn from Paul's use of these expressions? It is going beyond the evidence to conclude that these opening salutations prove that Paul regards Jesus as God. Barrett may also be pressing the evidence too hard in observing that the very juxtaposition of θεός and Χριστός lacks any indication that they belong to a different order of being from each other. (What would this imply about James' self-understanding, as reflected in Acts 15.28: ἔδοξεν γὰρ τῷ πνεύματι τῷ ἁγίῳ καὶ ἡμῖν?)

But there is another important text to be noted here. In 1 Thessalonians there occurs a prayer-wish which, in its formulation, is unique in Paul's letters:[3] αὐτὸς δὲ ὁ θεὸς καὶ πατὴρ ἡμῶν καὶ ὁ κύριος ἡμῶν Ἰησοῦς κατευθῆναι τὴν ὁδὸν ἡμῶν πρὸς ὑμᾶς (3.11). Although it does not correspond exactly with the definition of the linguistic pattern (a shared preposition) under discussion here, it is clearly relevant. The singular verb has been noted by all commentators.[4] Whiteley observes that

> this construction... is extremely rare, and is normally found when the two subjects are very closely connected, as at Mt. 5.18, where the two pairs of subjects 'heaven and earth' and 'one letter... and one stroke of a letter' (NRSV) both govern verbs in the singular.[5]

Holtz also notes the singular verb: 'In a more emphatic way God and the Lord are comprehended as a unity'.[6] He rejects, however, the

1. Barrett, *2 Corinthians*, p. 56 (the quotation within the quotation coming from Barrett's commentary on 1 Corinthians, pp. 34-35).
2. Thus, rightly, Rigaux, *Epîtres*, p. 353.
3. There is a close parallel in the deutero-Pauline 2 Thess. 2.16, discussed in Appendix 4.
4. So also Kreitzer, *Paul's Eschatology*, p. 110.
5. Whiteley, *Theology*, p. 55.
6. Holtz, *An die Thessalonicher*, p. 142.

parallels cited by Best from Mt. 24.35 and 1 Cor. 15.50, where 'heaven and earth' and 'flesh and blood' are followed by singular verbs. He prefers, rather, to speak of an identity of action: insofar as God acted in Christ, there exists an identity between them. He goes on to emphasize that it is a one-sided identity *(die Identität eine einseitig gerichtete*— that is, God acted in Christ—the sentence cannot be reversed).

It is interesting to observe that Paul nowhere else uses an expression of this kind. Rom. 15.5-6 and 15.13 are prayer-wishes directed only to God. Similarly, as O'Brien has shown[1] Paul's thanksgivings are deeply Jewish in form and even content. It is possible that here Paul's use of πατήρ has 'attracted' the reference to 'our Lord Jesus' since πατήρ is rarely used by Paul except in the context of a reference to Jesus.

The problem of ascertaining Paul's theological presuppositions here is compounded by his reference to ὁ κύριος in the following verse: ὑμᾶς δὲ ὁ κύριος πλεονάσαι καὶ περισσεύσαι τῇ ἀγάπῃ εἰς ἀλλήλους καὶ εἰς πάντας καθάπερ καὶ ἡμεῖς εἰς ὑμᾶς. Commentators are divided over whether ὁ κύριος refers to God or to Jesus. The context, with the preceding and following references to 'our Lord Jesus' (vv. 11 and 13) suggests that it must be a reference to Jesus. Some scholars resist this conclusion, pointing out that Paul rarely, if ever, prays to Jesus.[2] There are, however, a few parallels between Paul's God- and Lord-language[3] which suggest that the first Christians probably prayed to 'the Lord' as well as to God. Certainly the grammatical pattern we have observed here of God- and Christ- or Lord-language sharing the same preposition, and, in one instance, the same verb, suggests at the very least a close unity and, indeed, identity of action. But it is important to note that in this particular pattern we do not have Christ-language alone; the references are to '*the Lord* Jesus Christ'.

Pattern 2: Christ is the Object of a Verb Governed by θεός

The great majority of the examples under this heading refer to the death or to the resurrection of Jesus, and so are 'the other half' (grammatically speaking) of the Christ sayings referring to the cross and resurrection in

1. O'Brien, *Introductory Thanksgivings.*

2. Thus Holtz, *An die Thessalonicher*, p. 143-44. Best, *Commentary*, p. 148, however, refers to 2 Thess. 3.5, 16; 2 Cor. 12.8 and 1 Cor.16.22, the last of which Holtz rejects as an example of prayer, while 2 Cor. 12.8 occurs in an exceptionally personal context.

3. See section 3 below.

which 'Christ' is the subject (see section 1). It is not part of the purpose of this discussion to offer a detailed exegesis of all these passages. Instead, I shall explore the function of Paul's statements about God in these contexts, and their significance. (Many of these statements are almost certainly pre-Pauline. Pokorny has recently attempted to trace the development of such pre-Pauline formulae.[1] However, a diachronic approach is not relevant here.)

Paul's language about the resurrection is more uniform than his language about the death of Christ. Frequently, as we saw in the previous section, Paul uses a divine passive.[2] Sometimes he uses the active tense of ἐγείρω, with God as the subject[3] or in participial phrases referring to God. Thus the letter to the Galatians begins: Παῦλος ἀπόστολος... διὰ Ἰησοῦ Χριστοῦ καὶ θεοῦ πατρὸς τοῦ ἐγείραντος αὐτὸν ἐκ νεκρῶν.[4] The only exceptions to these theocentric expressions are 1 Thess. 4.14, where the verb used is ἀνίστημι (ὅτι Ἰησοῦς ἀπέθανεν καὶ ἀνέστη), and Rom. 14.9 (εἰς τοῦτο γὰρ Χριστὸς ἀπέθανεν καὶ ἔζησεν...). In the second instance the context requires the verb ζάω.[5] In the case of 1 Thess. 4.14, it is tempting to wonder whether in this early letter Paul has not yet refined his theological language, preferring in later letters to use more obviously theocentric expressions.

Another variation in Paul's resurrection language occurs in Phil. 2.9, not surprisingly perhaps as it is part of a possibly pre-Pauline hymn. Here the verb with reference to God's exaltation of Jesus is ὑπερύψωσεν.

By contrast, there is more variation in the various words and formulae used to describe the death of Christ. Most frequently the simple aorist ἀπέθανεν (or aorist participle) is used.[6] Nearly always, these expressions with Χριστός as subject occur in the context of a governing θεός

1. P. Pokorny, *The Genesis of Christology* (Edinburgh: T. & T. Clark, 1987), pp. 63-109.

2. Rom. 4.25; 6.4, 9; 7.4; 8.34; 1 Cor. 15 *passim*; 2 Cor. 5.15.

3. Rom. 10.9; 1 Cor. 6.14; 1 Thess. 1.10.

4. Gal. 1.1; cf 2 Cor. 4.14; 5.15; Rom. 4.24 and 8.11. Rom. 4.17 and 2 Cor. 1.9 have similar participial phrases, but referring to God's power to raise the dead without particular reference to Christ.

5. Cf. also 2 Cor. 13.4.

6. 1 Thess. 4.14; 5.10; Gal. 2.21; 1 Cor. 8.11; 15.3; 2 Cor. 5.15; Rom. 5.6-8; 6.10; 8.34; 14.9 and 15.

(section 1 above). When Χριστόν is the object, θεός naturally is the subject. The 'sending formula' is especially noteworthy.[1] There are two instances of this formula with the verb to send (Gal. 4.4, ἐξαπέστειλεν, and Rom. 8.3, πέμψας), each referring to God's 'Son'. Under this same heading of the 'sending formula' we should probably include[2] Paul's use of the verb παραδίδωμι: God 'handed over' Jesus (Rom. 8.32, and in the passive voice the pre-Pauline Rom. 4.25 and 1 Cor. 11.23). At 2 Cor. 5.21 the striking expression 'He (sc. God) made sin (ἁμαρτίαν ἐποίησεν) him who did not know sin (Christ) for us'. Finally in Rom. 3.25 Paul writes of how God 'put (Christ) forward as an expiation' (ὃν προέθετο ὁ θεὸς ἱλαστήριον). The only variation from this otherwise deeply theocentric language occurs in Gal. 2.20, with its reference to τοῦ υἱοῦ τοῦ θεοῦ τοῦ ἀγαπήσαντός με καὶ παραδόντος ἑαυτὸν ὑπὲρ ἐμοῦ.

There is thus a remarkable uniformity about the God- and Christ-language in this particular grammatical pattern: with only one exception (Gal. 1.16, with its reference to the call of the apostle) all refer to either the death or the resurrection of Jesus. Christ, then, in death and resurrection was the 'object' of divine action.[3] Thus far, then, we have two quite different patterns: the first pattern reflecting a certain kind of equality of Christ with God, and the second reflecting his subordination to God.

Pattern 3: Χριστός *in a Prepositional Phrase Accompanies a Reference or Implied Reference to God*

It is not possible to review each of these individually, nor is it necessary here since most of the examples of this particular pattern include either the phrase ἐν Χριστοῦ Ἰησοῦ or διὰ τοῦ κυρίου ἡμῶν Ἰησοῦ Χριστοῦ (and their variations) reviewed in the first section of this

1. Cf. A. Hultgren, *Christ and his Benefits* (Philadelphia: Fortress Press, 1987), pp. 49-50.

2. Thus Hultgren, *Christ and his Benefits.*

3. Once again, the range of words used by Paul reflect a mixture of old and new. Thus παραδίδωμι is frequent in the LXX (although often of wrathful action, as when God hands over Israel into the hands of her enemies, Ezek. 39.23 etc.) and ἐξαποστέλλω, translating שׁלח, frequently refers to divine action. On the other hand, occurrences of προτίθημι in the LXX are few, although MSS variants complicate the matter, copyists often confusing this word with προστίθημι (Hatch and Redpath, *Concordance*, *ad loc.*)

chapter. It is important, however, to summarize the main theological themes which emerge from this very frequent pattern. The most important point to be made is that God is almost always the expressed or implied subject, most often as the origin and instigator, and in particular as the one who calls, gives and justifies. The main categories, therefore, are *soteriological* and *ecclesiological*.

The grace of God operated, and operates, in and through Christ (Rom. 5.21; 1 Cor. 1.4). Similarly the righteousness of God was effected in and through Christ (Rom. 3.21-26; cf. 2 Cor. 5.21; Phil. 3.9). Consequently, the activity most frequently predicated of God in these contexts is *justification*. The fact that it is *God* who justifies is partly obscured by the frequency with which Paul uses the passive of this verb (Gal. 2.16-17; 3.24; Rom. 2.13; 3.20, 24, 28; 4.2; 5.1, 9; 1 Cor. 6.11). That these are all 'divine passives', however, is made abundantly clear by other texts (Gal. 3.8; Rom. 3.26, 30; 4.5; 8.30, 33, where ὁ θεός is the explicit subject of δικαιῶ). In Paul, it is always God who justifies ἐκ or διὰ πίστεως Χριστοῦ. It is never Christ who justifies, and yet a person is not justified ἐὰν μὴ διὰ πίστεως Ἰησοῦ Χριστοῦ (Gal. 2.16).

This pattern continues in the nature, direction and outcome of Christian living: all is 'of God through or in Christ'. Thus Paul speaks of God continuing to work in the believer, and of ultimately bringing his work to completion.[1] Just as all comes from God, so there is a 'return' movement to God. Thus thanksgivings are directed to God;[2] to God the Christian is ultimately accountable (1 Thess. 3.13), and it is by God, indeed, that all will be judged 'through Jesus Christ' (Rom. 2.16).

This is one of the two most frequent patterns of God- and Christ-language in Paul. The soteriological and ecclesiological character of the texts are the clue to understanding how the Christ-language functions. In both it denotes the locus or means of divine action. Thus one may speak of a divine *concentration* on Christ, reflected in the linguistic dependence here of God-language on Christ-language. It is clear that Paul could only articulate what he had to say about God by juxtaposing these two kinds of language. Whether this language can be called 'exclusive' (ἐὰν μὴ διὰ πίστεως Ἰησοῦ Χριστοῦ) raises important questions about religious experience contemporary with Paul (as reflected, for

1. Thus 1 Thess. 5.18; 2 Cor. 1.21; Phil. 4.7,19.
2. 1 Cor. 15.57.

example, in the Qumran language of justification), but here I can only draw attention to the question.

Pattern 4: θεός, *often in a Prepositional Phrase or in the Dative Case, Follows or 'Enlarges' a Reference to Christ*

This pattern can be seen in a group of texts where 'Christ' or 'the Lord' is associated with 'the will of God'. Paul himself is an apostle of Jesus Christ διὰ θελήματος θεοῦ.[1] The most important example of this word association, however, occurs in Gal. 1.4, where Paul writes of Jesus Christ τοῦ δόντος ἑαυτὸν ὑπὲρ τῶν ἁμαρτιῶν ἡμῶν...κατὰ τὸ θέλημα τοῦ θεοῦ καὶ πατρός. The juxtaposition of διὰ τοῦ κυρίου Ἰησοῦ (1 Thess. 4.2), and the following statement τοῦτο γάρ ἐστιν θέλημα τοῦ θεοῦ (v. 3) suggests that the will of God is conveyed or mediated through or by the Lord Jesus. Similarly, the formula in 1 Thess. 5.18 (τοῦτο γὰρ θέλημα θεοῦ ἐν Χριστῷ Ἰησοῦ εἰς ὑμᾶς) seems to mean that God's will is actualized or expressed 'in Christ'.[2]

Secondly, such θεός phrases, combined with references to Christ, are used in a doxological context. Thus Paul addresses the Christians at Philippi as those who are πεπληρωμένοι καρπὸν δικαιοσύνης τὸν διὰ Ἰησοῦ Χριστοῦ εἰς δόξαν καὶ ἔπαινον θεοῦ (1.11) and of the universal confession of Christ Jesus as Lord εἰς δόξαν θεοῦ πατρός (2.11; cf. Rom. 15.7 and, more implicitly, 1 Thess. 3.8).

It is clear, therefore, that the work of Christ and Christian living are 'according to the will of God' and 'to the glory of God'. These particular prepositional phrases, in other words, confirm the pattern so widespread in Paul's writings: God as initiator or instigator, God as warrant,[3] and God as final goal or destiny.

Other examples of this linguistic pattern bring out more clearly the relationship of Christ to God. Christ did not act as his own agent, but became 'a servant of the Jewish people' ὑπὲρ ἀληθείας θεοῦ (Rom. 15.8); he does not live by any power of his own, rather ζῇ ἐκ δυνάμεως θεοῦ (2 Cor. 13.4). Indeed, the place of his exaltation is ἐν δεξίᾳ τοῦ θεοῦ (Rom. 8.34).

Once again, the interdependence of Paul's God- and Christ-language

1. 1 Cor. 1.1 and 2 Cor. 1.1; cf. Eph. 1.1; Col. 1.1; 2 Tim. 1.1

2. Cf. 2 Cor. 8.5.

3. As reflected, for example, in some of the texts where Paul refers to 'the will of God'. On this see p. 182 n. 5.

is clear. God-language is necessary to *explain* Christ. But the converse is also true: Christ-language is needed to explain God. Yet while in this pattern God-language might seem a mere adjunct to Christ-language, the reality to which it points is quite different. It is no coincidence that two of the leading themes in this relatively small group of texts are the will of God (corresponding to the fundamental ἐκ θεοῦ) and the glory of God (corresponding to the equally fundamental εἰς θεόν). It is within this theistic framework that the 'equality' of Christ with God, as seen in Pattern 1, must be interpreted.

Pattern 5: Other Juxtapositions

Several of these have been examined in earlier chapters, and require little comment here. The main point to observe once again is the continuation of the pattern we have observed so far. The prepositions used with θεός denote origin, direction and accountability. Thus Paul speaks of the righteousness τὴν διὰ πίστεως Χριστοῦ τὴν ἐκ θεοῦ δικαιοσύνην (Phil. 3.9), of speaking 'in Christ' (ἐν Χριστῷ), 'in the sight of God' (κατέναντι θεοῦ) as 'commissioned by God' (ἐκ θεοῦ) (2 Cor. 2.17; cf. 12.19), of boasting 'in' and 'to God' 'through' and 'in' Jesus Christ (Rom. 5.1, 11; 15.17; cf. 2 Cor. 3.4).[1]

A variation in this pattern can be seen in texts where θεός and Χριστός govern juxtaposed nouns or as adjectives. For example, in 1 Cor. 4.1 Paul writes: οὕτως ἡμᾶς λογιζέσθω ἄνθρωπος ὡς ὑπηρέτας Χριστοῦ καὶ οἰκονόμους μυστηρίων θεοῦ. Commentators tend to focus on words other than Χριστοῦ and θεοῦ.[2] Yet texts such as these help to illuminate the way in which Paul thought of the relationship between God and Christ.[3] Here he clearly assumes that to be a servant of Christ *is* to be a 'steward of the mysteries of God'.[4]

A more difficult example of this kind of expression occurs in

1. See the earlier reference to Rom. 15.17 in the previous section.

2. Thus, for example, Conzelmann, *1 Corinthians*, p. 83; and Barrett, *1 Corinthians*, p. 100.

3. Compare 1 Thess. 3.2, where Paul refers to Timothy as συνεργὸν τοῦ θεοῦ ἐν τῷ εὐαγγελίῳ τοῦ Χριστοῦ. Best, *Commentary*, pp. 132-33, and Rigaux, *Epîtres*, p. 468, rightly defend the reading συνεργόν. It is more questionable whether Holtz, *An die Thessalonicher*, p. 126 n. 611, is correct in describing Χριστοῦ as a *genitivus auctoris*. More probably it is an objective genitive.

4. Rom. 15.16 carries a similar thought: Paul is a minister (λειτουργόν) of Christ Jesus *in* the priestly service (λειτουργοῦντα) of the gospel of God.

1 Cor. 9.21, where Paul, speaking of his apostleship describes himself as μὴ ὢν ἄνομος θεοῦ ἀλλ' ἔννομος Χριστοῦ. This is a difficult phrase to translate, let alone interpret.[1] Understandably, interest has been focused on what Paul is saying here about his own relationship to the Law. But what is implied here about the relationship between God and Christ, and between Christ and the Law? Other passages in Paul[2] make it clear that for Gentile Christians Christ now stands, as it were, in place of the Law. This expression, of course, does not show that for Paul Christ stands *in loco Dei*, and yet the very fact that he can use the words God and Christ in such close juxtaposition shows, at the very least, that his thought is moving in that direction.

It will be seen that these texts comprise a somewhat heterogeneous group in which we encounter Pauline presuppositions, rather than explicit statements about, the God–Christ relationship. But the evidence is suggestive. 1 Cor. 4.1 and 1 Thess. 3.2 indicate an *identity of interest* between God and Christ: thus, to align oneself with the gospel of Christ is *ipso facto* to be the servant or co-worker of God. In 1 Cor. 9.21, too, the God–Christ relationship is not Paul's main concern. But the parallelism of expression ἄνομος θεοῦ...ἔννομος Χριστοῦ is reminiscent of the opening salutations, suggesting quasi-equality.[3]

Pattern 6: God is Defined by Reference to Christ, and Christ is Defined by Reference to God

I have chosen to describe this group of texts in this way, rather than to use the, in this context, more familiar word 'titles'. In fact, although the word πατήρ (used of God), and the title υἱὸς τοῦ θεοῦ (used of Jesus), account for the great majority of instances here, this pattern is rather broader than titles alone. But the fact that we are dealing here with *relational* words shows that this particular pattern of juxtapositions, while clearly overlapping with Pattern 1, is qualitatively different from the other patterns reviewed here.

First, Christ is defined with reference to God in the following ways: he is 'the power and wisdom of God' (1 Cor. 1.24); he is 'wisdom from

1. Barrett, *1 Corinthians*, p. 212, paraphrases, 'He is not free of legal obligation to God...but under legal obligation to Christ...'

2. Notably Gal. 6.2.

3. When God and Christ occur *as subjects* in juxtaposed clauses or sentences, Paul appears to use ὁ κύριος rather than ὁ Χριστός (1 Cor. 3.5-6; cf 4.5). Paul's κύριος-language will be discussed in the next section of this chapter.

God' (1 Cor. 1.30); he is 'the image of God' (2 Cor. 4.4). All these definitions take their shape from the context addressed: for example, Christ 'the image of God' reflects the divine glory 'in his face' (2 Cor. 4.6), thus superceding the earlier revelation through Moses (3.7-18). Elsewhere, Christ-language is juxtaposed with the title 'Son of God'.[1] Paul uses this title more often without explicit reference to 'Christ', but in order to appreciate its significance in his writings, I shall need briefly to review its occurrences.

The 15 occurrences of the title are not spread evenly across the seven genuinely Pauline letters. It does not occur at all in Philippians or Philemon, only once in 1 Thessalonians (1.10), and once in 2 Corinthians (1.19). Of the remaining instances, 11 occur in Galatians and Romans,[2] the other instances being 1 Cor. 1.4 and 15.28.[3]

The predominant themes are subordination and obedience. As the Son, Christ is the object of the divine action. In particular, he is sent (Gal. 4.4; Rom. 8.3) to fulfil God's purpose by his sacrificial death (Rom. 5.10; 8.32). Because the sacrificial death of the Son is so central to Paul's message, that message can be summarized quite simply by reference to the Son. Thus in Rom. 1.9 Paul refers to 'the gospel of his Son', and in Gal. 1.16 to the revelation of the Son through him (i.e. Paul).[4]

All of this suggests that Paul's language here is both functional and wholly theocentric. As Kümmel says: 'That God the Father himself is working salvation in that which has happened and will happen through Jesus Christ is what Paul wants to emphasize when he speaks of the Son of God'.[5] Yet there are hints of later christological developments. In 2 Cor. 1.19 there is a strong hint that the Son reflects the character of God, whose trustworthiness (referred to in v. 18: πιστὸς δὲ ὁ θεός) is evidenced by the Son: ὁ τοῦ θεοῦ γὰρ υἱὸς Ἰησοῦς Χριστός..., οὐκ

1. 1 Cor. 1.9; 2 Cor. 1.19; and (less immediately) Rom. 1.3-4.

2. Gal. 1.16; 2.20; 4.4, 6; Rom. 1.3-4, 9; 5.10; 8.3, 29, 32.

3. It is clear from Rom. 1.3-4, and possibly from Gal. 4.4 and Rom. 8.3 (see Hultgren, *Benefits*, p. 47) that the title belonged to traditions which Paul himself received. At 1 Thess. 1.10, the title may have replaced an earlier ὁ υἱὸς τοῦ ἀνθρώπου.

4. I assume, with Lightfoot, *Galatians*, p. 83, against Bruce, *Galatians*, pp. 92-93, that ἐν here is instrumental.

5. Kümmel, *Theology*, p. 161.

ἐγένετο ναὶ καὶ οὒ ἀλλὰ ναὶ ἐν αὐτῷ γέγονεν.[1]

In sum, the title 'Son of God', although relatively infrequent in Paul's writings, conforms to the predominant pattern of Paul's Christ-language, that of functional subordination. Yet here, too, there are hints of identity-in-subordination which contain the germ of later christological developments.

Secondly, we are concerned here with the ways in which Paul defines God by reference to Christ, although, unlike John's Gospel with its ubiquitous ὁ πέμψας με, Paul does not often define God in this way. To begin with, the participial clauses where ἐγείρας is used should be noted. Delling, in the study to which reference has already been made,[2] notes the prevalence of both καλῶν and ἐγείρας in such participial constructions, claiming that καλῶν is the divine characteristic in the New Testament which parallels ἁγιάζων in the Old Testament,[3] while ὁ ἐγείρας becomes virtually 'God's name', since this word 'proclaims God directly as the one who was active in the saving event in Christ'.[4] There are several examples in Paul: Rom. 4.25, 8.11 (twice); 2 Cor. 1.9, 4.14; Gal. 1.1.

The most important defining word used of God, however, is πατήρ. It may seem surprising that Paul only three times addresses or refers to God as 'Father of our Lord Jesus Christ',[5] two of these instances occurring in doxological contexts. Almost all Paul's references to God as πατήρ, in fact, occur either in the opening salutations of letters or in prayers and doxological contexts.[6] These contexts give the word a significance not immediately indicated by its relative infrequency in Paul.[7] Its usage, indeed, indicates that for Paul it is *the* distinctively Christian way of referring to and addressing God. This is shown not only by its appearance in all the opening salutations,[8] but also by its

1. The title 'Son' occurs elsewhere in conjunction with the πιστὸς ὁ θεός formula—1 Cor.1.9.

2. Chapter 1, section 1.

3. Delling, 'Partizipiale', p. 31.

4. Delling, 'Partizipiale', p. 33.

5. 2 Cor. 1.3; 12.31; Rom. 15.6.

6. These categories include Rom. 1.7; 6.4 (διὰ τῆς δόξης τοῦ πατρός), 8.15; 15.6; 1 Cor. 1.3; 2 Cor. 1.3; Gal. 1.1.3-4; 4.6; Phil. 1.2; 2.11; 4.20; 1 Thess. 1.1, 3; 3.11, 13; Phlm. 3.

7. Compared, for example, with the frequency of θεός in Paul, or with πατήρ in John.

8. Is it significant that in the letter to the church whose Christian birthright is

occurrence in the credal formula of 1 Cor. 8.6: ἀλλ' ἡμῖν εἷς θεὸς ὁ πατήρ[1] and by its use in two similar contexts: ὅτι δέ ἐστε υἱοί, ἐξαπέστειλεν ὁ θεὸς τὸ πνεῦμα τοῦ υἱοῦ αὐτοῦ εἰς τὰς καρδίας ἡμῶν κράζον αββα ὁ πατήρ (Gal. 4.6); οὐ γὰρ ἐλάβετε πνεῦμα δουλείας πάλιν εἰς φόβον ἀλλὰ ἐλάβετε πνεῦμα υἱοθεσίας ἐν ᾧ κράζομεν αββα ὁ πατήρ (Rom. 8.15). A full discussion of these verses is not possible here, but two observations may be made. First, although God-language here is not juxtaposed immediately with Christ-language, the *implicit* connection is very clear.[2] Secondly, the phrase αββα ὁ πατήρ means that αββα was understood as 'an emphatic state form', rendered literally as '*the* father'.[3] This fits in not only with the credal formula of 1 Cor. 8.6, but also the saying attributed to Jesus in Mt. 23.9: καὶ πατέρα μὴ καλέσητε ὑμῶν ἐπὶ τῆς γῆς, εἷς γάρ ἐστιν ὑμῶν ὁ πατὴρ ὁ οὐράνιος. Thus the word πατήρ becomes not only the distinctively Christian word, but acquires also an exclusive character which precludes all other fathers. We are justified, therefore, in speaking of a distinctively Christian expression of Jewish monotheism.

Thirdly, this does not mean that πατήρ or αββα was unique to Jesus[4] or the first Christians, but in contrast with (a) the marginal position of πατήρ in the LXX and in later Jewish writings, and (b) its use by Philo, derived from the Stoics, with reference to God as universal creator, the title and appellation 'father' becomes a central, defining God-word with a soteriological root. This development is reflected in Paul's own use of πατήρ.

Summary

The survey of the juxtapositions of God- and Christ-language in Paul's letters has now been completed. The main conclusions to be drawn are these:

1. Not only is most of Paul's language about Christ deeply theocentric, most of his language about God is explicitly or implicitly shaped or coloured by his belief in and experience of Christ. There is not only the implicit Christology contained in expressions such as ἡ ἐκκλησία,

most threatened, πατήρ is used three times in the opening greeting?

1. On this verse, see also section 5 below.

2. The parallelism of Gal. 4.4 and 4.6 shows this (cf. Rom. 8.11).

3. J. Barr, 'Abba Isn't Daddy', *JTS NS* 39.1 (1988), p. 40.

4. On this see not only Barr's article, but also G. Vermes, *Jesus the Jew* (London: Collins 1973), pp. 210-13.

but also the 'Christianizing' in other contexts of much of the God-language used of non-Christian Jews and Gentiles in Romans 1–2.

2. Some of the patterns (2, 3 and 4) confirm the findings of section one of this chapter, namely the subordination of Christ to God. But this in turn means that Christ, in his death and resurrection, becomes the expression and focus of God's will, the means of God's call and glory, and the agent by whom God justified Jew and Gentile alike and through whom thanksgivings are directed to God.

3. Pattern 1, where the title 'Lord' usually occurs with 'Christ', shows that Paul had begun to think of God and Christ in such close intimacy that the same qualities and actions could be attributed to both. Pattern 5, to a lesser extent, indicates a parallelism and community of interest between God and Christ.

4. Pattern 6 led us to explore some key relational expressions, in particular, ὁ υἱὸς (τοῦ θεοῦ) and πατήρ. The theme of Jesus' sonship in Paul reflects the subordination and obedience of Christ which is reflected in so much of Paul's 'theological grammar', but at the same time hints at a likeness between God and Christ, suggesting, perhaps, that what may be predicated of God may *to some extent* be predicated of Christ (to this subject I turn in the next section). Finally, the contexts in which πατήρ occurs suggest that for Paul this has become a central, defining God-word.

3. *Transference or Overlap between Paul's Language about Christ and his Language about God*

There is a further area to be explored in this investigation into the relationship between Paul's language about God and his language about Christ. It is the question of the extent to which language used about God is *transferred* to Christ. (We must also be alert to the possibility of linguistic interchange occurring in the opposite direction—that is, of language used of Christ being transferred to God.)

The aim of L. Kreitzer in his recent monograph *Jesus and God in Paul's Eschatology*[1] is very similar to the aim of this chapter: How does Paul relate theo- and christocentricity in his thinking?[2] Kreitzer notes four ways in which scholars have attempted to do this:

1. Kreitzer, *Jesus and God.*
2. Kreitzer, *Jesus and God*, p. 15.

1. by a thematic approach—e.g. the study of 'Wisdom Christology',
2. by a study of Paul's use of Old Testament texts,[1]
3. by liturgical and sacramental texts and hymns (and Kreitzer adds to these the openings of Paul's letters),
4. by a study of Paul's doctrine of the atonement.

Kreitzer's own approach is to explore 'the mutual interpenetration of Paul's eschatology and Christology'.[2] He begins by examining what he calls a 'conceptual overlap'[3] between God and the messiah in Jewish Pseudepigrapha. The phrase 'conceptual overlap', in fact, is harder to substantiate than 'functional overlap',[4] a phenomenon which is fairly clear from the texts which Kreitzer surveys. Nevertheless, Kreitzer demonstrates that certain expressions were shared by God and the messiah: for example, the Similitudes of Enoch describe both God and the messiah as sitting 'on the throne'.[5] Kreitzer then proceeds to an analysis of Pauline eschatological language. For example, he lists[6] the various terms used to refer to, or in conjunction with, the concept of the day of the Lord and, as with the Jewish Pseudepigrapha, finds that they indicate 'a referential confusion and conceptual overlap between God and his messianic representative'. From these and other passages, Kreitzer believes that three kinds of 'transference' can be discerned in Paul's writings here:

1. a referential shift of 'Lord' from God to Christ, 'a very early phenomenon indeed',[7]
2. a referential shift of pronouns from God to Christ,[8]
3. a referential shift of the description of the Day of the Lord from God to Christ.[9]

1. Kreitzer draws attention to an outright substitution of christocentrism for theocentrism 'within many of the OT quotes in the NT' (*Jesus and God*, pp. 18-19).

2. Kreitzer, *Jesus and God*, p. 23.

3. Kreitzer, *Jesus and God*, p. 29.

4. Kreitzer, *Jesus and God*, p. 90.

5. Of God at 47.3 and 60.1-3, and of the messiah at 45.3-6; 51.3; 55.4; 61.8; 62.2-5; 69.29 (Kreitzer, *Jesus and God*, p. 106).

6. Kreitzer, *Jesus and God*, pp. 112-13.

7. Kreitzer, *Jesus and God*, p. 114.

8. Kreitzer notes the addition of ἐπ' αὐτῷ—not in all copies of the LXX—in Rom. 9.33 (*Jesus and God*, p. 124).

9. ὁ ῥυόμενος in Rom. 11.26 refers to God, τὸν ῥυόμενον in 1 Thess. 1.10

From all this Kreitzer concludes that there is a 'conceptual ambiguity' in Paul's eschatological teaching which indicates, or is symptomatic of 'the delicate balance between theocentricity and christocentricity in Paul's thought'.[1] Nevertheless, while Kreitzer draws attention to some important details in the Pauline texts, is he right in his evaluation of them? The 'functional overlap' between God and Christ to which Kreitzer points does not necessarily mean the identification of God and his agent.[2] But before we can do justice to this and other related questions, it will be necessary to extend the scope of Kreitzer's inquiry.

The question before us is this: to what extent does Paul attribute to Christ the same qualities, functions or actions that he attributes to God?

Our earlier studies have suggested that such an area of linguistic interchange will not be very great, since it has become clear that, in some respects, Paul's God- and Christ-language are complementary. For example, θεός is rarely the object of a verb, Χριστός is rarely the subject (except in a few clearly defined contexts). Thus we should hardly expect to find the same actions directly predicated of God and of Christ;[3] in other words, θεός and Χριστός do not swap verbs.[4] But what of the many genitival expressions which Paul uses? Here four important words must be noted.

1. χάρις is used frequently with both θεός[5] and with Χριστός.[6] The frequency of these expressions is significant, although they are only 'the tip of the iceberg'. The opening greetings of Paul's letters ('Grace…from God our Father and the Lord Jesus Christ'), and the use of χάρις absolutely, particularly in Romans,[7] show the centrality of this

refers to Christ (Kreitzer, *Jesus and God*, pp. 125-26).

1. Kreitzer, *Jesus and God*, p. 129.

2. Thus also J.D.G. Dunn in his review of Kreitzer's book ('L.J. Kreitzer—Review', *ExpTim* 100.1 [1988], p. 32, *contra* Kreitzer, *Jesus and God*, e.g. p. 170).

3. This is not necessarily applicable to Paul's κύριος-language, on which see below.

4. The only exceptions are προσλαμβάνω (Rom. 14.1; 15.7), κατεργάζομαι (Rom. 15.18; 2 Cor. 5.5) and (ἐξ)αποστέλλω (1 Cor. 1.17; Gal. 4.4, 6).

5. Rom. 5.15, 1 Cor. 1.4; 3.10; 15.10; 2 Cor. 6.1; 9.14; Gal. 2.21.

6. Rom. 16.20, 24; 1 Cor. 16.23; 2 Cor. 8.9; 13.13, Gal. 1.6; 6.18; Phil. 4.23; 1 Thess. 5.28.

7. Rom. 4.4, 16; 5.17.20-21; 6.1, 14-15; 11.5-6.

theme in Paul's thought. Clearly 'grace' may be predicated either of God or Christ.[1]

I have already observed (section 1 above) that the expression χάρις τοῦ θεοῦ does not occur in the LXX at all, although it must be emphasized again that this does not mean that the *idea* or *experience* of grace is absent. It is also a relatively infrequent expression elsewhere in the New Testament. There is much to be said for the view that χάρις τοῦ θεοῦ was a phrase created by Paul to give expression to the undeserved favour of God,[2] embracing Gentiles as well as Jews. It was a term open to misunderstanding and abuse, as Rom. 6.1 indicates. In fact, its pagan use, denoting the benevolence of the emperor, meant that *gratia* and χάρις could easily be associated with corruption.

Paul, then, can readily predicate χάρις of God or Christ, because, as the *enthymeme* of Gal. 2.21 shows,[3] the argument seems to be

A. The Law did not bring righteousness
B. Christ did not die for nothing
C. God's grace was at work in Christ's death
D. Paul's law-free gospel does not annul the grace of God.
E. God's grace was at work in Christ.

2. ἀγάπη and ἀγαπῶ. Paul can speak of ἡ ἀγάπη τοῦ Χριστοῦ,[4] and of ἡ ἀγάπη τοῦ θεοῦ.[5] In section 1 of this chapter it was pointed out that the word ἀγάπη acquires a prominence which it did not have in the LXX, even though the idea and experience of it are by no means absent. And, again, there is a close connection with the death of Christ (esp. Rom. 5.8; 8.35, 37, 39; Gal. 2.20).

3. δύναμις. Power also is predicated of both God and Christ. The range of contexts in which Paul uses this word is suggestive. First, it

1. In the deutero-Pauline 2 Thessalonians we have the expression κατὰ τὴν χάριν τοῦ θεοῦ ἡμῶν καὶ κυρίου Ἰησοῦ Χριστοῦ (1.12). See Appendix 4 for further examples of this kind of language in the deutero-Paulines.

2. Rom. 4.4 and 11.6 bring out particularly clearly the meaning of χάρις (cf. 1 Cor. 15.10).

3. See Lightfoot, *Galatians*, p. 12.

4. Rom. 8.35; cf. Gal. 2.20 and 2 Cor. 5.14, where the genitive τοῦ Χριστοῦ, though ambiguous, is probably subjective (see the discussion in Martin, *2 Corinthians*, p. 128).

5. 2 Cor. 13.13; cf. Rom. 5.8; 8.39, and, more generally, 2 Cor. 9.7. The unusual διὰ τῆς ἀγάπης τοῦ πνεύματος in 15.30 is probably to be understood as the love *given by* the Spirit (thus Barrett, *Romans*, p. 279).

seems, power is an attribute which belongs supremely, if not solely, to God. The word δύναμις is used nearly always of God's power. Where it is not so used, it is implied that power is derived from, delegated by and subordinate to God (as in 1 Cor. 15.24), and so whatever 'powers' there are, they cannot separate the believer from God (Rom. 8.38). Secondly, there is the closest possible correspondence between the power of God and the power of Christ. Only twice does Paul speak of the power of God without speaking, explicitly or implicitly, of Christ: (1) in the Old Testament quotation of Rom. 9.17, and (2) in his reference to creation in Rom. 1.20 (ἥ τε ἀΐδιος αὐτοῦ δύναμις καὶ θειότης). Elsewhere, Paul declares that the gospel is the power of God,[1] that Christ himself is the power of God.[2] But thirdly, and more precisely, the power of God is demonstrated or revealed in the resurrection of Christ,[3] and also in the raising to new life of those who come to faith.[4] Fourthly, Paul's language of power implies that it is the same power (sometimes called the power of the Holy Spirit) which is at work in his ministry and in the life of the Christian community.[5]

The correlation between the power of God and the power of Christ emerges in Paul's catalogue of his sufferings.[6] His prayer 'to the Lord' received the answer ἡ γὰρ δύναμις ἐν ἀσθενείᾳ τελεῖται (12.9b). It is striking that there is no possessive pronoun with δύναμις in this oracular saying, but since a reference to 'the power of Christ' immediately follows (v. 9), 'the power' here can only be Christ's.[7]

It is clear that the language of power in Paul's writings provides another example of 'interchange': an attribute of God becomes an attribute of Christ. It is vital to recall, however, the conclusion of Chapter 2 that Paul's understanding of divine power cannot be separated from the cross.

4. δόξα. Paul normally writes of the glory *of God*.[8] But three times

1. Rom. 1.16; cf. 1 Cor. 1.18, where the same statement is made of 'the word of the cross'.
2. 1 Cor. 1.24.
3. Rom. 1.4, 2 Cor. 13.4.
4. 1 Cor. 6.14, 2 Cor. 13.4, Phil. 3.10; cf. Rom. 6.4.
5. Rom. 15.13, 19; 1 Cor. 2.4-5; 5.4; 2 Cor. 4.7, 6.7; cf. Gal. 3.5.
6. 2 Cor. 11.22–12.10.
7. Thus, e.g. Martin, *2 Corinthians*, p. 419.
8. Rom. 1.23; 3.23; 4.20; 5.2; 15.7; 1 Cor. 10.31; 2 Cor. 4.6, 15; Phil. 1.11; 2.11; cf., for example, 1 Thess. 2.12, 20; Gal. 1.5.

Paul writes of the glory *of Christ*. In 2 Cor. 8.23 'our brothers' are described as ἀπόστολοι ἐκκλησιῶν, δόξα Χριστοῦ. Whether Martin is right to paraphrase this last phrase with 'an honor to Christ'[1] is perhaps questionable, but this is clearly not an example of the linguistic interchange I am investigating here. The other two occurrences to Christ's glory, however, are. But both, in different ways, are strongly 'subordinationist'. At 2 Cor. 4.4 Paul, after referring to 'the gospel of the glory of Christ', immediately goes on to describe Christ as 'the image of God'. The subsequent expression in v. 6 helps to bring out more clearly the nature of Christ's glory: it is a *reflected* glory: πρὸς φωτισμὸν τῆς γνώσεως τῆς δόξης τοῦ θεοῦ ἐν προσώπῳ ('Ιησοῦ) Χριστοῦ (v. 6). Similarly, at Phil. 3.21 the transformation of believers in conformity with 'his glorious body' (τῷ σώματι τῆς δόξης αὐτοῦ) happens κατὰ τὴν ἐνέργειαν τοῦ δύνασθαι αὐτὸν καὶ ὑποτάξαι αὐτῷ τὰ πάντα.

Thus far, then, I have examined four examples of linguistic interchange: χάρις, ἀγάπη, δύναμις and δόξα. That is to say, the grace, love, power and glory of God are effected through Christ and demonstrated in Christ. Paul's use of χάρις and ἀγάπη makes clear the connection of these divine attributes with the death of Christ. This is also true in a more indirect way of his use of δύναμις and δόξα. The revelation and experience of God's power 'in this age' cannot be known except through the weakness and poverty epitomized by the cross. Similarly, the glory of God cannot be appropriated, except by those in Christ, that is to those determined by the fact that Jesus Christ died and rose.

One other example of what appears to be linguistic interchange deserves special consideration here, and that is Paul's use of the phrase 'the name of the Lord Jesus Christ'.[2] The expression τὸ ὄνομα τοῦ

1. Martin, *2 Corinthians*, p. 277.

2. Before turning to Paul's κύριος-language, I note briefly other examples of linguistic interchange. The juxtaposition of πνεῦμα θεοῦ and πνεῦμα Χριστοῦ at Rom. 8.9 has been frequently commented on, and need only be noted here. Similarly, Kreitzer's study (*Jesus and God*, pp. 107-12) has drawn attention to the parallel expressions τῷ βήματι τοῦ θεοῦ (Rom. 14.10) and τοῦ βήματος τοῦ Χριστοῦ (2 Cor. 5.10). Here, clearly, there is a transference of function, if not, as Kreitzer has argued, a 'conceptual overlap'. Interchange also occurs in a group of ecclesial words. Thus Paul writes of ministers (διάκονοι) of God (2 Cor. 6.4) and ministers of Christ (Rom. 15.8; 2 Cor. 11.23). (The διάκονος θεοῦ of Rom. 13.4 refers to 'the authority'. For this reason λειτουργός does not belong to the material

θεοῦ occurs in Paul only in an Old Testament quotation,[1] although there are three further references to the divine name in Old Testament quotations in Romans.[2] The phrase 'the name of the Lord Jesus Christ' is confined entirely to 1 Corinthians, occurring mainly in prepositional phrases.[3] But does the 'name of the Lord Jesus Christ' function in any way as a parallel with, or substitute for, the name of God? The most important verses to be discussed in this respect are Rom. 10.13, where

which we are reviewing, since λειτουργοὶ θεοῦ at Rom. 13.6 also refers to the authorities, whereas Paul uses the phrase λειτουργὸς Χριστοῦ of himself at Rom. 15.16.) The word ἐκκλησία, however, *does* provide another example of linguistic interchange, even though Paul normally refers to 'the church *of God*' (ἐκκλησία τοῦ θεοῦ), referring to 'all the churches of Christ' only at Rom. 16.16. (But see also 'the churches of God in Judaea *in Christ Jesus*', 1 Thess. 2.14; cf. Gal. 1.22).

Other apparent examples of this kind of linguistic interchange are not exact parallels. For example, in the expressions to εὐαγγέλιον τοῦ θεοῦ (e.g. 1 Thess. 2.8) and τὸ εὐαγγέλιον τοῦ Χριστοῦ (Rom. 15.19) θεοῦ is a subjective genitive, and Χριστοῦ is an objective genitive. (So also γνῶσις with θεοῦ [Rom.11.33], and with Χριστοῦ [Phil. 3.8]). πίστις is a special case in that, where it occurs with τοῦ θεοῦ (Rom. 3.3), it refers to the faithfulness of God, when it occurs with Χριστου (e.g. Gal. 2.16) it refers *either* to the faithfulness of *the man* Jesus (see the earlier discussion on this) or Χριστοῦ is an objective genitive, giving to πίστις a different meaning ('faith in Christ').

Paul's use of ἀλήθεια with (τοῦ) θεοῦ (only in Romans at 1.25, 3.7 and 15.8) and with Χριστοῦ (only at 2 Cor. 11.10) is likewise not an example of linguistic interchange, in that the expression ἀλήθεια τοῦ θεοῦ derives from the Hebrew אֱמֶת (So, e.g., Dunn, *Romans*, I, p. 136), whereas at 2 Cor. 11.10 the expression ἀλήθεια Χριστοῦ functions as an oath-formula. This, however, may point to another form of 'interchange': Martin, *2 Corinthians*, p. 347, paraphrases here 'As certain as God's truth is on my side', referring to a change of the divine name. Furnish cites Romans 9.1 as a parallel (*2 Corinthians*, p. 493). Paul writes of 'the law *of God*' (Rom. 2.23; 7.22, 25; 8.7) and of 'the law of Christ' (Gal. 6.2). Although this last expression is probably polemical, we cannot talk of a direct transference here, since for Paul Christ himself, rather than the law of Christ, now replaces the 'law of God' (e.g. Rom. 10.4). The use of ἐντολή with both θεοῦ (1 Cor. 7.19) and κυρίου (1 Cor. 14.25; cf 7.25) is noteworthy, but when used with κυρίου it has a specific reference, whereas with θεοῦ it has a wider more general application (NB the plural ἐντολῶν).

1. Rom. 2.24.
2. 9.17; 10.13; 15.9.
3. 1.2 (σὺν πᾶσιν τοῖς ἐπικαλουμένοις τὸ ὄνομα...), 1.10 (παρακαλῶ δὲ ὑμᾶς...διὰ τοῦ ὀνόματος...) 5.4 (ἐν τῷ ὀνόματι...συναχθέντων ὑμῶν) and 6.11 (ἐδικαιώθητε ἐν τῷ ὀνόματι...).

Joel 3.5 is quoted[1] and Phil. 2.10, the only Pauline verse outside 1 Corinthians where the expression 'the name of Jesus' occurs.[2] I shall need to return to these verses in the discussion of Paul's κύριος-language, to which I now turn. But two preliminary observations need to be made.

1. There is an uneven spread of the title ὁ κύριος in Paul's letters. It occurs only six times in Galatians,[3] presumably because the central issue at Galatia, in Paul's view, was the significance of *Christ's* redemptive work, and therefore the Galatians' very identity as Christians. In Romans the use of κύριος occurs (1) in prepositional phrases with Ἰησοῦς Χριστός,[4] (2) in Old Testament quotations,[5] (3) in the paraenetic context of ch. 14, and twice elsewhere with δουλεύω,[6] (4) in ch. 16 in the phrase ἐν κυρίῳ.[7] Very different from both Galatians and Romans is 1 Corinthians, the variety and extent of whose κύριος-language can hardly be summarized in brief.[8]

The other epistles fall between these two extremes, and require no

1. 1 Cor. 1.2 also seems to echo the Joel verse.

2. For the sake of completeness, however, we should note the expression at Rom. 1.5, ὑπὲρ τοῦ ὀνόματος αὐτοῦ, where the reference is clearly to Christ.

3. 1.3; 1.19; 4.1 (where, however it is used of a secular κύριος); 5.10 (although the Uncial B omits ἐν κυρίῳ here); 6.14 and 6.18.

4. With διά at 5.1, 11, 21; 7.25 and 15.30; with ἐν at 6.23; 8.39; (cf.14.14), and with ἀπό at 1.4.

5. 4.8; 9.28, 29; 10.13, 16; 11.3, 34; 12.19; 15.11.

6. 12.11; 16.18.

7. The greetings formula ἡ χάρις τοῦ κυρίου ἡμῶν Ἰησοῦ (Χριστοῦ) occurs in some MSS at 16.20 and 24.

8. 67 occurrences, compared with 47 in Romans, and 29 in 2 Corinthians (Morgenthaler, *Statistik*, p. 115). The frequency of κύριος-language in 1 Corinthians may seem to tell against the view put forward in Chapter 2 that the 'Christ party' at Corinth tended to allow Christ to eclipse God. It should be noted, however, that the κύριος-language of 1 Corinthians has some striking features: first, the remarkable concentration of the expression 'the Lord Jesus Christ' in the opening verses of the Epistle (1.2, 3, 7, 8, 9, 10). Weiss (*Körintherbrief*, pp. 10-11) notes the 'ugliness' of language, and recognizes the possibility that the name of Christ is being 'hammered' home as much as possible in order, perhaps, to remind the Corinthians of the full content of the title 'the Lord'; secondly, the uniquely subordinationist ὁ δὲ θεὸς καὶ τὸν κύριον ἤγειρεν (6.14) and the use of ὁ κύριος, referring to the earthly Jesus at 7.10, 12; 9.5, 14; 11.23-27. These account for about half the total number of such uses of ὁ κύριος in the New Testament (the others are 1 Thess. 2.15; Gal.1.19; 2 Tim. 1.8; Heb. 2.3; 1 Pet. 2.13; Acts 20.35).

special comment here.[1] (I noted in Chapter 4 the frequency of the phrase ἐν κυρίῳ in Philippians.)[2]

2. κύριος-language and θεός-language rarely occur together in Paul's writings.[3] This suggests that they are alternative kinds of language. But why is this so? What are the differences in function and meaning between these two kinds of language? And what is the relationship of Paul's κύριος-language to his θεός-language? Should κύριος-language be regarded as *part of* Paul's language about God? Or does it in some way serve as a *substitute* for θεός-language? Finally, are there any examples of linguistic interchange, that is to say, of attributes or actions attributed to God being transferred to 'the Lord'?

W. Förster in his article on κύριος[4] claims that 'the name of κύριος implies a position equal to that of God'[5] and that Christ 'is the One who exercises God's sovereignty in relation to the world'.[6] So far, one may agree: if the κύριος Christ acts *in loco Dei*, this helps to explain why θεός- and κύριος-language are rarely juxtaposed; they are, in a sense, alternative kinds of language. Similarly, one may agree with Förster's observation that Χριστός appears 'when there is reference to 'the work of redemption', and that 'κύριος refers to the exalted Lord who is (*sic*) authority'.[7] When, however, he goes on to say 'Paul then does not make any distinction between θεός and κύριος as though κύριος were an intermediate god' this is misleading. It is true that there is no hint in Paul's language that Paul ever thought of Christ as an 'intermediate God', but the distribution of both the words θεός and κύριος in Paul's writings suggests that Paul differentiates very clearly between the two.[8]

But this is not the whole picture. We cannot avoid the question whether the title κύριος would have been *heard* as God-language. And here the linguistic situation is complicated, to say the least. First, scholars

1. See the statistics on p. 280 n. 8. (For the sake of completeness, we should note the 24 occurrences of κύριος in 1 Thessalonians, and its absence from the short Philemon [Morgenthaler *Statistik*, p. 115]).

2. 1.14; 2.19; 2.24, 29; 3.1; 4.1, 2, 4, 10. Only in Rom. 16 is there a comparable concentration.

3. 1 Cor. 6.13-14, 8.6 and 12.3-4 are rare examples.

4. *TWNT*, III, pp. 1088-92.

5. *TWNT*, III, p. 1089.

6. *TWNT*, III, p. 1090.

7. *TWNT*, III, p. 1090.

8. So also Kramer, *Christ*, p. 159; J.D.G. Dunn, 'Was Christianity a Monotheistic Faith from the Beginning?', *SJT* 35.4 (1982), p. 328.

now rightly reject the views of earlier generations (a) that the title κύριος was first applied to Jesus in a Gentile Greek-speaking environment,[1] and (b) that it derived from the LXX.[2] There is now clear evidence that the Hebrew word *adon*, the Aramaic words *mare* and *marya*, as well as the Greek κύριος, were used in a variety of contexts to refer either to God or to secular lords.[3] Thus there is no reason why Jesus could not have been, and strong evidence that he was, referred to by the absolute designation 'the Lord' in his lifetime.[4] But that, of course, was not necessarily to call Jesus God, and indeed the New Testament's remarkable reticence in calling Jesus God *tout simple*[5] indicates strongly that this was not the significance of calling, or addressing Jesus as 'Lord'.

The vital question with reference to this inquiry must be: what difference did the LXX make? Here again the views of scholars have changed in the light of new evidence. Fragments of the LXX dating from the first century BCE show that the tetragrammaton YHWH was still read in the text.[6] In G.F. Howard's view the tetragram was what Paul originally wrote in LXX quotations, the abbreviations θς and κς being substituted in Christian usage of the LXX (and therefore in quotations of the LXX) by the beginning of the second century.[7] In Howard's view this helps to explain the many MSS variants at, for example, Rom. 10.16-17, 14.10-11, 1 Cor. 2.16 and 10.9, since the change would have caused

1. Bousset's *Kyrios Christos* is the classic statement of this view, but the *maranatha* prayer of 1 Cor. 16.22 was always its Achilles' heel, and more recent linguistic evidence, discussed below, makes Bousset's original thesis untenable.

2. The same objection applies here as to the Bousset theory. The influence of the LXX, however, cannot be entirely discounted.

3. See, for example, the summaries by J.A. Fitzmyer in *The Gospel According to Luke* (2 vols.; New York, Doubleday, 1981), I, pp. 201-202, and *To Advance the Gospel* (New York: Crossroad, 1981), pp. 218-35; cf. Vermes, *Jesus*, especially pp. 113-14, 121-22; and G.H. Parke-Taylor, *Yahweh: the Divine Name in the Bible* (Waterloo, Ontario: Wilfred Laurier University Press, 1975), especially pp. 100-103, where Parke-Taylor suggests that the substitution of *adonay* for YHWH within Judaism meant that there was a shift in emphasis to the concept of sovereignty and lordship.

4. So Vermes, *Jesus*, pp. 103-27.

5. For a discussion of the most important texts see, for example, V. Taylor, *New Testament Essays* (London: Epworth, 1970), pp. 83-89.

6. Fitzmyer, *Luke*, I, p. 201.

7. Cf. G. Howard, 'The Tetragram and the New Testament', *JBL* 96 (1977), pp. 63-66.

ambiguity—i.e. was the reference to God or to Christ?[1] Nevertheless, whatever was originally *written* in the LXX quotations which refer to 'the Lord', the question must still be asked: what was *read* (aloud) at these points in the text? Pokorny[2] has argued, on the basis of Philo's discussion in *De Mutatione Nominum* 20, 21 and 23 that the tetragram was read as κύριος.[3]

The position, therefore, seems to be this: (1) while the disciples of Jesus called him 'the Lord' from the earliest days,[4] this did not compromise their monotheistic Jewish faith, and that the distinction between 'God' and 'the Lord' is clearly maintained in much of Paul's writings, and (2) under the influence of the LXX, some overlap between 'God-language' and language applied to Christ developed. The extent of that overlap must now be examined.

The most important examples occur in LXX quotations. The use of 'Lord' in these quotations has been discussed by Cerfaux[5] and Kramer.[6] Here I refer to their findings only where I differ in my estimate of the extent to which LXX κύριος-language is applied to Jesus, and of its significance. First, both scholars exaggerate the number of LXX κύριος quotations or fragments which apply to Jesus. The view taken here is that only Rom. 10.13,[7] 1 Cor. 1.31 (and 2 Cor. 10.17), 10.21, 22 apply

1. Howard, 'Tetragram', pp. 74-75.

2. Pokorny, *Genesis*, p. 76 n. 32; cf. C.F.D. Moule, *The Origin of Christology* (Cambridge: Cambridge University Press, 1977), p. 40.

3. Philo is referring here to Exod. 6.29, where the MT has YHWH. A. Pietersma, however, in an essay 'Kyrios or Tetragram? A Renewed Quest for the Original LXX', in A. Pietersma and G. Cox (eds.), *De Septuaginta* (Ontario: Benben Publications, 1984), pp. 85-101, utters a cautionary note about this method, asking how faithfully texts in Philo and other ancient authors testify to the text of the LXX. But he goes on to argue, citing the work of P.W. Skehan, that there was an archaizing tendency, beginning perhaps in the second century BCE, substituting the tetragram for κύριος (pp. 99-101).

4. See, however, R.N. Longenecker, *The Christology of Early Jewish Christianity* (London: SCM Press, 1970), who notes (pp. 129-31) the restraint of the evangelists in referring to Jesus as 'Lord' or 'the Lord' in pre-resurrection narratives.

5. '"Kyrios" dans les citations pauliniennes de l' Ancient Testament', in Cerfaux, *Recueil*, pp. 173-88.

6. Kramer, *Christ*, pp. 156-59.

7. The majority of commentators take 'the Lord' of Rom. 10.13 to refer to Christ—e.g. Dunn, *Romans*, II, p. 617, who notes the 'striking' use of Joel 2.32 (LXX 3.5). Ziesler, *Romans*, p. 264, is more non-committal.

to Christ.[1] But, secondly, Kramer underestimates the significance of the LXX quotations which apply to Jesus. To say that 'the places at which Kyrios refers to Jesus merely give us fragments of quotations or isolated phrases which are not acknowledged as quotations'[2] is to ignore the importance of Rom. 10.13, which he then goes on to discuss. This verse πᾶς γὰρ ὃς ἂν ἐπικαλέσηται τὸ ὄνομα κυρίου σωθήσεται is a literal quotation from the LXX (Joel 3.5). Kramer notes the use elsewhere in the New Testament of the phrase 'call on the name' (that is, of Christ),[3] but in his evaluation of this development (reflected also in the christological application of two other LXX echoes or phrases in 1 Cor. 10.21, 22)[4] Kramer curiously overlooks the significance of the transfer to Christ of language used directly of God.

When we turn to 1 Cor. 1.31 (and 2 Cor. 10.17), the situation is rather different. Here Paul does not quote exactly, although in the 1 Corinthians passage he indicates that he is quoting Scripture: ἵνα καθὼς γέγραπται ὁ καυχώμενος ἐν κυρίῳ καυχάσθω.[5] The passage to which he alludes is Jer. 9.24: ἀλλ' ἢ ἐν τούτῳ καυχάσθω ὁ καυχώμενος, συνιεῖν καὶ γινώσκειν ὅτι ἐγώ εἰμι κύριος ὁ ποιῶν ἔλεος. A comparison of Paul's 'quotation' of Jeremiah suggests that, for him, to boast 'in the Lord' (that is, in Christ) is the equivalent of boasting of the sovereign reality of *God* 'who exercises mercy' and so on.

There is an interesting parallel to Paul's use of Scripture here at Phil. 2.11. In an earlier chapter[6] I noted Paul's quotation of Isa. 45.24, where clearly the κύριος referred to is Yahweh. In Philippians the context is much more explicitly christological, the echo of the Isaiah verse coming as the climax of the christological hymn which Paul has

1. Against Cerfaux and Kramer, the κύριος in 1 Thess. 4.6 and at 2 Cor. 3.16 and 18 apply to God (see Chapter 4, section 3, and Chapter 3, section 3 respectively for earlier discussions of these verses), and I agree with Cerfaux (against Kramer) in regarding 1 Cor. 10.26 as a reference to God.

2. Kramer, *Christ*, p. 157.

3. 1 Cor. 1.2, Acts 2.21; 9.14, 21; 22.16 (Kramer, *Christ*, p. 157).

4. The phrase 'the table of the Lord' echoes Mal.1.7,12, while Paul's question in v. 22, ἢ παραζηλοῦμεν τὸν κύριον, echoes Deut. 32.21, although the title Lord is added here by Paul (a point noted also by Kramer, *Christ*, p. 161).

5. At 2 Cor. 10.17 Paul gives exactly the same quotation, but without the preceding καθὼς γέγραπται, or any equivalent phrase.

6. Chapter 4, section 2.

quoted here (vv. 6-11). It will be as well to set out the relevant words from both Paul and Isaiah:

> Paul: ἵνα ἐν τῷ ὀνόματι Ἰησοῦ / πᾶν γόνυ κάμψῃ / ἐπουρανίων καὶ ἐπιγείων καὶ καταχθονίων / καὶ πᾶσα γλῶσσα ἐξομολογήσηται ὅτι / κύριος Ἰησοῦς Χριστὸς / εἰς δόξαν θεοῦ πατρός.
> Isaiah: ὅτι ἐμοὶ κάμψει πᾶν γόνυ καὶ ἐξομολογήσεται πᾶσα γλῶσσα τῷ θεῷ, λέγων, Δικαιοσύνη καὶ δόξα πρὸς αὐτὸν ἥξουσιν, καὶ αἰσχυνθήσονται πάντες οἱ ἀφορίζοντες ἑαυτούς (vv. 24-25).

It will be seen that in Paul's version ἐν τῷ ὀνόματι Ἰησοῦ appears to have replaced ἐμοί. This does not mean that for Paul Jesus is now to be identified with Yahweh, but rather that 'bending the knee' at the name of Jesus is now the new way of acknowledging that Yahweh is God. The remainder of Paul's adaptation of Isaiah elaborates this point. In place of 'every tongue' 'swearing' by God, Paul has (that) 'every tongue may confess *that Jesus Christ is Lord*'. Thus swearing by God[1] is replaced by the confession that 'Jesus Christ is Lord'. Finally the words attached to the Old Testament oath 'that righteousness and glory will come to him' (that is, to God) find an echo in Paul's concluding phrase εἰς δόξαν πατρός.

In neither 1 Cor. 1.31 nor in Phil. 2.10-11 is there a transfer of language used in the Old Testament of God to Jesus. Rather, Paul's use of the Old Testament here shows that Jewish monotheism is now to be expressed and confessed *christologically* . 1 Cor. 8.6, therefore, with its 'expansion' of the Jewish *shema* remains paradigmatic for the proper understanding of the relationship between Paul's theology and his Christology.[2]

1. A practice interestingly condemned in the Sermon on the Mount (Mt. 5.33-37), although we do no know whether this teaching would be known to Paul or not.

2. The reference to God bestowing on Jesus τὸ ὄνομα τὸ ὑπὲρ πᾶν ὄνομα supports rather than contradicts the argument here. R.P. Martin, *Carmen Christi: Philippians 2.5-11 in Recent Interpretation and in Early Christian Worship* (Cambridge: Cambridge University Press, 1967), pp. 235-39, notes three lines of interpretation of the phrase τὸ ὄνομα τὸ ὑπὲρ πᾶν ὄνομα. First, he rightly rejects the view that τὸ ὄνομα is the word θεός, since as we have observed the New Testament is very reticent about calling Jesus God. Secondly, the view put forward by E. Käsemann and others that the name means 'the manifested character' of God founders on the fact that the contrast in the hymn cannot lie solely or primarily in the fact that Christ, though already God's equal in his pre-incarnate state (ἐν μορφῇ θεοῦ), was as such the hidden God, whereas through his exaltation he is now *Deus*

Paul's use of the LXX, therefore, in the texts we have examined is twofold. First, there is a little evidence (Rom. 10.13 above all, but also 1 Cor. 10.21-22) that LXX references to God could be and were transferred directly to Jesus as 'the Lord'. But, secondly, Paul's Old Testament adaptations at 1 Cor. 1.31 (and 2 Cor. 10.17) and Phil. 2.10-11 suggest that for Paul the universal Lordship of Jesus is the new expression of Jewish monotheism. The tension at the heart of this twofold use of the Jewish Scriptures contains *in nuce* a great deal of later christological development.

Apart from Paul's LXX quotations, what other evidence is there in the apostle's writings of the transference of God-language to Jesus in the range of Paul's κύριος-language? The great difficulty here lies in determining whether 'the Lord' refers to God or to Jesus. But there are several instances where the context suggests that the reference is to Jesus. I examine them briefly below, indicating where the context leaves open the question of whether 'the Lord' is God or Jesus. But first, it will be as well to acknowledge the difficulty in evaluating, and therefore appropriately describing, the evidence here. They may be instances of the *transference* of God-language to Jesus. But it may be more appropriate to use the word 'overlap', as a way of acknowledging that there are parallel expressions in Paul's God-language and his κύριος-language, which may have arisen without any conscious awareness by Paul that he was thereby 'transferring' God-language to Jesus.

1. There is the eschatological language to which Kreitzer has drawn attention—including the Old Testament expression 'the day of the Lord' (1 Cor. 5.5).[1] Similarly, Paul can speak of *God* judging (e.g. Rom. 2.16), but also of '*the Lord*' (e.g. 1 Cor. 11.32; cf. 4.4),[2] and of 'the fear of *God*' (Rom. 3.18, 2 Cor. 7.1), and 'the fear of *the Lord*' (2 Cor. 5.11).

2. In Paul's references to his travels and travel plans parallel expressions occur. Thus he can speak of travelling by 'the will of God' (ἐν τῷ

revelatus. Paul's language in v. 9 ὑπερύψωσεν clearly suggests that Christ received a *higher* status than before (a point apparently not noted by Martin). It seems best, therefore, to adopt a third view that 'the name above every name' refers to the office of lordship, noting the comment of Lightfoot, *Philippians*, p. 111, that we should probably look here to a very common Hebrew sense of 'name', 'not meaning a definite appellation, but denoting office, rank, dignity.'

1. Cf. ἡμέρα κυρίου at 1 Thess. 5.2.

2. The contexts in both cases here make it likely that 'the Lord' refers to Christ.

θελήματι τοῦ θεοῦ, Rom. 1.10; διὰ θελήματος θεοῦ, Rom. 15.32)[1] but he speaks too of travel plans 'if the Lord wills' (ἐὰν ὁ κύριος ἐπιτρέψῃ, 1 Cor. 4.19), or 'if the Lord allows' (ἐὰν ὁ κύριος ἐπιτρέψῃ, 1 Cor. 16.7; the reference here to Jesus is less certain). It is tempting to see here adaptations by Paul to the prevailing language of the church to which he is writing; certainly the preponderance of θεός-language in Romans is striking.

3. Paul writes once of pleasing *the Lord* (1 Cor. 7.32), admittedly in a context where κύριος-language is to be expected. Elsewhere he writes of pleasing *God* (Rom. 8.8, 1 Thess. 2.15; 4.1).

4. Normally in Pauline writings *God* is the subject, expressed or implied, of the verb ἐλεῶ (e.g. Rom. 11.32), but in 1 Cor. 7.25 he uses the expression (of himself) ὡς ἠλεημένος ὑπὸ κυρίου. The occurrence of κύριος here may be by process of attraction, Paul having just used the expression ἐπιταγὴν κυρίου.[2]

5. Two prepositions are used with both θεός and κύριος: the Corinthians grieved κατὰ θεόν (2 Cor. 7.11); Paul on another occasion speaks οὐ κατὰ κύριον...ἀλλ' ὡς ἐν ἀφροσύνῃ (2 Cor. 11.17).[3] Furnish[4] rightly compares the two, paraphrasing κατὰ θεόν as 'as God wills'.

6. Paul writes of 'the commandments of *God*' (1 Cor. 7.19), and of 'the command of *the Lord*' (1 Cor. 14.37), significantly here of his own letter. (Cf. 1 Cor. 7.25 where Paul writes more indefinitely of a 'charge from the Lord' [ἐπιταγὴν κυρίου].)

7. Paul writes both of living for *God* (ζῶντας δὲ τῷ θεῷ, Rom. 6.11; cf. Gal. 2.19) and of living for, or to *the Lord* (τῷ κυρίῳ ζῶμεν, Rom. 14.8, cf. 2 Cor. 5.15). These verses provide important and clear examples of the phenomenon we are examining. Paul probably thought of the Christian as living for and belonging to 'the Lord' in the immediacy of everyday life (as in Rom. 14), but generally and ultimately to God (as disclosed and made possible by baptism—Rom. 6).[5]

1. Cf. 1 Cor. 16.12, where the reference to θέλημα may be to *God's* will.

2. For this expression, see pp. 278-79 n. 2, and no. 6 in the main text here.

3. Martin, *2 Corinthians*, p. 362, incorrectly paraphrases 'on the Lord's authority'; more correctly Furnish, *2 Corinthians*, p. 496, translates 'according to the Lord' comparing 'speaking in Christ' (2.17 and 12.19b).

4. Furnish, *2 Corinthians*, p. 496.

5. Cf. the reference in 2 Cor. 8.5 to the Corinthians giving themselves 'to the Lord', a context where the accompanying phrase θελήματος θεοῦ makes it clear

8. Paul writes of loving *God* (1 Cor. 8.3) but also of loving *the Lord* (εἴ τις οὐ φιλεῖ τὸν κύριον, ἤτω ἀνάθεμα, 1 Cor. 16.22).

9. As has often been pointed out, Paul normally refers to praying to *God* (e.g. Rom. 10.1), but in 2 Cor. 12.8, where Paul refers to his prayer for deliverance from 'the thorn in the flesh', κύριος-language is used: ὑπὲρ τούτου τρὶς τὸν κύριον παρεκάλεσα ἵνα ἀποστῇ ἀπ' ἐμοῦ. As I argued earlier in this section, the reference to ἡ δύναμις τοῦ Χριστοῦ in v. 9 makes it very probable that 'the Lord' here is Christ.

10. In 1 Thess. 5.27 Paul uses an oath formula which he uses nowhere else: ἐνορκίζω ὑμᾶς τὸν κύριον.[1] Elsewhere Paul uses oath formulae which appeal to God.[2]

11. There is a close correlation in Paul's writings between *God* and *the Lord* giving to Paul his apostolic authority. Thus Paul twice (in virtually identical language at 2 Cor. 10.8 and 13.10) writes of the authority, ἧς ἔδωκεν ὁ κύριος εἰς οἰκοδομὴν καὶ οὐκ εἰς καθαίρεσιν ὑμῶν.[3]

Summary of Paul's κύριος*-Language*

1. θεός-language and κύριος-language occur together quite rarely. Thus there is a *prima facie* case for the view that κύριος-language functions as θεός-language. That does not mean that there is a simple identification of Christ with God. Rather, the exalted Lord stands *in loco Dei*.

2. The extent to which LXX references to 'the Lord' have been transferred to Christ is limited. Nevertheless, Rom. 10.13 is evidence of it. There is no such transference at work in Phil. 2.10-11, where ἐν τῷ ὀνόματι Ἰησοῦ has replaced the ἐμοί, referring to Yahweh, of Isa. 45.24. This means that for Paul the universal lordship of Jesus is the new expression of Jewish monotheism.

3. The extent of overlap between the θεός- and κύριος-language is significantly greater than that between θεός- and Χριστός-language.

that 'the Lord' here must be understood as Christ.

1. Holtz, *An die Thessalonicher*, p. 274, notes the uniqueness of the expression in Paul, and the extreme rarity of ἐνορκίζω in biblical Greek.

2. Rom. 1.9; 2 Cor. 11.11, 31; Gal. 1.20; Phil. 1.8; 1 Thess. 2.5, 10. See, however, Furnish's classification of 2 Cor. 11.10 ('As Christ's truth is in me', cf. Rom. 9.1), as an oath-formula (*2 Corinthians*, p. 493).

3. In 2 Cor. 13.10 Paul has ἥν and omits ὑμῶν, but otherwise there is a remarkable identity of expression here.

The overlap occurs in contexts where the theme of the Lord's authority (and above all his authority over the believer who belongs to him) is prominent. These parallels are important in that they show the readiness with which Christians could attribute functions or actions (e.g. answering prayer, or directing journeys) which they normally associated with God to Christ. But the extent of this linguistic transference is still quite limited, occurring, outside the language of eschatology, mainly in a small number of personal contexts (personal obedience, travel, prayer and, in 1 Thess. 5.27, an oath). The differences between Paul's θεός- and κύριος-language are much greater: Paul never writes, for example, of 'the righteousness of the Lord' or 'the wrath of the Lord'. Conversely, he does not write of 'the day of God', and only very rarely uses the expression 'in God'.

Summary to Section 3

This section has been concerned primarily with the scope and significance of what I have called 'linguistic interchange', investigating the extent of the 'mutual interpenetration' (Kreitzer's phrase) of the language Paul uses about God and about Christ. It has become clear that a distinction must be drawn between the function of Paul's Christ-language and that of his κύριος-language. Both relate to, and are affected by, Paul's God-language in different ways, reflecting different facets of Paul's total understanding of Jesus Christ.

I noted in section 2 of this chapter the way in which Paul's Christ-language was grammatically complementary to his God-language, that it was deeply theocentric and at the same time focused above all on what God did through the cross and resurrection of Christ, and was doing in the community of those 'in Christ'. Because of this wider linguistic context, the linguistic interchange which occurs, although limited in extent, is deeply significant. Important attributes of God are transferred to Christ—notably God's grace, love, power and glory. (The expressions πνεῦμα Χριστοῦ and πνεῦμα θεοῦ are also used interchangeably in Rom. 8.9.) The nature of this interchange reflects the mediating role of Christ: through him God's grace, love, and so on were both demonstrated and made effective, first in the death and resurrection of Christ, and secondly in the life of the believer. Of these, we observe that two, 'power' and 'glory', have a strong Old Testament pedigree; the remaining two, 'grace' and 'love', acquire a new prominence and importance in God-language. And all four words, directly or indirectly, focus on the cross and resurrection.

Paul's κύριος-language does not alternate with his God-language in the same way at all. The fact that the two kinds of language are rarely used together suggests that ὁ κύριος functions in some sense *in loco Dei*. But 'the Lord' must not be identified *tout court* with God, as the full range and variety of Paul's language shows. Rather, Jesus' lordship is the new expression of Jewish monotheism; people bow the knee at the name of Jesus εἰς δόξαν πατρός (Phil. 2.11).

This use of the LXX in Philippians (cf. 1 Cor. 1.31 and 2 Cor. 10.17) reflects one of the two ways in which LXX texts are reinterpreted by Paul in the light of Christ's lordship. In this instance, Christ's lordship *stands for, but does not replace* the sovereignty of God. On the other hand, Rom. 10.13 may indicate that a LXX text referring to Yahweh could be straightforwardly applied to Christ.

The kind of linguistic interchange which we found in Paul's κύριος-language was again limited but significant. But whereas Paul's Christ-language reflects the transfer of divine attributes to Christ, Paul's κύριος-language shows that the exalted Lord shares in the authority and, to some extent, the functions of God.

4. *2 Corinthians 5.19: God in Christ*

In any survey of the relationship in Paul's letters between the apostle's language about God and his language about Christ, there is one passage which demands particular attention. 2 Cor. 5.11-21 has been widely regarded as summarizing Paul's message about God and Christ. Following Thüsing,[1] I note that this passage is more theocentric than at first sight appears. But other features of the passage also merit some comment, particularly the remarkable language of v. 19.

First Paul seems to have reverted to a more polemical, or at the very least a more apologetic style, returning to one of the central themes of 2.14–4.15—that is, a justification of his own apostolic ministry. Thus 5.11-12 pick up the themes of earlier verses (notably 3.1 and 4.2). Significantly, the words πάντες/πάντων figure prominently in the next stage of the argument:

> ἡ γὰρ ἀγάπη τοῦ Χριστοῦ συνέχει ἡμᾶς, κρίναντας τοῦτο, ὅτι εἷς ὑπὲρ πάντων ἀπέθανεν, ἄρα οἱ πάντες ἀπέθανον· καὶ ὑπὲρ

1. Thüsing, *Per Christum*, pp. 101-105.

> πάντων ἀπέθανεν, ἵνα οἱ ζῶντες μηκέτι ἑαυτοῖς ζῶσιν ἀλλὰ τῷ ὑπὲρ αὐτῶν ἀποθανόντι καὶ ἐγερθέντι (vv. 14-15).

Thus Paul is laying out the theological grounds for his ministry to Gentiles, for Christ has rendered old distinctions null and void. (It is noteworthy how many echoes of Galatians occur here—for example the reference to καινὴ κτίσις at v.17a and Gal. 6.15.)[1] In fact, the reference to knowing Christ κατὰ σάρκα (v. 16) may be a further point of contact with Galatians, if Paul is thinking here of Christ's Jewishness. (It is true that Paul does not use this precise expression in Galatians, but the equation of 'the flesh' with subjection to the Law is prominent.)

After the polemical assertion of the new state of affairs brought about by Christ (v. 17), Paul moves towards a summary of the whole argument with an emphatic τὰ δὲ πάντα:

> τὰ δὲ πάντα ἐκ τοῦ θεοῦ τοῦ καταλλάξαντος ἡμᾶς ἑαυτῷ διὰ Χριστοῦ καὶ δόντος ἡμῖν τὴν διακονίαν τῆς καταλλαγῆς, ὡς ὅτι θεὸς ἦν ἐν Χριστῷ κόσμον καταλλάσσων ἑαυτῷ, μὴ λογιζόμενος αὐτοῖς τὰ παραπτώματα αὐτῶν καὶ θέμενος ἐν ἡμῖν τὸν λόγον τῆς καταλλαγῆς (vv. 18-19).

There are a number of interpretative problems about vv. 19-21, and it will be necessary to deal with them insofar as they affect our understanding of Paul's God-language here.

First, the widely accepted view that Paul is quoting a pre-Pauline tradition does not seem soundly based. Martin offers three reasons for the view that Paul is quoting traditional teaching.[2] He argues that what Paul goes on to say does not fit the context. The command 'Be reconciled to God' in v. 20 is evangelistic rather than pastoral. However, it is important to observe that Paul does not say 'We beg *you*',[3] and similarly, there is no ὑμᾶς stated as the direct object of παρακαλοῦντος (sc. τοῦ θεοῦ). For what Paul is doing here is telling the Corinthians what his ministry involves. He goes about urging people 'Be reconciled to God'. That is his message everywhere. It is not in this context a direct command to the Corinthians.

Secondly, Martin believes that its literary structure shows that it is substantially pre-Pauline.[4] There are no good grounds, however, for

1. Cf. the εἰς κενόν of 2 Cor. 6.1 with Gal. 2.2 (cf. Gal. 2.22 and 4.11).
2. Martin, *2 Corinthians*, pp. 152-54.
3. δεόμευθα has no object here.
4. Martin cites Rom. 3.24-26, Phil. 2.6-11 and Col. 1.15-20 as examples

regarding καταλλάσσω as pre-Pauline. It occurs in the New Testament only at Rom. 5.10, 1 Cor. 7.11 and here in vv. 18 and 20.[1]

Thirdly, Martin claims that while v. 19b (μὴ λογιζόμενος αὐτοῖς τὰ παραπτώματα αὐτῶν) and v. 20c (δεόμεθα ὑπὲρ Χριστοῦ, καταλλάγητε τῷ θεῷ) seem strongly Pauline, the use of δικαιοσύνη θεοῦ does not. Against this, however, we note 1 Cor. 1.30, which is closely similar in thought, and the fact that the theme of 'interchange' expressed in v. 21 is almost certainly Pauline.[2]

Other arguments that v. 19 is partly or entirely un-Pauline are unconvincing. Furnish contends that the plural παραπτώματα is uncharacteristic of Paul, occurring elsewhere only at Rom. 4.23 (a probably pre-Pauline verse) and Rom. 5.16 where 'the plural is required to make the point'.[3] Furnish does not note, however, that the singular is required to make the point in almost all the contexts where it occurs.[4]

Two other points remain to be dealt with. What is the significance of ὡς ὅτι in v. 19? It is not necessarily an indication that Paul is quoting a tradition. He does not give such an indication in Rom. 1.3-4, 3.24-26 or 4.25, all of which are widely regarded as containing pre-Pauline tradition. (The significance of ὡς ὅτι I shall return to below.)

The outstanding question is the translation of v. 19a. Is ἐν Χριστῷ the equivalent of διὰ Χριστοῦ?[5] But despite the occurrence of ἐν in its Semitic sense of 'by' at, for example, Rom. 5.9 (ἐν τῷ αὐτοῦ αἵματι σωθησόμεθα),[6] I can find no examples in Paul's writing of ἐν Χριστῷ being used in this sense. In fact, after the ἐν Χριστῷ of v. 17 and διὰ Χριστοῦ of v.18, it would be confusing, to say the least, if Paul did not intend ἐν Χριστῷ to have its normal meaning in v. 19.[7]

of Paul quoting and explaining other hymns.

1. Similarly the noun καταλλαγή occurs only at Rom. 5.11, 11.15 and 2 Cor. 5.18-19.

2. Contrast the fundamentally pre-Pauline πίστις formula (cf. Pokorny, *Genesis*, pp. 63-70).

3. Furnish, *2 Corinthians*, p. 329.

4. Thus, of Adam's transgression at Rom. 5.15, 17, 18 and of Israel's (in rejecting the gospel) at 11.11-12.

5. Thus Martin (*Carmen Christi*), Furnish (*2 Corinthians*), Bultmann (*Zweite Brief*), commentaries *ad loc.*

6. Cf. Gal.1.16 ('...to reveal his Son ἐν ἐμοί').

7. Furnish, *2 Corinthians*, p. 318, suggests that 'in Christ' here does not have 'the full eschatological meaning' present in v.17, but it is difficult to see how ἐν Χριστῷ in this context can *lack* its full eschatological meaning.

How then is v.19a to be translated? Furnish lists three possibilities:

1. 'God was in Christ, reconciling...'
2. 'In Christ God was reconciling...'
3. (reading 'God' as a predicative nominative)[1] 'it was God who in Christ was reconciling...'

Of these, (2) may be ruled out on the grounds I have argued, namely that this is not a pre-Pauline tradition, and moreover, as Furnish himself notes, the periphrastic construction is not often used by Paul. But of (1) and (3), which is to be preferred ?

A question which seems to have been largely overlooked[2] is whether the absence of the definite article with θεός is significant. The evidence here is revealing. While it seems that Pauline usage is *sometimes* dictated by stylistic reasons (especially in prepositional phrases, where, for example, Paul may write παρὰ θεῷ or παρὰ τῷ θεῷ),[3] this is not true of the nominative θεός. Paul uses the nominative 106 times, almost always with the definite article.[4] The exceptions are easily explained: the use of εἷς with θεός at 1 Cor. 8.6 (cf. οὐδεὶς θεός at 8.4); the oath formula at 1 Thess. 2.5 (θεὸς μάρτυς),[5] while in the other remaining examples θεός seems to be used predicatively, and usually emphatically with a participial clause in 2 Cor. 1.21, 5.5, Rom. 8.33, 9.5 and Phil. 2.13.[6] There can be little doubt, therefore, that θεός is both predicative and emphatic.[7]

But does ἐν Χριστῷ belong with ἦν or with καταλλάσσων? Furnish[8] acknowledges that the word order favours the former, but

1. Thus Barrett, *2 Corinthians*, p. 177.

2. Barrett is a rare exception.

3. See the discussion in C.F.D. Moule, *An Idiom Book of New Testament Greek* (Cambridge: Cambridge University Press, 1968 [1953]), pp. 111-17, where, however, Moule demonstrates his claim that 'in some instances it is hard to avoid the impression that usage is arbitrary' with reference to ἀλήθεια, πνεῦμα and νόμος, but *not* θεός.

4. 2 Cor. 4.4 and Phil. 3.19 may be discounted as the latter does not, and the former probably does not, refer to God.

5. Paul, however, usually retains the definite article in similar oath formulae.

6. The only other example in Paul's writings of θεός occurring anarthrously is in the Old Testament quotation of 2 Cor. 6.16 (καὶ ἔσομαι αὐτῶν θεός).

7. The absence of the definite article cannot be attributed to the fact that the preceding word ends with a short vowel, as 1 Cor. 1.27-8 show.

8. Furnish, *2 Corinthians*, p. 318.

rejects this on the grounds that 'the idea of God's "being in" (*einai en*) Christ is not present elsewhere in Paul's letters, and an incarnational emphasis is not otherwise present in this context'.[1] These objections would have some force, if it were not for the introductory ὡς ὅτι, and to that I must now turn.

The occurrence of ὡς ὅτι here is problematical because of its occurrence in 2 Cor. 11.21 and 2 Thess. 2.2, where Paul and 'pseudo-Paul' use it with a reference to a statement from which they are distancing themselves. Thus at 2 Cor. 11.21 Paul is ironically conceding the charge (by a section of the Corinthian church presumably) that he had been weak: κατὰ ἀτιμίαν λέγω, ὡς ὅτι ἡμεῖς ἠσθενήκαμεν. On this construction Plummer comments as follows: 'In ὡς ὅτι the ὡς intimates that what is introduced by ὅτι is given as the thought of another, for the correctness of which the speaker does not vouch'.[2] Similarly, at 2 Thess. 2.2 the writer is referring to a letter ὡς δι' ἡμῶν, with a message ὡς ὅτι ἐνέστηκεν ἡ ἡμέρα τοῦ κυρίου. The problem with the occurrence of ὡς ὅτι at 2 Cor. 5.19 is obvious, for the two other occurrences of ὡς ὅτι in letters attributed to Paul are, in fact, the only instances in the entire New Testament. We cannot therefore take refuge in the observation that in later Greek ὡς ὅτι is virtually the equivalent of ὅτι.[3] Barrett recognizes the difficulty: 'The difficulty is that the statement made in verse 19a is not one on which Paul would wish to cast doubt'.[4] Barrett himself, with reservations, adopts the solution of the Vulgate (*quoniam quidem*) in giving the words 'a causal sense'. But the question must be asked: would Paul have found such a statement as unproblematical as Barrett supposes?

It is possible that Paul is here using a phrase which is not his own, but which, with reservations, he decides to employ in this context. The phrase is 'God in Christ', and its origin is more likely to have been the Gentile churches than the Aramaic-speaking churches of Palestine, or, indeed, any of the predominantly Jewish churches. For the fact is that there is no parallel in Paul to this kind of language, nor would there have been any precedent in pre-Pauline tradition. James Barr, discussing the relationship of Jesus and the gospel to the Old Testament, points out that

1. Cf. Bultmann, *Zweite Brief*, p. 161, and Martin, *2 Corinthians*, p. 147.

2. A. Plummer, *A Critical and Exegetical Commentary on the Second Epistle of Saint Paul to the Corinthians* (Edinburgh: T. & T. Clark, 1915), p. 317.

3. Moulton and Milligan, p. 703.

4. Barrett, *2 Corinthians*, p. 176.

Christianity is not 'a mere mild modification of Judaism nor a supplement to the Old Testament...but something radically new...'[1] He goes on to illustrate this with reference to the idea of incarnation. Such an idea became 'possible and meaningful' only in a Jewish context, since the Old Testament's sharp distinction between human and divine differentiated it from non-Jewish mythologies. But, Barr goes on, the Old Testament also made 'combinations of the divine and the human impossible, unthinkable and forbidden...In fact, incarnation is one part of Christian belief for which the Old Testament (and, still more, post-biblical Judaism) had furnished little positive preparation.'

I am suggesting, therefore, that Paul's use of ὡς ὅτι in 2 Cor. 5.19 gives us a remarkable glimpse into the mind of a Jew struggling to express the 'radically new' and coming, in the process, to the very brink of incarnational language:

> All this (has come)[2] from God, who has reconciled us to himself through Christ and has given to us the ministry of reconciliation, namely that (as some put it) it was 'God in Christ', reconciling the world to himself, not reckoning people's misdeeds against them, and placing (lit. having placed) among us the word of reconciliation (vv. 18-19).

Two further points may be briefly made here. First, Paul's tentative adoption of such incarnational language is the logical outcome of the christological and soteriological language which he uses elsewhere. If, that is to say, God's call had been effected *in* Christ, if he had liberated Jew and Gentile *through* Christ, if Christ's death and resurrection was the manifestation of God's grace and power, then, sooner or later, the Church was bound to affirm 'God was in Christ'.[3]

Secondly, it might be asked why Paul, having ventured to use incarnational language once, does not do so again. Romans, however, is the only major letter, perhaps the only surviving complete letter written after 2 Corinthians and, as we have had occasion to note more than

1. J. Barr, *Holy Scripture, Canon and Authority* (Oxford: Oxford University Press, 1983), p. 16.

2. There is no verb here in the Greek.

3. It is noteworthy that Colossians, although probably written by a disciple of Paul, moves in this direction in 1.19 (ὅτι ἐν αὐτῷ εὐδόκησεν πᾶν τὸ πλήρωμα) and 2.9 (ὅτι ἐν αὐτῷ κατοικεῖ πᾶν τὸ πλήρωμα). There are some important linguistic and exegetical questions in these verses, which cannot be gone into here, but there can be little doubt that they represent a significant step in the direction of the incarnational language of subsequent generations.

once in the course of this study, Paul's language in Romans seems more traditionally Jewish than it is in the Corinthian correspondence.

2 Cor. 5.19 comprises, in my judgment, a unique example of the interaction of Paul's God- and Christ-language. It does not conform to the more common patterns which I have reviewed so far in this chapter, and to which I return in the next section. (This may be the reason why it has frequently been misconstrued.) But this does not mean it is unimportant. Indeed, I have argued that 'incarnational' language of this kind was the logical corollary of Paul's other statements that juxtapose God- and Christ-language. In this respect, too, the seeds of later christological development have already been sown.

5. *1 Corinthians 8.6 and Theological* Inclusio *in Paul*

ἀλλ' ἡμῖν εἷς θεὸς ὁ πατὴρ
ἐξ οὗ τὰ πάντα καὶ ἡμεῖς εἰς αὐτόν,
καὶ εἷς κύριος Ἰησοῦς Χριστὸς
δι' οὗ τὰ πὰντα καὶ ἡμεῖς δι' αὐτοῦ.

The importance of 1 Cor. 8.6 for both Pauline theology and Christology has been widely recognized. It is almost certainly pre-1 Corinthians, probably being a formula coined by Paul himself.[1] Whatever the case, it summarizes crucial elements in Paul's understanding of God and of Jesus.[2]

First, the Jewish background of the phrase εἷς θεός (v. 6a) is obvious.[3] Two particularly striking parallels to the whole verse, however, occur in Josephus, who refers to θεὸς εἷς καὶ τῶν Ἑβραίων γένος ἐν (*Ant*. 4.201), and to εἷς ναὸς ἑνὸς θεοῦ κοινὸς ἁπάντων κοινοῦ θεοῦ (*Apol*. 2.166).[4] It is also probable that the formulation owes

1. Thus, for example, Thüsing, *Per Christum*, p. 225. Dunn (*Christology*, pp. 179-83) thinks that this verse is an *ad hoc* formula put together by Paul from elements which are pre-Pauline and pre-Christian. Contrast W.L. Willis, *Idol Meat in Corinth* (Chico, CA: Scholars Press, 1985), pp. 84-87, who thinks that vv. 4-6 are a quotation by Paul of the Corinthians' views.

2. So also Thüsing, *Per Christum*, p. 225, who finds here the essential outlines (*'wesentlichen Linien'*) of Pauline theology (cf. p. 257), although his own lines of inquiry and emphases are rather different from those developed here.

3. Thus Conzelmann, *1 Corinthians*, p. 144; and Dunn, *Christology*, pp. 179, 329.

4. Both references cited by D.A. Schlatter, *Wie sprach Josephus von Gott?* (Gütersloh: C. Bertelsmann, 1910), p. 16.

something to Stoic influence, particularly its use of prepositions.[1]

It is the prepositions, in fact, which immediately concern us. As Cullmann points out, Father and Son are distinguished not by their sphere of operation but by the prepositions.[2] The first section of this chapter explored the frequency of διά + genitive in Paul's Christ-language; it is clear that the second διά used here, ἡμεῖς δι' αὐτοῦ, has many parallels in Paul. The first διά (δι' οὗ τὰ πάντα) is a theme less common.[3] Thüsing draws attention to the similar phrases in Rom. 11.36 (ἐξ αὐτοῦ καὶ δι' αὐτοῦ καὶ εἰς αὐτὸν τὰ πάντα), and suggests that this parallel, together with the link here with v. 6a shows that v. 6b means 'an aspect of Christ's work which is wholly cosmic...his mediation in creation'.[4]

Another interpretation is possible, however, for two reasons. First, Rom. 11.36 refers to *God*, not to Christ. Secondly, as Thüsing himself observes, the meaning of τὰ πάντα in Paul varies according to context. Thus at 1 Cor. 11.12 it seems to refer to creation, but at 2 Cor. 5.18 to God's salvific work. The possibility that τὰ πάντα is to be interpreted differently in its two occurrences in 1 Cor. 8.6 is strengthened by the fact that 'we' (ἡμεῖς) are perceived from two different perspectives. We were created 'for God' (εἰς αὐτόν) (v. 6a); we were redeemed 'through' Christ (ἡμεῖς δι' αὐτοῦ). The verbs, of course have to be supplied, but this clearly seems to be Paul's thought here. This suggests that the first τὰ πάντα indicates God's creative work, the second his salvific work through Christ. If this interpretation is correct, it means that there is very little trace of 'Wisdom Christology' in the undisputed Pauline writings. 1 Cor. 1.24, 30 should be noted of course, although here the language is rhetorical rather than ontological. (I argued in Chapter 2[5] that when Paul described Christ as 'the power of God and the wisdom of God' [1 Cor. 1.24], he meant that the proclamation of Christ *embodies* the wisdom of God and *conveys* the power of God.) It

1. Grant, *Early Christian Doctrine*, finds here and in several other Pauline passages (Rom. 1.19-21; 11.36; Gal. 4.8-10; cf. 1 Tim. 1.7) what he calls 'bridges' towards 'philosophical doctrines of God'.

2. O. Cullmann, *The Christology of the New Testament* (London: SCM Press, 1963 [1959]), pp. 247, 326; cf. *TWNT*, IX, p. 550.

3. See, however, Col. 1.16, Heb. 1.2 and Jn 1.3.

4. Thüsing, *Per Christum*, p. 229. The parallel with Rom. 11.36 is noted also by Conzelmann, *1 Corinthians*, p. 145 n.48.

5. Chapter 2, section 4.

is doubtful, therefore, whether according to 1 Cor. 8.6 Christ 'embodies the creative power of God',[1] and still more doubtful that there is a reference here to the pre-existence of Christ.

But what is the relationship of Paul's Christology to his theology here? I have drawn attention to the significance of the prepositions in 1 Cor. 8.6. Now it must be observed that their use here seems to be typical of Paul's wider usage. The previous paragraph referred to two verses (1 Cor. 11.12b; 2 Cor. 5.18a) where Paul uses the expression τὰ πάντα. In both contexts τὰ πάντα belongs to a larger verb-less phrase: τὰ δὲ πάντα ἐκ τοῦ θεοῦ. Other passages with ἐκ or ἀπὸ θεοῦ indicate Paul's conviction that God is the origin and goal of the church. God as author of salvation seems to be particularly emphasized by the use of ἀπὸ θεοῦ at 1 Corinthians and Phil. 1.28.[2] ἐκ or ἀπὸ θεοῦ is also used to denote the source of judgment (Rom. 2.29; 1 Cor. 4.5).

The phrase εἰς θεόν occurs less often.[3] However, there is the frequent εἰς δόξαν (τοῦ) θεοῦ at Rom. 15.7, 1 Cor. 10.31, 2 Cor. 4.15, Phil. 1.9 and 2.11.[4]

I shall return to the implications of these prepositions, and the 'pattern' which they give to Pauline theology, but before doing so I must note some further features of 1 Cor. 8.6.

First, the threefold ἡμῖν-ἡμεῖς-ἡμεῖς gives a strongly experiental note to the formula. Conzelmann is surely correct in saying that the

1. *Contra* Dunn, *Christology*, pp. 182-83. In his discussion of Wisdom Christology in Paul (pp. 176-96), Dunn sets aside 1 Cor. 10.4 and Rom. 10.6-10 as less than certain examples, focusing instead on 1 Cor. 8.6 and Col. 1.15-20. But I am suggesting that there has been a tendency in New Testament scholarship to interpret 1 Cor. 8.6 in the light of Col. 1.15-20 and to ignore (a) the possibility, if not probability, that Colossians is deutero-Pauline and (b) the varying meaning of τὰ πάντα in Paul.

2. Cf. Schenk, *Philipperbriefe*, pp. 87-88, who refers to von Dobschütz's observation of the application of ἀπό to God and διά to Jesus, thus identifiying God as 'Creator of all gifts'.

3. In a negative sense, ἔχθρα εἰς θεόν at Rom. 8.7.

4. The phrase πρὸς τὸν θεόν in Paul's writings is a more general phrase, usually used with reference to prayer (Rom. 10.1; 15.30; 2 Cor. 13.7; Phil. 4.6). It is used at Rom. 5.1 of peace with God (εἰρήνην πρὸς τὸν θεόν) and at 2 Cor. 3.4 of confidence 'in' or 'before' God (thus Barrett, *2 Corinthians*, p. 110). Here, however, διὰ τοῦ Χριστοῦ is not used (*contra* Furnish, *2 Corinthians*, p. 183) as a phrase equivalent with 'in the Lord'. At Rom. 14.14, Gal. 5.10 and Phil. 1.14 and 2.24, Paul is referrring to convictions or opinions rather than confidence or trust in God.

ἡμῖν removes this affirmation from the category of a metaphysical or ontological judgment.[1] It is, rather, a question of 'adopting an attitude'. It is more than this, however, as the context makes clear. Here the divine passive of v. 3 should be noted: εἰ δέ τις ἀγαπᾷ τὸν θεόν, οὗτος ἔγνωσται ὑπ' αὐτοῦ. In fact, Paul seems to prefer the passive 'being known' rather than the active 'knowing God'. The passive is used here in the eschatological context of 1 Cor. 13.12 and, most signficantly of all, as a corrective to the active participle at Gal. 4.9: νῦν δὲ γνόντες θεόν, μᾶλλον δὲ γνωσθέντες ὑπὸ θεοῦ.[2]

The use of the pronoun 'we', then, gives this credal formula an experiential emphasis. We must now go on to ask whether πατήρ must be interpreted in this light, and whether, indeed, it owes anything to Christology. It may be correct to see ὁ πατήρ here as filling out the content of θεός.[3] But does it anticipate the Christology of v. 6b? In the light of the context, and even more, Paul's use of πατήρ elsewhere, Demke[4] is probably right to insist that πατήρ is not simply indicating that the one God is Creator. He correctly stresses the importance of the context, arguing that 'Father' here is a *name*, and because God can be called 'Father' 'all things are yours'. But all this happens only insofar as we are known (that is, chosen). And *both* discovering that all is from him *and* that we are 'for Him' come to us through Jesus Christ. Demke concludes that 1 Cor. 8.1-6 implies the 'unequivocalness' (*Eindeutigkeit*) of God: God's Fatherhood thus comes to light in the death of Jesus.[5]

Demke may be reading rather too much of Paul's theology into this short passage. He is, however, surely right to stress the christological foundation of Paul's use of πατήρ here, as elsewhere.[6] This means that already we have a measure of 'interaction' between a fundamental affirmation about God and Christ.

That brings us, finally, to the question of the relationship between the

1. Conzelmann, *1 Corinthians*, p. 145 (cf. Weiss, *Körintherbrief*, p. 223, and Lindemann, *Die Rede von Gott*, pp. 365-66, who emphasizes that ἡμῖν εἷς θεός is not a statement about our choice, nor an exhortation, nor a theoretical knowledge, but rather an 'expression of a concrete, existential experience').

2. The active verb is used with a negative at 1 Thess. 4.5, Gal. 4.8 and 1 Cor. 1.21, and in a negative context at Rom. 1.21.

3. Thus Conzelmann, *1 Corinthians*, p. 144.

4. C. Demke, 'Ein Gott und viele Herren', *EvT* 36.5 (1976), pp. 473-84.

5. Demke, 'Ein Gott', pp. 482-83.

6. On Paul's use of πατήρ see section 3 above.

twin affirmations about the 'one God' and the 'one Lord'. Clearly, no simple identification of Christ with God is being made.[1] Nor is Christ being described as 'a vice-regent for God'.[2] As so often in Paul, as we saw in section 2 of this chapter, God-phrases and Christ-phrases are simply set side by side, and the relationship between the two is not spelled out. Dunn writes here of how Paul 'splits the Shema' in a way that has 'no earlier parallels'.[3] Or would it be more correct to say that Paul expands or amplifies the *shema*? Or is the difference between these descriptions of what Paul is doing here insignificant? Here, above all, Thüsing's question of the relation between Paul's Christocentricity and his monotheism is sharply focused.

In an important but apparently neglected article, E. Rohde argued that for Paul the juxtaposition *(Zusammenstellung)* of God and 'the Lord' in this way was brought about by the resurrection.[4] This is why God may be defined as the one who raised Jesus. Therefore, Rohde concludes: 'In the confession "One God and one Lord" "Lord" signifies a statement about God. By the addition of "the Lord", God is characterized in a particular way.'[5] This conclusion thus indicates another way in which 1 Cor. 8.6 is paradigmatic for Paul's theology, particularly the interrelation between his language about God and his language about Christ: the lordship of Christ *is* for Paul the expression of his (Jewish) monotheism. As Rohde argues, faith in Christ is an abbreviation for faith in God 'beside whom is Christ'.[6]

1. Thus, e.g., Cullmann, *Christology*, p. 193, and Lindemann, *Die Rede von Gott*, p. 366. Contrast Hurtado, *One God, One Lord*, who assumes without discussion the 'binitarian' nature of this verse (pp. 1-3). M. Davies, 'Review of L. Hurtado's *One God One Lord*', *New Blackfriars* (Jan. 1990), pp. 51-52, rightly notes that 'lord' 'has a wide range of possible meanings from which Hurtado selects one without discussion'. P.A. Rainbow, 'Jewish Monotheism as the Matrix for New Testament Christology. A Review Article', *NovT* 33.1 (1991) also tends to assume, like Hurtado, that Jesus was venerated as God in early Jewish Christianity (pp. 83-84), but his reference to 1 Cor. 8.6 and Phil. 2.9–11 as the earliest datable evidence for 'the use of monotheistic language as a christological category' suggests that he has over-simplified the evidence of these texts.

2. Lindemann, *Die Rede von Gott*, p. 367.

3. Dunn, *Christology*, p. 180.

4. E. Rohde, 'Gottesglaube und Kyriosglaube bei Paulus', *ZNW* 22 (1923), p. 52.

5. Rohde, 'Gottesglaube', p. 53.

6. Rohde, 'Gottesglaube', pp. 54-55.

When we ask what is the *effect* on Paul's understanding of God and of Christ by this striking juxtaposition in this verse, Rohde claims that the result is the Christianizing of Paul's concept of God: 'The synthesis of God and Christ indicates in Paul a struggle within the apostle over his concept of God. The result of the synthesis is the Christianizing of his concept of God, not the divinizing (*Vergottung*) of Christ.'[1] This is a somewhat misleading over-simplification. While it is one of the main contentions of this chapter that Paul's understanding of God has indeed been affected by his faith in Christ, it is important not to offer any hostages to Marcionism! The evidence I have marshalled in the preceding sections shows that language about Christ complements language about God and, in so doing, provides the basis for a new (but not totally new) concept of God.

I return now to the implications of the prepositions in 1 Cor. 8.6, which, as we have seen, are particularly identified with θεός and Χριστός in Paul's letters. The contention of the remainder of this section is that the prepositions are a particular grammatical expression of what is a deeper and more widespread pattern in Paul's writings. This pattern may be set out diagrammatically as

$$\theta \rightarrow X \rightarrow X \rightarrow \theta$$

and therefore merits the description of a 'theological *inclusio*'.

This, of course, corresponds with the observation made by many commentators that God is the source and goal, Christ the mediator or instrument. What seems not to have been noticed is the extent to which this pattern emerges in units, large and small, of Paul's letters. Only a summary of the evidence can be given here, with one or two examples.

First, Romans 9–11 provide an example of the kind of theological *inclusio* we are discussing. The emphasis of 9.1-29 on the divine freedom and call is well epitomized in the phrase ἐκ θεοῦ; 9.30–10.21 provides the christological 'heart' of Paul's argument; and the overall thrust of 11.1-36 is εἰς θεόν. The doxology, therefore, with which Paul concludes these chapters is eminently suitable, in that all three prepositions—ἐκ, διά and εἰς—which play such a crucial role in his God- and Christ-language occur here: ὅτι ἐξ αὐτοῦ καὶ δι' αὐτοῦ καὶ εἰς αὐτὸν τὰ πάντα αὐτῷ ἡ δόξα εἰς τοὺς αἰῶνας, ἀμήν (v. 36).[2]

1. Rohde, 'Gottesglaube', p. 56.

2. If the question of why there is no διὰ Χριστοῦ here, the reason must be partly stylistic, but also perhaps linked with Paul's strategy as an apologist; in these

Two other large units in Paul's letters which show a similar theological structure are Rom. 14.1–15.13 and (although this is not quite so clear) 1 Cor. 8.1–11.1.

The pattern of 'theological *inclusio*'—from God through Christ to God—which is discernible in these three extended arguments can also be discerned in smaller units. It may be significant that it can be identified in several units of the Corinthian correspondence. I pointed out in an earlier chapter that Paul places special emphasis on the word θεός, particularly in the early chapters of 1 Corinthians,[1] and I suggested that the 'Christ party', referred to in 1 Cor. 1.12 may have developed a kind of Christology which totally or partially eclipsed *theo*-logy. So it is surely significant that 1 Cor. 8.6 seems to be the theological paradigm for several units in these letters. Here one example must suffice.

It is possible to subdivide the section 1 Cor. 15.12-28 into smaller units, as the commentaries do. But it is clear from the structure of the argument, and from the language itself, that vv. 12-28 can be regarded as a unit.[2] It is important, when we consider the language of these verses, not to set up a false antithesis between theocentrism and Christocentrism.[3] The passage is both theocentric and Christocentric. The reason lies in the underlying theological structure which we have identified elsewhere. A simple word count of 'Christ' and 'God' would be misleading, since vv. 12-22 contain many divine passives, notably the perfect passive of ἐγείρω (vv. 12, 13, 14, 16, 17, 20).[4] From v. 23, however, there is an explicit alternation of Christ- and God-language. In v. 23 the focus is primarily on Christ: ἀπαρχὴ Χριστός, ἔπειτα οἱ τοῦ Χριστοῦ ἐν τῇ παρουσίᾳ αὐτοῦ (v. 23b). But God-language is introduced in the next verse: εἶτα τὸ τέλος, ὅταν παραδιδῷ τὴν βασιλείαν τῷ θεῷ καὶ πατρί, ὅταν καταργήσῃ πᾶσαν ἀρχὴν καὶ πᾶσαν ἐξουσίαν καὶ δύναμιν (v. 24).[5]

chapters Paul is being 'a Jew to Jews' (On this, see H. Chadwick, '"All Things to All Men". 1 Cor. 9.22', *NTS* 1 [1954–55], pp. 261-75), *passim*.

1. See especially Chapter 2, sections 2 and 3. See Chapter 4, section 2.

2. Both vv. 12 and 29 introduce new sections by references to Corinthian belief and practice.

3. Thus also Kreitzer, *Jesus and God*, p. 148, quoting J.C. Beker.

4. Verse 15 makes explicit the subject of ἐγείρω (τοῦ θεοῦ ὅτι ἤγειρεν τὸν Χριστόν). Note also the further divine passive in v. 22, ζῳοποιηθήσονται (cf. 2 Cor. 3.6 and Rom. 8.11).

5. The use of καταργέω with Christ as subject is noteworthy, but the context and structure preclude God being the subject. Thus, e.g., Kreitzer, *Jesus and God*,

The subject of v. 25 is Christ: the context requires it, although, as Kreitzer notes,[1] this means that 'an Old Testament function of God described in Psalm 110.1 becomes the activity of Christ' in this verse.

There is more disagreement about the subject of the next active verb: πάντα γὰρ ὑπέταξεν ὑπὸ τοὺς πόδας αὐτοῦ (v. 26b). Several commentators take the view that the subject is Christ, contending that the correction of v. 27 would not be necessary if the subject of ὑπέταξεν were God.[2] This objection falls to the ground, however, because (a) the subject of ὑπέταξεν is not explicit anyway, and is therefore open to misunderstanding, and (b) the subject of the participles ὑποτάξαντος and ὑποτάξαντι (vv. 27 and 28) is clearly God.[3] It is thus likely that the subject of ὑπέταξεν in v. 27a is God, rather than Christ, and if that is so this section ends with a resounding emphasis upon God. We may note the rather laboured correction of v. 27b,[4] the emphatic καὶ αὐτὸς ὁ υἱός of v. 28 and the final phrase ἵνα ᾖ ὁ θεὸς (τὰ) πάντα ἐν πᾶσιν. Thüsing is right in claiming that v. 28 (and v. 24, 'when he delivers the kingdom to God the Father') are in line with Pauline theology elsewhere.[5] Although the pattern here is rather more complicated than the simple θ χ θ which can be discerned in other units of Paul's letters, it remains true that God is both the alpha and the omega of the argument.

This literary pattern of 'theological *inclusio*' can be seen in other units in the Corinthian correspondence, notably 1 Cor. 1.18-25, 6.12-20, and 2 Cor. 1.18-22, 4.7-15 and 5.11-21.[6] It is, however, much more

p. 150; Barrett, *1 Corinthians*, p. 357; Conzelmann, *1 Corinthians*, p. 271.

1. Kreitzer, *Jesus and God*, p. 150.
2. Thus Lietzmann, cited by Conzelmann, *1 Corinthians*, p. 274 n.108.
3. Thus also Kreitzer, *Jesus and God*, p. 150.
4. Barrett, *1 Corinthians*, p. 360, notes the possibility of a Corinthian belief 'that at his exaltation Christ became the one supreme God'. Surprisingly, in view of the evidence we have reviewed in this study (Chapter 2, section 3), Barrett says that 'we have no other evidence' for this belief.
5. Thüsing, *Per Christum*, p. 244. However, it is unnecessary to argue with Thüsing (p. 244), that πάντα is an accusative. Thüsing is clearly anxious to avoid a pantheistic-sounding sentence, but the accusative of relation which he cites from 1 Cor. 10.33 offers no real parallel, and the parallels in wording quoted by Conzelmann both from Jewish and Hellenistic sources (the parallel from Sirach is especially striking: 'τὸ πᾶν ἐστιν αὐτός...' 43.27-28), makes the nominative overwhelmingly probable (Conzelmann, *1 Corinthians*, p. 275 n.113).
6. 2 Cor. 1.18-22 has an impressive cluster of θεός occurrences (vv. 18, 19,

pervasive, although not always as explicit as in the texts we have examined.[1]

Summary

In this section I have attempted to show how Paul's language about God and about Christ corresponds to a chiastic pattern, frequently appearing in individual units of his letters as a kind of 'theological *inclusio*'. For this pattern 1 Cor. 8.6 (and particularly its prepositions) serves, in effect, as a paradigm. This is a vitally important feature of Paul's theological grammar. His thinking begins and ends with God. Yet between the 'movement' from God and back to God there is Christ. Thus Paul's language about God has been opened up, amplified, explicated, justified, by language about Christ.

The grammar of this language reflects the theological reality. Whereas the word θεός occurs only rarely in the accusative, Χριστός is rarely found in the nominative except as the subject of verbs referring to the cross and resurrection. Much more common are the prepositional phrases διὰ ('Ιησοῦ) Χριστοῦ and ἐν ('Ιησοῦ) Χριστῷ, corresponding closely with the movement from and back to God. Clearly, God is not eclipsed by Christ in Paul's thought. Rather, in most of the contexts where Christ-language occurs, God is explicitly or implicitly origin, author, prime mover and goal.

What can be said of God's action in Christ is said in varying ways of Paul's own ministry. Here God is the framework, environment, warrant, ultimate reference-point of that ministry. Christ-language 'fills out' the framework by demonstrating the pattern, particularly of suffering and resurrection.[2]

6. *Conclusions*

1. Much of the traditional God-language used by Paul has been 'baptized into Christ'. That is to say, it has become implicitly christological by virtue of the contexts in which it is used and, where appropriate, of the people to whom it is applied. This process could be observed in some detail in the case of words and phrases used by Paul of non-Christian Jews and Gentiles in Romans 1–2.

20 [twice], 21, and three participial clauses referring to God).

1. See especially 1 Thess. 3.11-13; 5.23-24; 1 Cor. 3.18-23; Rom. 5.1-11; 8.31-39.

2. 2 Cor. 4.7-12; cf. 12.10; 13.3-4; Rom. 8.35-39.

2. Much of Paul's Christ-language is grammatically complementary to and subordinate to his God-language. Χριστός is rarely the subject of verbs other than those referring to Christ's death and resurrection. (In the latter case Paul nearly always uses the passive of ἐγείρω.) Paul's use of the phrases ἐν Χριστῷ and διὰ Χριστοῦ is also strongly theocentric, reflecting grammatically the subordination of Christ to God.

3. Several linguistic patterns were distinguished in the juxtapositions of God- and Christ-language. The grammatical interdependence of θεός and Χριστός was clear: statements about Christ are almost always set in a theistic frame of reference; conversely, statements about God are often particularized, either by an implicitly christological context or by explicit christological language. Yet the interdependence is not of an equal kind; throughout 'God' functions as origin, author, warrant and goal, 'Christ' as the agent or means.

4. Alongside the strongly subordinationist relationship of Christ to God, reflected in many of the linguistic patterns, a quasi-equal relationship is discernible, especially in the opening salutations.

5. The most significant interaction (rather than juxtaposition) of language about God and about Christ occurs in two key relational terms: πατὴρ (τοῦ Ἰησοῦ Χριστοῦ κυρίου ἡμῶν) and υἱὸς (τοῦ θεοῦ). While the term υἱὸς does not have the range of meaning found in later Christian writers, reflecting primarily the obedience and subordination of the son, the word πατήρ has become an important defining term, distinctive in its centrality and in its soteriological implications in Christian God-language.

6. Linguistic interchange was of two kinds. Attributes of God, notably God's grace, love, power and glory, are transferred to 'Christ', while Paul's κύριος-language shows that certain *functions* of God, especially in statements referring to the future judgment or, in the present, to personal obedience and piety, are transferred to 'the Lord'.

7. Paul's use of the LXX was twofold. Most references in LXX quotations to 'the Lord' are to God. Thus 'God' and 'the Lord' (when used outside the LXX quotations) are differentiated. But Rom. 10.13 (and 1 Cor. 10.21-22) show that LXX references to 'the Lord' could sometimes be transferred to Christ. This twofold development anticipates a substantial part of the later christological agenda of the Church.

8. The concentration of divine action in Christ, reflected in the interplay between God- and Christ-language, receives unique expression in 2 Cor. 5.19. This was the logical result of Paul's other christological and

soteriological language. Yet Paul, as a Jew, prefaces such startlingly incarnational language by ὡς ὅτι, suggesting that the words are those of others, not his own.

9. 1 Cor. 8.6 has good claim to be a paradigm of both Paul's God-language and his language about Christ, (a) in the affirmation of the one creator God who, by virtue of his saving work, 'we' can call Father, (b) in the unique mediatorial role and lordship of Jesus Christ, through whom came our salvation—an interpretation of δι' οὗ τὰ πάντα which, if correct, puts a large question-mark against the presence of 'Wisdom-Christology' in Paul, (c) in the stark juxtaposition of εἷς θεός and εἷς κύριος, and (d) in the 'theological *inclusio*' reflected in the prepositions, and finding expression in several units, large and small, in Paul's writings.

The conclusions of this chapter have, I believe, wider implications for our understanding of the New Testament and of early Christianity. In particular, I note the following points.

1. The interdependence of God- and Christ-language has important consequences for the methodology of New Testament studies. New Testament 'Christology', although perhaps necessary as a term of convenience, is an artificial concept. The 'Christology' of Paul can only be discovered by careful attention to the wider 'theological grammar' in which explicit statements about Christ are set.

2. The different linguistic patterns within Paul's language referring to Christ anticipate the christological agenda with which the Christian community has subsequently wrestled. Strongly subordinationist language co-exists with language in which occasionally the name Χριστός, and still more, the title ὁ κύριος, *function* as God-words. This, together with the incarnational language, however hesitant, of 2 Cor. 5.19, suggests that the gap between Pauline theology and the classical christological formulations of later creeds and councils is not as great as has often recently been alleged.

3. The alternatives for the early Christians, as posed by Röhde, of either worshipping Christ or of Christianizing their concept of God, reflect a serious over-simplification. First, the 'Christianizing' of the concept of God may indicate a Marcion-like approach which fails to do justice to the profound continuity between the old and the new. Secondly, the question of whether the early Christians worshipped Christ is not easily answered. But the patterns of linguistic interchange which I have discussed make it more rather than less probable that they

did, and further, that in so doing, they were not thereby displacing God.

4. The interplay between Paul's language about God and his language about Christ shows that the first Christians did not simply 'slot' the Christian kerygma into a pre-existing theistic framework which remained unaltered. Pre-existing framework there was, but no interpretation of the linguistic evidence can avoid the conclusion that in Paul's language about and understanding of God there is both continuity and discontinuity. If it is true that Paul uses God-language in order to interpret and 'define' Christ, it is also true that language about Christ in turn redefines the identity of God. Not only is the 'call' of God refocused, but his power is experienced through the unprecedented medium of the *kerygma* of the crucified Christ. This new experience of God brings into prominence two key words, χάρις and ἀγάπη. And while the grace and love of God are *not* alien to the Old Testament and later Jewish tradition, they are 'revealed' in a new way in the cross and resurrection, with powerfully new, creative effects.

SUMMARY AND CONCLUSIONS

In Romans 9–11 Paul has used traditional language about God in new contexts and new ways. Although in many respects Paul is here being 'a Jew to Jews', much of this traditional language is turned upside-down; Israel's zeal for God, for example, is criticized, not praised (10.2), Gentiles are the recipients of God's mercy and kindness (9.23-26; 11.22), and Israel is the object of God's longsuffering and wrath (9.22).

One of the most important God-words in Paul's writings is the verb καλέω, which is the key word running through the midrashic sections 9.6-13 and 9.14-26. To 'call', therefore, is a central defining activity of God.

God's call now, as in the past, is selective (κατ' ἐκλογήν, 9.11; cf. 1 Cor. 1.26-29). Yet this selection is totally unrelated to the merit or race of the person(s) called. In this matter God demonstrates his sovereign freedom (9.11, 18).

The Scriptures bear witness to this radical understanding of divine grace. (Although the word χάρις does not occur in Romans 9, the concept of grace is implicit, as 11.5-6 show.) But paradoxically and tragically the ethnocentricity and piety created by this divine selectivity had obscured or compromised such an understanding. The many character references, whether positive (of Abraham and Jacob) or negative (of Esau and Pharoah) in Jewish writings provide a marked contrast with the stark theocentricity of Paul.

The 'righteousness' of God is another crucial God-word redeployed and re-defined χωρὶς νόμου by Paul in response to the Judaizing crisis. It thus becomes an important 'bridge-word' between the old and the new, affirming the consistency of God yet pointing to the universal scope of his call and his primary, justifying action (3.21-26, 10.3-4). Here, too, there is an inversion process at work, Israel now finding herself on the outside, Gentiles, through no merit of their own, within the covenant.

Severe God-language is plentiful in Romans 9–11. But here, too, there is evidence of re-minting. God's 'wrath' was traditionally understood as having an educative and reforming function in relation to Israel, but, like God's righteousness, it must now be understood in a non-particularist way (9.17-24). It remains both an historical and an eschatological reality. (Paul especially emphasizes the latter.) The divine wrath works in and through history to bring everyone to the divine mercy (11.32). No-one may presume upon this mercy (9.14-16; 11.19-22), but no-one is irrevocably beyond it either. Even the 'hardening' process which is a consequence of this wrath is not beyond the promise of healing (11.8-32). (In this Paul is similar to the prophets.)

The closing doxology, though similar in style and content to other near-contemporary Jewish doxologies, functions differently by virtue of its context. The sense of mystery and praise contrasts with (a) the anguished bewilderment and (b) the joy at final victory over the nation's enemies which we find in *2 Baruch*.

Although language about Christ is infrequent, 10.1-13 is the central, pivotal section, indicating that the cause of the re-minting of traditional God-language is eschatological and christological.

The problems reflected in 1 Cor. 1.18–3.23 were due to pagan secular, rather than Jewish or Gnostic, influences.

Paul's solution is thoroughly theocentric, yet his theology is informed at every point by a distinction between 'this age' and the new age, and by the cross of Christ.

This whole passage contains remarkable 'clusters' of God-language, and many instances of θεός used in emphatic positions and phrases. A likely explanation for this lies in the Christ party (1.12), and its tendency to allow the figure of Christ to eclipse God.

Paul corrects Corinthian pretensions to wisdom and power by an appeal to Old Testament election, wisdom, and prophetic traditions (1.19, 26-29, 31; 3.19-20), and by employing the motif of the cross as 'un mot de rupture'. Thus Scripture (especially the put-down language of the Wisdom tradition), the cross and God-language exercise jointly a critical function in this passage.

Paul's God-language is marked by the two antitheses of wisdom/foolishness and power/weakness. This antithetical language must be understood eschatologically: what is weak and foolish in this age is strong and wise in the new age, and *vice versa*. The cross and resurrection of Christ are the origin of these eschatological affirmations and antitheses. But Paul does not say that the cross is the power of God. He says that *the word* of the cross is the power of God (1.18; cf. vv. 21, 25).

Despite Paul's indebtedness here to Old Testament traditions, there seems to be no parallel in Jewish traditions for the paradoxical language of 1.25: τὸ μωρὸν τοῦ θεοῦ and τὸ ἀσθενὲς τοῦ θεοῦ. The cross is the origin and explanation of such language, and at the same time the source of a new understanding of God.

Paul's own self-understanding as an apostle (1 Cor. 4.9-13; 2 Cor. 4.7-12; 6.3-10) shows the same antitheses which mark his God- and Christ-language in 1 Cor. 1.18-25. Paul himself therefore must be understood as an εἰκὼν τοῦ θεοῦ, and what he says of himself thus reflects his understanding of God.

In 2 Corinthians the section 2.14–4.6 has a polemical function, countering Jewish-Christian criticisms of Paul's gospel and ministry. Thus θεός-, πνεῦμα- and δόξα-language are all used polemically. θεός-language indicates God as final arbiter and judge, the word πνεῦμα is used in a series of sharp antitheses, contrasting the old dispensation with the new, and the δόξα of Moses is compared unfavourably with that of the apostles (3.12) and of Christians in general (3.18).

Despite frequent assertions by scholars to the contrary, Paul's use of πνεῦμα-language is better explained as having a polemical, rather than an eschatological, emphasis. The eschatological emphasis in Paul's teaching about the Spirit comes in later, not earlier letters (2 Cor. 1.22; 5.5; Rom. 8.23).The most formative influences on his use of πνεῦμα-language were his mission to the Gentiles and the Judaizing crisis.

The reasons for this polemical use of God-language lay, as in Paul's use of δικαιοσύνη θεοῦ, in the Judaizing crisis, and in the Jewish belief that God's Spirit operated only in a limited way (that is, in Jewish enclaves) outside Palestine.

The theological understanding behind this polemical use of Spirit-language provides a close link with the preaching and ministry of Jesus.

In much of his paraenetical teaching, Paul's language is strongly theocentric, the word 'God' frequently having a warranting function. This is particularly clear in Rom. 12.1-15.13.

Not all Paul's God-language is distinctively Christian, but much of it is implicitly christological by virtue of its context. Other God-language is juxtaposed with or alternates with Χριστός-language and κύριος-language, indicating a vital interdependence of language about God and language about Christ.

There is a little evidence (notably in Rom. 13.1-7; 1 Thess. 4.3-8; 1 Cor. 6.12-20) that concentrations of God-language occur where resistance to the teaching in question is expected.

In Galatians, because of its polemical character, God-language is less prominent and Christ-language has a strongly polemical, differentiating function.

Other letters, notably Philippians (but also 1 Corinthians) contain paraenetical teaching much more tightly interwoven throughout the letters. In this respect, the form reflects the message, and Paul's understanding of life lived ὑπὸ χάριν and εἰς δικαιοσύνην.

While sharing with Jewish paraenesis the frequent use of theological warrants, Paul has relatively fewer future tenses, and his aorists have a new focus and content.

Graeco-Roman paraenesis contrasts sharply with Pauline paraenesis in its emphasis on *natura*, its frequent use of prudential and moralistic warrants, and in the common alternation of 'God' and 'gods'.

Not only is much of Paul's God-language implicitly, if not explicitly, christological in content, it is also dependent upon his language about Christ. Indeed, Paul's language about God and about Christ are thoroughly interdependent, but that interdependence is not straightforwardly reciprocal: Paul's Χριστός-language is grammatically subordinate to his θεός-language (the language pattern reflecting theology) while θεός-language points to God as origin, author, warrant and goal.

Yet a kind of equality between God and Christ is implied in the form of the opening salutations, in the exercise by the exalted κυριός of divine functions and prerogatives, and in the occasional application to Christ of a LXX text referring to God.

Certain divine attributes, notably grace, power, love and glory, are attributed also to Christ, indicating God as the source, Christ the means.

In the many juxtapositions of language about God and Christ, two relational terms are outstandingly important, not by their frequency but because of the contexts in which they occur. These are ὁ υἱὸς τοῦ θεοῦ and ὁ πατήρ, the latter becoming a central, defining word in Christian language about God.

2 Cor. 5.19 contains a unique combination of God- and Christ-language ('God in Christ...'), language which Paul the Jew distances himself from by the prefacing ὡς ὅτι.

1 Cor. 8.6 is paradigmatic, pointing to a pattern of 'theological *inclusio*' (God–Christ–God) which is pervasive in Pauline thought and language.

The question with which I have been concerned throughout the course of this study has been the question of whether Paul's language about and understanding of God was affected and changed by his Christian experience. This particular question was prompted, not only by its own intrinsic importance, but also by the remarkable neglect in New Testament scholarship of what the New Testament teaches about God, and the striking difference of opinion among New Testament scholars about whether a new understanding of God is indeed reflected in the writings of Paul. I offer the following conclusions.

1. An imbalance has been created in our understanding of New Testament theology by the tendency to impose artificial distinctions on the New Testament material. While the words eschatological and christological are useful shorthand terms, it is a grave mistake to study 'eschatology' and 'Christology' without regard to the wider 'theological grammar' in which they are set.

2. Paul's thought and writings are *both* theocentric *and* Christocentric; Paul's language about God and his language about Christ are so intertwined that neither can properly be understood without the other. This fact renders invalid the reasons for the neglect of what the New Testament has to say about God. These reasons, referred to in the introduction to this study, were three in number: the Christocentricity of Paul's thought, the assumption that his teaching about God was not distinctive and, thirdly, the belief that Paul could take for granted the theistic world-view of those to whom he was writing.

3. There is abundant evidence in Paul's use of God-language, much of which he inherited from the traditions in which he grew up, to support the contention of John Barton (Introduction, p. 5), that the newness of the Christian faith 'does have an effect on texts. It draws them into fresh conjunctions, destroys existing threads of connection, and establishes new ones'. In short, Paul reworked traditional God-language.

4. This reworking of traditional God-language means that in Paul's language about and understanding of God there is both continuity and discontinuity with the Old Testament and later Jewish language about and understanding of God. This, I submit, explains the divergence of views among New Testament scholars—some, like Sanders, stressing

the continuity but overlooking the discontinuity, others, like Röhde, appearing to verge on a Marcionite view of the God of Israel, and thus neglecting the continuity. Paul does not, however, discard Old Testament language of 'hardening' and 'wrath'. Such language is neither marginal in Paul's writings, nor a relic of his 'Jewish past' (a highly misleading idea), and needs to be interpreted in contemporary expressions of Christian theism.

5. The fact that there *is* discontinuity raises the question of what this discontinuity was. In other words, what was the new understanding of God given to Paul by his faith in Christ?

What we have found in Paul's language about God and about Christ, particularly when compared against the language of Jewish contemporaries and near contemporaries,[1] is evidence that, for Paul, Christ *universalized and radicalized* the Old Testament understanding of the grace and love of God.

1. Limitations of space prevented the inclusion of further detailed comparisons of Paul's language about God with that of his Jewish contemporaries and near-contemporaries. But it can be shown that

a. Paul is strikingly selective in his use of the God-language of the Septuagint,
b. Even the Wisdom of Solomon, for all its bold Hellenistic language, and its universalist *Tendenz* (though it is no more than that), does not break the particularist mould,
c. The elaborate gradations of God-language in Philo, together with his portraits of the good man, point to an understanding of the nature of God different from Paul's in important respects,
d. There is a different 'centre of gravity' in Paul's God-language, compared with the more elaborate names for God, the many differentiating epithets qualifying θεός, and the more frequent theological generalizations found in other Jewish Hellenistic writers,
e. The situation of the Qumran community, as a sect under pressure, shaped its God-language in a way quite different from that of Paul; the language of grace is prominent but it is also particularist language, expressed sometimes in harshly predestinarian terms,
f. The Psalms of Solomon and apocalyptic writings such as *1 Enoch*, *4 Ezra* and *2 Baruch* were in many ways the products of a deepening crisis: the sharp differentiation of 'the righteous' and 'the wicked' reflects a different view of the righteousness of God, while the prayers of the apocalypses reflect a situation in which inherited theological convictions were under severe pressure.

a. The universal dimension of Paul's understanding of God needs little further comment. It can be seen not only in the explicit statement of Rom. 3.29, but also in the total disappearance from his God-language of the particularist expressions which are so plentiful in the Old Testament and in a good deal of later Jewish writing. This may also be the explanation for the absence of military imagery from Paul's God-language.

b. The radicalization of the Old Testament understanding of God's grace and love is both harder to define and more controversial. It must be stressed that here, too, there is continuity and discontinuity. The Abraham argument of Romans 4 shows that Paul did not believe that his statement about the justification of the ungodly was something new; rather, it was rooted in Israel's own self-understanding as reflected in the Scriptures. But this is the first dimension of his 'radicalization' of the Old Testament message. Paul went back to its roots, and, unlike much of contemporary Jewish tradition, did not allow either ethnocentricity or pious veneration of the patriarchs, or perfectly natural criticisms of, for example, Pharaoh, to obscure or compromise the divine freedom working 'by grace' (Rom. 11.5-6) and 'by selection' (Rom. 9.11).

But there is a second dimension to Paul's radicalization of the Old Testament understanding of God's grace and love. This stems from his belief that a new 'initiative' or action had been undertaken by God 'in' and 'through' Christ. The epicentre of that action was the cross and resurrection,which thus constitute the primary source of Paul's new understanding of God. That understanding can best be seen

1. in the restatement of what God in his righteousness *does*—that is, transforms wicked people into righteous people,
2. in the antitheses of power and weakness, wisdom and foolishness by which Paul interprets the cross, and in the light of which he interprets his own life and ministry,
3. in the emphasis on God's mission to the unclean (reflected in Paul's polemical use of πνεῦμα-language),
4. in the sharing by the believing community in the life of God, reflected in the application to the community of the language of grace, love, righteousness, power and glory,
5. in the prominence of the words χάρις, ἀγάπη and πατήρ in his language about God.

There is 'no great gulf fixed' between the theology of Paul and the later theology of the creeds and councils of the patristic period. It is vital that the New Testament be heard on its own terms, and that later doctrines are not read back into New Testament texts. Yet Paul's emphasis on the lordship of Christ as the new and final expression of Jewish monotheism, the incarnational implications of much of his language about Christ, together with the explication of his God-language by its association with Christ-language and Spirit-language, suggest that the later doctrines of the Incarnation and Trinity were the logical consequences of his theological grammar.

Appendix 1

πνεῦμα IN PRE-PAULINE TRADITIONS

The paucity of references to the Spirit in the teaching of Jesus has often been observed. I confine myself here to the Synoptic traditions, inclining to the view that Johannine references to the Spirit, including 'the Paraclete', comprise mostly later material coming from the 'Johannine circle' or the evangelist himself.[1] When due allowance has been made for the editorial work of the evangelists, especially Luke, and for synoptic parallels,[2] we are left with only one or two sayings about the Spirit which may be authentic *logia* of the historical Jesus. These are Mk 13.11 and Lk. 12.10.

Mk 13.11 forms part of the eschatological discourse of ch. 13:

> καὶ ὅταν ἄγωσιν ὑμᾶς παραδίδοντες, μὴ προμεριμνᾶτε τί λαλήσητε, ἀλλ' ὃ ἐὰν δοθῇ ὑμῖν ἐν ἐκείνῃ τῇ ὥρᾳ τοῦτο λαλεῖτε· οὐ γάρ ἐστε ὑμεῖς οἱ λαλοῦντες ἀλλὰ τὸ πνεῦμα τὸ ἅγιον.

Barrett, however, is one scholar who has claimed that the Lukan parallel to this verse (Lk. 21.14-15), which has no reference to the Spirit (θέτε οὖν ἐν ταῖς καρδίαις ὑμῶν μὴ προμελετᾶν ἀπολογηθῆναι), is the oldest form of the saying.[3] That may well be so, but Barrett's observation of the Hebraism in Luke (θέτε ἐν ταῖς καρδίαις ὑμῶν), is not conclusive, since Luke was quite capable of writing Semitic Greek when occasion required it (for example, Lk. 9.51). Marshall[4] notes the debate but his statement that it is 'arbitrary' to say that Mark's reference to the Spirit is 'naturally of Christian origin' rather begs the question of how much Jesus did indeed refer to the Spirit.

The other saying about the Spirit which has the greatest claim to authenticity is Lk. 12.10 (cf. Mt. 12.32): καὶ πᾶς ὃς ἐρεῖ λόγον εἰς τὸν υἱὸν τοῦ ἀνθρώπου, ἀφεθήσεται αὐτῷ· τῷ δὲ εἰς τὸ ἅγιον πνεῦμα βλασφημήσαντι οὐκ ἀφεθήσεται. It is outside the scope of this study to explore fully the difficulties of this saying. Behind the synoptic variants (cf. Mk 3.28-29 and Mt. 12.32) may well

1. See especially C.K. Barrett, *The Holy Spirit and the Gospel Tradition* (London: SPCK, 1947).

2. Editorial references to the Spirit in Luke probably include the following: 1.15, 35, 41, 67, 80; 2.25-27; 4.1, 14, 18; 10.21 (contrast Mt. 11.25).

3. Barrett, *Holy Spirit*, pp. 131-32.

4. I.H. Marshall, *The Gospel of Luke* (Exeter: Paternoster, 1978), pp. 768-69.

lie a reference to the Spirit in the *ipsissima verba Jesu*, but the obscurity of the sayings, and the very existence of the variants, mean that our conclusions are bound to be tentative. Even if the reference to the Spirit is original, it does not seem to provide a basis for the traditional view that Paul's understanding of the Spirit was predominantly eschatological. I suggest, therefore, that there are very few certain references to the Spirit in the teaching of Jesus, and that it is necessary to look elsewhere if we are to find pre-Pauline traditions about the Spirit which Paul may have drawn upon, or which may have shaped his own thought about the Spirit.[1]

What of the period between the crucifixion of Jesus and the writing of the letter to the Thessalonians? What evidence do we have that 'the Spirit' played a prominent part in Christian thought and vocabulary? In the resurrection narratives, Mt. 28.19 and Jn 20.22 seem to be clearly redactional references to the Spirit. The only probably pre-Pauline reference to the Spirit in the writings of Paul occurs in the credal formula quoted by the apostle in Rom. 1.3-4 (κατὰ πνεῦμα ἁγιωσύνης). (I return to the Pauline evidence for this period in a moment.) This leaves, therefore, the evidence of Acts.

While it is not possible to deal fully with all the references to the Spirit in Luke–Acts, it is important for this argument to observe that there are good grounds for thinking that we are dealing primarily with Luke's own editorial work. His hand seems evident in the words attributed to the risen Christ (Lk. 24.44-49), with their reference to 'power from on high' (v. 49), and in the references to the Spirit at Acts 1.2 and 1.8. What, then, remains? Thus far I have argued that all the references to the Holy Spirit either in the resurrection narratives of the Gospels, or in Acts 1, are likely to be redactional. But what of the Lukan account of Pentecost (Acts 2.1-13), and the sermon of Peter which follows (2.14-39), with its references to the Holy Spirit?

It is important to emphasize that the *reality* of the disciples' *experience* is not being questioned here. (That is partly a faith question anyway, not to be decided solely on literary-historical grounds.) I am, however, investigating the extent to which *language* about the Spirit formed a prominent part of Christian vocabulary in the pre-Pauline period. Many commentators have recognized in the Lucan narrative of Acts 2.1-13 a carefully crafted, highly stylized narrative.[2] It is possible that, just as Luke is often said to have distinguished the ascension from the resurrection (there being originally simply the concept of Jesus' exaltation), so he may also have 'made' two events, the resurrection and Pentecost, out of what was originally one event, or at least one complex of events. This is the impression given by John's version (Jn 20.19-23); the probability that most, if not all, the Johannine references to the Spirit are redactional does not rule out the possibility that in this respect John is

1. Isaacs, *Concept*, pp. 139-42, takes issue with scholars such as Barrett who see little evidence of references to the Spirit in the teaching of Jesus, but her argument is somewhat insubstantial: individual *logia* are not discussed in detail ('Jesus could well have...').

2. Haenchen, *Acts*, pp. 173-75, though generally too sceptical of the historical value of Acts, is probably correct here in stressing Luke's purpose and style in crafting this narrative.

nearer to the original nature of the event than Luke is.[1]

Here the Pauline evidence may be said to favour John rather than Luke. First, there is the intriguing statement in 1 Cor. 15.45 that 'the last Adam *became* (sc. ἐγένετο from earlier in the verse) a life-giving Spirit' (εἰς πνεῦμα ζῳοποιοῦν), suggesting that Paul does not always distinguish clearly between the risen Christ and the Spirit.[2] The pre-Pauline tradition which the apostle quotes in 1 Cor. 15.3-7 contains no reference to the outpouring of the Spirit. More important still, Paul includes himself in the list of people to whom the risen Christ appeared (vv. 5-8). There has been much debate about the precise meaning of ἐκτρώματι[3] in this context; but whether it implies that there was a gap in time between the earlier appearances of the risen Christ and his appearance to Paul, Paul's inclusion of himself in this list has important consequences for our interpretation of Luke's version of events, and, probably, for Pauline chronology. Jewett, in a study of Pauline chronology, notes early Christian and Gnostic traditions that the resurrection appearances lasted over a period of 18 months.[4] Although he goes on to describe the historical basis of this datum as 'extremely tenuous', nevertheless Jewett concludes that the conversion of Paul should probably be dated about 18 months, and certainly less than two years, after the crucifixion.[5]

To summarize, when chronological factors are taken into account, together with the paucity of pre-Pauline references to the Spirit in the New Testament, we are faced with a picture rather different from that originally painted. We may at least wonder whether, in the light of the evidence adduced in Chapter 3 (section 3) about the Spirit and *geographical* factors, it was the mission of Paul to the Gentiles and the consequent Judaizing controversy which made the Spirit an issue in Christian theology.

The crucial question then becomes: how prominent was an eschatological understanding of the Spirit in the Old Testament and in Jewish writings and thought at the time of Christian origins? Space precludes an extensive enquiry, but the following points may be made.

First, reference was made in Chapter 3 (p. 166), to Isaacs's conclusion that Jewish Diaspora writers tended to associate the activity of God's Spirit with the past rather than the future; even in the eschatological thought of Palestinian Judaism, God's *ruach* appears not to have featured very prominently. Secondly, the chief question which remains concerns the place of the Spirit in the Old Testament and *the influence of those texts both in Jewish and Christian circles*. Isaacs herself lists the following passages where, in her view, the Spirit is associated with eschatological renewal or fulfilment: Isa. 4.4; 11.4; 32.15; 44.3; Ezek. 11.19; 36.26; 37;

1. Again, I am positing a distinction between the original *experience* in which, I suggest, the experience of the risen Christ and that of the Spirit were indistinguishable, and, on the other hand, the later written accounts.

2. The resurrection seems to have been thought of in a variety of ways. For example, was Jesus raised *by* the Spirit (Rom. 1.3-4), or did he *become* life-giving Spirit (see Conzelmann, *1 Corinthians*, pp. 286-87)?

3. See, for example, Conzelmann, *1 Corinthians*, p. 259.

4. Jewett, *Paul's Life*, pp. 29-30.

5. Jewett, *Paul's Life*.

Joel 2.28-29; Zech. 12.10. This list, however, is almost certainly too long,[1] and attention should probably be focused on only five texts: Isa. 32.15; 44.3; Ezek. 36.26; 37.6 and Joel 2.28. It seems strange that, apart from the Acts 2 passage which we have already discussed, these texts seem not to have featured in Pauline[2] or, as far as we can tell, pre-Pauline Christian thought.

A strand of Jewish thought which was probably more influential in the very earliest Christian days than the Old Testament texts to which we have just referred was the belief that God's messiah would possess the Spirit.[3] That is a likely origin for the first Christian reflections on the Spirit but, as I have suggested, it remains at least probable that it was Paul's mission into Gentile territory which first made the Spirit a theological issue in Jewish and Christian circles.

1. Isa. 4.4 refers to the purging of blood from Zion ἐν πνεύματι κρίσεως καὶ πνεύματι καύσεως. 11.4 is by no means a certain reference to God's Spirit, since πνεύματι here seems to be used with the meaning 'breath' ('breath of the lips'); Ezek. 11.19 is probably a later addition, imitating as it does the later passage in Ezek. 36 (cf. W. Eichrodt, *Ezekiel* [London: SCM Press, 1970], p.111); Zech. 12.10 refers to πνεῦμα χάριστος καὶ οἰκτίρμου, although the use of ἐκχέω here suggests that this may be a reference to the Spirit of God.

2. Even the *catena* of Old Testament quotations at 2 Cor. 6.16-18 including, as it does, words from Ezek. 37, does not include a reference to the Spirit.

3. E.g. *Ps.Sol.* 17.3; 18.7.

Appendix 2

GOD-LANGUAGE IN THE PARAENESIS OF OTHER NEW TESTAMENT EPISTLES

The paraenesis of other New Testament epistles provides interesting similarities with and differences from Pauline paraenesis. Three examples may be briefly mentioned.

First, in the *Haustafeln* of Colossians (3.18–4.1) and Ephesians (5.21–6.9) there are no theological warrants involving the word θεός.

1. In Colossians wives are instructed to submit to their husbands ὡς ἀνῆκεν ἐν κυρίῳ (3.18); children are to obey their parents in everything, τοῦτο γὰρ εὐάρεστόν ἐστιν ἐν κυρίῳ (3.20); references to 'the Lord' similarly underpin the instruction to slaves to obey their lords (3.22, 23, 24, 25). Finally, masters are instructed to be fair as they remember ὅτι καὶ ὑμεῖς ἔχετε κύριον ἐν οὐρανῷ (4.1).

2. In Ephesians the references throughout are to 'Christ' (5.21, 23, 24, 25-27, 29-30, 32; 6.5-6), or 'the Lord' meaning Christ (5.22; 6.1, 4, 7-9. Verses 8-9 could refer to God, but the context makes this unlikely). The only reference to 'God' here occurs in the reference to 'the will of God' in 6.6, a phrase not found in the parallel passage in Colossians which was probably the model for Ephesians.

A number of observations may be made here. First, the versions of the *Haustafeln* found in Colossians and Ephesians[1] are more christological than those in the Pastorals (1 Tim. 2.8-15; 6.1-2, Tit. 2.1-10).[2] Secondly, this raises the question as to whether the writers of Colossians and Ephesians have taken over well-known traditions, adding distinctively Christian warrants. The fact that there are both Jewish and Hellenistic precedents[3] for the New Testament *Haustafeln* gives added point to the inquiry. Apart from the New Testament writers' occasional use of of the concept of 'what is fitting', or an appeal to 'nature', there are no parallels in Hellenistic

1. This is true of Colossians and Ephesians generally (see Appendix 4).

2. The warrants in the Pastorals' versions of the Household Code have a distinctive character of their own: it is the (good) name of God and of the faith which is at stake (1 Tim. 6.1; Tit. 2.5, 10), or else the appeal is to what is 'fitting' (e.g. 1 Tim. 2.10). Here G.E. Cannon (*The Use of Traditional Materials in Colossians* [Macon, GA: Mercer University Press, 1983]) is probably correct in seeing greater Stoic influence in the Pastorals, although he notes that the same motif occurs in Col. 3.18.

3. Cannon, *Traditional Materials*, p.111 .

paraenesis to the theological and christological warrants of the New Testament.[1] More surprisingly, in passages in the Jewish Wisdom literature which seem to anticipate the Household Code, there are few or no theological warrants.[2]

Ethical warrants in the Pastorals are on the whole less theocentric than in Paul's letters. For example, the passage in 1 Timothy outlining the qualities desirable in overseers and deacons (3.1-13) begins with a quotation (πιστὸς ὁ λόγος), and an untheological one at that, and ends with what sounds very much like a pragmatic or utilitarian warrant: 'For those who serve well as deacons gain a good standing for themselves and also great confidence in the faith which is in Christ Jesus' (v. 13). This is typical of other passages in the Pastorals where warrants tend to be prudential rather than theocentric.[3] But while there are a few examples of theocentric warrants,[4] Donelson's observation seems correct: 'the author's perception of God and Jesus as saviours cannot produce specific standards of behaviour'.[5] The author's solution lies in invoking the authority of Paul (and hence of tradition) by the device of pseudonymity, and, secondly, by the authority he invests in the church leaders with whom he is concerned.[6]

Thus there are two patterns discernible in the deutero-Pauline literature: first, a trend towards a more Christocentric perspective (Colossians and Ephesians—and also 2 Thessalonians, see Appendix 4), and secondly, signs of greater secular influences, combined with a stress on tradition and apostolic authority (the Pastorals). The patterns, however, are not uniform: we noted the addition of *theo*logical language in Ephesians, compared with the parallel in Colossians, and warrants in the Pastorals which are tersely theological.

Of the non-Pauline Epistles in the New Testament, 1 Peter most closely resembles the main body of the Pauline literature in the frequency and functions of its God-language, notably its warranting function in paraenesis. 'Wherever the causal ὅτι occurs in 1 Peter, it introduces the theological ground of an ethical injunction.'[7] Usually, the ὅτι is followed by an Old Testament quotation (1.16, 24-25; 2.6; 3.10-12; 5.5, cf. Jas 4.6), whereas Paul resorts to Old Testament quotations quite rarely as warrants for conduct, and when he does so they seldom provide a *theological* reason for the conduct advocated. In this respect, the letter to the Hebrews is closer to 1 Peter than to Paul, with theological warrants derived from Scripture (at 10.30, 37-38; 12.5b, 6, 29; 13.5b, 6). The letter of James, however, is an intriguing mixture. In 4.1-10 theological warrants come thick and fast (vv. 4, 6, 8, 10), with an Old Testament quotation (v.6) or language in the style of the Old Testament (vv. 8 and 10).[8] On the other hand, the description in James 3.1-12 on the dangers of the

1. See the discussion in Chapter 4, section 5.
2. Cannon, *Traditional Materials*, p.117.
3. Cf. 1 Tim. 2.2, although a theological warrant follows.
4. In, e.g., 1 Tim. 5.4.
5. Donelson, *Pseudepigraphy*, p. 155.
6. Donelson, *Pseudepigraphy*, pp. 171 and 198.
7. Selwyn, *1 Peter*, p. 217.
8. See J. Davids, *The Epistle of James* (Grand Rapids, MI: Eerdmans, 1982), pp. 166 and 168 for parallels.

tongue seems more akin to Graeco-Roman moralists with its descriptions, illustrations and moralizing.[1]

Other Epistles, therefore, illustrate still further the rich variety of paraenetic material in the New Testament. Some, like Colossians and Ephesians, are more Christocentric in their emphasis and warrants; others, notably 1 Peter and Hebrews, quote the Jewish Scriptures; others such as the Pastorals reflect rather more secular influence, while still retaining traces of the theological warrants of earlier Jewish and Pauline tradition.

1. Cf. 1.23-24.

Appendix 3

RELIGION IN THE GRAECO-ROMAN WORLD

The clearest expression from Paul himself of the wider religious background in his day is to be found in 1 Cor. 8.5: καὶ γὰρ εἴπερ εἰσὶν λεγόμενοι θεοὶ εἴτε ἐν οὐρανῷ εἴτε ἐπὶ γῆς, ὥσπερ εἰσὶν θεοὶ πολλοὶ καὶ κύριοι πολλοί. We do not, however, glean much else from Paul's pen. It is clear that most of Paul's converts were converts from paganism, but about that paganism Paul says practically nothing.[1] There is a little information elsewhere in the New Testament about the religious background of this period, notably in Acts,[2] but it does not amount to very much. Not surprisingly, the writers of the New Testament did not wish to take up valuable space with unedifying details with which their readers were only too familiar, unless it was directly relevant to their purpose. This appendix, therefore, looks beyond Jewish and Christian literature in order to obtain, in broad outline, the religious trends and theological ideas current in this period.

When we do so, it soon becomes apparent that a fundamental distinction needs to be made between the religious views or 'theo-logy' of an intellectual, or upper-class, minority, and the religious views of the majority. Much of the surviving literature reflects the former; the latter is to be found in the inscriptions, papyri, and hymns of the period.[3] Among those writing on religion in, or about, the time of Paul were Cicero,[4] Plutarch and Seneca.[5] The work of such men may be the basis for Nilsson's assertion that the late Hellenistic period saw the spread of a 'vague

1. 1 Thess. 1.9 refers to what they worshipped before as 'idols', and Gal. 4.8 as 'beings that by nature are not gods' (1 Cor. 10.20 appears to equate idols with demons). Nock, *Conversion*, p. 300 (in a note on the text of p. 221) categorizes the Jewish view of pagan gods as one of the following: (1) angels set by God over the 70 peoples of the world, (2) devils, (3) deified dead men (this in Hellenistic Judaism), and (4) nothing. We must assume that Paul's view approximated to one or more of these. Whether Paul believed that the statues or idols actually *were* the gods cannot be determined. As Grant (*Gods and the One God*, pp. 46-47) points out, this was a matter of debate in the early Christian period.

2. Notably Acts 8.10; 14.8-18; 17.22-31; 19.23-40; 28.8.

3. R. McMullen, *Paganism in the Roman Empire* (New Haven: Yale University Press, 1981), p. 77.

4. 106–43 BCE.

5. See Chapter 4, section 5 for further discussion of Plutarch's and Seneca's God-language.

deism',[1] although the warning against concentrating on only a few writers needs to be heeded.[2]

There are a number of general points which may be made about the religion of the intellectual élite.[3] First, they were well aware of the social function of religion. Cicero in his *De Natura Deorum* argues that 'the disappearance of piety towards the gods will entail the disappearance of loyalty and social union amongst men as well'.[4] It is not surprising that the Roman Empire saw the rise of the Caesar cult, which was not so much a new religious phenomenon as a powerful political expression of old religious traditions such as the Greek apotheosis of heroes, the *parousia* of victorious generals (Greek and Roman), and the Roman cult of the dead, particularly the honouring of statesmen, whether in their lifetime or after their death.[5]

Two particular features of the God-language which appears in this literature are important. One, the tendency to use the words 'god' and 'nature' as virtually synonymous, was noted in an earlier chapter.[6] The other is the bewildering alternation between 'god' and 'gods'.[7] The reason for this lay, in part at least, in the Greek understanding of θεός, to which I return later. But perhaps it is not surprising, in the light of this tendency to assimilate 'god' and 'nature', and to alternate between 'god' and 'gods', that the most contentious theological question of the day was whether the gods did nothing and directed nothing, or whether they determined everything.[8]

1. M. Nilsson, *Greek Piety* (Oxford: Oxford University Press, 1948), p. 118. Much depends on how deism is defined; F.G. Downing, *Strangely Familiar* (Manchester: F.G. Downing, 1985), p. 131, is probably correct in saying of this period that 'deism does not seem to be considered; there is no idea of a creator God who sets things going and then simply lets them run'.
2. R. Lane-Fox, *Pagans and Christians* (London: Viking, 1986), pp. 64-65. Although Lane-Fox's study covers the period from the beginning of the second century CE to Constantine, the slow rate of change to which I refer in this appendix justifies drawing on it (and, e.g., Philostratus) here.
3. Such religion was often virtually indistinguishable from philosophy. Scholars have varied in their views of the impact of these philosophies on the writers of the New Testament. W. Jaeger, *Early Christianity and Greek Paideia* (Oxford: Oxford University Press, 1962), p. 105 n. 2, rejected the nineteenth-century view that Greek philosophy had a direct impact on the New Testament, and particularly on Paul, taking the view that this happened with later writers. Grant (*Early Christian Doctrine*, p. 5) finds 'bridges' in the New Testament towards philosophical doctrines of God. That is a different point from Jaeger's, of course, but the recent researches of Malherbe and others suggest that the gap between Paul and Greek philosophy might not have been, in some respects, as great as Jaeger supposed.
4. 1.1.14 ; cf. H. Liebeschuetz, *Continuity and Change in Roman Religion* (Oxford: Oxford University Press, 1979), p. 50, who notes the Roman view that the success of the community depended on morals (cf. pp. 91-100).
5. S. Weinstock, *Divus Julius* (Oxford: Oxford University Press, 1971), pp. 287-96, and esp. pp. 296-300.
6. See the earlier section on Graeco-Roman paraenesis (Chapter 4, section 5). Cf. Sevenster, *Paul and Seneca*, p. 39. Sevenster cites Ep. 71.16 and many other passages as evidence that Seneca equated the will of God and the laws of nature.
7. Thus also Plutarch in his *De Superstitione*. Such alternation may occur within the same sentence, as in Philostratus's *Vita Apollonii*, 8.7.7: 'they were aware that there is between men and God a certain kinship which enables him alone of all the animal creation to recognize the gods'.
8. So Cicero claimed in his *De Natura Deorum*, 1.1.3. Compare Grant, *Gods*, p. 49.

At the other end of the social scale, there is little doubt that superstition and magic were prominent components of religious belief and practice. Although the magical papyri which have survived and which have been edited and translated[1] come from Egypt and reflect a mainly Graeco-Egyptian syncretism,[2] it is not unreasonable to suppose that they are typical of folk religion elsewhere in the Roman Empire. Similarly, although they come from a wide period, ranging from the early Hellenistic period to late antiquity, there is no evidence of any significant change in popular 'manipulation' of the divine. What people prayed for most was health,[3] although according to Artemidorus' 'Dream Book' (second century CE) people expected more from the gods: 'wealth, health, skill in one's work or profession, happy marriage and safe-child-birth, maintenance of family relationships, emancipation from slavery, safe journeys...'[4]

But while there was a widespread Deuteronomic-like belief that morality and success could not be separated,[5] paganism testified to an element of unpredictability: 'Like an electric current, the power of the gods had great potential for helping and harming; unlike electricity, it was unpredictable'.[6] This is particularly evident in the magical papyri, where the traditional gods and goddesses are often portrayed as capricious, demonic, and even dangerous.[7] Perhaps for this reason the prayers and invocations in the papyri are usually elaborate, describing the god(s)/goddess(es) in careful detail, and often invoking a whole string of gods, or the same god, by many different names.[8]

This brings us to another prominent feature of religion in this period: the interchangeability of the names of gods, or the equation of one god with another. In a period in which 'polytheism knew no bounds',[9] foreign deities could be incorporated into the Graeco-Roman pantheon, either retaining their original names or changing them.[10] Thus the statement of Minucius Felix, *Nec Deo nomen quaeras. Deus nomen est* would have seemed paradoxical or senseless.[11] In such a situation it was not surprising that worshippers could move easily from temple to temple,[12] or that they

1. H.-D. Betz, *The Greek Magical Papyri in Translation* (Chicago: University of Chicago Press, 1986).
2. Betz, *Papyri*, p. xlv.
3. Grant, *Gods*, pp. 57-58.
4. Grant, *Gods*, p. 58.
5. *Philostratus* 1.11. Thus also Liebeschuetz, *Continuity and Change*, pp. 44-45, 91-100.
6. Lane-Fox, *Pagans*, p. 38.
7. Betz, *Papyri*, p. xlv.
8. Of the many examples which could be given from Betz I quote two: 'I call upon you, Zeus, Helios, Mithra, Sarapis, unconquered one, Meliouchos, Melikertes, Meligenetor...' (PGM V, 1-5, Betz, *Papyri*, p. 101); similarly, this prayer to the rising sun: 'Hail, fire's dispenser, world's far-seeing king, O Helios, with noble steeds the eye of Zeus which guards the earth, all-seeing one, Who travels lofty paths, O gleam divine, Who move through the heaven, bright unattainable...' (PGM II, 88-89, *Papyri*, p. 15).
9. E. Bickerman, *Studies in Jewish and Christian History* (Leiden: Brill, 1976), p. 271.
10. Bickerman, *Studies*, pp. 270-73, pp. 273-74.
11. Bickerman *Studies*, p. 270.
12. *Philostratus* 4.40 (although Apollonius was blamed for moving from temple to temple).

spoke of 'choosing' a god. There is a telling phrase in Philostratus's *Vita Apollonii* where Apollonius, recounting the deliverance of Ephesus from plague, attributes the miracle to Hercules because 'I chose him to help me' (ξυνεργὸν δ' αὐτὸν εἱλόμην, ἐπειδὴ σοφός τε καὶ ἀνδρεῖος ὤν).[1].

This polytheism 'without bounds' may help to explain the increasing popularity of the cult of παντὲς καὶ πᾶσαι θεοί in the Greek world of the Hellenistic-Roman period,[2] a feature of this cult being the dedication of altars to ἀγνώστοις θεοίς (Acts 17.23 has ἀγνώστῳ θεῷ). Such a practice may well have been a catch-all insurance policy in the face of a bewildering polytheism, although it is questionable whether this supports the description of the period by E.R. Dodds as 'The Age of Anxiety'.[3]

A widespread consequence of this religious pluralism was an easy-going tolerance. (It is not difficult to see why Jews and Christians were social irritants.) All the more noteworthy is the inscription from Sardis, quoted by Horsley,[4] according to which officials of the cult of Zeus were forbidden to participate in the mysteries of Sabrazios, Agdistis and Ma (Phrygian and Cappadocian deities). (Nor does this seem to have been a short-lived ban, since this edict, probably promulgated in Aramaic in the 4th century BCE, seems to have been translated into Greek some 500 years later.) Nevertheless, one swallow does not make a summer, and the overall picture is one of pluralism, tolerance and tendencies to syncretism.

Such religious complexity should probably be regarded not as evidence of decline, but of a certain life and vitality. According to one recent survey of religion in the early Roman Empire, paganism was experiencing something of a revival.[5] Certainly pagan festivals (according to Apollonius, there is nothing more dear or pleasing to the gods[6]) were for centuries lively foci of social and cultural activity, as well as religious experience.

Other studies support the view that many of the cults of this period were flourishing. In particular, the cults of Asclepius, Isis, Sarapis, and Dionysius spread from the east,[7] while even ancient regional cults lived on. The cult of Baal Shamir,

1. *Philostratus* 8.7.9. Cf. 4.19, where Apollonius advises the religious man on how he can 'best adapt his sacrifice, his libation or prayers to any particular divinity'.

2. Der Horst's essay 'The Unknown God', in R. Van Den Broek (ed.), *Knowledge of God in the Graeco-Roman World* (Leiden: Brill, 1988), pp. 27 and 34.

3. The evidence offered by Lane-Fox, *Pagans*, while showing that anxiety was a factor in *some* of the religious experience of this period, suggests that paganism was far from being totally dominated by fear and anxiety. See especially his chapter 'Seeing the Gods' (pp. 102-67).

4. G.H.R. Horsley, *New Documents Illustrating Early Christianity I* (North Ryde, New South Wales: Macquarie University Press, 1981), pp. 21-23.

5. Lane-Fox, *Pagans*, pp. 34, 74-75. The word 'paganism' deserves a brief comment: Lane-Fox (pp. 30-31), favours the view that *pagani* was originally the Christian slang for the unbaptised—i.e. 'civilians', but the term is used here to denote the mass of religious belief and practice which was neither Jewish nor Christian.

6. *Philostratus* 8.18. Cf. the important summary in Lane-Fox, *Pagans*, p. 259, and McMullen's description of the customs of Stratonicea in SW Asia Minor (McMullen, *Paganism*, pp. 46-48).

7. Grant, *Gods*, pp. 29-42.

for example, persisted in Syria and Phoenicia,[1] while at Thessalonica there was the mystery cult of Cabirus,[2] which was absorbed into the civic cult, maintained by oligarchs in league with Rome, in the Augustan period.[3] The reasons for this were almost certainly political and social.

It is impossible to explore at length the nature and extent of continuity and change in what we have called 'paganism'. As far as continuity is concerned, it is helpful to recall E.R. Dodds's borrowing of Gilbert Murray's image of 'the Inherited Conglomerate' to describe inherited religious ideas and beliefs, for 'religious growth is geological... A new belief-pattern very seldom effaces completely the pattern that was there before'.[4] Changes, however, did occur, and these, together with the great variety already noted, make generalizations hazardous. Nevertheless, a few widespread theological ideas may be discerned.

First, the concept of divine power was ubiquitous. A papyrus catechism which concluded, 'What is a god? That which is strong. What is a king? He who is equal to the divine' was no doubt typical of much religious thought.[5] The concept of divine power was popularly associated with answers to prayer. Inscriptions testify to strong and widespread belief that the gods answer prayers (the themes of which were noted earlier). This was undoubtedly a fundamental reason for the enduring popularity of the pagan cults.[6]

It is difficult to say to what extent ancient concepts of divine power changed over the centuries. Nilsson[7] argued that the 'new cosmology' of the late Hellenistic period and the contemporary concept of power were very closely connected. Particularly interesting for the purpose of this study is his discussion of the appearance of the plural δυνάμεις in religious contexts. This concept seems to have served as a kind of intermediary between the gods and the world, or as a substitute for the presence of the gods themselves.[8] It is one indication of a major difference between Paul and his

1. J. Teixidor, *The Pagan God: Popular Religion in the Graeco-Roman Near East* (Princeton: Princeton University Press, 1977), *passim*, drawing on the evidence of inscriptions and archaeology.

2. Jewett, *Correspondence*, pp. 126-32. Jewett notes also the presence of the mystery religions of Serapis and Dionysius.

3. Jewett, *Correspondence*, p. 131, thinks that this may have created a vacuum for Christianity.

4. E.R. Dodds, *The Greeks and the Irrational* (Berkeley: University of California Press, 1951), p. 179. Murray's own criticism of these 'conglomerates' ('practically no chance of being true or even sensible' [quoted by Dodds on p. 192]) is too sweeping, but the image is a valid one.

5. Nock, *Conversion*, p. 91. A rather similar definition of 'the gods' is given in *Philostratus* 1.11, where a priest identifies the difference between gods and humans not in the fact that the gods are just and wise, but in that humans 'because of their own frailty do not understand their own concerns whereas the gods have the privilege of understanding the affairs both of men and of themselves'.

6. Thus Teixidor, *Pagan God*, p. 14.

7. Nilsson, *Piety*, p. 99 .

8. Nilsson, *Piety*, p. 106, notes the use of δύναμις in Philo, arguing that 'Philo used the word δύναμις to include a single concept the properties and actions of the Jewish God... representing

contemporaries. For them divine power was diffused; for Paul it was not.

The anger of the gods was another leading concept in paganism, although, again, generalizations are hazardous. Lane-Fox, however, links the anger of the gods with their 'honour', and regards these as central to paganism and pagan cults.[1] Some believed that the anger of the gods was capricious,[2] but there were also more thoughtful voices, professing to see a pattern or logic in divine punishments.[3] But co-existing with these beliefs in divine power and anger was a widespread, if often vague, belief in the goodness of the gods. Philostratus, for example, has Apollonius say that God (τὸ θεῖον) cares for the human race.[4]

While it is not possible to enter here into a full evaluation of differences between Paul's language about God and contemporary pagan beliefs and practices, one crucial factor should be noted. The Graeco-Roman religious scene lacks what McMullen calls 'radical monotheism', defined as the kind of monotheism that took power away from every other god.[5]

This brings us to one of the most elusive 'theological' ideas of paganism, namely the meaning of the word θεός. 'The Greek gods are simply basic forms of reality.'[6] The sweeping simplicity of this statement is somewhat elusive but it can serve as a starting point for the observation that in the ancient world there seems not to have been what Kierkegaard was later to call an 'infinite qualitative difference' between gods and humans. Whether Pindar's famous line ἑν ἀνδρῶν, ἑν θεῶν γένος ἐκ μιᾶς δὲ πνέομεν ματρὸς ἀμφότεροι[7] was true of later thinking is difficult to determine, but it almost certainly represents a pervasive, persistent strand in pagan thinking. Thus there is a readiness to speak of humans being 'gods'.[8] Even in more monotheistic thought, 'God' can be both identified with 'the things that are' and also differentiated from them.[9]

What is much clearer than the theological presuppositions behind the language about God and the gods is the social consequences of it. The theological fundamental for the Jews that 'there is but one God with power to determine finally all human affairs, judging all by transcendent standards and showing no partiality' was the basis for their social distinctiveness.[10] This was true also for the Christians, although

them as active powers and intermediaries between God and the world, and now and then identifying them with the angels' (cf. Rom. 8.38).

1. Lane-Fox, *Pagans*, pp. 38, 95, 694.
2. Betz, *Papyri*, p. xlv.
3. Plutarch, *De Sera Num.* 551C, quoted by Downing, *Strangely Familiar*, p. 153.
4. *Philostratus* 2.5.
5. McMullen, *Paganism*, p. 88.
6. *TWNT*, III, p. 68.
7. Quoted in *TWNT*, III, p. 71. Cf. *Philostratus* 8.7.7.
8. Thus, e.g., *Philostratus* 3.31. Kleinecht (*TWNT*, III, p. 68) notes that statesmen and emperors could be called 'gods'.
9. Thus Apollonius in his letter to Valerius (Ep. LVIII, *Philostratus* II, pp. 455-61), identifies the 'first essence' (πρώτην οὐσίαν) and the eternal God (θεὸς ἀΐδιος), but a few sentences further on speaks of (the) God who is in charge of reality: εἰ τάξις δὲ τῶν ὄντων ἔστι δέ, καὶ θεὸς ἐπιστατεῖ ταύτης...
10. Meeks, *Moral World*, p. 92.

the inclusiveness which they showed (Gal. 3.28), combined with their 'radical monotheism',[1] was no doubt a baffling mixture to many of their contemporaries.

1. It is difficult to be sure exactly what Paul means in 1 Cor. 8.5-6. Does he deny the existence of other 'gods'? Does the ἡμῖν mean, in effect, 'in our experience' (cf. Chapter 5, section 5)? Perhaps, as a recent writer has suggested (B. Lang in C. Geffré and J.-P. Jossna, *Concilium*: *Monotheism* [Edinburgh: T. & T. Clark, 1985], pp. 41-49), it would be more appropriate to speak of a soteriological monotheism at this stage, rather than a dogmatic monotheism.

Appendix 4

CHRIST-LANGUAGE IN THE DEUTERO-PAULINES.

It is not my purpose here to analyse in detail the language which the deutero-Pauline letters use about Christ. There are, however, some significant differences from the genuine Pauline letters which are relevant to this study and therefore worth summarizing here. Two preliminary points about method should be made first of all. First, I simply assume the deutero-Pauline authorship of 2 Thessalonians, Colossians and Ephesians and the Pastorals. Such an assumption is based on a wide consensus in New Testament scholarship, although, in the case of Colossians and perhaps 2 Thessalonians, the consensus is not as great as it is in the case of Ephesians and the Pastorals.[1] Secondly, I am not using the evidence set out below to 'prove' non-Pauline authorship. To label any word or characteristic as 'unPauline' must always be a hazardous undertaking. In each instance the case for non-Pauline authorship is a cumulative one. But the evidence of this section may at least be cited as a small part of that cumulative case.

Some deutero-Paulines show a small but marked shift away from God-language to Christ-language. The trend is clearest in 2 Thessalonians, but can be seen also in Colossians and Ephesians. First, in 2 Thessalonians there are several christological expressions not found in Paul. Thus we have:

1.8: τῷ εὐαγγελίῳ τοῦ κυρίου ἡμῶν Ἰησοῦ. Paul has both 'the gospel of God' and 'the gospel of Christ' (see the earlier reference in Chapter 5, pp. 278-79 n. 2). But whereas in Paul Χριστοῦ is almost certainly an objective genitive, here it is probably subjective.[2]

1.9: ἀπὸ προσώπου τοῦ κυρίου. Marshall[3] comments, 'it is significant that language originally used of Yahweh is here applied to Jesus'.

2.14: εἰς περιποίησιν δόξης τοῦ κυρίου ἡμῶν Ἰησοῦ Χριστοῦ. Although Paul frequently has 'the glory of God' (for example, 1 Cor. 10.31) or 'the glory of the Father' (for example, Phil. 2.11), Paul writes of 'the glory of Christ' only as a

1. For recent studies arguing that 2 Thessalonians and Colossians are deutero-Pauline, see G.S. Holland, *The Tradition that you Received from us: 2 Thessalonians in the Pauline Tradition* (Tübingen: Mohr, 1988) and M. Kiley, *Colossians as Pseudepigraphy* (Sheffield: JSOT Press, 1986). For the traditional view, see Marshall, *1 and 2 Thessalonians*, and P. O'Brien, *Colossians and Ephesians* (Waco, TX: Word Books, 1982) respectively.

2. Contra Marshall, *1 and 2 Thessalonians*, p. 178.

3. Marshall, *1 and 2 Thessalonians*, pp. 179-80.

description of apostles (2 Cor. 8.23) and at 2 Cor. 4.4, where, significantly, he goes on to describe Christ as εἰκὼν τοῦ θεοῦ.

3.1: ὁ λόγος τοῦ κυρίου. This expression occurs in Paul's writings only at 1 Thess. 1.8. Commenting on this verse, Holtz contends that early Jewish-Christianity preferred λόγος with θεοῦ.[1]

The most significant evidence, however, comes in those verses which offer close parallels with 1 Thessalonians, and which, on the assumption of deutero-Pauline authorship, are presumably modelled on 1 Thessalonians. These are:

2.13: ἠγαπημένοι ὑπὸ κυρίου (A few later witnesses have θεοῦ). The earlier part of this verse closely parallels 1 Thess. 2.13, but earlier in that letter (1.4) Paul, in a thanksgiving for the Thessalonians' faith, refers to them as ἠγαπημένοι ὑπὸ (τοῦ) θεοῦ.

2.16-17: αὐτὸς δὲ ὁ κύριος ἡμῶν Ἰησοῦς Χριστὸς καὶ (ὁ) θεὸς ὁ πατὴρ ἡμῶν ὁ ἀγαπήσας ἡμᾶς...παρακαλέσαι ὑμῶν τὰς καρδίας καὶ στηρίξαι ἐν παντὶ ἔργῳ καὶ λόγῳ ἀγαθῷ. There is a close parallel to this prayer-wish in 1 Thess. 3.11-13, where, however, the reference to God precedes the reference to Jesus. Marshall[2] suggests that Jesus is mentioned first because 'Paul's thought in the preceding verses tends to be centred on Jesus'. But this is hardly correct, θεός occurring in vv. 11 and (twice) 13.

3.3: πιστὸς δέ ἐστιν ὁ κύριος. This expression is in striking contrast with the Pauline πιστὸς δέ ἐστιν ὁ θεός used by the apostle at 1 Cor. 10.13 and 2 Cor. 1.18 (cf. 1 Thess. 5.24: πιστὸς ὁ καλῶν).

3.16: αὐτὸς δὲ ὁ κύριος τῆς εἰρήνης. Paul has ὁ θεὸς τῆς εἰρήνης, and similar expressions at Rom. 15.33, 1 Cor. 14.33, 2 Cor. 13.11, Phil. 4.9 and, in a verse which provides the model here, 1 Thess. 5.23 (αὐτὸς δὲ ὁ θεὸς τῆς εἰρήνης).[3]

This shift from God to Christ is less marked in Colossians and Ephesians. Nevertheless in Colossians we have:

3.11: ἀλλὰ (τὰ) πάντα καὶ ἐν πᾶσιν Χριστός. This resounding phrase ends an extended reference to the kind of life expected in the new community of Christ, where (ὅπου) 'there cannot be Greek and Jew, circumcised and uncircumcised, barbarian, Scythian, slave, freeman, but Christ...' In 1 Cor. 15.28 Paul applies the same phrase to God (ἵνα ᾖ ὁ θεὸς [τὰ] πάντα ἐν πᾶσιν).[4]

1. Holtz, *An die Thessalonicher*, p. 51 n.132.

2. Marshall, *1 and 2 Thessalonians*, p. 211.

3. Marshall, *1 and 2 Thessalonians*, p. 230, commenting on 2 Thess. 3.16, writes of 'a certain tendency in this letter to ascribe to Jesus qualities or activities elsewhere ascribed to the Father', but does not relate this to the question of authorship (cf. p. 40). Holland, *The Tradition*, identifies five 'major' tendencies within 2 Thessalonians which he thinks mark it out as un-Pauline. One of these is 'the exaltation of the figure of Christ and the consequent eclipse of the Father in 2 Thessalonians' (p. 85). This is to overstate the case, but Holland in my view is substantially correct. His own list of texts (pp. 85-86) coincides very closely with that given here, although I have omitted 2 Thess. 1.12b (κατὰ τὴν χάριν τοῦ θεοῦ ἡμῶν καὶ κυρίου Ἰησοῦ Χριστοῦ), where the phraseology is ambiguous. (Marshall, however [p. 40], dismisses it a little too easily).

4. Eph. 1.23 has a reference to τὸ πλήρωμα τοῦ τὰ πάντα ἐν πᾶσιν πληρουμένου. Here,

3.15: ἡ εἰρήνη τοῦ Χριστοῦ. This is almost certainly the original reading despite some variant readings with θεοῦ, and contrasts with Phil. 4.7 which has ἡ εἰρήνη τοῦ θεοῦ.[1]

3.16: ὁ λόγος τοῦ Χριστοῦ. Again, Χριστοῦ is probably the original reading, despite the MSS variants κυρίου and θεοῦ. Although (as noted in the previous section) Paul uses the expression ὁ λόγος τοῦ κυρίου, he nowhere has ὁ λόγος τοῦ Χριστοῦ.

4.3: τὸ μυστήριον τοῦ Χριστοῦ. Here the MSS variants are far fewer. (Cf. Eph. 3.4, where the same expression occurs.) We should not, however, overlook Col. 2.2, where the probable reading—here there are many variants—is τοῦ μυστηρίου τοῦ θεοῦ, Χριστοῦ. In the undisputed Paulines the phrase 'the mystery of Christ' does not occur. Instead we have τὸ μυστήριον τοῦ θεοῦ at 1 Cor. 2.1.

Three more examples are relevant here in that they contain expressions different from the genuine Paulines:

3.13: καθὼς καὶ ὁ κύριος ἐχαρίσατο ὑμῖν. This is a less weighty example (even if Χριστός is read here), since Paul has καθὼς καὶ ὁ Χριστὸς προσελάβετο ἡμᾶς at Rom. 15.7. The contexts, however, are different, as the other Christ-language in Colossians quoted here shows (cf. also Rom. 14.3).

3.17: καὶ πᾶν ὅ τι ἐὰν ποιῆτε ἐν λόγῳ ἢ ἐν ἔργῳ, πάντα ἐν ὀνόματι κυρίου Ἰησοῦ. A very similar sentiment is expressed in 1 Cor. 10.31, but without the reference to Christ: εἴτε τι ποιεῖτε, πάντα εἰς δόξαν θεοῦ ποιεῖτε. The references to τῷ θεῷ, however, in vv. 16 and 17 of the Colossians passage must not be overlooked.

3.24: τῷ κυρίῳ Χριστῷ δουλεύετε. Again, despite MSS variants, this seems to be the original reading, but the expression ὁ κύριος Χριστός does not occur in Paul.

It needs to be borne in mind that the writer of Ephesians almost certainly used Colossians as a 'model' or 'base' for his own letter.[2] Thus the phrase ἐν τῷ μυστηρίῳ τοῦ Χριστοῦ (3.4) seems to be a borrowing from Col. 4.3. But in one instance the writer alters the wording of Colossians in a more *theo*-logical direction: where Colossians has καθὼς καὶ ο κύριος ἐχαρίσατο ὑμᾶς (3.13), Ephesians has καθὼς καὶ ὁ θεὸς ἐν Χριστῷ ἐχαρίσατο ὑμῖν (4.32). On the whole, however, Ephesians reflects the same pattern we have detected in 2 Thessalonians and Colossians, and we note the main examples below.

4.5-6: εἷς κύριος, μία πίστις, ἓν βάπτισμα, εἷς θεὸς καὶ πατὴρ πάντων. Here there is a reversal of the order found in the credal formula at 1 Cor. 8.6, which referred first to εἷς θεός, and secondly to εἷς κύριος.

5.5: ἐν τῇ βασιλείᾳ τοῦ Χριστοῦ καὶ θεοῦ. The word order here (the probable

however, it is not certain whether the reference is to God or to Christ. (See Houlden, *Paul's Letters*, p. 277).

1. The uncial A has Χριστοῦ here, but the weight of the evidence is strongly in favour of reading θεοῦ.

2. C.L. Mitton, *The Epistle to the Ephesians* (Oxford: Oxford University Press, 1951).

reading, despite the evidence of a few MSS reading τοῦ θεοῦ καὶ Χριστοῦ) is indicative of the trend we are observing in the deutero-Paulines.[1]

5.10: δοκιμάζοντες τί ἐστιν εὐάρεστον τῷ κυρίῳ. Normally εὐάρεστον is followed by τῷ θεῷ in Paul (Rom. 12.1; 14.18; Phil. 4.18), although Col. 3.20 has τοῦτο γὰρ εὐάρεστόν ἐστιν ἐν κυρίῳ.

5.17: τὸ θέλημα τοῦ κυρίου. θέλημα always with τοῦ θεοῦ, expressed or understood, in Paul (for example, 1 Thess. 5.18).

5.19: ψάλλοντες τῇ καρδίᾳ ὑμῶν τῷ κυρίῳ. Here there is a contrast with Col. 3.16, which refers to singing to *God*. Both Col. 3.17 and Eph. 5.20, however, have a reference to giving thanks to God.

These are the most striking, although not the only[2] examples in Colossians and Ephesians of a shift from theocentric to Christocentric language.

The Pastorals, it has often been remarked, seem to operate on a rather more mundane level than either Paul or the interpreters of Paul whom we have so far considered. This may be to do less than justice to the particular genre to which they belong.[3] Nevertheless the relative infrequency of θεός-, Χριστός-, κύριος- and πνεῦμα-language compared with other letters bearing the name of Paul is unmistakable.[4] Pauline words occur, but in phrases or contexts very different from those in which they occur in the undisputed Paulines (for example, 'Timothy' is exhorted to 'pursue' δικαιοσύνη, 1 Tim. 6.11; 2 Tim. 2.22). The pattern we have discerned in 2 Thessalonians, Colossians and Ephesians, however, is not so clear here. But there are a few new expressions which may reflect the same shift to a rather more Christocentric theology. Again, I list the most obvious examples:

1 Tim. 1.12: χάριν ἔχω τῷ ἐνδυναμώσαντί με Χριστῷ Ἰησοῦ τῷ κυρίῳ ἡμῶν. This expression is noteworthy, since in Paul's writings the apostle always expresses thanks to God, whether in the more exclamatory χάρις τῷ θεῷ (as in 2 Cor. 9.15), or with the verb εὐχαριστῶ (as in Phil. 1.3).

1 Tim. 1.14: ὑπερπλεόνασεν δὲ ἡ χάρις τοῦ κυρίου ἡμῶν. This probably refers to Christ, in view of the earlier reference (v. 12) to 'Christ Jesus our Lord', and in spite of the immediately following reference to 'the faith and love which are in

1. Col. 1.13 refers to the kingdom τοῦ υἱοῦ τῆς ἀγάπης αὐτοῦ, but Eph. 5.5 seems to be a development of an older paraenetic tradition, used by Paul at Gal. 5.21 and 1 Cor. 6.9-10, which refers to 'inheriting' the kingdom of God.

2. In Appendix 2 I noted briefly the predominance of Christ-language of the *Haustafeln* (Col. 3.18–4.1; Eph. 5.21–6.9) in contrast with the, on the whole, more theocentric character of Pauline paraenesis.

3. On this, see, for example, Donelson, *Pseudepigraphy*.

4. Morgenthaler, *Statistik*, gives the following statistics:

θεός: 1 Timothy 22 occurrences, 2 Timothy 13, Titus 13 (compare 36 and 31 for 1 Thessalonians and Galatians respectively).

Χριστός: 1 Timothy 15 occurrences, 2 Timothy 13, Titus 4 (compare 10 and 37 for 1 Thessalonians and Galatians respectively).

κύριος: 1 Timothy 6 occurrences, 2 Timothy 16, Titus 5 (compare 24 and 6 for 1 Thessalonians and Galatians).

πνεῦμα: 1 Timothy 3 occurrences, 2 Timothy 3, Titus 1 (compare 5 and 18 for 1 Thessalonians and Galatians).

Christ Jesus'. The language recalls that of Romans 5, especially vv. 15 and 20. But here Paul speaks of ἡ χάρις τοῦ θεοῦ (v. 15), for which ἡ χάρις elsewhere in this passage is an abbreviation, references to Christ usually being preceded by ἐν or διά.[1]

1 Tim. 5.21: Διαμαρτύρομαι ἐνώπιον τοῦ θεοῦ καὶ Χριστοῦ Ἰησοῦ (cf. 6.13 and 2 Tim. 4.1). Here we have the appearance of an oath formula referring to both God and Jesus (although always in that order). Paul mostly refers to God in oath-formulae, but the remarkably strong expression of 1 Thess. 5.27 should not be overlooked (Ἐνορκίζω ὑμᾶς τὸν κύριον), κύριον almost certainly referring, in this personal context, to Christ.[2]

2 Tim. 4.17: ὁ δὲ κύριός μοι παρέστη καὶ ἐνεδυνάμωσέν με.[3] This verse may be further evidence of a tendency to use κύριος-language where Paul would probably have referred to 'God'.

Tit. 2.13: τῆς δόξης τοῦ μεγάλου θεοῦ καὶ σωτῆρος ἡμῶν Ἰησοῦ Χριστοῦ. As with 2 Thess. 1.12, it is impossible to be certain that this is a reference to God *and* to Christ, but both verses may be among the very few instances in the New Testament where Jesus is called God .[4]

In conclusion, we must be careful in evaluating this evidence that we do not speak of theocentric and Christocentric approaches as if they were antithetical. John's Gospel is an example of a document which is both theocentric and christocentric. So, too, as this study has shown, are the writings of Paul. Nevertheless, the evidence of the deutero-Paulines seems to point towards a growth in κύριος- and Χριστός-language. The milieux from which these letters came seem to have been ones where more κύριος and Χριστός expressions were used in contexts where a generation of Christian believers closer to its Jewish roots would probably have referred to 'God'.

1. See the discussion in section 1 of Chapter 5.
2. See p. 290 in Chapter 5.
3. 2 Cor. 12.8 should not be forgotten, but the *ambiguity* of κύριος-language in 2 Timothy (there are no examples in Titus, and in 1 Timothy κύριος hardly ever occurs except in the title 'our Lord Jesus Christ') is noteworthy: it is often not clear whether the reference is to Jesus or to God (e.g. 2 Tim. 1.16, 18; 2.7, 14, 22, 24; 3.11; 4.8, 14, 17, 18, 22). There are similar ambiguities in Acts, but proportionately fewer in Paul.
4. See Taylor, *New Testament Essays*, pp. 83-89.

Appendix 5

THE ἐν κυρίῳ FORMULA

The ἐν κυρίῳ formula occurs over 30 times altogether in the genuinely Pauline letters, most often in Romans 16 and, given its length, in Philippians. Käsemann considers the expression parallel to 'in Christ', and thinks that it was probably coined by Paul himself. With reference to this enquiry I note the following points:

1. Although Paul rarely uses the expression ἐν θεῷ, it occurs occasionally—notably in the opening greeting of 1 Thessalonians (τῇ ἐκκλησίᾳ Θεσσαλονικέων ἐν θεῷ πατρί) (cf. 2 Thess. 1.1).

2. The expression ἐν κυρίῳ, although very rare in the LXX, occurs occasionally, as in 1 Sam. 2.1 in the Song of Hannah: Ἐστερεώθη ἡ καρδία μου ἐν κυρίῳ, and in an oath formula in 1 Sam. 24.22: καὶ νῦν ὄμοσόν μοι ἐν κυρίῳ (cf. 1 Kgs 28.10, although not all MSS have ἐν κυρίῳ here). Other examples of ἐν κυρίῳ are 1 Sam. 10.22 and 2 Sam. 19.7 and 1 Kgs 2.8. It occurs also in Wis. 5.15 in the statement ἐν κυρίῳ ὁ μισθὸς αὐτῶν.

But although there are a few LXX parallels (in the literal sense), the phrase should be understood in the light of the discussion in Chapter 5—that is, to be 'in the Lord' is to acknowledge (with one's life and being) the sovereignty of the Lord Christ, a lordship which, as we have seen, is the new and universal expression of the sovereignty of the God of Israel.[1]

Yet before we oversimplify the matter by identifying 'the Lord' too closely with God, we should note the observation of F. Büchsel,[2] that there are 'distinctive parallels' (p. 158) between ἐν κυρίῳ and ἐν νόμῳ which in his view cannot be accidental, since for Paul Christ stands in Christian faith where the law stands in Judaism. There is thus a *twofold* process of 'transference' occurring in Paul's κύριος-language: the title κύριος functions at times parallel with, and as a substitute for, ὁ θεός, and, secondly, if Büchsel is correct, it functions in the ἐν κυρίῳ formula as a subsitute for the law.

1. Cf. Grayston, *Dying We Live*, p. 390.
2. F. Büchsel, '"In Christus" bei Paulus', *ZNW* 42 (1943), pp. 141-58.

BIBLIOGRAPHY

Primary Texts and Principal Sources

Aberbach, M., and B. Grossfeld (eds.), *Targum Onkelos to Genesis* (New York: Ktav, 1982).

Babbit, F.C. (ed.), *Plutarch's Moralia*, II (Loeb translation; London: Heinemann, 1928).

Basore, J.W. (ed.), *Seneca's Moral Essays*, I (Loeb translation; London: Heinemann, 1928).

Betz, H.-D. (ed.), *The Greek Magical Papyri in Translation* (Chicago: University of Chicago Press, 1986).

Brenton, L.L. (trans.), *The Septuagint Version of the Old Testament* (London: S. Bagster & Sons, n.d.).

Charlesworth, J.H. (ed.), *Old Testament Pseudepigrapha* (2 vols.; London: Darton, Longman & Todd, 1983, 1985).

Colson, F.H., G.H. Whitaker *et al.* (eds.), *Philo* (12 vols.; Loeb translation; London: Heinemann, 1929–53).

Conybeare, F.C. (ed.), *The Life of Apollonius of Tyana* (2 vols.; Loeb translation; London: Heinemann, 1912).

Danby, H. (ed.), *The Mishnah* (Oxford: Oxford University Press, 1933).

Déaut, R. le (ed.), *Targum du Pentateuque Tome i Genèse* (Paris: Les Editions du Cerf, 1978).

Freedman, H., and M. Simon (eds.), *Midrash Rabbah* (10 vols.; London: Soncino Press, 1939).

Gummere, R.M. (ed.), *Seneca Epistulae Morales*, I–III (Loeb translation; London: Heinemann, 1925–34).

Helmbold, W.C. (ed.), *Plutarch's Moralia*, VI (Loeb translation; London: Heinemann, 1939).

Horsley, G.H.R. (ed.), *New Documents Illustrating Early Christianity I* (North Ryde, New South Wales, Macquarie University Press, 1981).

Hübner, H. (ed.), *Wörterbuch zur Sapientia Salomonis* (Göttingen: Vandenhoeck & Ruprecht, 1985).

Lauterbach, J.Z. (ed.), *Mekilta* (3 vols.; Philadelphia: Jewish Publication Society of America, 1933–35).

Nestle, E. (ed.), *Novum Testamentum Graece* (Stuttgart: Deutsche Bibelgesellschaft,, 1979).

Oldfather, W.A. (ed.), *Arrian's Discourses of Epictetus* (2 vols.; Loeb translation; London: Heinemann, 1925, 1928).

Staniforth, M. (ed.), *Early Christian Writings* (Harmondsworth: Penguin, 1968).

Stevenson, J. (ed.), *A New Eusebius* (London: SCM Press, 1968).

Vermes, G. (ed.), *The Dead Sea Scrolls in English* (Harmondsworth: Pelican, 1962, 1975).

Except where otherwise stated, quotations in translation from the Old Testament, Apocrypha and New Testament are taken from the NRSV.

General Bibliography

Allo, E.B., *Saint Paul: Seconde épître aux Corinthiens* (Paris: Gabalda, 2nd edn, 1956).
Anderson, A.A., *Psalms* (2 vols.; London: Marshall, Morgan & Scott, 1972).
Arrington, F.L., *Paul's Aeon Theology in 1 Corinthians* (Washington, DC: University Press of America, 1978).
Aune, D.E., *The New Testament in its Literary Environment* (Cambridge: J. Clarke, 1988).
Badenas, R., *Christ the End of the Law: Romans 10.4 in Pauline Perspective* (Sheffield: JSOT Press, 1985).
Bailey, K.E., 'Recovering the Poetic Structure of 1 Corinthians 1.17–2.2', *NovT* 17.4 (1975), pp. 265-96.
Barclay, J.M.G., *Obeying the Truth: A Study of Paul's Ethics in Galatians* (Edinburgh: T. & T. Clark, 1988).
Barr, J., *Holy Scripture, Canon and Authority* (Oxford: Oxford University Press, 1983).
—'Abba Isn't Daddy', *JTS* NS 39.1 (1988), pp. 28-47.
Barrett, C.K., *The Holy Spirit and the Gospel Tradition* (London: SPCK, 1947).
—*The Epistle to the Romans* (London: A. & C. Black, 1957).
—*The Pastoral Epistles* (Oxford: Clarendon Press, 1963).
—*The First Epistle to the Corinthians* (London: A. & C. Black, 1968).
—*The Second Epistle to the Corinthians* (London: A. & C. Black, 1973).
—*Essays on Paul* (London: SPCK, 1982).
Bartlett, J.R., *Jews in the Hellenistic World: Josephus, Aristeas, the Sibylline Oracles, Eupolemus* (Cambridge: Cambridge University Press, 1985).
Barton, J., *People of the Book?* (London: SPCK, 1988).
Bassler, J.M., *Divine Impartiality* (SBLDS 59; Chico, CA: Scholars Press, 1982).
Bauckham, R., 'The Apocalypses in the New Pseudepigrapha', *JSNT* 26 (1986), pp. 97-117.
Baumann, R., *Mitte und Norm des Christlichen: Eine Auslegung von 1 Korinther 1.1–3.4* (Münster: Aschendorff, 1968).
Beale, G.K., 'The Old Testament Background of Reconciliation in 2 Corinthians 5–7 and its Bearing on the Literary Problem of 2 Corinthians 6.14–7.1', *NTS* 35.4 (1989), pp. 550-81.
Beker, J.C., *Paul the Apostle* (Edinburgh: T. & T. Clark, 1980).
Best, E., *1 Peter* (London: Marshall, Morgan & Scott, 1971).
—*A Commentary on the First and Second Epistles to the Thessalonians* (London: A. & C. Black, 1972).
—'The Use and Non-Use of *Pneuma* by Josephus', *NovT* 3, pp. 218-25.
Best, E., and R.McL. Wilson (eds.), *Text and Interpretation: Studies in the New Testament Presented to M. Black* (Cambridge: Cambridge University Press, 1979).
Betz, H.-D., 'The Literary Composition and Function of Paul's Letter to the Galatians', *NTS* 21 (1975), pp. 353-79.

—*Galatians: A Commentary on Paul's Letter to the Churches in Galatia* (Philadelphia: Fortress Press, 1979).

Bickerman, E., *Studies in Jewish and Christian History*, III (Leiden: Brill, 1976).

Black, M. (ed.), *The Scrolls and Christianity* (London: SPCK, 1969).

Black, M., *Romans* (London: Marshall, Morgan & Scott, 1973).

—'The Christological Use of the Old Testament in the New Testament', *NTS* 18 (1972), pp. 1-14.

Boer, W. den, *Private Morality in Greece and Rome* (Leiden: Brill, 1979).

Boers, H., *What is New Testament Theology?* (Philadelphia: Fortress Press, 1979).

—'The Form-Critical Study of Paul's Letters. 1 Thessalonians as a Case-Study', *NTS* 22, pp. 140-58.

Bonhoeffer, D., *Letters and Papers from Prison* (London: Fontana, 1963).

Bornkamm, G., *Early Christian Experience* (London: SCM Press, 1969).

Bornstad, R.G., 'Governing Ideas of the Jewish War of Flavius Josephus' (dissertation, Yale University, 1979).

Borret, M. (trans.), *Origène: Homélies sur l'exode* (Paris: Editions du Cerf, 1985).

Borse, U., *Der Brief an die Galater* (Regensburger Neues Testament; Regensburg: Pustet, 1984).

Bousset, W., *Kyrios Christos* (Nashville: Abingdon Press, 1970).

Branick, V.P., 'Source and Redaction Analysis of 1 Corinthians 1–3', *JBL* 101 (1982), pp. 251-69.

Brinsmead, B.H., *Galatians—Diaological Response to Opponents* (Chico, CA: Scholars Press, 1982).

Broek, R. Van Den (ed.), *Knowledge of God in the Graeco-Roman World* (Leiden: Brill, 1988).

Bruce, F.F., *The Acts of the Apostles* (London: Tyndale, 1951).

—*The Epistle to the Galatians* (Exeter: Paternoster, 1982).

—*1 and 2 Thessalonians* (WBC 45; Waco, TX: Word Books, 1982).

Büchsel, F., '"In Christus" bei Paulus', *ZNW* 42 (1943), pp. 141-58.

Bultmann, R., *Jesus* (London: Collins, 1958).

—*Theology of the New Testament* (2 vols.; London: SCM Press, 1952, 1955).

—*Der zweite Brief an die Körinther* (Göttingen: Vandenhoeck & Ruprecht, 1985).

Bünker, M., *Briefformular und rhetorische Disposition im Korintherbrief* (Göttingen: Vandenhoeck & Ruprecht, 1983).

Buren, P. van, *The Edges of Language* (London: SCM Press, 1972).

Byrne, B., *'Sons of God'—Seed of Abraham* (Rome: Biblical Institute Press, 1979).

Cadbury, H., *The Peril of Modernizing Jesus* (London: SPCK, 1962 [1937).

Campbell, W.S., 'Why Did Paul Write Romans?', *ExpTim* 85.9 (1974), pp. 264-69.

—'The Romans Debate', *JSNT* 10 (1981), pp. 19-28.

—'The Freedom and Faithfulness of God in Relation to Israel', *JSNT* 13 (1984), pp. 27-45.

Cannon, G.E., *The Use of Traditional Materials in Colossians* (Macon, GA: Mercer University Press, 1983).

Carrez, M., *La deuxième épître de Saint Paul aux Corinthiens* (Geneva: Labor et Fides, 1986).

Carrington, P., *The Primitive Christian Catechism* (Cambridge: Cambridge University Press, 1940).

Carson, D.A., and H.G.M. Williamson (eds.), *It is Written: Scripture Citing Scripture* (Cambridge: Cambridge University Press, 1988).
Cerfaux, L., *Recueil Lucien Cerfaux*, II (Paris: Gembloux, 1954).
—*Christ in the Theology of St Paul* (New York: Herder & Herder, 1959).
Chadwick, H., '"All Things to All Men". 1 Corinthians 9.22', *NTS* 1 (1954–55), pp. 261-75.
—'St Paul and Philo of Alexandria', *BJRL* 48 (1966), pp. 286-307.
Chouinard, L., 'Gospel Christology: A Study of Methodology', *JSNT* 39 (1987), pp. 21-37.
Clarke, E.G., *The Wisdom of Solomon* (Cambridge: Cambridge University Press, 1973).
Clements, R.E., *Old Testament Theology: A Fresh Approach* (London: Marshall, Morgan & Scott, 1978).
—'The Ten Commandments. Law and Social Ethic', *EpwRev* 16.3 (1989), pp. 71-81.
Collange, J.-F., *Enigmes de la deuxième épître aux Corinthiens: Etude exégétique de 2 Cor. 2.14–7.4* (Cambridge: Cambridge University Press, 1972).
—*The Epistle of Saint Paul to the Philippians* (London: Epworth, 1979).
Collins, J., *Between Athens and Jerusalem* (New York: Crossroad, 1983).
Collins, R.F., *Studies in the First Letter to the Thessalonians* (Leuven: Leuven University Press, 1984).
Conzelmann, H., *An Outline of the Theology of the New Testament* (London: SCM Press, 1969 [1968]).
—*1 Corinthians* (Philadelphia: Fortress Press, 1975).
Coppens, J. (ed.), *La notion biblique de Dieu: Le Dieu de la bible et le Dieu des philosophes* (Leuven: Leuven University Press, 1976).
Cranfield, C.E.B., *The Epistle to the Romans* (2 vols.; ICC; Edinburgh: T. & T. Clark, 1975, 1979).
Crenshaw, J.L. (ed.), *Theodicy in the Old Testament* (Philadelphia: Fortress Press, 1983).
—*Old Testament Wisdom* (Atlanta: John Knox Press, 1981; London: SCM Press, 1982).
Cullmann, O., *The Christology of the New Testament* (London: SCM Press, 1963 [1959]).
Dalbert, P., *Die Theologie der hellenistisch-jüdenischen Missions-Literatur unter Ausschluss von Philo und Josephus* (Hamburg: Evangelischer Verlag, 1953).
Daniélou, J., *Philon d'Alexandrie* (Paris: Librairie Arthème Fayard, 1958).
Daube, D., *Ancient Jewish Law* (Leiden: Brill, 1981).
Davenport, G.L., *The Eschatology of the Book of Jubilees* (Leiden: Brill, 1971).
Davies, M., Review of L. Hurtado's *One God, One Lord*, *New Blackfriars* (Jan. 1990), pp. 51-52.
Davies, W.D., *Paul and Rabbinic Judaism* (London: SPCK, 1970).
—*Christian Origins and Judaism* (London: Darton, Longman & Todd, 1962).
—*The Gospel and the Land* (Berkeley: University of California Press, 1974).
—*Jewish and Pauline Studies* (London: SPCK, 1984).
Davis, J.A., *Wisdom and Spirit: An Investigation of 1 Corinthians 1.18–3.20 against the Background of Jewish Sapiental Traditions in the Graeco-Roman Period* (Lanham, MD: University Press of America, 1984).
Deidun, T.J., *New Covenant Morality in Paul* (Rome: Biblical Institute Press, 1981).
Deissmann, A., *St Paul: A Study in Social and Religious History* (London: Hodder & Stoughton, 1926).

Delling, G., 'Partizipiale Gottesprädikationen in den Briefen des Neuen Testaments', *ST* 17 (1963), pp. 1-59.
Demke, C., 'Ein Gott und viele Herren', *EvT* 36.5 (1976), pp. 473-84.
Dibelius, M., *A Fresh Approach to the New Testament and Early Christian Literature* (Westport, CT: Greenwood, 1979 [1936]).
Dibelius, M. (with H. Greeven), *James* (Philadelphia: Fortress Press, 1976 [1949]).
Dobschütz, E. von, *Die Thessalonicherbriefe* (Göttingen: Vandenhoeck & Ruprecht, 1909).
Dodd, C.H., *The Epistle to the Romans* (London: Hodder & Stoughton, 1932).
—*The Bible and the Greeks* (London: Hodder & Stoughton, 1935).
Dodds, E.R., *The Greeks and the Irrational* (Berkeley: University of California Press, 1951).
Donfried, K.P. (ed.), *The Romans Debate* (Minneapolis: Augsburg, 1977).
Donelson, L.R., *Pseudepigraphy and Ethical Argument in the Pastoral Epistles* (Tübingen: Mohr [Paul Siebeck], 1986).
Doty, W.G., *Letters in Primitive Christianity* (Philadelphia: Fortress Press, 1973).
Doughty, D., 'The Priority of ΧΑΡΙΣ. An Investigation of the Theological Language of Paul', *NTS* 19 (1973), pp. 163-68.
Downing, F.G., *Jesus and the Threat of Freedom* (London: SCM Press, 1987).
—*Strangely Familiar* (Manchester, 1985).
Drane, J., *Paul—Libertine or Legalist?* (London: SPCK, 1975).
Drummond, J., *Philo Judaeus or the Jewish–Alexandrian Philosophy in its Development and Completion* (2 vols.; London: Williams & Norgate, 1888).
Dunn, J.D.G., '2 Cor. iii 17—"The Lord is the Spirit"', *JTS* 21 (1970), pp. 309-20.
—*Christology in the Making* (London: SCM Press, 1980).
—'Was Christianity a Monotheistic Faith from the Beginning?', *SJT* 35.4 (1982), pp. 303-36.
—'L.J. Kreitzer—Review', *ExpTim* 100.1 (1988), p. 32.
—*Romans* (2 vols.; Waco, TX: Word Books, 1988).
Eckardt, A.R. (ed.), *The Theologian at Work* (London: SCM Press, 1968).
Ellis, E.E., *Paul's Use of the Old Testament* (Edinburgh: Oliver & Boyd, 1957).
Farmer, W.R., C.F.D. Moule and R. Niebuhr (eds.), *Essays in Christian History and Interpretation* (Cambridge: Cambridge University Press, 1967).
Feldman, L.H., *Josephus and Modern Scholarship (1937–80)* (Berlin: de Gruyter, 1984).
Fitzgerald, J.T., *Cracks in an Earthen Vessel: An Examination of the Catalogues of Hardships in the Corinthian Correspondence* (Atlanta: Scholars Press, 1988).
Fitzmyer, J.A., *To Advance the Gospel* (New York: Crossroad, 1981).
—*The Gospel According to Luke* (2 vols.; New York: Doubleday, 1981).
—*Paul and his Theology* (Princeton, NJ: Prentice-Hall, 1987).
Foerster, W., 'Der Heilige Geist im Spätjudentum', *NTS* 8, pp. 117-34.
Ford, D., and F. Young, *Meaning and Truth in 2 Corinthians* (London: SPCK, 1987).
Franxman, T.W., *Genesis and the Jewish Antiquities of Flavius Josephus* (Rome: Biblical Institute Press, 1979).
Fretheim, T.E., *The Suffering of God: An Old Testament Perspective* (Philadelphia: Fortress Press, 1987).
Fritsch, C.T., *The Anti-Anthromorphisms of the Greek Pentateuch* (Princeton: University Press, 1943).

Furnish, V.P., 'Fellow-Workers in God's Service', *JBL* 80 (1961), pp. 364-70.
—*Theology and Ethics in Paul* (Nashville: Abingdon, 1968).
—*II Corinthians* (New York: Doubleday, 1984).
Gamble, H., Jr, *The Textual History of the Letter to the Romans* (Grand Rapids, MI: Eerdmans, 1977).
Garland, D.E., 'The Composition and Unity of Philippians: Some Neglected Factors', *NovT* 27.2 (1985), pp. 141-73.
Garnett, P., *Salvation and Atonement in the Qumran Scrolls* (Tübingen: Mohr, 1977).
Gärtner, B.E., 'The Pauline and Johannine Idea of "To Know God" against the Hellenistic Background', *NTS* 14 (1968), pp. 209-31.
Gasque, W.W., and R.P. Martin (eds.), *Apostolic History and the Gospel* (Exeter: Paternoster, 1970).
Geffré, C., and J.-P. Jossna, *Concilium: Monotheism* (Edinburgh: T. & T. Clark, 1985).
Georgi, D., *The Opponents of Paul in 2 Corinthians* (Edinburgh: T. & T. Clark, 1986).
Goppelt, L., *Theology of the New Testament* (2 vols.; Grand Rapids, MI: Eerdmans, 1981, 1982).
Grant, F.C., *Roman Hellenism and the New Testament* (Edinburgh: Oliver & Boyd, 1962).
Grant, R.M., *The Early Christian Doctrine of God* (Charlottesville, 1966).
—*Gods and the One God: Christian Theology in the Graeco-Roman World* (London: SPCK, 1986).
Grayston, K., 'Not with a Rod', *ExpTim* 78.1 (1976), pp. 13-16.
—*Dying We Live* (London: Darton, Longman & Todd, 1990).
Haenchen, E., *The Acts of the Apostles* (Oxford: Basil Blackwell, 1971).
Hafemann, S.J., *Suffering and the Spirit* (Tübingen: Mohr, 1986).
Hallender, H.W., *Joseph as an Ethical Model in the Testaments of the Twelve Patriarchs* (Leiden: Brill, 1981).
Hamerton-Kelly, R., and R. Scroggs (eds.), *Jews, Greeks and Christians* (Leiden: Brill, 1976).
Hansen, G.W., *Abraham in Galatians: Epistolary and Rhetorical Contexts* (Sheffield: JSOT Press, 1989).
Hanson, A.T., *The Wrath of the Lamb* (London: SPCK, 1957).
—*Grace and Truth* (London: SPCK, 1975).
—'The Midrash in II Corinthians 3: A Reconsideration', *JSNT* 80 (1980), pp. 2-28.
—*The Image of the Invisible God* (London: SCM Press, 1982).
—*The Paradox of the Cross in the Thought of St Paul* (Sheffield: JSOT Press, 1987).
Hanson, R.P.C., 'St. Paul's Quotations of the Book of Job', *Theology* 53 (1950), pp. 250-53.
Harvey, A.E., *Jesus on Trial: A Study in the Fourth Gospel* (London: SPCK, 1976).
Hawthorne, G.F., *Philippians* (Waco, TX: Word Books, 1983).
Hawthorne, G.F., and O. Betz (eds.), *Tradition and Interpretation in the New Testament* (Grand Rapids, MI: Eerdmans, 1987).
Haymes, B., *The Concept of the Knowledge of God* (London: Macmillan, 1988).
Hemer, C.J., *The Book of Acts in the Setting of Hellenistic History* (Tübingen: Mohr, 1989).
Hengel, M., *Judaism and Hellenism* (2 vols.; London: SCM Press, 1974).
—*Crucifixion* (London: SCM Press, 1977).
—*Acts and Early Christianity* (Philadelphia: Fortress Press, 1980).

—*The Zealots* (Edinburgh: T. & T. Clark, 1989).
Hermann, I., *Kyrios und Pneuma: Studien zur Christologie der paulinischen Hauptbriefe* (Munich: Kösel, 1961).
Heschel, A.J., *The Prophets* (London: Harper, 1962).
Hill, D., *New Testament Prophecy* (London: Marshall, Morgan & Scott, 1979).
Holbrook, C.A., *The Iconoclastic Deity—Biblical Images of God* (Lewisburg: Bucknell University Press, 1984).
Holl, K., *The Distinctive Elements in Christianity* (Edinburgh: T. & T. Clark, 1937).
Holladay, C.H., *Theios Aner in Hellenistic Judaism* (Missoula, MT: Scholars Press, 1977).
Holland, G.S., *The Tradition that you Received from us: 2 Thessalonians in the Pauline Tradition* (Tübingen: Mohr, 1988).
Holtz, T., *Der erste Briefe an die Thessalonicher* (Zürich: Benzinger Verlag, 1986).
Hooker, M.D. (ed. with S.G. Wilson), *Paul and Paulinism* (London: SPCK, 1982).
—'ΠΙΣΤΙΣ ΧΡΙΣΤΟΥ', *NTS* 35.3 (1989), pp. 321-42.
Hordern, W., *Speaking of God* (London: Epworth, 1964).
Houlden, J.L., *Paul's Letters from Prison* (London: Pelican, 1970).
Howard, G., 'The Tetragram and the New Testament', *JBL* 96 (1977), pp. 63-83.
Hughes, P., *Paul's Second Epistle to the Corinthians* (Grand Rapids, MI: Eerdmans, 1962).
Hultgren, A., *Christ and his Benefits* (Philadelphia: Fortress Press, 1987).
Hurd, J.C., *The Origin of 1 Corinthians* (London: SPCK, 1965).
Hurd, J.C. (ed. with P. Richardson), *From Jesus to Paul* (Waterloo, Ontario: Wilfrid Laurier University Press, 1984).
Hurst, L.D., and N.T. Wright (eds.), *The Glory of Christ in the New Testament* (Oxford: Oxford University Press, 1987).
Hurtado, L., *One God, One Lord* (Philadelphia: Fortress Press, 1988).
Isaacs, M.E., *The Concept of the Spirit* (London: Heythrop College, 1976).
Jaeger, W., *Early Christianity and Greek Paideia* (Oxford: Oxford University Press, 1962).
Jaubert, A., *1 Clement: Epître aux Corinthiens* (Paris, 1971).
Jellicoe, S., *The LXX and Modern Study* (Oxford: Oxford University Press, 1968).
Jervell, J., *The Unknown Paul: Essays in Luke–Acts and Early Christian History* (Minneapolis: Augsburg, 1984).
Jervell, J. (with W.A. Meeks), *God's Christ and his People* (Oslo: Universitetsforlaget, 1977).
Jewett, R., *Paul's Anthropological Terms* (Leiden: Brill, 1971).
—*Dating Paul's Life* (London: SCM Press, 1979).
—(ed.), *Semeia: Christology and Exegesis: New Approaches* (Atlanta: Scholars Press, 1985).
—*The Thessalonian Correspondence* (Philadelphia: Fortress Press, 1986).
Johnson, E.E., *The Function of Apocalyptic and Wisdom Traditions in Romans 9–11* (Atlanta: Scholars Press, 1987).
Jonge, M. de, *The Testaments of the Twelve Patriarchs* (Leiden: Brill, 1953).
—(ed.), *Studies in the Testaments of the Twelve Patriarchs* (Leiden: Brill, 1975).
Jüngel, E., *God as the Mystery of the World* (Edinburgh: T. & T. Clark, 1983).
Käsemann, E., *New Testament Questions for Today* (London: SCM Press, 1969).
—*Commentary on Romans* (London: SCM Press, 1980).

Kaufman, G., *God the Problem* (Cambridge, MA: Harvard University Press, 1972).
Keck, L.E., 'Towards the Renewal of New Testament Christology', *NTS* 32 (1986), pp. 362-67.
Kelly, J.N.D., *A Commentary on the Pastoral Epistles* (London: A. & C. Black, 1978 [1963]).
Kennedy, G.A., *Classical Rhetoric and its Christian and Secular Tradition from Ancient to Modern Times* (London: Croom Helm, 1980).
—*New Testament Interpretation through Rhetorical Criticism* (Chapel Hill: University of North Carolina Press, 1984).
Kiley, M., *Colossians as Pseudepigraphy* (Sheffield: JSOT Press, 1986).
Knox, W.L., *St Paul and the Church of the Gentiles* (Cambridge: Cambridge University Press, 1939).
Kramer, W., *Christ, Lord, Son of God* (London: SCM Press, 1966 [1963]).
Kreitzer, L., *Jesus and God in Paul's Eschatology* (Sheffield: JSOT Press, 1987).
Kümmel, W.G., *Theology of the New Testament* (London: SCM Press, 1974 [1972]).
Lampe, G.W.H. (ed.), *A Patristic Greek Lexicon* (Oxford: Oxford University Press, 1961).
Lane-Fox, R., *Pagans and Christians* (London: Viking, 1986).
Lash, N., *A Matter of Hope* (London: Darton, Longman & Todd, 1981).
Leaney, A., 'The Experience of God in Qumran and in Paul', *BJRL* 51, pp. 431-52.
—*The Jewish and Christian World* (Cambridge: Cambridge University Press, 1984).
Liebeschuetz, H., *Continuity and Change in Roman Religion* (Oxford: Oxford University Press, 1979).
Lieu, J., '"Grace to You and Peace": The Apostolic Greeting', *BJRL* 68.1 (1985), pp. 161-85.
Lightfoot, J.B., *St Paul's Epistle to the Philippians* (London: Macmillan, 2nd edn, 1885).
—*Saint Paul's Epistle to the Galatians* (London: Macmillan, 1896).
Lindemann, A., 'Die Rede von Gott in der paulinische Theologie', *Theologie und Glaube* 69.4 (1979), pp. 357-76.
Longenecker, B.W., 'Different Answers to Different Issues: Israel, the Gentiles and Salvation History in Romans 9–11', *JSNT* 46 (1989), pp. 95-123.
—*Eschatology and the Covenant: A Comparison of 4 Ezra and Romans 1–11* (Sheffield: JSOT Press).
Longenecker, R.N., *The Christology of Early Jewish Christianity* (London: SCM Press, 1970).
Lührmann, D., *Das Offenbarungsverständnis bei Paulus und in paulinischen Gemeinden* (WMANT, 16; Neukirchen–Vluyn: Neukirchener Verlag, 1965).
—*Der Brief an die Galater* (Zürich: Theologischer Verlag, 1978).
—'Paul and the Pharisaic Tradition', *JSNT* 36 (1989), pp. 75-94.
Lull, D., *The Spirit in Galatia* (Chico, CA: Scholars Press, 1980).
Lyons, G., *Pauline Autobiography—Towards a New Understanding* (Atlanta: Scholars Press, 1985).
Macholz, C., 'Das "Passivum Divinum"—seine Anfänge im Alten Testament und der "Hofstil"', *ZNW* 81 (1990).
Mackinnon, D.M., *Themes in Theology: The Threefold Cord* (Edinburgh: T. & T. Clark, 1987).
MacQuarrie, J., *God-Talk* (London: SCM Press, 1967).

—*In Search of Deity* (London: SCM Press, 1984).
Maddox, R., *The Purpose of Luke–Acts* (Edinburgh: T. & T. Clark, 1982).
Malherbe, A.J., 'Exhortation in 1 Thessalonians', *NovT* 25.3 (1983), pp. 238-56.
—*Moral Exhortation: A Graeco-Roman Source-Book* (Philadelphia: Westminster Press, 1986).
Malina, B.J., *The New Testament World* (London: SCM Press, 1983).
Manson, T.W., 'C.T. Fritsch's *The Anti-Anthropormorphisms of the Greek Pentateuch*', *JTS* 46 (1945), pp. 78-80.
—*Studies in the Gospels and Epistles* (Manchester: Manchester University Press, 1962).
Marcus, R., 'Divine Names and Attributes in Hellenistic Jewish Literature', *Proceedings of the American Academy for Jewish Research* 3 (1932), pp. 43-120.
Marmorstein, A., *Studies in Jewish Theology* (Oxford: Oxford University Press, 1950).
Marshall, I.H., *The Gospel of Luke* (Exeter: Paternoster, 1978).
—*1 and 2 Thessalonians* (London: Marshall, Morgan & Scott, 1983).
Marshall, P., *Enmity in Corinth: Social Conventions in Paul's Relations with the Corinthians* (Tübingen: Mohr, 1987).
Martin, R.P., *Carmen Christi: Philippians 2.5-11 in Recent Interpretation and in Early Christian Worship* (Cambridge: Cambridge University Press, 1967).
—*Colossians and Philemon* (London: Marshall, Morgan & Scott, 1978 [1974]).
—*The Epistle of Paul to the Philippians* (London: Marshall, Morgan & Scott, 1976).
—*2 Corinthians* (WBC, 40; Waco, TX: Word Books, 1986).
Martyn, J.L., 'Apocalyptic Antinomies in Paul's Letter to the Galatians', *NTS* 31.3 (1985), pp. 410-24.
Marxen, W., *Introduction to the New Testament* (Philadelphia: Fortress Press, 1968).
Mays, J.L., *Amos* (London: SCM Press, 1969).
McCasland, S.V., 'The Image of God according to Paul', *JBL* 69 (1950), pp. 85-100.
McDonald, J.I.H., 'Romans 13.1-7: A Test Case for New Testament Interpretation', *NTS* 35 (1989), pp. 540-49.
McMullen, R., *Paganism in the Roman Empire* (New Haven: Yale University Press, 1981).
McNamara, M., *The New Testament and the Palestinian Targum* (Shannon: Irish University Press, 1968).
Meeks, W., *The Moral World of the First Christians* (London: SPCK, 1987).
Michel, O., *Der Brief an die Römer* (Göttingen: Vandenhoeck & Ruprecht, 1978).
Mitton, C.L., *The Epistle to the Ephesians* (Oxford: Oxford University Press, 1951).
Moore, A.L., *1 and 2 Thessalonians* (London: Marshall, Morgan & Scott, 1969).
Moore, G.F., *Judaism in the First Centuries of the Christian Era: The Age of the Tannaim* (3 vols.; Cambridge, MA: Harvard University Press, 1927–30).
Morgan, R., and J. Barton, *Biblical Interpretation* (Oxford: Oxford University Press, 1988).
Morgenthaler, R., *Statistik des neutestamentlichen Wortschatzes* (Zürich: Gotthelf-Verlag, 1958).
Moule, C.F.D., *An Idiom Book of New Testament Greek* (Cambridge: Cambridge University Press, 1968 [1953]).
—*The Origin of Chrstology* (Cambridge: Cambridge University Press, 1977).
Moxnes, H., *Theology in Conflict* (Leiden: Brill, 1980).
Mullins, T.Y., 'Petition as a Literary Form', *NovT* 5 (1962), pp. 46-54.
Munck, J., *Christ and Israel* (Philadelphia: Fortress Press, 1967).

—*Paul and the Salvation of Mankind* (London: SCM Press, 1959).
Mussies, G., *Dio Chrysostom and the New Testament* (Leiden: Brill, 1972).
Mussner, F., *Der Galaterbrief* (Frieburg: Herder, 1977).
Newton, M., *The Concept of Purity at Qumran and in the Letters of Paul* (Cambridge: Cambridge University Press, 1985).
Nickelsburg, G.W.E., *Jewish Literature between the Bible and the Mishnah* (London: SCM Press, 1981).
Nickle, W., *The Collection* (London: SCM Press, 1966).
Nilsson, M., *Greek Piety* (Oxford: Oxford University Press, 1948).
Nineham, D.E. (ed.), *Studies in the Gospels* (Oxford: Basil Blackwell, 1955).
Nock, A.D., *Conversion: The Old and the New in Religion from Alexander the Great to Augustine of Hippo* (Oxford: Oxford University Press, 1933).
—*St Paul* (Oxford: Oxford University Press, 1938 [rev. 1946 and 1948]).
Norris, R.A., *God and the World in Early Christian Tradition* (London: A. & C. Black, 1966).
O'Brien, P., *Colossians and Ephesians* (Waco, TX: Word Books, 1982).
O'Brien, P.T., *Introductory Thanksgivings in the Letters of Paul* (Leiden: Brill, 1977).
O'Day, G.R., 'Jeremiah 9.22-3 and 1 Corinthians 1.26-31: A Study in Inter-textuality', *JBL* 109.2 (1990), pp. 259-67.
O'Neill, J.C., *Paul's Letter to the Romans* (Harmondsworth: Penguin, 1975).
Orr, W.F., and J.A. Walther, *1 Corinthians* (New York: Doubleday, 1976).
Parke-Taylor, G.H., *Yahweh: The Divine Name in the Bible* (Waterloo, Ontario: Wilfred Laurier University Press, 1975).
Pearson, B.A., *The Pneumatikos–Psychikos Terminology* (Missoula, MT: Scholars Press, 1973).
Pedersen, S. (ed.), *Die paulinische Literatur und Theologie* (Arhus: Forlaget Aros, 1980).
Pfister, W., *Das Leben im Geist nach Paulus* (Freiburg: Universitätsverlag, 1963).
Piper, J., *The Justification of God: An Exegetical and Theological Study of Romans 9.1-23* (Grand Rapids, MI: Baker, 1983).
Plummer, A., *A Critical and Exegetical Commentary on the Second Epistle of Saint Paul to the Corinthians* (Edinburgh: T. & T. Clark, 1915).
Pobee, J., *Persecution and Martyrdom in the Theology of Paul* (Sheffield: JSOT Press, 1985).
Pokorny, P., *The Genesis of Christology* (Edinburgh: T. & T. Clark, 1987).
Prestige, G.L., *God in Patristic Thought* (London: SPCK, 2nd edn, 1987).
Provence, T.E., '"Who is Sufficient for These Things?" An Exegesis of 2 Corinthians 2.15–3.18', *NovT* 24.1 (1982), pp. 54-81.
Rad, G. von, *Genesis* (London: SCM Press, 1963 [1961]).
—*Old Testament Wisdom* (London: SCM Press, 1972).
Rahner, K., *Theological Investigations 1* (London: Darton, Longman & Todd, 1965).
Rainbow, P.A., 'Jewish Monotheism as the Matrix for New Testament Christology. A Review Article', *NovT* 33.1 (1991), pp. 78-91.
Rajak, T., *Josephus, the Historian and his Society* (London: Duckworth, 1983).
Ramsey, I.T. (ed.), *Words about God* (London: SCM Press, 1971).
Räisänen, H., 'Paul's Conversion and the Development of his View of the Law', *NTS* 33.3 (1987), pp. 404-19.
—*The Torah and Christ* (1986).

Reumann, J., *Righteousness in the New Testament* (Philadelphia: Fortress Press, 1982).
Rigaux, B., *Saint Paul: Les épîtres aux Thessaloniciens* (Paris: Gembloux, 1956).
Rist, J.M., *A Study in Ancient Philosophical Ethics* (Leiden: Brill, 1982).
Robertson, A., and A. Plummer, *A Critical and Exegetical Commentary on the First Epistle of St Paul to the Corinthians* (Edinburgh: T. & T. Clark, 1914).
Robinson, J.A., *St Paul's Epistle to the Ephesians* (Cambridge: J. Clarke, 1903).
Robinson, J.A.T., *Wrestling with Romans* (London: SCM Press, 1979).
Roetzel, C.J., *The Letters of Paul: Conversations in Context* (London: SCM Press, 1983).
Rohde, E., 'Gottesglaube und Kyriosglaube bei Paulus', *ZNW* 22 (1923), pp. 43-57.
Romaniuk, C., 'Le livre de la sagesse dans le Nouveau Testament', *NTS* 14 (1968), pp. 503-13.
Roon, A. Van, 'The Relation between Christ and the Wisdom of God according to Paul', *NovT* 16 (1974), pp. 207-39.
Rowley, H.H., *Job* (London: Marshall, Morgan & Scott, 1976).
Runia, D.T., *Philo of Alexandria and the Timaeus of Plato* (Leiden: Brill, 1986).
—'God and Man in Philo of Alexandria', *JTS* 39.1, pp. 48-75.
Sanday, W., and A.C. Headlam, *The Epistle to the Romans* (Edinburgh: T. & T. Clark, 1902).
Sanders, E.P., *Paul and Palestinian Judaism* (London: SCM Press, 1977).
—(ed. with A.L. Baumgarten and A. Mendelson), *Jewish and Christian Self-Definition* II (London: SCM Press, 1981).
—*Paul, the Law and the Jewish People* (Philadelphia: Fortress Press, 1983).
—(with M. Davies), *Studies in the Synoptic Gospels* (London: SCM Press, 1989).
Sanders, J.T., *Ben Sira and Demotic Wisdom* (Chico, CA: Scholars Press, 1983).
Sandmel, S., *Judaism and Christian Beginnings* (Oxford: Oxford University Press, 1978).
—*Philo of Alexandria: An Introduction* (Oxford: Oxford University Press, 1978).
Sayler, G.B., *Have the Promises Failed? A Literary Analysis of 2 Baruch* (Chico, CA: Scholars Press, 1984).
Schechter, S., *Studies in Judaism* (New York: Meridian Books Inc. and the Jewish Publication Society of America, 1958).
Schenk, W., *Die Philipperbriefe des Paulus* (Stuttgart: Kohlhammer, 1984).
Schlatter, D.A., *Wie sprach Josephus von Gott?* (Gütersloh: C. Bertelsmann, 1910).
Schlier, H., *Der Römerbrief* (Freiburg: Herder, 1977).
Schmidt, L., *Die Ethik der alten Griechen I* (Berlin: Hertz, 1882).
Schmithals, W., *Gnosticism in Corinth: An Investigation of the Letters to the Corinthians* (Nashville: Abingdon, 1971).
Schnabel, E.K., *Law and Wisdom from Ben Sira to Paul* (Tübingen: Mohr, 1985).
Schneider, G., 'Urchristliche Gottesverkündigung in hellenisticher Umwelt', *ZNW* 13 (1969), pp. 59-75.
Schubert, P., *Form and Function of the Pauline Thanksgivings* (BZNW; Berlin: Töpelmann, 1939).
Schürer, E., *The History of the Jewish People in the Age of Jesus Christ* (Edinburgh: T. & T. Clark, 1987).
Schütz, J.H., *Paul and the Anatomy of Apostolic Authority* (Cambridge: Cambridge University Press, 1975).

Schweitzer, A., *The Mysticism of Paul the Apostle* (London: A. & C. Black, 1931).
Schweizer, E., *Neo-Testamentica* (German and English Essays 1951–63; Zürich/Stuttgart: Zwingli Verlag, 1963).
—*The Holy Spirit* (Philadelphia: Fortress Press, 1980).
—*The Letter to the Colossians* (London: SPCK, 1982).
Seifrid, M.A., *Justification by Faith: The Origin and Development of a Central Pauline Theme* (Leiden: Brill, 1992).
Selwyn, E.G., *1 Peter* (London: Macmillan, 1949).
Senft, C., *La première épitre de Saint-Paul aux Corinthiens* (Neuchâtel: Delachaux & Niestlé, 1979).
Sevenster, J.N. (with W.C. van Unnik [eds.]), *Studia Paulina* (in Honorem J. de Zwaan) (Haarlem: Bohn, 1953).
—*Paul and Seneca* (Leiden: Brill, 1961).
Shanor, J., 'Paul as Master Builder: Construction Terms in 1 Corinthians', *NTS* 34 (1988), pp. 461-71.
Siegert, F., *Argumentation bei Paulus* (Tübingen: Mohr, 1985).
Slingerland, H.D., *The Testaments of the Twelve Patriarchs: A Critical History of Research* (Missoula, MT: Scholars Press, 1977).
—'The Levitical Hallmark within the Testaments of the Twelve Patriarchs', *JBL* 103 (1984), pp. 531-37.
—'The Nature of *Nomos* (Law) within the Testaments of the Twelve Patriarchs', *JBL* 105 (1986), pp. 39-48.
Smit, J., 'The Letter of Paul to the Galatians: A Deliberative Speech', *NTS* 35.1 (1989), pp. 1-26.
Stegner, W.R., 'Romans 9.6-29—A Midrash', *JSNT* 22 (1984), pp. 37-52.
Stendahl, K. (ed.), *The Scrolls and the New Testament* (London: SCM Press, 1958).
—*Paul among Jews and Gentiles* (London: SCM Press, 1977).
Stockhausen, C.K., *Moses' Veil and the Glory of the New Covenant: The Exegetical Substratum of II Corinthians 3.11–4.6* (AnBib, 116; Rome: Pontificio Instituto Biblico, 1989).
Stowers, S.K., *The Diatribe and Paul's Letter to the Romans* (Chico, CA: Scholars Press, 1981).
Strack, H.L., and P. Billerbeck, *Kommentar zum Neuen Testament aus Talmud und Midrasch* (München: C.H. Beck'she, 1922–28).
Sumney, J.L., 'The Bearing of a Pauline Rhetorical Pattern on the Integrity of 2 Thessalonians', *ZNW* 81 (1990), pp. 192-204.
—*Identifying Paul's Opponents. The Question of Method in 2 Corinthians* (Sheffield: JSOT Press, 1990).
—'The Bearing of a Pauline Rhetorical Pattern', *ZNW* 81. 3/4 (1990), pp. 192-204.
Swete, H., *An Introduction to the Old Testament in Greek* (Cambridge: Cambridge University Press, 1900).
Talbert, G., 'Tradition and Redaction in Romans 12.9-21', *NTS* 16 (1970).
Taylor, V., *New Testament Essays* (London: Epworth, 1970).
Teixidor, J., *The Pagan God: Popular Religion in the Graeco-Roman Near East* (Princeton: Princeton University Press, 1977).
Theissen, G., *Biblical Faith* (London: SCM Press, 1984).
—*Psychological Aspects of Pauline Theology* (Edinburgh: T. & T. Clark, 1987).

Thompson, A.L., *Responsibility for Evil in the Theodicy of IV Ezra* (Missoula, MT: Scholars Press, 1987).
Thüsing, W., *Per Christum in Deum: Studien zum Verhältnis von Christozentrik und Theozentrik in den paulinischen Hauptbriefen* (Münster, 1965).
Vanhoye, A. (ed.), *L'apôtre Paul: Personalité, style et conception du ministère* (Leuven: Leuven University Press, 1986).
Varneda, V.I., *The Historical Method of Flavius Josephus* (Leiden: Brill, 1986).
Vermes, G., *Jesus the Jew* (London: Collins, 1973).
Verner, D.C., *The Household of God* (Atlanta: Scholars Press, 1983).
Vouga, F., 'Zur rhetorischen Gattung des Galaterbriefes', *ZNW* 9.3-4 (1988), pp. 291-92.
Watson, F., *Paul, Judaism and the Gentiles—A Sociological Approach* (Cambridge: Cambridge University Press, 1986).
Wedderburn, A.J.M., *The Reasons for Romans* (Edinburgh: T. & T. Clark, 1988).
—'Paul and Jesus: Similarity and Continuity', *NTS* 34.2 (1988), pp. 161-82.
Weinstock, S., *Divus Julius* (Oxford: Oxford University Press, 1971).
Weiss, J., *Der erste Körintherbrief* (Göttingen: Vandenhoeck & Ruprecht, 1910).
Welborn, L.L., 'On the Discord in Corinth: 1 Corinthians 1–4 and Ancient Politics', *JBL* 106.1 (1987), pp. 85-111.
Westermann, C., *Isaiah 40–66* (London: SCM Press, 1974).
White, J.L., *The Form and Function of the Body of the Greek Letter* (Columbia, MO: SBL, 1972).
—*The Form and Structure of the Official Petition—A Study in Greek Epistolography* (Columbia, MO: SBL, 1972).
—*Light from Ancient Letters* (Philadelphia: Fortress Press, 1986).
Whiteley, D.E.H., *The Theology of St Paul* (Oxford: Basil Blackwell, 1964).
Whybray, R.N., *Isaiah 40–66* (London: Marshall, Morgan & Scott, 1975).
—*The Intellectual Tradition in the Old Testament* (Berlin: de Gruyter, 1974).
Wilckens, U., *Der Brief an die Römer* (3 vols.; Zürich: Benziger Verlag; Neukirchen-Vluyn: Neukirchenes Verlag, 1978, 1980, 1982).
Williams, S.K., 'The "Righteousness of God" in Romans', *JBL* 99/2 (1980), pp. 241-90.
Willis, W.L., *Idol Meat in Corinth* (Chico, CA: Scholars Press, 1985).
—'The Mind of Christ in 1 Corinthians 2.16', *Bib* 70.1 (1989), pp. 110-22.
Winston, D., *The Wisdom of Solomon* (New York: Doubleday, 1979).
Winter, J.G., *Life and Letters in the Papyri* (Ann Arbor: University of Michigan Press, 1933).
Wire, A.C., 'Pauline Theology as an Understanding of God: The Explicit and the Implicit' (unpublished PhD dissertation, Claremont, 1974).
Witt Hughes, F., *Early Christian Rhetoric and 2 Thessalonians* (Sheffield: JSOT Press, 1989).
Witt, N.D. de, *St Paul and Epicurus* (Minneapolis: University of Minnesota, 1954).
Wolfson, H.A., *Philo: Foundation of Religious Philosophy in Judaism, Christianity and Islam* (2 vols.; Cambridge, MA: Harvard University Press, 1947).
Wright, N.T., *The Climax of the Covenant: Christ and the Law in Pauline Theology* (Edinburgh: T. & T. Clark, 1991).
Wuellner, W., 'Haggadic Homily Genre in 1 Corinthians 1–3', *JBL* 89 (1970), pp. 199-204.

Yarborough, O.L., *Not Like the Gentiles: Marriage Rules in the Letters of Paul* (Atlanta: Scholars Press, 1985).

Ziesler, J.A., *The Meaning of Righteousness in Paul* (Cambridge: Cambridge University Press, 1972).

Ziesler, J.A., *Paul's Letter to the Romans* (London: SCM Press, 1989).

INDEXES

INDEX OF REFERENCES

OLD TESTAMENT

APOCRYPHA

INDEX OF AUTHORS

JOURNAL FOR THE STUDY OF THE NEW TESTAMENT

Supplement Series

1 THE BARREN TEMPLE AND THE WITHERED TREE
William R. Telford
2 STUDIA BIBLICA 1978
II. PAPERS ON THE GOSPELS
Edited by E.A. Livingstone
3 STUDIA BIBLICA 1978
III. PAPERS ON PAUL AND OTHER NEW TESTAMENT AUTHORS
Edited by E.A. Livingstone
4 FOLLOWING JESUS:
DISCIPLESHIP IN THE GOSPEL OF MARK
Ernest Best
5 THE PEOPLE OF GOD
Markus Barth
6 PERSECUTION AND MARTYRDOM IN THE THEOLOGY OF PAUL
John S. Pobee
7 SYNOPTIC STUDIES:
THE AMPLEFORTH CONFERENCES OF
1982 AND 1983
Edited by C.M. Tuckett
8 JESUS ON THE MOUNTAIN:
A STUDY IN MATTHEAN THEOLOGY
Terence L. Donaldson
9 THE HYMNS OF LUKE'S INFANCY NARRATIVES:
THEIR ORIGIN, MEANING AND SIGNIFICANCE
Stephen Farris
10 CHRIST THE END OF THE LAW:
ROMANS 10.4 IN PAULINE PERSPECTIVE
Robert Badenas
11 THE LETTERS TO THE SEVEN CHURCHES OF ASIA IN THEIR LOCAL SETTING
Colin J. Hemer
12 PROCLAMATION FROM PROPHECY AND PATTERN:
LUCAN OLD TESTAMENT CHRISTOLOGY
Darrell L. Bock
13 JESUS AND THE LAWS OF PURITY:
TRADITION HISTORY AND LEGAL HISTORY IN MARK 7
Roger P. Booth
14 THE PASSION ACCORDING TO LUKE:
THE SPECIAL MATERIAL OF LUKE 22
Marion L. Soards

15 HOSTILITY TO WEALTH IN THE SYNOPTIC GOSPELS
Thomas E. Schmidt

16 MATTHEW'S COMMUNITY:
THE EVIDENCE OF HIS SPECIAL SAYINGS MATERIAL
Stephenson H. Brooks

17 THE PARADOX OF THE CROSS IN THE THOUGHT OF ST PAUL
Anthony Tyrrell Hanson

18 HIDDEN WISDOM AND THE EASY YOKE:
WISDOM, TORAH AND DISCIPLESHIP IN MATTHEW 11.25-30
Celia Deutsch

19 JESUS AND GOD IN PAUL'S ESCHATOLOGY
L. Joseph Kreitzer

20 LUKE
A NEW PARADIGM (2 Volumes)
Michael D. Goulder

21 THE DEPARTURE OF JESUS IN LUKE–ACTS:
THE ASCENSION NARRATIVES IN CONTEXT
Mikeal C. Parsons

22 THE DEFEAT OF DEATH:
APOCALYPTIC ESCHATOLOGY IN 1 CORINTHIANS 15 AND ROMANS 5
Martinus C. de Boer

23 PAUL THE LETTER-WRITER
AND THE SECOND LETTER TO TIMOTHY
Michael Prior

24 APOCALYPTIC AND THE NEW TESTAMENT:
ESSAYS IN HONOR OF J. LOUIS MARTYN
Edited by Joel Marcus & Marion L. Soards

25 THE UNDERSTANDING SCRIBE:
MATTHEW AND THE APOCALYPTIC IDEAL
David E. Orton

26 WATCHWORDS:
MARK 13 IN MARKAN ESCHATOLOGY
Timothy J. Geddert

27 THE DISCIPLES ACCORDING TO MARK:
MARKAN REDACTION IN CURRENT DEBATE
C. Clifton Black

28 THE NOBLE DEATH:
GRAECO-ROMAN MARTYROLOGY
AND PAUL'S CONCEPT OF SALVATION
David Seeley

29 ABRAHAM IN GALATIANS:
EPISTOLARY AND RHETORICAL CONTEXTS
G. Walter Hansen

30 EARLY CHRISTIAN RHETORIC AND 2 THESSALONIANS
Frank Witt Hughes

31 THE STRUCTURE OF MATTHEW'S GOSPEL:
A STUDY IN LITERARY DESIGN
David R. Bauer

32 PETER AND THE BELOVED DISCIPLE:
FIGURES FOR A COMMUNITY IN CRISIS
Kevin Quast

33 MARK'S AUDIENCE:
THE LITERARY AND SOCIAL SETTING OF MARK 4.11-12
Mary Ann Beavis

34 THE GOAL OF OUR INSTRUCTION:
THE STRUCTURE OF THEOLOGY AND ETHICS
IN THE PASTORAL EPISTLES
Philip H. Towner

35 THE PROVERBS OF JESUS:
ISSUES OF HISTORY AND RHETORIC
Alan P. Winton

36 THE STORY OF CHRIST IN THE ETHICS OF PAUL:
AN ANALYSIS OF THE FUNCTION OF THE HYMNIC MATERIAL
IN THE PAULINE CORPUS
Stephen E. Fowl

37 PAUL AND JESUS:
COLLECTED ESSAYS
Edited by A.J.M. Wedderburn

38 MATTHEW'S MISSIONARY DISCOURSE:
A LITERARY CRITICAL ANALYSIS
Dorothy Jean Weaver

39 FAITH AND OBEDIENCE IN ROMANS:
A STUDY IN ROMANS 1–4
Glenn N. Davies

40 IDENTIFYING PAUL'S OPPONENTS:
THE QUESTION OF METHOD IN 2 CORINTHIANS
Jerry L. Sumney

41 HUMAN AGENTS OF COSMIC POWER:
IN HELLENISTIC JUDAISM AND THE SYNOPTIC TRADITION
Mary E. Mills

42 MATTHEW'S INCLUSIVE STORY:
A STUDY IN THE NARRATIVE RHETORIC OF THE FIRST GOSPEL
David B. Howell

43 JESUS, PAUL AND TORAH:
COLLECTED ESSAYS
Heikki Räisänen

44 THE NEW COVENANT IN HEBREWS
Susanne Lehne

45 THE RHETORIC OF ROMANS:
ARGUMENTATIVE CONSTRAINT AND STRATEGY AND PAUL'S
DIALOGUE WITH JUDAISM
Neil Elliott

46 THE LAST SHALL BE FIRST:
THE RHETORIC OF REVERSAL IN LUKE
John O. York

47 JAMES AND THE Q SAYINGS OF JESUS
Patrick J. Hartin

48 TEMPLUM AMICITIAE:
ESSAYS ON THE SECOND TEMPLE PRESENTED TO ERNST BAMMEL
Edited by William Horbury

49 PROLEPTIC PRIESTS
PRIESTHOOD IN THE EPISTLE TO THE HEBREWS
John M. Scholer

50 PERSUASIVE ARTISTRY:
STUDIES IN NEW TESTAMENT RHETORIC
IN HONOR OF GEORGE A. KENNEDY
Edited by Duane F. Watson

51 THE AGENCY OF THE APOSTLE: A DRAMATISTIC ANALYSIS OF PAUL'S
RESPONSES TO CONFLICT IN 2 CORINTHIANS
Jeffrey A. Crafton

52 REFLECTIONS OF GLORY:
PAUL'S POLEMICAL USE OF THE MOSES–DOXA TRADITION IN
2 CORINTHIANS 3.12-18
Linda L. Belleville

53 REVELATION AND REDEMPTION AT COLOSSAE
Thomas J. Sappington

54 THE DEVELOPMENT OF EARLY CHRISTIAN PNEUMATOLOGY
WITH SPECIAL REFERENCE TO LUKE–ACTS
Robert P. Menzies

55 THE PURPOSE OF ROMANS:
A COMPARATIVE LETTER STRUCTURE INVESTIGATION
L. Ann Jervis

56 THE SON OF THE MAN IN THE GOSPEL OF JOHN
Delbert Burkett

57 ESCHATOLOGY AND THE COVENANT:
A COMPARISON OF 4 EZRA AND ROMANS 1–11
Bruce W. Longenecker

58 NONE BUT THE SINNERS:
RELIGIOUS CATEGORIES IN THE GOSPEL OF LUKE
David A. Neale

59 CLOTHED WITH CHRIST:
THE EXAMPLE AND TEACHING OF JESUS IN ROMANS 12.1–15.13
Michael Thompson

60 THE LANGUAGE OF THE NEW TESTAMENT:
CLASSIC ESSAYS
Edited by Stanley E. Porter

61 FOOTWASHING IN JOHN 13 AND THE JOHANNINE COMMUNITY
John Christopher Thomas

62 JOHN THE BAPTIZER AND PROPHET:
A SOCIO-HISTORICAL STUDY
Robert L. Webb

63 POWER AND POLITICS IN PALESTINE:
THE JEWS AND THE GOVERNING OF THEIR LAND 100 BC–AD 70
James S. McLaren

64 JESUS AND THE ORAL GOSPEL TRADITION
Edited by Henry Wansbrough

65 THE RHETORIC OF RIGHTEOUSNESS IN ROMANS 3.21-26
Douglas A. Campbell

66 PAUL, ANTIOCH AND JERUSALEM:
A STUDY IN RELATIONSHIPS AND AUTHORITY IN EARLIEST CHRISTIANITY
Nicholas Taylor

67 THE PORTRAIT OF PHILIP IN ACTS:
A STUDY OF ROLES AND RELATIONS
F. Scott Spencer

68 JEREMIAH IN MATTHEW'S GOSPEL:
THE REJECTED-PROPHET MOTIF IN MATTHAEAN REDACTION
Michael P. Knowles

69 RHETORIC AND REFERENCE IN THE FOURTH GOSPEL
Margaret Davies

70 AFTER THE THOUSAND YEARS:
RESURRECTION AND JUDGMENT IN REVELATION 20
J. Webb Mealy

71 SOPHIA AND THE JOHANNINE JESUS
Martin Scott

72 NARRATIVE ASIDES IN LUKE–ACTS
Steven M. Sheeley

73 SACRED SPACE
AN APPROACH TO THE THEOLOGY OF THE EPISTLE TO THE HEBREWS
Marie E. Isaacs

74 TEACHING WITH AUTHORITY:
MIRACLES AND CHRISTOLOGY IN THE GOSPEL OF MARK
Edwin K. Broadhead

75 PATRONAGE AND POWER:
A STUDY OF SOCIAL NETWORKS IN CORINTH
John Kin-Man Chow

76 THE NEW TESTAMENT AS CANON:
A READER IN CANONICAL CRITICISM
Robert Wall and Eugene Lemcio

77 REDEMPTIVE ALMSGIVING IN EARLY CHRISTIANITY
Roman Garrison
78 THE FUNCTION OF SUFFERING IN PHILIPPIANS
L. Gregory Bloomquist
79 THE THEME OF RECOMPENSE IN MATTHEW'S GOSPEL
Blaine Charette
80 BIBLICAL GREEK LANGUAGE AND LINGUISTICS: OPEN QUESTIONS IN CURRENT RESEARCH
Edited by Stanley E. Porter and D.A. Carson
81 THE LAW IN GALATIANS
In-Gyu Hong
82 ORAL TRADITION AND THE GOSPELS: THE PROBLEM OF MARK 4
Barry W. Henaut
83 PAUL AND THE SCRIPTURES OF ISRAEL
Edited by Craig A. Evans and James A. Sanders
84 FROM JESUS TO JOHN: ESSAYS ON JESUS AND NEW TESTAMENT CHRISTOLOGY IN HONOUR OF MARINUS DE JONGE
Edited by Martinus C. De Boer
85 RETURNING HOME: NEW COVENANT AND SECOND EXODUS AS THE CONTEXT FOR 2 CORINTHIANS 6.14–7.1
William J. Webb
86 ORIGINS OF METHOD: TOWARDS A NEW UNDERSTANDING OF JUDAISM AND CHRISTIANITY—ESSAYS IN HONOUR OF JOHN C. HURD
Edited by Bradley H. McLean
87 WORSHIP, THEOLOGY AND MINISTRY IN THE EARLY CHURCH: ESSAYS IN HONOUR OF RALPH P. MARTIN
Edited by Michael Wilkins and Terence Paige
88 THE BIRTH OF THE LUKAN NARRATIVE
Mark Coleridge
89 WORD AND GLORY: ON THE EXEGETICAL AND THEOLOGICAL BACKGROUND OF JOHN'S PROLOGUE
Craig A. Evans
90 RHETORIC IN THE NEW TESTAMENT
ESSAYS FROM THE 1992 HEIDELBERG CONFERENCE
Edited by Stanley E. Porter and Thomas H. Olbricht
91 MATTHEW'S NARRATIVE WEB: OVER, AND OVER, AND OVER AGAIN
Janice Capel Anderson
92 LUKE: INTERPRETER OF PAUL, CRITIC OF MATTHEW
Eric Franklin
93 ISAIAH AND PROPHETIC TRADITIONS IN THE BOOK OF REVELATION: VISIONARY ANTECEDENTS AND THEIR DEVELOPMENT
Jan Fekkes
94 JESUS' EXPOSITION OF THE OLD TESTAMENT IN LUKE'S GOSPEL
Charles A. Kimball

95 THE SYMBOLIC NARRATIVES OF THE FOURTH GOSPEL:
THE INTERPLAY OF FORM AND MEANING
Dorothy A. Lee
96 THE COLOSSIAN CONTROVERSY:
WISDOM IN DISPUTE AT COLOSSAE
Richard E. DeMaris
97 PROPHET, SON, MESSIAH
NARRATIVE FORM AND FUNCTION IN MARK 14–16
Edwin K. Broadhead
98 FILLING UP THE MEASURE:
POLEMICAL HYPERBOLE IN 1 THESSALONIANS 2.14-16
Carol J. Schlueter
99 PAUL'S LANGUAGE ABOUT GOD
Neil Richardson